For

Miju, Eugene, Mulan, Aqma Aqda, and my extended families

For

the Hani Nationality and the Akha People

云南省红河州世界遗产管理局"红河州哈尼族自然圣境与哈尼梯田生态文明调研"项目
（项目编号：HHSJYC2016001）资助出版

Sacred and Contested Landscapes
Dynamics of Natural Resource Management by the Akha People in Xishuangbanna

神圣与竞争的景观
西双版纳阿卡人自然资源管理模式变迁

Wang Jianhua
王建华 / 著

图书在版编目（CIP）数据

神圣与竞争的景观：西双版纳阿卡人自然资源管理模式变迁 = Sacred and Contested Landscapes：Dynamics of Natural Resource Management by the Akha People in Xishuangbanna：英文/王建华著. —北京：知识产权出版社，2018.2
ISBN 978-7-5130-5269-6

Ⅰ.①神… Ⅱ.①王… Ⅲ.①哈尼族—自然资源—资源经济—研究—西双版纳—英文 Ⅳ.①F127.742

中国版本图书馆 CIP 数据核字（2017）第 276596 号

内容提要

通过认真梳理其迁徙史诗和族谱，参考相关历史文献、考古和民族志资料，本书把哈尼族的文化起源地追溯到天山天池和吐鲁番一带。作者认为哈尼族的万物有灵信仰和众生共同体的世界观早在其采集狩猎的远古时期就已经形成。哈尼族先民经历了几千年的往南迁徙史，先后参与了炎帝部落的农业文明、古蜀国文明、古夜郎国文明和古滇国文明，最后在元江流域形成了自己的加滇地方政权，从事水稻农业。作者认为阿卡支系的形成与加滇政权有密切关系，而加滇政权被元朝蒙古军所灭直接导致阿卡人的主体从元江流域往南迁徙到澜沧江—湄公河流域，成为该地区一个主要的山地民族群体，从事以种植旱稻为主的轮歇农业，并用其在加滇时期形成的传统民族法典"昂桑活"管理其神圣的景观。中华人民共和国成立以后，其神圣景观与国家的生产和管控导向的景观发生了互动，导致其向市场经济转型，并以种植橡胶、茶叶等长期经济作物为主。本书分析了自然资源管理模式的变迁对阿卡人社会经济和文化及其生态环境所产生的影响。最后讨论了影响可持续发展的因素。

责任编辑：兰　涛　　　　　　　　责任校对：谷　洋
封面设计：郑　重　　　　　　　　责任出版：刘译文

神圣与竞争的景观：西双版纳阿卡人自然资源管理模式变迁
Sacred and Contested Landscapes：Dynamics of Natural Resource Management by the Akha People in Xishuangbanna
王建华　著

出版发行：知识产权出版社有限责任公司	网　　址：http://www.ipph.cn
社　　址：北京市海淀区气象路 50 号院	邮　　编：100081
责编电话：010-82000860 转 8325	责编邮箱：lantao625@163.com
发行电话：010-82000860 转 8101/8102	发行传真：010-82000893/82005070/82000270
印　　刷：北京嘉恒彩色印刷有限责任公司	经　　销：各大网上书店、新华书店及相关专业书店
开　　本：720mm×1000mm　1/16	印　　张：22.5
版　　次：2018 年 2 月第 1 版	印　　次：2018 年 2 月第 1 次印刷
字　　数：245 千字	定　　价：68.00 元
ISBN 978-7-5130-5269-6	

出版权专有　侵权必究
如有印装质量问题，本社负责调换。

Selected Pictures and Figures

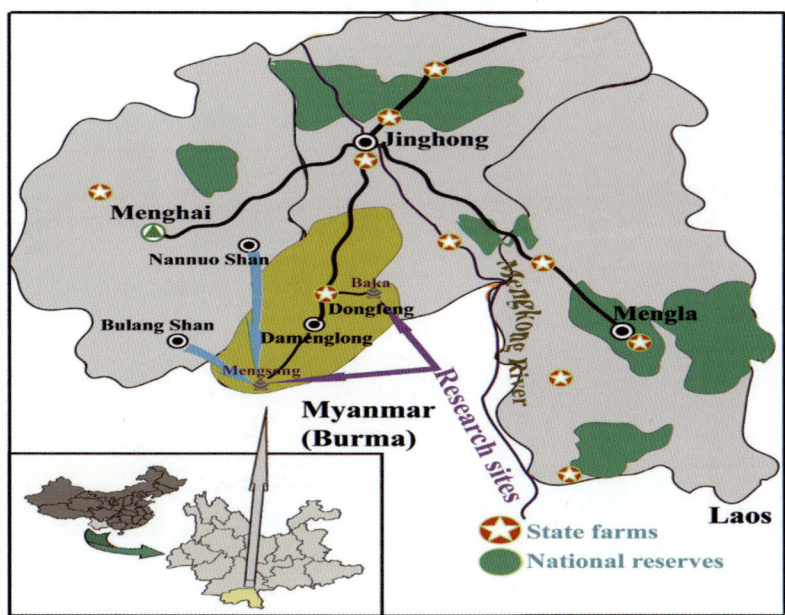

Figure 2 Research Sites in Xishuangbanna, Yunnan Province, Southwest China (P12)

Picture 27 Baka Village Surrounded by Rubber Plantations (Dry Season) (P180)

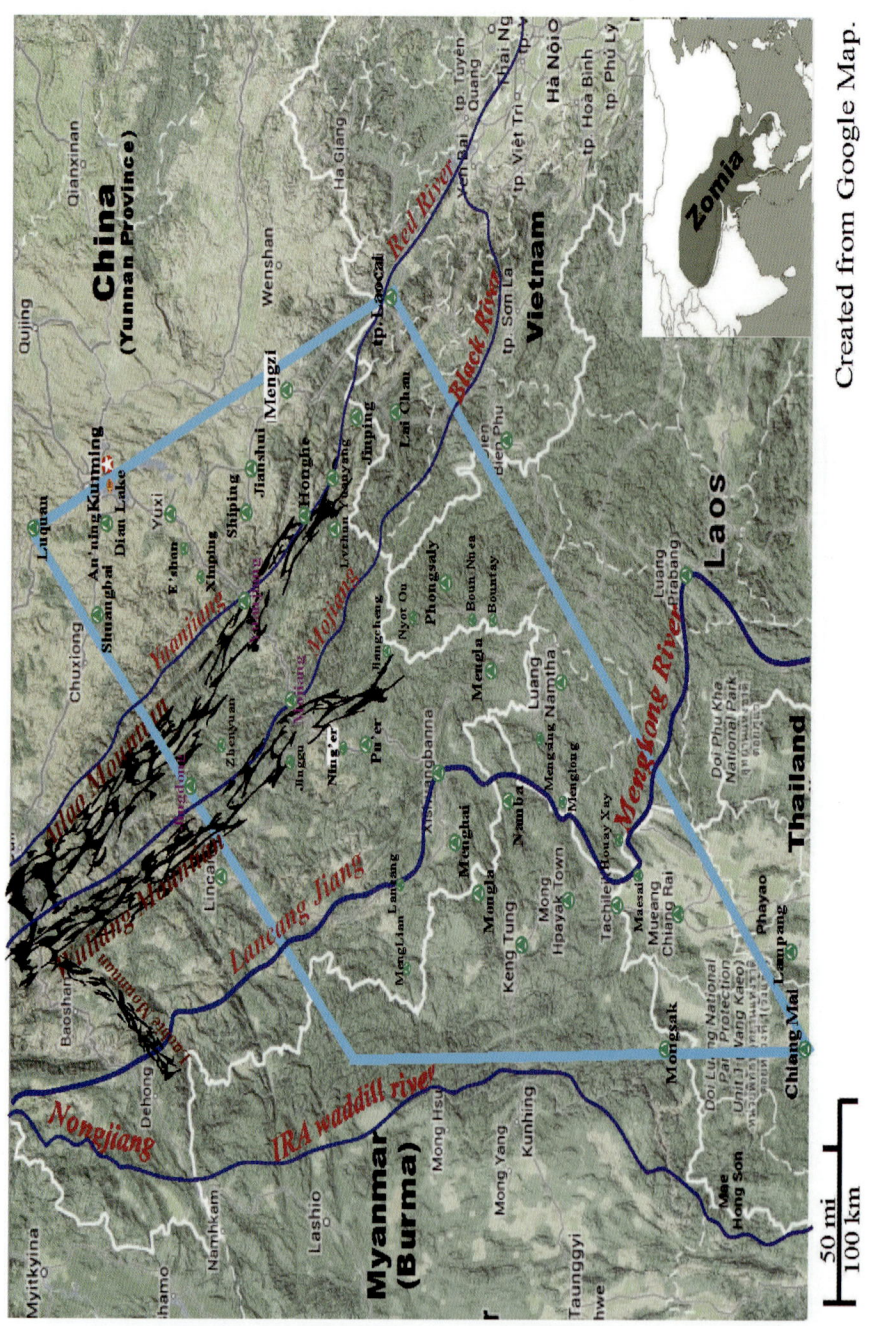

Figure 3 A Quadrangle Region of the Hani-Akha in Zomia (P23)

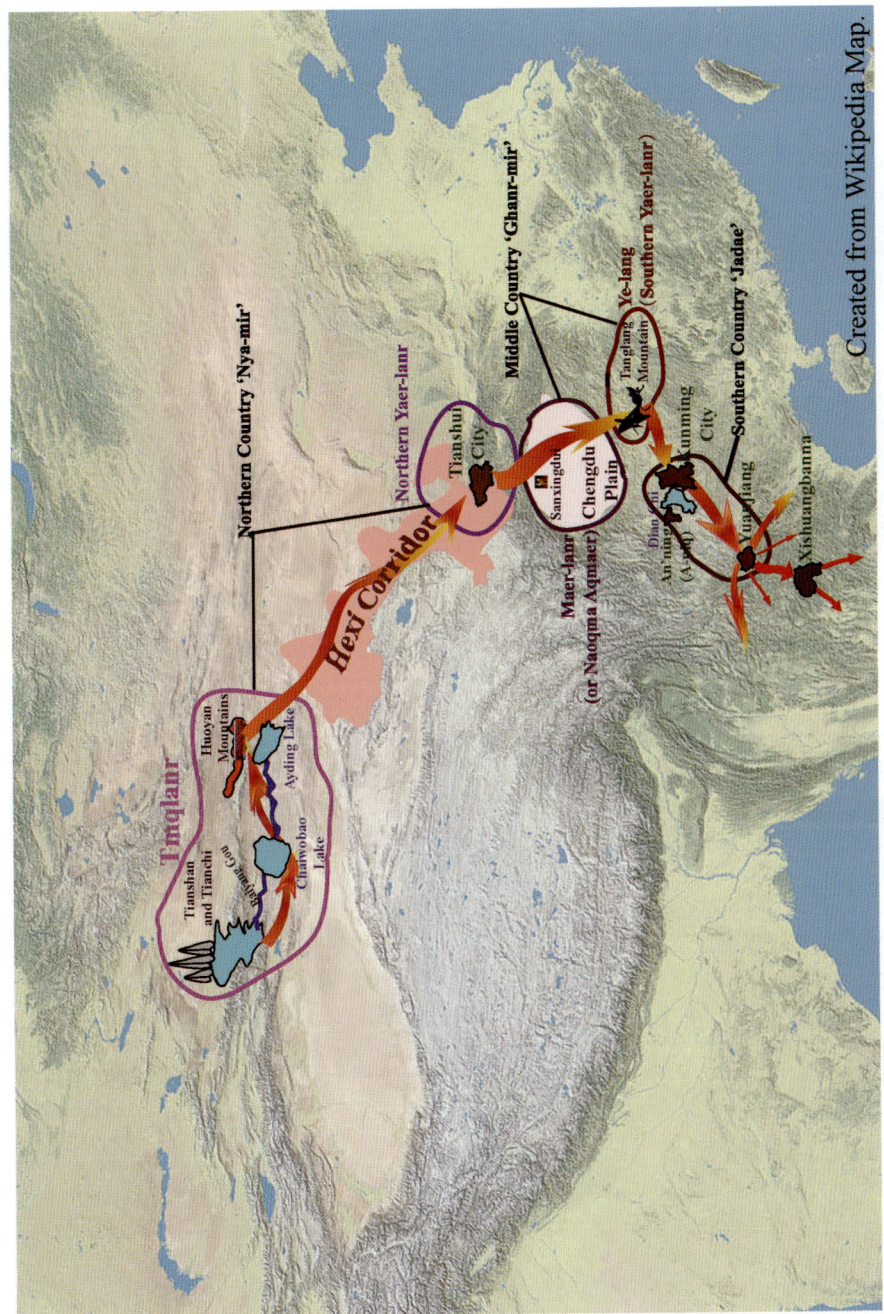

Figure 4 A hypothesized route of the Hani-Akha migration (P32)

Picture 2 Huoyanshan (courtesy of Yang Jiaxing, Department of Culture and Media, Chongqing University of Arts and Sciences, Chongqing, China) (P34)

Figure 16 Map of current land uses in Baka village (P205)

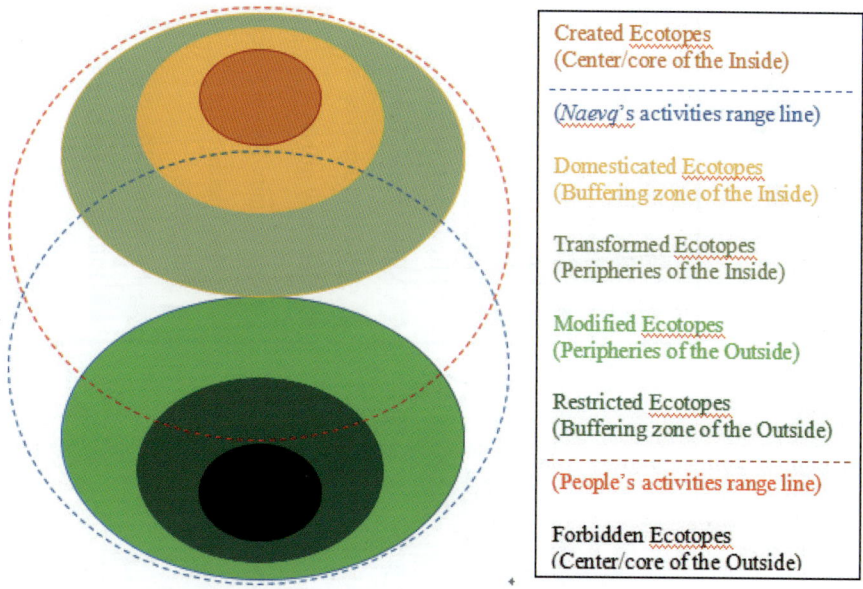

Figure 6 A mental map of Akha sacred landscapes (P80)

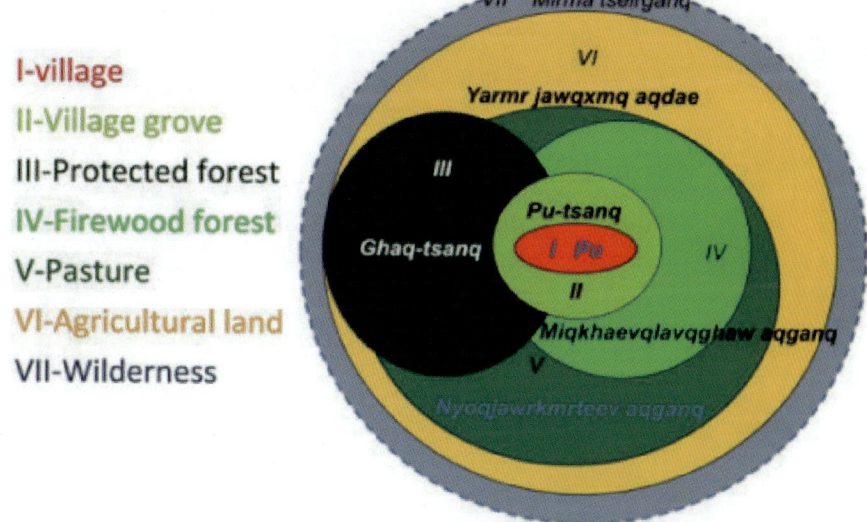

Figure 7 Six zones of land use in a traditional Akha village (P81)

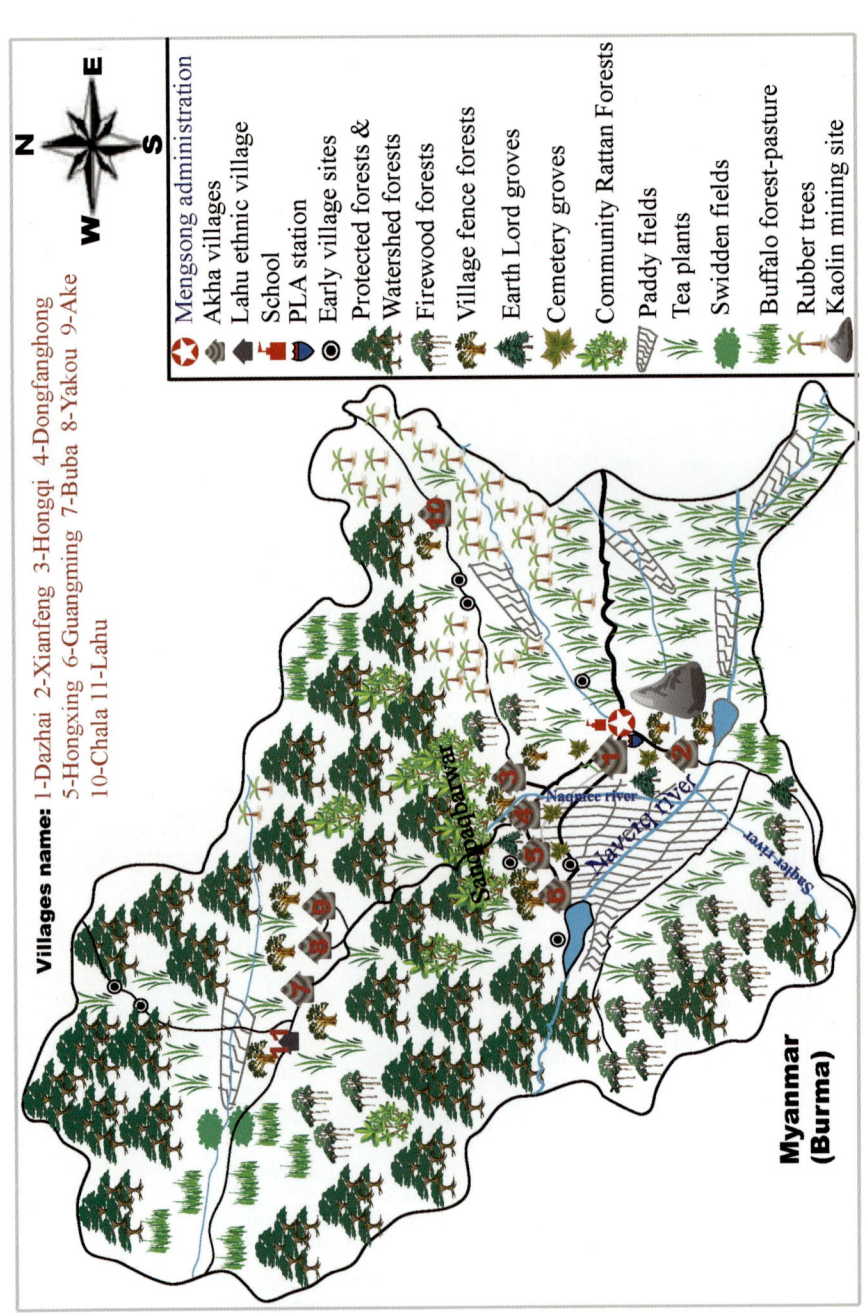

Figure 5 Mengsong Administrative Village (P71)

Figure 11 Mengsong Community and Current Land Use Map (P173)

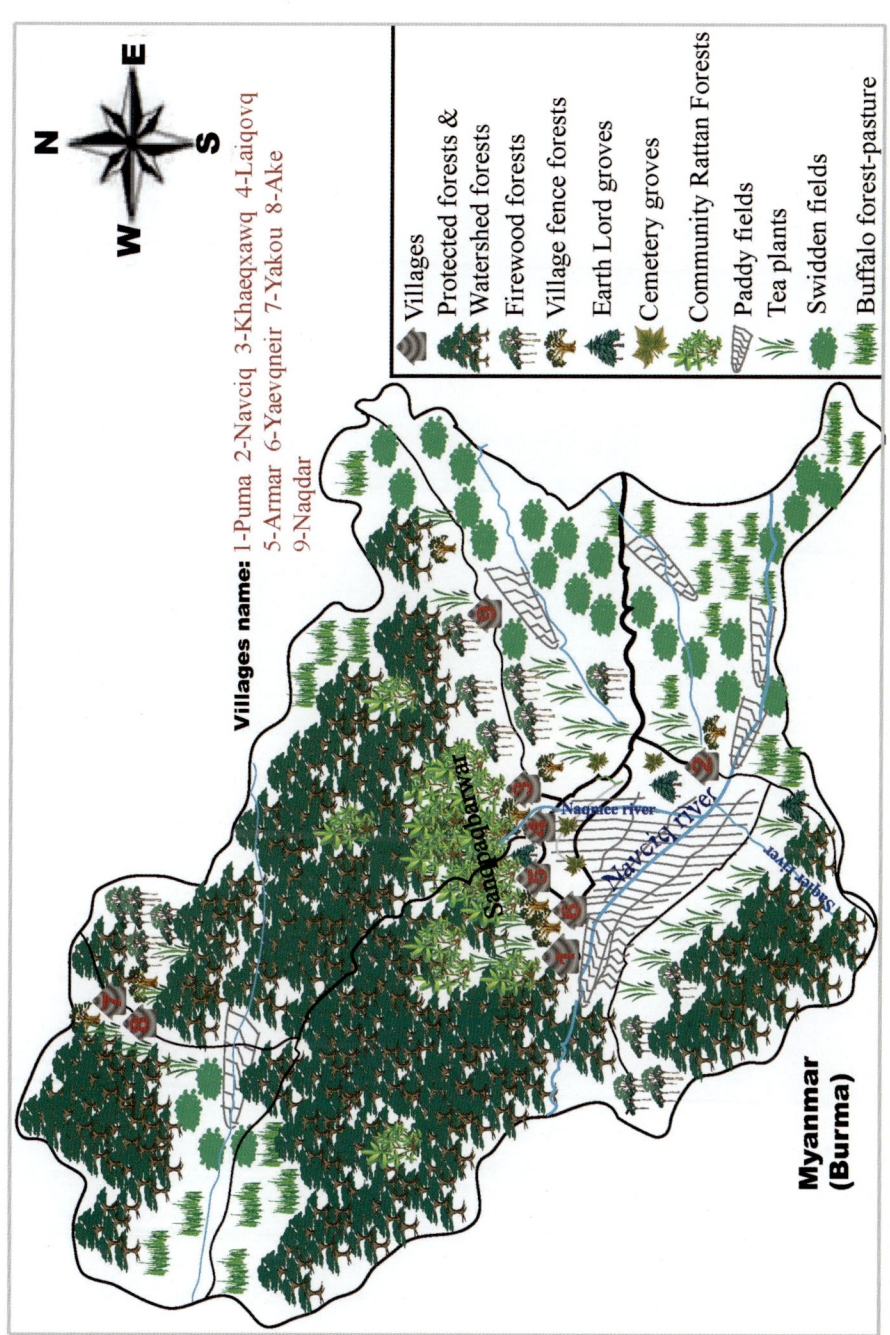

Figure 9 Mengsong community and land use map prior to 1950 (P138)

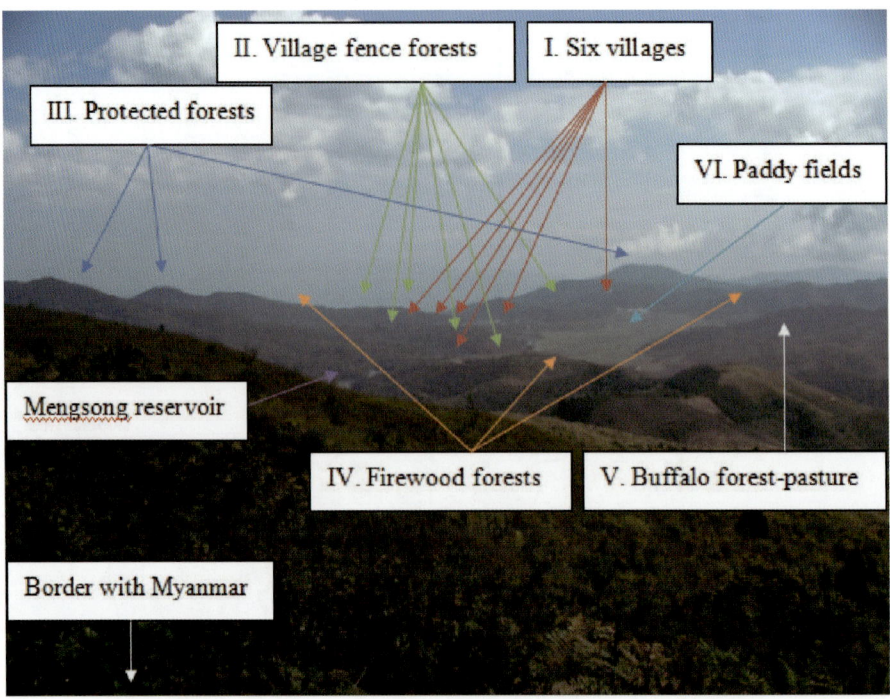

Picture 4 Six zones of land uses in Mengsong Akha community (partial) (P82)

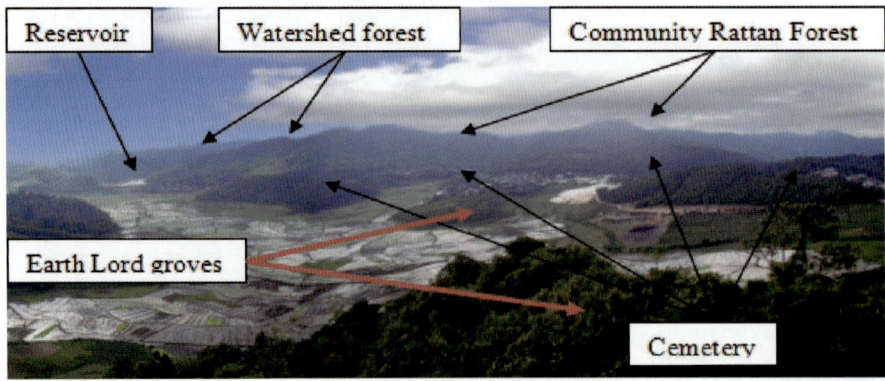

Picture 5 Restricted ecotopes of Mengsong (partial) (P84)

Picture 7 The Earth Lord Grove of Hongxing village (P88)

Picture 9 Forest reserved in agricultural zone (P101)

Picture 6 An Akha village gate lanrkanq at Doichang, Chiang Rai, Thailand (above left) (P86)

Picture 8 An altar in a Earth Lord grove, Doi Chang village, Chiang Rai, Thailand (above right) (P89)

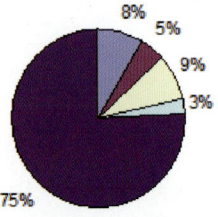

Figure 10 Xishuangbanna Reforestation in the Natural Forest Project (1998-2006) (P160)

Picture 13 A site of the Natural Forest Protect Project at Mengsong, Damenglong Township, Jinghong City. (P161)

The sign in Chinese reads: "Jinghong City 2002 Natural Forest Protect Project: Natural Reforestation Area". But later, the area also became the Land Conversion Project target area, under which tea plantation was conducted since 2004.

Picture 14 Both rubber (above left) and tea (above right) plantations are identified as ecological forests since they are intercropped with Cajanus cajan. (P163)

Picture 15 The Land Conversion Project in Mengsong I (above left) (P164)
(Naturally reforested fallow lands were cleaned for tea plantation in order to get subsidy)
Picture 16 The Land Conversion Project in Mengsong II (above right) (P164)
(Naturally vegetated wastelands were cleaned for tea and Chinese fir plantations in order to get subsidy)

Picture 17 Freehold household forests were cleaned for tea plantation under the influence of Land Conversion Project in Mengsong (above left) (P164)
Picture 18 Understorey of the State forests in Mengsong cleaned for tea plantation (above right) (P164)

Picture 19 Mengsong Dam construction site (above left) (P165)
Picture 20 Navciq River on which Mengsong Dam will be built (above right) (P165)

Picture 21 150 mu of paddy fields and 3000 mu forests will be submerged by the new Mengsong Reservoir (above left) (P166)

Picture 22 It is estimated that about 15,000 tea trees in the forests will be submerged too (above right) (P166)

Picture 23 A kaolin mining factory in Mengsong (above left) (P166)

Picture 24 A kaolin mining site used to be covered by forests. The trees and topsoil were all striped in order to mine kaolin (above right) (P166)

Picture 25 A land slide occurred at a kaolin mining site (above left) (P166)

Picture 26 Kaolin mining is threatening paddy fields (above right) (P166)

Foreword

E. N. Anderson

Professor Emeritus of Anthropology

University of California, Riverside

Jianhua "Ayoe" Wang has documented here some of the best environmental care in the world. The peoples of the mountainous regions of northern Southeast Asia, a region known as "Zomia" to many, have for millennia faced a problem of high population density and lack of central government in a fragile environment. They have developed many sustainable ecological adjustments to the region. Among the most successful is the system developed by Ayoe's own ethnic group, the Akha, speakers of a Tibeto-Burman language, living in the area where Yunnan, Burma, Thailand, and Laos meet.

Dr. Wang explains in this book the basis of the system in mutual respect. Humans respect other lives, both animal and plant. The Akha concept of *taqheeq-e* is actually wider than respect: it includes a caring, protective attitude as well as the respect owed to elders and family members. Spirits, especially forest spirits, have a mutual respect relationship with humans. In mythic time, humans and spirits divided the world; humans got the fields and farms, spirits got the forests and woods. Forests must be protected and conserved, because the spirits need their share. They will help rather than harm, if this is maintained. Ceremonies maintain the connection. There are not only ceremonies for the spiritual lords of the game, there is even a ceremony to placate the souls of earthworms killed in plowing.

These beliefs give the Akha a different view of "nature" and "culture" from the usual Western one. The Akha world is divided into the realm of forest spirits—still human-affected and to some extent human-managed—and the realm of humans, the villages and cultivated fields. These too have their tame and wild plants and animals, their own spirits, and their own rules. Instead of sharply separated "natural" and "cultural" worlds, the Akha see one world with interpenetrating realms—each one distinct but affecting, and, indeed, dependent on the other. This view is strikingly similar to that of the Yucatec Maya of Mexico, for whom the world is divided into *kaah* "village" with its *kool* "fields", and the *k'aax* "forest", a realm with its own spirit guardians but heavily managed by humans (Anderson 2005). Traditional Chinese had yet another view, one of concentric rings: town, hamlets, close-by fields, remote fields, managed forests, and the actual "wild" (*ye*). And some Native Americans simply contrast their own world—animals, plants, mountains, rivers, humans, all one society—with the worlds of their different-language neighbors. No nature/culture opposition exists, or if it does it is dwarfed in importance by us/them dichotomy. Often, mountains, waters and winds are seen as people, with their own minds and agency (Anderson 2014; Ojalehto 2016).

Similar accounts of excellent environmental management based on beliefs in forest spirits that guard the game and protect the trees come from other areas in southeast Asia (Pinkaew, 2001; Yos, 2003). Even the modern Thai state has had dramatic confrontations between traditional Buddhists and "modernizing" agents of environmental destruction, with victory often going to the traditional conservers (Sponsel, 2012). More widely, the concept of "respect" is reported as the basic moral concept of many good environmental regimes around the world, from Mongolia to Rumania (Anderson, 2014). Most cultures, worldwide, had varying degrees of respect for their environments, at least to the point of preventing frank suicide through destruction of their resource bases.

Conversely, European culture includes a subcurrent of fear and hate of "nature" and anything natural. It was never dominant enough in rural Europe to lead to environmental suicide, but it is dominant in many modern urban and political arenas, and it has unfortunately propagated in recent decades in the rest of the world. It lies behind the modern economic myth—far from universal but still widely shared—that destruction of natural things counts as "progress", while conservation is not counted as a benefit. Related to this is the idea that traditional cultures are "backward", and their sustainable management of resources—when it occurs—is anti-"growth". China during the Planned Economy Period adopted these alien ideas, to the confusion and the sorrow of many. The slogan saying "struggle against nature" was far from Chinese (let alone Akha) tradition, but it was enforced nationwide. This led to appalling damage (Economy, 2005; Shapiro, 2001), including, in Akha territory, cutting down vast swaths of spirit forests to plant rubber trees and grain. During Cultural Revolution, Chinese government also opposed traditional culture, seeing it as "feudal" and "superstitious". Dr. Wang describes how these campaigns led to erosion of conservation and sustainable management throughout the Akha lands. Restrictions on hunting and overcollecting dissolved along with beliefs in forest spirits. Fortunately, both China and the world have changed and improved their perceptions recently, and Yunnan is the target of highly contested and debated but still often successful conservation efforts.

A sub-theme of the book is the story of the lost Jadae polity, an orally transmitted memory of a past Akha state whence the Akha radiated outward. In recent history, the Akha were stateless, being more or less subjected to surrounding kingdoms or else left alone. The loss of a state polity reminds us of the alternation of state and non-state in Edmund Leach's study of *gumsa* and *gumlao* politics among the distantly related Jinghpaw (Leach, 1973). It also recalls James Scott's work, *The Art of Not Being Governed* (2009), on the fondness of Zomia societies for abandoning or rejecting state organization to live "free in the forest" (Hickey, 1982).

Yunnan was a refuge, with its incredibly rugged terrain, remote valleys, and endemic malaria; the horrors of dealing with a malarial environment in Imperial times are the subject of a brilliant new study by David Bello (2016: 190 – 218). Scott may well be exaggerating, but certainly the societies of Zomia have a long history of oscillating between state and nonstate politics, and Dr. Wang's book brings us a new and particularly nuanced and sensitive account of how the people on the ground perceive and talk about such matters. Interference by top-down government, without understanding, creates problems, but Zomian independence may yet prevail.

Along the way, Dr. Wang describes the rich, full, satisfying life of the old-time villages, with dances, ceremonies, courting rituals, local foods and drinks, and above all a full consciousness of the beauty and power of the world around the communities.

Dr. Wang's book stands as an extremely well-grounded, factual, thorough, and dispassionate account of a traditional Zomian society. It shows that a large, complex community, with a long and involved history, can manage resources sustainably and create a brilliant, dynamic culture built around sustainable resource management and respect for all beings. It is a message of hope for a world where many now despair. Ordinary humans can use common sense, respect, and everyday morality to manage the world well and live good lives in it.

References

[1] Anderson, E. N. Political Ecology of a Yucatec Maya Village. Tucson: University of Arizona Press, 2005.

[2] Anderson E. N. Caring for Place. Walnut Creek, CA: Left Coast Press, 2014.

[3] Economy, Elizabeth C. The River Runs Black: The Environmental Challenge to China's Future. Ithaca, NY: Cornell University Press, 2005.

[4] Hickey, Gerald Cannon. Free in the Forest: Ethnohistory of the Vietnamese Central Highlands (1954 – 1976) New Haven: Yale University Press, 1982.

[5] Leach, Edmund R. Political Systems of Highland Burma: A Study of Kachin Social Structure. London: London School of Economics, Monographs in Social Anthropology #44, 1973.

[6] Ojalehto, Bethany. Who's at Stake? Nonhuman Agency Concepts and Cultural (Folk) Ecologies. Ph. D. thesis, Northwestern University, Dept. of Psychology, 2016.

[7] Pinkaew Laungaramsri. Redefining Nature: Karen Ecological Knowledge and the Challenge to the Modern Conservation Paradigm. Chennai, India: Earthworm Books, 2001.

[8] Scott, James C. The Art of Not Being Governed: An Anarchist History of Upland Southeast Asia. New Haven: Yale University Press, 2009.

[9] Shapiro, Judith. Mao's War against Nature: Politics and the Environment in Revolutionary China. Cambridge: Cambridge University Press, 2001.

[10] Spencer, J. E. Shifting Cultivation in Southeast Asia. Berkeley: University of California Press, 1966.

[11] Sponsel, Leslie E. Spiritual Ecology: A Quiet Revolution. Santa Barbara, CA: Praeger

(Imprint of ABC - CLIO), 2012.

[12] Yos Santasombat. Biodiversity, Local Knowledge and Sustainable Development. Chiang Mai, Thailand: Regional Center for Social Science and Sustainable Development, Chiang Mai University, 2003.

Introduction to Prof. E. N. Anderson: E. N. Anderson is a Professor Emeritus of Anthropology, University of California, Riverside. Prof. Anderson received his Ph. D in Anthropology at University of California, Berkeley in 1967, and served once as president of Society of Ethnobiology. Prof. Anderson published numerous articles at prestigious academic journals as well as authored or co - authored/edited over 20 books, including but not limited to, The Food of China (1988), Ecologies of the Heart (1996), The Pursuit of Ecotopia (2010), Ethnobiology (2011), Caring for Place (2014).

ABSTRACT

Through careful analyses of rich oral texts of their migratory history, genealogies and rituals, as well as using historical records in Chinese, archaeological evidence, and ethnographic data, this study traces the history of Akha people, a Tibeto-Burman speaking group in Zomia, back to their original homeland *Tmqlanr* where their ancestors were hunter-gathers. The author hypothesizes the *Tmqlanr* refers to Tianchi (Sky Lake) in Tianshan or Sky Mountain, northwest China. The author argues that their animist belief and community-of-beings worldview were well developed when they were hunter-gathers. A huge wild fire forced the ancestors of the Akha to leave their original homeland and started their millennia long southward migration.

It is evident that the Akha ancestors became agriculturalists and were involved in building several ancient Tibeto-Burman states and contributed to several ancient civilizations in Southwest China and eventually established their own polity *Jadae*, centered in Yuanjiang valley of the Red River, roughly in AD1054 through AD1274 when it was conquered by the Mongol Empire of the Yuan Dynasty. The author argues that the Akha identity was formed in the process of building, defending and losing the *Jadae* polity. Rice cultivation in irrigated paddy fields was the economic basis of the *Jadae* polity. Collapse of the *Jadae* polity forced the Akha people to migrate further southward; they became one of the biggest shifting cultivating groups in highlands of Zomia, where they still reproduced sacred landscapes composed of six patches including forbidden, restricted, modified, transformed, domesticated, and created ecotopes, according to the worldview developed by their hunting - gathering ancestors and managed their natural resources through a holistic body of customary law *Ghanrsanrkhovq* standardized in the *Jadae* polity.

As Akha people migrated into Xishuangbanna area, they were forced to move up to live in mountains and became more specialized in shifting cultivation and rotations of dozens varieties of rice and other hundreds species of crops gradually, and even cash crops such as opium later on and agroforestry (of tea, bamboo, rattan, and indigo), supplemented with home gardening, hunting and gathering. The Chinese, and other (Thai), governments often blame Akha and other highland groups for deforestation due to their practices of shifting cultivation. My case study demonstrates, however, that the Akha had sustainably managed their natural resources and played an undeniable role in conserving local biodiversity until the onset of China's modernization programs in the 1950s. Thus it is the state that has been most responsible for deforestation. Among all the state development programs and policies, rubber plantations have contributed foremost to the deforestation and loss of biodiversity in Xishuangbanna.

Traditionally the Akha people had sustainably managed their natural resources (especially forests and forest-related animals and plants) not because they were culturally nature lovers, nor due to their animist belief as some cultural ecologists might assume, but rather because their livelihoods (e. g. shifting cultivation as well as hunting and gathering) had been by and large based on forests, and their survival as highlanders of Zomia had been dependent on sustainable management of forests and forest-related resources for centuries. In doing so, Akha societies had accumulated a rich body of ecological knowledge regarding natural resource management as they become swidden agriculturalists in Zomia. As an oral culture without writing scripts, their Traditional Ecological Knowledge (TEK) was vividly recorded and presented in proverbs and a phenomenological calendar, and was represented in a lot of stories (including fairy tales) and myths. Through reciting those proverbs and the calendar and retelling those stories and myths constantly, the Akha TEK had been taught and transmitted from generation to generation for centuries. More importantly, their TEK had been efficiently applied in their practices of natural resource management (such as forest management, agricultural activities, home gardening, collecting plants, hunting and fishing, among others) through embedding them in landscapes. This efficiency had been not only guaranteed by the village elders' council (i. e. an internal government led by a chief *dzoeqma*) who monitored and enforced their customary laws (*Ghanrsanrkhovq* which included environmental rules of natural resource uses) but also, and more importantly, enhanced through the religious representations and moral transactions of their natural resource management. In other words, besides being embedded in landscape, Akha TEK was also represented in their belief system and worldview as environmental taboos and rules, and integrated into their moral system as environmental ethics. Those taboos and rules are observed in their practices of natural resource management and enforced as religious rituals which are repeatedly conducted. Almost all forbidden and restricted ecotopes of the Akha are ecologically significant locations that are vital to maintain healthy local ecosystems. For instance, figs are key species in the ecosystem of tropical rain forests as they play key roles in maintenance and re-establishment of the ecosystem when it is disturbed (Xu, 1994), and the Akha forbidden ecotopes protect these fig species. Another protected species *loqkawv* tree

(*Terminalia myriocarpa*) in Akha forbidden ecotopes is a dominant and representative species in tropical rain forests (Wang et al., 1999). Akha forbidden ecotopes tend to protect water sources, which are vital for the health of tropical/subtropical forests. Furthermore, forbidden and/restricted ecotopes are not only animal friendly, but in particular many sacred animals and birds (e. g. hornbills, loris) protected by the Akha are only found in primitive forests (Wang, 1997). And last, but not least, some forbidden ecotopes contain ecologically fragile locations (such as landslide, rocky area, water springs and/or ponds on the mountains). These taboos were effective measures that would minimize any possible harmful damages of Akha swidden agriculture to the ecosystem. Observation of these taboos guaranteed that practices of swidden agriculture could only open limited dispersed plots in the jungle—which was the case prior to 1950.

It is strikingly interesting to note the parallel between the Akha landscape and concept of a modern natural reserve. For instance, the forbidden ecotopes (*yawkhawr*) are equivalent to cores of natural reserves; the restricted ecotopes are equivalent to buffering zones of natural reserves; and modified ecotopes are similar to peripheries of natural reserves. The difference between the two systems is that the Akha use terms that conform to their worldview to describe their ecological knowledge, while the ecologists use scientific terms to describe it. For instance, a fig tree (*Ficus religiosa*) is called *nyirdzanr* in Akha, literally meaning "village of the outside beings". The name reflects their knowledge gained from their observation that the fig trees are important to a lot of other beings (plants and animals), and so, they should be respected and protected. But Akha do not say this directly, instead they classify it in a religious term, *yawkhawr*, "awesome, sacred, and dangerous". The purpose of doing this is to protect fig tree by using emotionally powerful symbol of "*yawkhawr* ". Therefore, I use the term "ecology of sacred landscape", following Berkes' (1999) "sacred ecology", to describe natural resource management system by traditional societies through religious representation. And I think the term "ecology of sacred landscape" is better than "sacred ecology", because people interact with their environment through landscape. Furthermore, I argue that the widely used definition of Traditional Ecological Knowledge by Berkes (1999) confuses knowledge with its practice and representation. Alternatively, I suggest that Traditional Ecological Knowledge should be redefined as *a cumulative body of knowledge of a people, evolving by adaptive processes in practices, represented in their belief system and/or worldview, embedded in their landscape, and handed down through generations by cultural transmission, about the relationship of living beings (including humans) with one another and with their environment.*

Due to those taboos and rules, Akha traditional shifting cultivation just opened small patches of forests at any given time. As a result, it was evident that over 60% of Xishuangbanna lands were still covered by forests in 1950 (Xishuangbanna Forestry Bureau 1998). However, majority of these forests has disappeared as a result of new ways of natural resource management promoted by the Chinese government under the name of development. First of all, large scale shifting cultivation, involving massive clearance of forests without observing those taboos and rules, were encouraged as a form of commune economy during the Planned Economy Period of China (1949 – 1977). Indeed, those sacred forests were destroyed intentionally in the "anti - superstition" campaign. All those religious rituals and related cultural activities were forbidden. In other world, the fact, that the traditional natural resource management system was abandoned along with their TEK and sacred forests, is a major reason of deforestation and loss of biodiversity in Xishuangbanna.

Another major factor that contributed to deforestation and loss of biodiversity in Xishuangbanna was rubber plantations. The newly born government of China needed to produce this strategic but unavailable industrial material rubber within its own territory for the sake of national security during the cold war. From the state's point of view, Xishuangbanna tropical natural forests were wasteful that needed to be reclaimed and traditional shifting cultivation were unproductive that needed to be replaced, and both were uncontrollable (untaxable). Rubber plantations were justified by the belief of Chinese that the plantations were forests which would provide environmental/ecological services as those natural forests do. So it was just "forests for forests" and would kill two birds with one stone. Therefore, eight state-run rubber plantation farms have been established in Xishuangbanna under the Reclaim Bureau of Yunnan Province since 1956. Since local indigenous people were viewed backward and thus unqualified for this new job of modern productivity, the farm workers were recruited from Han populations in other parts of China, and indeed most first batch workers were retired veterans. Thus rubber plantations seemed to be a perfect new technology which would allow the state to control over local resources and indigenous people.

These new landscapes of productivity and control, i. e. rubber plantations, have created huge tensions with those of traditional sacred ecology. Great expansion of rubber plantations has been achieved at the expenses of rainforests as well as forested lands used for shifting cultivation by local people, which allows Xishuangbanna to become the second national biggest base for rubber production but forces local people to farm less desirable lands, and indeed leaves less lands not enough for continuing traditional shifting cultivation in many Akha villages. Local governments tried to promote rubber plantations as alternative to shifting cultivation for economic development in Akha villages in the 1960s and 1970s, but all of these efforts failed as Akha people neither liked this new alien crop nor did they have the technology. In the early 1980s, the neighbor state farms helped some Akha villages to develop collective rubber plantations through a "*lianying*" (co-farming) system in which Akha villages provided free labor and lands while the state farms provided free seedlings and technology, then they shared the products when the rubber trees started to be tapped later. Local government also financed to set up many collective rubber plantation farms during the same period of time. As Akha people, and other local groups, started learning the technology and getting economic benefits, smallholder's private rubber plantations by local people boomed in the 1990s. And by the time the local governments tried to stop the expansion of private rubber plantations in the late 1990s, it was too late to do so as local people had adopted a new way of life adaptive to rubber plantations. Cash is what they need most in current market-oriented economy as everything they need is available at the markets. Rubber plantations could provide what they need now just as forests used to provide to them before. What have been lost are rainforests, forest-dwelled animals and plants, traditional ways of life, TEK, and a healthy ecosystem. What Akha people have gained is an empowerment deprived from increasing cash income, which allows them to renegotiate their identities and their political relationships with other ethnic groups such as Dai and with the state.

It is very interesting to examine how Akha people explain all of these changes within their own animistic worldview. During Planned Economy Period, that destroying sacred forests without being punished as they used to believe led to the belief of Akha people that forest spirits were disappearing, that Han Chinese were like wandering spirits Akha people had to deal instead, and that Chairman Mao was the supreme God governing all creatures including spirits. They started to worship Chairman Mao and believe that they would not get punished if they follow Chairman Mao's and the communist's order. Death of Mao caused a big panic to Akha people who started worrying of returning of those powerful forest spirits. However, having tasted the power of money, some Akha youths dare to challenge the very notion of spirits by expanding rubber plantations on even most sacred lands. A new form of religion that would worship money as powerful spirits is forming.

It concludes that Akha societies and their natural resource management have involved as they adapt to dynamic changes of two sets of forces. When natural forces are the major challenges, Akha natural resource management system tends to be more sustainable ecologically; while social - political forces surpassed natural ones, Akha people tend to adopt a new strategy of natural resource management which would provide best interests to them, in doing so, negative ecological consequences may follow. Therefore, to review a policy or a development project needs to examine its economic, social, and ecological impacts. Only and if only are benefits of those three domains balanced, would a sustainable development be achieved.

CONTENTS

Chapter 1 Introduction of Natural Resource Management and Sustainable Development ··· 1

1. 1 Background ·· 1
1. 2 Conceptual Framework: Ecology of Landscape ················· 6
1. 3 Research Area and Subject: Xishuangbanna and Akha ··· 13
1. 4 Research Objectives, Hypotheses and Methodology ········ 21
1. 5 Significance of the Study ·· 23

Chapter 2 Dynamic Politics of Akha Identities: A Brief History of the Akha ··· 25

2. 1 Introduction ·· 25
2. 2 Genealogies of the Hani-Akha ·· 31
2. 3 People of the Sky in North Country *Nya-mir* ···················· 35
2. 4 People of the Bamboo Kingdom in the Middle Country *Ghanr-mir* ··· 47
2. 5 *Jadae* polities and formation of Akha identity in the South Country *Gee-mir* ·· 55

2.6 Diasporic Period of Akha History ……………… 72
2.7 Discussion ………………………………………… 80

Chapter 3 Ecology of Sacred Landscape: Natural Resource Management of Akha People in China Prior to 1950 …………… 83

3.1 Introduction ……………………………………… 83
3.2 Akha Belief System ……………………………… 86
3.3 Akha Worldview and Sacred Landscapes …………… 88
3.4 Six Zones of Land Uses in Mengsong Akha Community … 98
3.5 Management of Forbidden Ecotopes ………………… 99
3.6 Management of Restricted Ecotopes—*putsanq* (village fence forest) and *ghaqtsanq* (protected forests) …………… 100
3.7 Management of Modified Ecotopes —*miqkhaevq lavqghaw aqganq* (firewood forest) and *nyoqjawr kmrteev aqganq* (fenced buffalo forest) ………………………………… 114
3.8 Management of transformed ecotopes—*yarmr jawqxmq aqdae* (swidden fields) ………………………………… 120
3.9 Management of Domesticated Ecotopes —*daema* (paddy fields) and *yark mr* (fenced gardens) ……………… 133
3.10 Management of Mobile Ecotopes—*bawrtsanq jeiqzaq* (wild animals) ……………………………………………… 136
3.11 Management of Created Ecotope—*pu* (village) ……… 146
3.12 Conclusion and Discussion: Ecology of Sacred Landscapes of the Akha ………………………………………… 154

Chapter 4 From Swidden Agriculture to Cash Crop Monoculture: A Case Study of Mengsong Community …………… 162

4.1 Introduction ……………………………………… 162

4.2	Period I (1949—1977)	170
4.3	Period II (1978—1998)	180
4.4	Period III (1998—up to date)	188
4.5	Other Activities in Mengsong	195
4.6	Conclusion	199

Chapter 5　Rubber Plantations and Transformations of Akha Society in Xishuangbanna, Southwest China: A Case Study of Baka Village ………… 210

5.1	Introduction	210
5.2	Rubber Plantations in Xishuangbanna: State *vs.* People	214
5.3	State Efforts to Eliminate Shifting Cultivation in Xishuangbanna	217
5.4	Rubber Plantations in Baka Village	220
5.5	Cultural Adaptations to Rubber Plantation in Baka	225
5.6	Conclusion	244

Chapter 6　Conclusions ………… 250

6.1	Revisiting Contested Landscapes in China	250
6.2	Cultural (Mal)adaptations to Frontiers by the Akha	261
6.3	Discussions and Suggestions on Sustainable Development and Bio-diversity Conservation in Xishuangbanna and Beyond	269

REFERENCES ………… 279

Appendix I　Preferred Timber Trees in Mengsong ………… 297

Appendix II A List of Plants and Crops in Mengsong
            Swidden Fields ·· 298

Appendix III A List of Plants in Mengsong Home garden ·········· 304

Appendix IV The Twelve Annual Ancestor Offerings of the Akha ··· 312

Appendix V Akha Lunar Calendar (*khovqtovq latovq*) ············ 316

Appendix VI Dynamics of Mengsong Land Uses ···················· 320
Acknowledgement ·· 322

Chapter 1

Introduction of Natural Resource Management and Sustainable Development

1.1 Background

Growing environmental crises and enlarging social inequalities concomitant of rapid economic growth in the second half of the twentieth century had forced our world leaders to think of a new way of development. Sustainable development is demonstrated in Agenda 21, which exclusively addresses themes related to sustainable development. It was issued by leaders of 178 governments at the United Nations Conference on Environment and Development (also known as Earth Summit), held in Rio de Janeiro from June 3rd to 14th, 1992. The most often-quoted definition of sustainable development is "development that meets the needs of the present without compromising the ability of future generations to meet their own needs", as defined by the World Commission on Environment and Development (WCED), in their report titled *Our Common Future* (1987:43). Sustainable development ties together concern for the carrying capacity of natural systems with the social challenges facing humanity (Meadows etc. , 1972; Stivers, 1976; Daly, 1991). The concept of sustainable development has often been broken into three constituent parts: environmental sustainability, economic sustainability, and social sustainability. More specifically, sustainable development simultaneously addresses balances among 1) economic growth and social equitability, 2) social development and environmental bearability, and 3) environmental health and economic viability (Munasinghe Institute for Sustainable Development, 2007). More recently, it has been suggested that a more consistent analytical breakdown is to distinguish four domains: economic, ecological, political and cultural sustainability (Hawkes, 2001; UCLG, 2009).

Making these balances, however, is a challenging task in any given society, because various stakeholders prioritize their agenda for their own better benefits under a given circumstance, and take various strategies when they come to interact and negotiate with each other. Different activities of a given society following various strategies may or may not lead to sustainable development. For instance, Elizabeth Economy (2004) and Kristen Day (2005) pointed out that great economic development of China in the past couple of decades was achieved at the huge environmental expenses — overdraft of resources, devastation of whole eco-systems, loss of species, water and air pollution, to name a few. These environmental crises, and over population, have become big challenges for the sustainable development of China. Therefore, some key questions we need to answer here are that why a society prioritizes certain activities over others in their agenda, what are the major factors that influence decision-making of various stakeholders, under which conditions a society would take a strategy that would more likely lead to a sustainable development, and how could various stakeholders (especially those with power and influence such as governments and international organizations/societies) create these favorable conditions. As an ethnobotanist and ecological anthropologist, since 1996, I have been trying to address these questions through examining historical dynamics of natural resource management by Akha people❶ in Xishuangbanna, Yunnan Province, Southwest China.

A study of natural resource management is not only a necessary part but also a very good entry point for studies of sustainable development, because a sustainable natural resource management regime is a prerequisite for sustainable development. Like the latter, the former also cuts across the four dimensions of nature, economy, society, and culture. Among the scholars who study natural resource management two groups are outstanding: cultural ecologists and political ecologists. Cultural ecologists' studies focus on interaction of traditional ecological knowledge and belief systems/worldviews in natural resource management by traditional societies (Anderson, 1996; Berkes, 1999; Nelson, 1983; Strang, 1997). They argue that these traditional societies have managed their natural resources in a sustainable way through religious representations of their traditional ecological knowledge (Berkes' notion of knowledge-practice-belief system, or Anderson's conservation ethics). However, these traditional management systems along with bio-diversity are disappearing as these societies integrate into modern nation-states and global market economy (Pei, 1996). Consequently, those cultural ecological studies of "isolated traditional societies" have been criticized for lack of attention to power and inequality and for exclusion of the dynamics of colonialism and the encroachment of a global capitalist economy, as "ecology without politics" (Peet and Watts, 1993). As an alternative, studies under the name of "political ecology" (Blaikie and Brookfield, 1987; Wolf, 1982) have burgeoned since the 1980s to examine the relationship of patterns of resource use to political-economic forces. Current political ecological studies, however,

---

❶ Akha people are officially identified as a branch of the Hani Minority Nationality in China. The historical and contemporary relationship of Akha people with other Hani groups will be elaborated in Chapter 2.

claimed to be a combination of cultural ecology and political economy, often focus on the latter and neglect the former, and have consequently been criticized as "politics without ecology" (Vayda and Walters, 1999).

My own study is a response to the call for integrating cultural ecology into current political ecological studies (Paulson et al., 2003). I argue that these traditional societies are not merely passive victims of national and/or international development projects and of a global capitalist market economy, as conventionally held, but rather they change their resource management strategies as they adapt to new social, economic and political environments of modern nation-states. Therefore, my study would fall into a "political ecology" that combines approaches of political economy, which examine the relationship of patterns of resource use to political-economic forces, with those of traditional cultural ecology, which emphasize cultural adaptations to local environments (Grossman, 1998; Sheridan, 1988).

A recent masterpiece of political ecological studies is Michael R. Dove's book *The Banana Tree at the Gate* (2011), in which Dr. Dove has challenged the conventionally held prevailing view of isolated resource-poor and economically marginal tropical forest communities who might need to be helped into the modernity of nation-states and global economic system, through his careful and deep studies of the Kantu, a member of an Ibanic-speaking tribe of Dayak who live in the northern and westerly headwaters of the Kapuas River in West Kalimantan, Indonesian Borneo. Dove shows that the involvement of Borneo's indigenous peoples in commodity production for global markets is not only ancient but also successful. Dove attributes Kantu's success to their development of a dual household economy, with distinct subsistence-and market-oriented sectors, which has historically made these smallholding farmers extremely competitive with the large-scale, heavily capitalized, state-supported plantation sector. Janet C. Sturgeon (2010) also demonstrates similar stories of Dai and Akha smallholding farmers in Xishuangbanna, Yunnan Province, Southwest China, who are more competitive than the state farms in a regionalized economy based on rubber plantations, and have become successful entrepreneurs to invest to develop more rubber plantations with their counterparts in northern Laos. Sturgeon attributes this success to the capability and agility of these smallholders to adapt to new crops, cropping strategies, markets, and labour opportunities.

In a similar line to works of Dove (2011) and Sturgeon (2010), I will show how Akha farmers in Xishuangbanna have been competing in using and managing natural resources (particularly lands and forests) with the state of China through contested landscapes. As Dove shows that the involvement of Kantu in the global market is not a modern event but rather ancient, I will also demonstrate that Akha people have been dealing with various polities for millennia (see Chapter 2). However, my case studies are different from those of Dove (2011) and Sturgeon (2010) in several ways. Firstly, I will use landscape (Sauer 1925), by which I mean perceived and culturally presented environment, natural or modified/created by people, as a key concept to examine the dynamics of natural resource management by the Akha people over space and time, which would be different theoretically and methodologically from those of Dove (2011) and Sturgeon (2010). Secondly, I will examine how the Akha have become cash crop farmers from swidden agriculturalists, as a result of negotiations between the Akha and state of China over the contested landscapes, which is different from Kantu who have been able to maintain dual economic systems (Dove, 2011). Thirdly, I will examine ecological, economic-political, social-cultural consequences of the transformations of the natural resource management systems, which might have a lot of similarities with those of Dove (2011) and Sturgeon (2010), but emphases on cultural (mal)adaptations to these transformations and discussions on implications of these changes in sustainable development should make my own studies distinct.

1.2 Conceptual Framework: Ecology of Landscape

The world in people's mind is not a perfect, total and exact representation of what the senses perceive, rather, people tend to organize and reinterpret the perceptions in the light of experiences as well as in terms of their wants and needs — not only needs for things like food and shelter, but also needs to see the world as hopefully as possible, to see it as simple and comprehensible, and to see it as ultimately *manageable* and *controllable* (Anderson, 1996). The way a people perceive and interpret the world is their cultural worldview, "the shared conceptual framework by means of which human experience is organized to create a common 'reality' or 'habitus' for the members of a given culture" (Callicott and Nelson, 2004: 6). I use the term *landscape* to refer to perceived and culturally presented environment, natural or modified/created by people. By contrast, *bio-physical environment* is far wider, including everything from sunlight to bacteria. People may know very little about their environment, but by definition, the landscape is what they see, know, and interact with.

This distinction between landscape and bio-physical environment is fundamental to the study of human-environmental interaction because different peoples may perceive the same environment differently, that is, they may "see" different landscapes over the same environment, which in turn will shape the way they further interact with the perceived environment. Every culture needs to "control" their environments and manage their resources in order to survive and continue. These control and management always involve two interdependent processes. The first is a cultural presentation or mental transformation of their bio-physical environment into a landscape. The second process is to physically manage and/or control their landscape, the perceived environment, ritually or physically. A ritual management would maintain a natural landscape while a physical management would result in a *modified* or built landscape, which is a physically modified or transformed environment. This modified or built landscape could be temporary — capable of being reversed back to a natural landscape (though not necessarily to the same as the previous natural landscape), or permanent — some of which are intentionally maintained by continuous human intervention. An example of a temporary built landscape could be a swidden agricultural system, and a permanent built landscape could be irrigated paddy fields or or an industrial monoculture such as rubber tree plantations. These two processes lead to a conclusion that landscape is both the *medium* and the *outcome* of human-environmental interactions. Therefore, a landscape is a perceived environment, natural or modified or created. And I use the term *ecology of landscape* to refer to the study of human-environment interactions in general and cultural-political ecology of natural resource management in particular.

All traditional societies with historical continuity in resource use on a particular land have accumulated a great amount of ecological knowledge about their environment. Berkes (1999) defines this traditional ecological knowledge as,

> "a cumulative body of knowledge, practice, and belief, evolving by adaptive processes and handed down through generations by cultural transmission, about the relationship of living beings (including humans)

Sacred and Contested Landscapes

with one another and with their environment."

The term *traditional ecological knowledge* came into widespread use only in the 1980s, though the practice of traditional ecological knowledge is as old as ancient hunter-gatherer cultures (Berkes, 1999). Berkes (1999: 13-14) provides a useful framework of analysis for traditional ecological knowledge, known as a knowledge-practice-belief complex, which can be analyzed at four interrelated levels: (1) local environmental knowledge; (2) a resource management system that uses local environmental knowledge and an appropriate set of practices, tools, and techniques; (3) social institutions; and (4) worldview. I think Berkes' analytical framework of the knowledge-practice-belief complex can be applied to general resource management of any society with some modifications (see Figure 1).

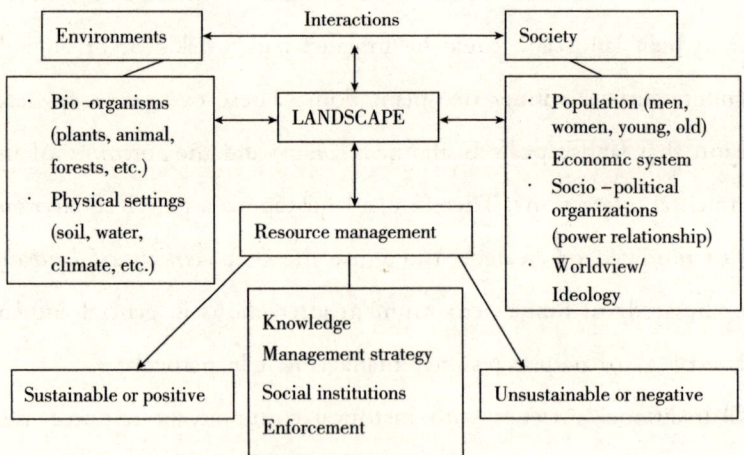

Figure 1   Analytical framework of natural resource management

Firstly, detailed and rich knowledge of local biophysical environments, that is, plants, animals, forests, soils, climates, etc., is fundamental for a sustainable resource management. By "sustainable resource management" I mean meeting our needs while ensuring that we leave healthy and viable natural resources for future generations. For the purpose of simplicity, I will limit my analysis of sustainability to renewable biological resources, or biological diversity, which is regarded vital for the survival and health of people and the Earth (UN, 1992). Maintenance (and creation) of a certain level of biodiversity is believed vital for the health of eco-systems and thus the key criterion for evaluating the sustainability of the management regime (Zhang, 1995). Bio-diversity is the full range of variety and variability within and among living organisms and the ecological complexes in which they occur, and encompasses genetic diversity, species diversity, and eco-system or community diversity (Reid and Miller, 1989). Genetic diversity is the genetic variation of a species. Varieties of a crop species will be used to evaluate the genetic diversity in this study. Species diversity is the variety and abundance of different types of organisms which inhabit an area. Eco-system diversity encompasses the variety of habitats that occur within a region, or the mosaic of patches found within an environment. Folk or cultural ecotopes (Johnson and Hunn, 2010) will be used to evaluate eco-system diversity in this study.

Local ecological knowledge includes knowledge of species identifications and taxonomy, their life histories, distributions, and behaviors — knowledge of ecological processes, such as the functional relationships among key species, their relationships with their environments (soils, climates, etc.), and forest succession. Such knowledge is both cumulative — based on experience and empirical observation, and transmitted over generations — and dynamic, adapting to changes, thus has obvious survival value for all traditional societies. But local ecological knowledge is not sufficient by itself to ensure the sustainable use of resources. There must be a resource management strategy by which local knowledge is applied with appropriate tools and technology to ecological practices. These ecological practices involve decision-making by different actors (individuals, households, community), and (when it applicable, states, among others), not only based on the information coming out of local ecological knowledge, but also influenced by socio-economic factors. To make an optimal decision, decision makers require complete and accurate information. However, such completeness and accuracy are rarely, if ever, met in actual resource management situations, because: firstly, environments constantly change, so it is very vital for local ecological knowledge to be dynamic (adapting to changes) and thus to be cumulative, which means it is never complete; secondly, local ecological knowledge tends to be distributed among different holders in a society rather than equally shared by its members—the more complex a society is, the more tendency of their knowledge is distributed, which requires effective means of communicating of information and sharing knowledge. Therefore, people always have to make decisions based on imperfect information (Anderson, 1996; Simon, 1960). Different societies have various specific difficulties when they make decisions. For a complex state like China in the 1950s, it was extremely difficult to make good decisions for a particular remote area such as Xishuangbanna, basically because the decision makers at the central government did not have enough information and knowledge about local environment at that time. It is the reason why the central government sent out an order to scientists (ecologists, agronomists, botanists, etc.) to study the feasibility of rubber plantations in Xishuangbanna in the 1950s. It is also often the case that the information and knowledge the decision makers at the central authority of a state might have is too general to be applicable to a particular local area, as in the case of the Land Conversion Program in China in the 1990s and the early 2000s (see Chapter 4). Even if they have enough information and knowledge about a particular area, they may still make an imperfect decision on that area for other obvious socio-economic or political reasons, such as establishment of state farms of rubber plantations in the 1950s (see Chapter 5). So, it is very important in resource management to leave a specific decision to the local population or at least to make sure that the local population participates in the process of decision making and that local knowledge is considered seriously. It does not necessarily mean, however, that local populations always make good decisions. Traditional societies may possess a great amount of knowledge about their environment, but the sheer quantity of information presents a major problem in systematizing, storing, and retrieving information because of their lack of a writing system. The solution lies partly in their powerful narratives—myths, legends, tales, and stories. Knowledge is given the absolute value in these sacred texts. For instance, in areas as locally disparate as aboriginal Australia and California, children in deserts learn the location of water sources through stories (Sutton and Anderson, 2004:119).

After a decision has been made, either individually or collectively, in order to implement it effectively appropriate social institutions (that is, rules and codes of social behavior and relationships) need to be made to guarantee adequate coordination and cooperation among interdependent hunters, fishers, agriculturalists, or whoever is involved in the ecological practices. The last level has to be the enforcement of these social rules and codes. There exist various means of enforcement, which can be sorted into two broad categories: internalized and externalized. Internalized controls are social controls through beliefs, values, and moralities deeply internalized in the minds of individuals. This includes religion, ethics, and more generally, belief systems including worldview. External controls, also known as *sanctions*, involve external enforcement through open coercion, designed to encourage conformity to social norms. Any society has both means of social controls available, though they may tend to rely more on one than another. State-based societies tend to rely more on external controls, which include law, judicial system, prison, police, military, and so forth. Traditional societies tend to rely more on internalized controls, among which religion and general belief systems are at central place, as E. N. Anderson (1996) argues:

> "all traditional societies that have succeeded in managing resource well, over time, have done it in part through religious or ritual representation of resource management. The key point is not religion per se, but the use of emotionally powerful cultural symbols to sell particular moral codes and management systems." (166)

As a matter of fact, religion, ethics, and practical knowledge are not separated in many traditional societies, rather, they are integrated into their worldview, which is depicted in their sacred narratives, particularly myths, as Malinowski's (1992:103) argument that "it [myth] expresses, enhances, and codifies belief; it safeguards and enforces morality; it vouches for the efficiency of ritual and contains practical rules for the guidance of man". Thus, study of these narratives becomes the most salient anthropological methodology for the study of worldview (Callicott and Nelson, 2004).

This brings us back to the beginning of process of a people's interaction with their environment, which involves the psychological transformation of environment in to landscape according to their worldview. According to Irving Hallowell (1963), all cultures have their own worldview,

> "which, by means of beliefs, available knowledge and language, mediates personal adjustment to the world through such psychological processes as perceiving, recognizing, conceiving, judging, and reasoning... which, intimately associated with a normative orientation, becomes the

basis for reflection, decision, and action... and a foundation for a consensus with respect to goals and values."(258)

Following the idea of Berkes' Sacred Ecology (1999), I am using the term *sacred landscape* to refer to the perceived and culturally presented/ transformed environments by traditional societies like Akha according to their worldview and/or belief systems. Documentation and analyses of the Akha sacred landscapes and management of them will be elaborated in Chapter 3. When different cultures come to interact with the same environment, they will perceive/imagine different landscapes and make different decisions on their management strategies accordingly, which could be cooperative, or, more often than not, produces conflicts between groups in their control over resources. This leads to my another concern of this research, that is, contested landscapes, their socio-economic contexts, and their social environmental consequences, which will be exemplified in two case studies in Chapter 4 and Chapter 5.

1.3 Research Area and Subject: Xishuangbanna and Akha

Xishuangbanna is a Dai Ethnic Minority[1] autonomous prefecture of Yunnan Province, Southwest China. Located between 21°08′−22°36′N, and 99°56′−101°50′E, with elevations ranging between 475 meters — 2429.5 meters above sea level, Xishuangbanna covers a total area of 19,125 square kilometers (Forestry Bureau of Xishuangbanna Prefecture, 1998:26). Lying at southern tip of Yunnan Province, it borders with Laos at its east and

---

[1] Dai Ethnic Minority is one of officially recognized 55 Minority Nationalities in China. There are several subgroups within the Dai Ethnic Minority. The majority of those in Xishuangbanna call themselves Tai Lue.

southeast and with Myanmar at its west and southwest. Mekong River, Known as Lancang Jiang in China, runs across Xishuangbanna from its northwest through southeast (see Figure 2).

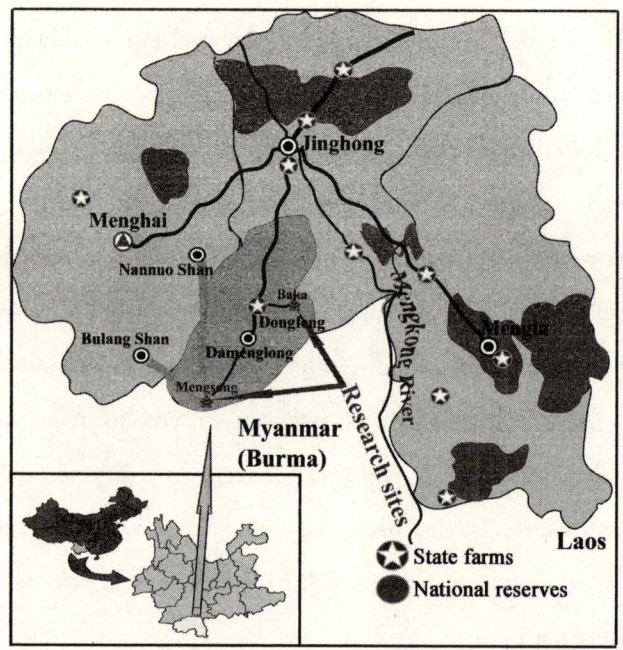

Figure 2   Research Sites in Xishuangbanna, Yunnan Province, Southwest China

Geographically, Xishuangbanna is divided among one county-level city (Jinghong), two counties (Menghai and Mengla), and ten county-level state farms (Jinghong, Dongfeng, Mengyang, Ganlanba, Dadugan, Liming, Mengla, Mengpeng, Mengman, and Mengsing) (see Figure 2). Administratively speaking, however, Xishuangbanna Dai Autonomous Prefecture (XDAP) governs only Jinghong Municipality and two other counties (Menghai and Mengla); while the ten county-level state farms had been state-subsidized enterprise governed directly by the Agricultural Reclamation Bureau of Yunnan Province until 2003, when they were hived off into parastatal companies belonging to the Yunnan Agricultural Reclamation Cooperation Limited.

This reform of the administrative system of the state farms was a result of China's entry into WTO in 2001, which requires curtailing state subsidies to industry.

Xishuangbanna is a special place to China in at least three ways.

Firstly, it is one of the biodiversity hot spots at a transitionary zone between the tropical and the subtropical in China and in the world. Due to its unique geographic and climate aspects, it contains the highest level of biodiversity per unit of land area in China. Although the area occupies less than 0.2% of total national land area, it comprises 4,000 vascular plant species, 102 mammal species, 400 bird species, 63 reptile species, 38 amphibian species and 100 fish species — which account for one fifth of vascular plant species and one fourth of animal species in the whole of China. Besides, more than 90% of China's wild elephant population is living in this region (UNESCO, 2007). Therefore, it is given the title of "Kingdom of Animals" and "Kingdom of Plants" in China. Most of these plants and animals are protected in Xishuangbanna Nature Reserve[1], one of the earliest established national natural reserves. Currently, it comprises the largest and most comprehensive tropical forests in China. However, many of these plants and especially animals are in very small populations or even in danger of extinction, and they comprise 12.5% of first-class, 32% of second-class, and 37% of third-class protected animals in China (Liu et al., 1990). Having realized its ecological and cultural significance and fragility, UNESCO has designated Xishuangbanna as one of biosphere preserve areas under the Man and the Biosphere Programme (MAB) since 1993 (UNESCO, 2007).

---

[1] Xishuangbanna Nature Reserve was established in 1958 by Yunnan Provincial Government and was upgraded as a national nature reserve in 1986. It comprises seven separated sections with a total area of 242,510 hectares, making up 12.68% of Xishuangbanna territory.

Secondly, Xishuangbanna is a strategic gateway to Southeast Asia. Lying at southern tip of Yunnan Province, Xishuangbanna borders with Laos at its east and southeast and with Myanmar at its west and southwest along 966 kilometers borderline. Mekong River, Known as Lancang Jiang in China, runs across Xishuangbanna from its northwest through southeast, before it runs as the sole international border between Laos and Myanmar, then partial borders between Laos and Thailand, as well as runs through Laos, Cambodia and Vietnam where it finally flows into the South China Sea. Historically, this region was governed by a Tai Lue polity, known as *Sipsong Panna* —literally meaning "twelve thousand paddy-fields"❶ in the Tai Lue language. Rulers of Sipsong Panna paid tribute to both Chinese and Burmese states, and maintained a kind of brotherhood relationships with other ancient Tai states in today's Laos, Shan state of Myanmar, and Northern Thailand (Hsieh, 1995). Xishuangbanna❷Dai Autonomous Prefecture (XDAP) was established in 1953 according to the Region Autonomous Law of China, because it was ruled by a Dai (Tai Lue) Tusi❸and the Dai (Tai Lue) were the majority in this area when it was liberated by the People's Liberation Army of P. R. China in 1950.

Xishuangbanna is a mountainous area where flat and slightly sloped lands can be found only at various basins, which make up only 5% of its total land area. Such basins are called "Muang" in Tai (written as "Meng" in Chinese) or "Bazi" in local Chinese. Historically, Tai Lue people had settled at these basins and turned these flat lands into irrigated paddy fields, while the

---

❶ *Panna* or "thousand paddy-fields" is an administrative unit of the Tai Lue feudal polity.

❷ Xishuangbanna is a Chinese transliteration of *Sipsong Panna*.

❸ *Tusi* , also known as Local Headmen or Chieftains or Rulers, were tribal leaders recognized as imperial officials by Chinese governments of the Yuan, Ming, and Qing dynasties, principally in Yunnan. The arrangement is generally known as the Native Chieftain System.

rest vast mountainous areas were occupied by other ethnic groups such as Akha, Lahu, Bulang, Yi, Jinuo, Yao (also known as Mien in Thailand), and among others whose economy was mainly based on swidden agriculture. Many of these highland groups are living in mountainous border areas of Mainland Southeast Asia today. Though the historical political relationships of this region and its peoples have been changed fundamentally since WWII, its economic and cultural connections have been maintained and even enhanced recently. The latter has been demonstrated through rubber boom in Luang Namtha, northern Laos under the influence and investments from Xishuangbanna (Shi, 2008) and establishment of Xishuangbanna Jinghong Industrial Zone—a cooperative development between China local government and Thailand's companies in Jinghong, capital city of Xishuangbanna in 2006 (Xishuangbanna Prefecture, 2008).

Thirdly, Xishuangbanna is one of a few tropical places where natural rubber is produced from plantation of Amazon rubber trees *Hevea brasiliensis* in China. Rubber along with steel, coal, and petroleum were defined as four strategic materials for national industries and defenses by the new-born People's Republic of China in 1949. These materials were embargoed to China by the United States-led capitalist countries in 1950 as a direct result of China's decision to involve in the American-Korean war. Though there were some rubber plantations in southern China, mainly in Hainan Island and Guangdong Province at that time, they produced too little rubber to meet huge demands for national industrialization and defense constructions. In order to break the US-led imperialist economic blockage and embargo policies, central government of China made a decision to expand rubber plantations at any possible places within its territories at the 100th session of Government Affairs Council of Central People's Government of China in

1951 (Yunnan Agricultural Reclamation Cooperation Ltd. and Yunnan Association of Tropical Crops, 2005). Xishuangbanna, as the national second biggest tropical frontier in China (following Hainan Island), was targeted for this historical and honorable mission. Consequently, numerous state rubber farms were established in Xishuangbanna since 1956. These state farms were incorporated into today's ten county-level farms by the early 1980s. Consequently, Xishuangbanna has become the second biggest basis of rubber production in China after Hainan Island. The total area of rubber plantations in Xishuangbanna is said to reach 173,133 hectares in 2004 (Statistics Bureau of Xishuangbanna Prefecture, 2005), which takes up about 9% of its total land (I believe this number is underreported; see Chapter 5).

An important concomitance of the establishment of rubber plantations in Xishuangbanna is demographic shift in its ethnic makeup (see Table 1). There were only 5,000 Han Chinese in Xishuangbanna in 1949, which was 2.5% of its total population. However, Han population soared to 17,905 in 1956, 185,894 in 1982, and 340,431 in 2010, which made up 6.9%, 28.3%, and 30.01% of its total population respectively. Most of them were recruited as workers in the state farms from other parts of China. As a result, Han Chinese has become the biggest ethnic group from a small negligible minority in Xishuangbanna. In contrast, proportion of Dai population had dropped from 52.1% in 1949 to 34.3% in 1982 and further to 27.9% in 2010, from a majority to the second biggest group in Xishuangbanna.

Due to its special geographic location as being laid out above, Xishuangbanna has been caught between contradictory national policies of economic development (particularly rubber plantations) and natural reserves since the 1950s. These two contradictory goals can be achieved only through appropriation of huge area of forested lands used for swidden agriculture by the indigenous peoples. They become cash crop farmers in this process. My study is to document and analyze this process by examining the dynamics of natural resource management by the Akha people in Xishuangbanna, particularly through two thorough case studies in Mengsong and Baka Akha communities, before and after 1950[1].

Table 1　Demographic Dynamics of Xishuangbanna (1949 – 2010)

Ethnic groups	1949	(%)	1956	(%)	1982	(%)	2010	(%)
Dai	105000	52.1	128700	49.8	225485	34.3	316151	27.9
Han	5000	2.5	17905	6.9	185894	28.3	340431	30.0
Hani-Akha	30000	14.9	46514	18.0	129198	19.7	215434	19.0
Lahu	13000	6.5	16203	6.3	33336	5.1	61504	5.4
Bulang	15000	7.4	19368	7.5	27664	4.2	47529	4.2
Yi	4500	2.2	6365	2.5	16495	2.5	66731	5.9
Jinuo	4000	2.0	5491	2.1	12405	1.9	22124	2.0
Yao	2500	1.2	6519	2.5	10958	1.7	22266	2.0
Others	22440	11.1	11575	4.5	15890	2.4	41345	3.6
Total	201440	100	258640	100	657325	100	1133515	100

Sources:

—1949 data is from Liu et al. (1990: 141).

—1956 data is from China's first national census

—1982 data is from China's third national census

—2010 data is from China's sixth national census

I have chosen Akha people as my study subjects for the following reasons. Firstly, national policies such as logging ban and shifting cultivation ban have brought more profound impacts on the highlanders than on the

---

[1] Although People's Republic of China was established in 1949, Xishuangbanna was not liberated and made part of its administrative region until 1950. Therefore, I use the year of 1950 as a turning point for my comparison study.

lowlanders (e. g. Dai or Tai Lue), and the Akha have been the biggest highland group whose economy was based on swidden agriculture in Xishuangbanna for centuries. Secondly, Akha is one of the major ethnic groups in the Southeast Asia mainland massif (Michaud, 2000), a geo-political region also known as Zomia (Van Schendel, 2001; Scott, 2009), with a total population of about 700, 000[1]. A majority of the Akha in Xishuangbanna have become rubber farmers, while the rest have become tea farmers, in the meanwhile, influenced by their counterparts in China, many Akha in Eastern Myanmar, Northern Laos, and Northern Thailand started growing rubber trees a decade or two ago, and more and more are following now. Experiences and lessons of the Akha in Xishuangbanna could be learned by those in neighbor countries. Thirdly, being born and having grown up in an Akha village in Xishuangbanna, I have personally experienced and witnessed socio-cultural, economic, and ecological transformations of Akha societies in last four decades. My membership of the Akha community, knowledge on Akha culture and language skill allow me insight into Akha societies and provide comprehensive understanding of those changes from an insider's perspectives.

---

[1] The total population of the Hani Minority Nationality in Yunnan was 1,660,000 in 2010 according to the Sixth National Census, among which the Akha population was 274,734, over three quarters of them are living in Xishuangbanna. According to Mr. Min Nyo, the director of Association of Traditional Akha in Myanmar, the population of Akha in Myanmar is about 250,000. A Lao PDR national census showed 90,698 Akha in Laos in 2005. According to Mr. Athu Pochae, the director of Akha Association for Education and Culture in Thailand (AFECT), the population of Akha in Thailand is about 80,000. I was informed by some Akha villagers and officials in Phongsaly of Laos that there were some Akha villages in Lai Chau Province of Vietnam along the border with Laos in 2002. Estimated numbers of Hani/Akha population in Vietnam range from 26,000 (Mr. Yang Youyi, from Cultural Department of Lao Cai Province of Vietnam, 2008, personal communication) to 40,000 (Huang, 2007:50), but the number of Akha is unknown in Vietnam.

Chapter 1 Introduction of Natural Resource Management and Sustainable Development

1.4 Research Objectives, Hypotheses and Methodology

Through documenting and analysing the dynamics of natural resource management systems by Akha people in Xishuangbanna and beyond over time, the overall goal and purpose of this research is to 1) understand the mechanism of cultural adaptation by the Akha to changing social and natural environments; and 2) explore how a sustainable natural resource management regime could be established. More specifically, this research aims to:

1) construct a brief history of Akha people in general and its socio-political relationships with various states, ancient and modern, in this region;

2) discover the traditional natural resource management system by the Akha people as swidden agriculturalists in Xishuangbanan prior to 1950;

3) trace dynamic changes of natural resource management strategies by the Akha people in last sixty years or so; and

4) examine the roles of national policies in the process through which Akha people have become cash crops farmers (particularly rubber and tea farmers) from traditional swidden agriculturalists.

My hypotheses of this study are:

1) Akha societies change their natural resource management strategies as cultural adaptive mechanism to changing environments, biophysical and socio-political.

2) Akha societies are more likely to adopt a more sustainable natural resource management regime when biophysical environment is the main external force with which they have to deal.

3) When socio-political environment becomes the main force with which Akha societies have to deal, they will adopt a natural resource management

system that would protect their best interests, which might have to be achieved at the expense of natural environment and biodiversity.

This thesis is based on many years of intensive fieldwork in two Akha communities — Mengsong and Baka in Xishuangbanna, particularly in 1996, 1998, 2004, 2006, and 2008, 2009, as well as extensive fieldwork in other Akha communities in Xishuangbanna and its neighboring countries in Greater Mekong Subregion (GMS) since 1996. In order to test my hypotheses and achieve my objectives, the following methods were deployed in my study:

1) reviewing relevant literature;

2) mining governmental archives and interviewing relevant officials regarding changes of national policies and their impacts on local/regional social and environmental situations;

3) collecting second-hand data and maps about the social and environmental (including climatic) changes in Xishuangbanna since 1949;

4) interviewing village-based key informants, such as village heads, religious specialists, folk botanists, folk zoologists, folk herb and/or medicinal specialists, and other cultural specialists particularly knowledgeable elders, for information on Akha traditional ecological knowledge, resource management systems, institutions, worldview, and landscapes;

5) interviewing focus groups to examine general community knowledge and how they talk about themselves, their environments, and national policies, how these change over time from their point of view and how their management strategies change accordingly;

6) observing (including participant observation) all major resource management activities;

7) using questionnaires and statistical analyses to collect and analyze data

on economic variables, knowledge distribution and transmission links;

8) collecting botanical specimens of relevant plants and get specialist help in their identification;

9) taking photographs (especially of ecologically relevant scenes—both scenes that I identify and scenes that local people point out as particularly illustrative or significant) and videos (especially of ceremonies);

10) encouraging people to draw their agricultural calendar and maps;

11) collecting the Akha origin myths and stories about plants, animals, and humans by using a tape-recorder;

12) collecting oral history of the Akha.

1.5 Significance of the Study

In general, this study of Akha resource management, combining traditional cultural ecology with political ecology approaches and insights from the newly emerging field of landscape studies, will contribute both theoretically and methodologically to current discourses in these fields.

Moreover, I think that documenting the detailed Akha traditional ecological knowledge and natural resource management system is not only necessary, as Dove (1999: 290) argues in saying that "... the detailed descriptions of vernacular technology and knowledge central to early ecological anthropology can now be read as politically empowering counter discourses;" but also urgent because the last Akha generations who possess this knowledge in some reasonably complete form are in their 1970s and 1980s now. This orally transmitted knowledge will be gone forever if it is not documented in the near future. I believe that traditional knowledge, as Berkes (1999: 179) put it, "is complementary to Western scientific knowledge, and not a replacement for it"; as such it remains important.

Finally, through evaluating the ecological impacts of different resource management strategies, this study will draw some lessons for China and the rest of world concerning how to construct a sustainable resource management regime, what conditions need to be taken into account, and how the state and/or a society can produce such conditions. These lessons should be particularly applicable to the Southeast Asian highlands (of which the Akha area is a part) since this geographically connected but politically separated region and its indigenous people, who are traditionally shifting cultivators, have been undergoing similar social and environmental transformations under the influences of different nation-states' development programs and of globalization of capitalist market economy during the last decades (Padoch, 2004).

Chapter 2

Dynamic Politics of Akha Identities: A Brief History of the Akha

2.1 Introduction

The term *Akha* is a self denomination for an extensive group of Tibeto-Burman-speaking people who also refer themselves by more ancient names such as *Zaq-niq*, *Yaq-niq*, *Aq-niq* or *Haq-niq* ❶ — pronunciation variants of the same term in the different dialects of these groups. The Akha are officially identified as part of the Hani Minority Nationality in China. The Hani Minority Nationality includes more than 20 various self-denominated subgroups, among which Akha is one (Jiang, 2007). These subgroups are usually sorted into three major dialectic groups: Ha-Ya, Bi-Ka and Hao-Bai. Akha belongs to the Ha-Ya dialectic group (Yunnan Provincial Editorial Committee on Local Chronicles, 2002; Jiang, 2007:133). The Hani Nationality (Akha included) is one of the major ethnic groups in the geographic area

---

❶ All Hani-Akha terms are written italicly in a Romanized Common Hani-Akha Orthography (CHAO) or known as *Khanq Haqniq Aqkaq Sanqbovq* (*KHAS*) in Hani-Akha, which was adopted by Akha representatives from China, Laos, Myanmar and Thailand, in Jinghong, Yunnan, China, on January 1st, 2009. Hani-Akha is a tonal language. It has three tones. In *KHAS*, low tone (11) is marked with the letter "q", high tone (55) is marked with the letter "r", while the middle tone (33) is not marked by any letter. In addition, there are two sets of vowels: oral and laryngealized (Lewis and Bai, 2002). The laryngealized vowels are marked by the letter "v".

Sacred and Contested Landscapes

known as Southeast Asia mainland massif[1] (Michaud, 2000), with a total population over two million people[2] living in a quadrangle region that spreads across the mountainous borderlands of five modern nation-states—Yunnan Province of China, Shan State of Eastern Myanmar, Northern Thailand, Northern Laos, and Northwestern Vietnam (see Figure 3). Elsewhere Akha are referred to as Ikaw/Ekaw in Thailand, Ikaw/Kaw in Myanmar (Burma), Ikaw/Ko in Laos and Hani/Ha Nhi in Vietnam (Kunstadter, 1967, Michaud, 2006). Akha is one of the biggest subgroups within the Hani Nationality and takes up about one-third of its total population.

Although there are a few scholars (Sun, 1991) who argue that the Hani originated in Yunnan and neighboring Southeast Asia, most historians (You, 1985; Mao, 1992; Huang, 2007) agree that the Hani (along with all Southern Loloish-speaking groups of the Tibeto-Burman family) originated from the Di or Di Qiang tribes[3] in the upstream of Yellow River. The latter has been supported by rich orally transmitted southward migratory epics possessed by the Hani and Akha, such as Ha Ni A Pei Cong Po Po (Yunnan Provincial

---

[1] Southeast Asia mainland massif is also known as Zomia, a geo-political term coined by Willem van Schendel (2001) and modified by James Scott (2009).

[2] In Yunnan Province, the population of the Hani Minority Nationality was 1,630,000 in 2010 (the Sixth National Census). According to Mr. Min Nyo, director of the Association of Traditional Akha in Myanmar (ATAM), there are about 250,000 Akha in Myanmar. According to Dr. Bai Yongfang from Yunnan University (personal communication), there are also about 180,000 Kado people (a subgroup of the Hani) in Northwest of Myanmar. According to the Directory of Highland Communities in 20 Provinces of Thailand, the Department of Social Development and Welfare, the Ministry of Social Development of Human Security of Thailand there were 68,653 Akha in 271 villages in Thailand in 2002. Considering dispersed Akha populations in towns and cities, Mr. Artuq Bawrcaeq, director of Association for Akha Education and Culture in Thailand (AFECT), estimates that the total number of Akha people in Thailand might be 80,000 persons. The total number of Hani/Akha in Laos is over 100,000 in 2012 (Wang et al., 2012). Estimated numbers of Hani/Akha population in Vietnam range from 26,000 (Mr. Yang Youyi, from Cultural Department of Lao Cai province of Vietnam, 2008, personal communication) to 40,000 (Huang 2007:50).

[3] Today, there are a people called Qiang concentrating in the northwest of Sichuan Province. They are a coordinate branch of Tibeto-Burman, not ancestral to the Hani and other Southern Loloish-speaking groups.

Chapter 2　Dynamic Politics of Akha Identities

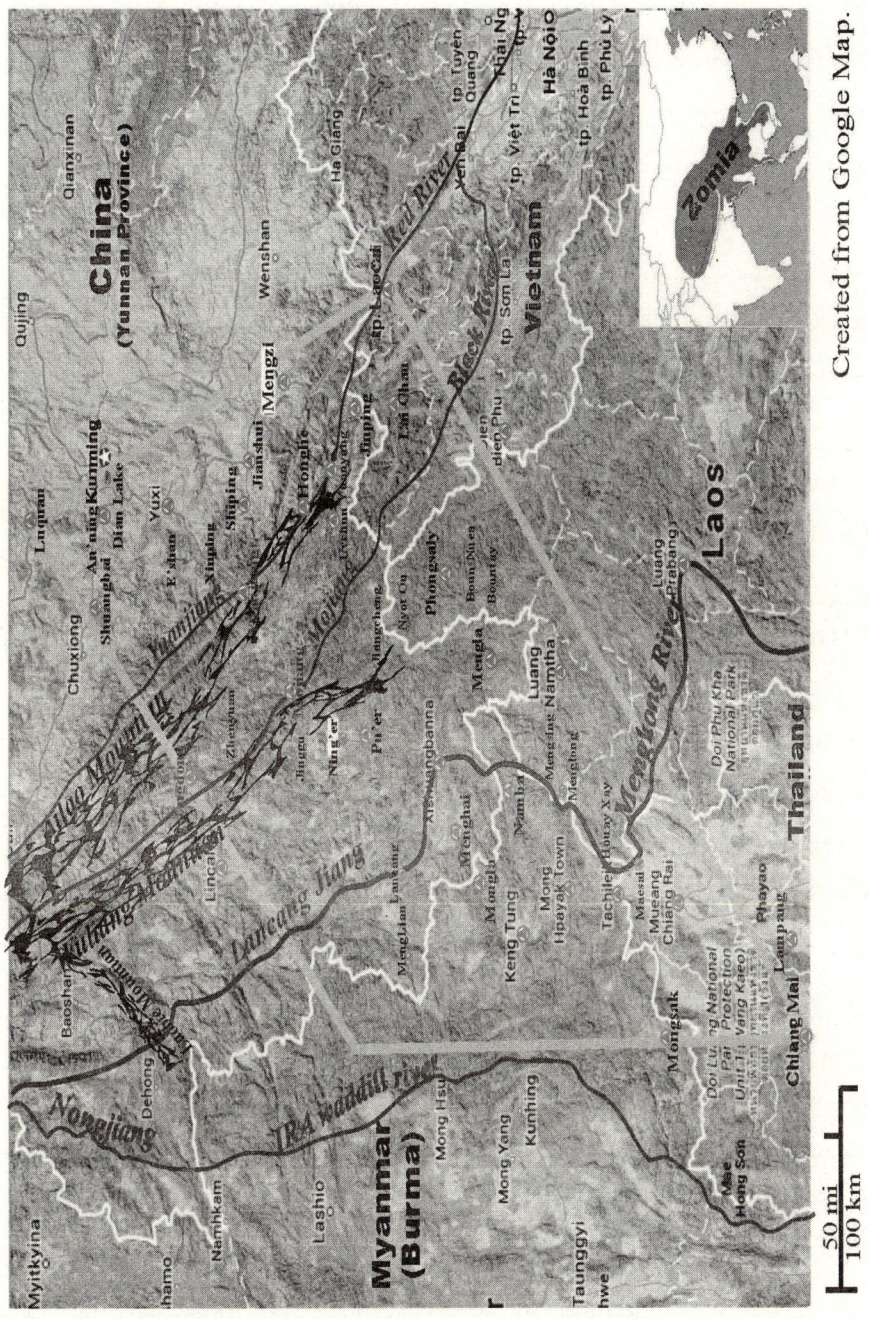

Figure 3　A Quadrangle Region of the Hani-Akha in Zomia

Office of Publication and Plan for Ethnic Minorities' Archaic Texts, 1986) and Ya Ni Ya Ga Zan Ga (Shida and Ahai, 1992), as well as by sporadic Chinese records (e. g. in Shang Shu) and archaeological discoveries. Various migratory epics possessed by different subgroups demonstrate different migratory routes and/or emphasize different historical events, and ethnic heroes/heroines, important to the survival of their tribes. However, historical studies of the Hani Nationality as a whole have drawn on the historical and ethnographic materials from other Hani groups than the Akha. This is due to two facts: firstly, most scholars of Hani studies in general and its history in particular are either Chinese or Hani nationals from subgroups other than the Akha; secondly, most Akha populations are living outside of China. So, the (historical) knowledge of the Akha has been by and large ignored by Chinese and Hani scholars, due to linguistic barriers as well as geographical and demographical marginality of the Akha in China. Therefore, I have found some of the conclusions from previous Hani studies particularly of its histories are not accurate or not applicable to Akha groups.

On the other hand, non-Chinese scholars who study Akha mostly in Thailand and some in Myanmar and Laos, such as Dr. Paul Lewis (1969, 1984, 1992, 2002), Dr. Cornelia Kammerer (1986, 1989, 1996a, 1996b, 1998, 2003), Dr. Deborah Tooker (1988, 1996a, 1996b, 1996c, 2004, 2012), Dr. Inga-Lill Hansson (1982, 1983), Dr. Mika Toyota (1999, 2000, 2005), Dr. Janet Sturgeon (2000, 2005, 2010), Dr. Panadda Boonyasaranai (2003, 2004), Dr. Paul Cohen (2000), and Dr. Chris Lyttleton (2008), have touched little or none on the ancient history of the Akha. The only exception is Dr. Leo Alting von Geusau (2000) who studied the internal history of the Akha, based on very limited information collected from Ulo Akha subgroup in Thailand. Akha societies are usually portrayed as either "tribal" peoples with "no extra-village political organization" (Tooker, 1988: 53; Kammerer, 1989:

277), or refugees fleeing various lowland oppressors, particularly Tai-speaking and/or Chinese states, or in some cases oppressive hierarchically structured Hani chiefdoms in Yunnan (Alting von Geusau, 2000). Following Mary Douglas (1966), Leo Alting von Geusau (2000) uses the terms marginalization or "encapsulation" to refer to the process by which the "Yani/Zani" (ancient self-referential terms of the Akha), became a self-declared "people of the middle" (Akha), situated between a number of other ethnic groups on the mid-slopes of mountains in Zomia. In addition, based on oral traditions collected from members of the Ulo Akha subgroup in Thailand where they represent the largest subgroup demographically, Alting von Geusau (2000) concludes that "the Ahka never had a regular Akha state system" (p.140) and are instead the diaspora of a non-state-based Akha alliance system. However, there are internal as well as external bodies of evidence to show that ancestors of the Hani-Akha were involved in and contributed to several ancient states and civilizations in Southwest China, which paved the foundations for the formation of the Hani Nationality. It is also evident that the Akha once established their own polity, *Jadae,* in the up-and middle-stream areas of the Red and Black Rivers in today's southern Yunnan Province from the middle eleventh century through mid-late thirteenth century. I argue that the formation of the Akha as a people who branched off from other Hani subgroups and their adoption of the self-referential term *Aqkaq* [1] are the direct results of their collective experiences in building the *Jadae* polity. Therefore, a main purpose of this chapter is to (re)discover the history of the Hani Nationality in general and of the Akha in particular, from Akha perspectives, which would be supplementary to the existed studies of Hani history in China, and provide non-Chinese scholars who are interested in the

---

[1] This is the way how Akha is written in KHAS, from whence the English term "Akha" is derived.

Hani Nationality and/or the Akha people a brief and yet relatively complete history of the Akha and historical relationships of the Akha with other Hani groups.

The Hani-Akha people divide their history into four major periods internally: *Nya-mir* (North Country), *Ghanr-mir* (Middle Country), *Gee-mir* (South Country), and *Lanr-byav-eq* (Diasporic)[1]. I will use their internal history as a basic line, and then try to identify places and times of the Hani and the Akha historical events through examining them with historical records mainly in Chinese and supplementarily in Yi and Dai (Tai Lue) when applicable, as well as archaeological and ethnographic evidence. I place particular emphasis on the formations of the Hani Nationality and Akha identity as well as the historical relations between the Hani and the Akha because these are the least understood aspects of Hani-Akha history and ethnicity. I will start with a brief introduction to Hani-Akha genealogies because they provide a basic internal historical line, followed by the four historical periods, and then conclude with discussion on studies of relationship between identities and places.

---

[1] If not otherwise cited, the information on the Akha oral history in this chapter is collected during my fieldwork, through interviewing numerous Akha *pirma*s (priests and reciters) and cultural specialists, including but not limited to, *Pirma Arkev Ceimeeqguq* (Thailand), *Aqbawr Panrlov Nyawrbyeivqguq* (China), *Aqbawr Jarwuq Byanlaeqguq* (China), *Ardov Aqyir Jeirbeeqguq* (China), *Aqbawr Govlawq Meeqbanguq* (China), *Aqbawr Yang Guangming* (China), *Ardov Artsaq Lartavguq* (Thailand), *Pirma Arnav Ceimeeqguq* (Myanmar), *Aqbawr Ardzev Ceimeeqguq* (Laos), and *Ardov Jaqtee Ceimeeqguq* (Thailand). Since the historical information or oral texts provided by these individuals are overlapping as well as supplementary, for the purpose of convenience, it would be better to cite them here all together one time collectively, rather than cite them individually throughout this Chapter.

2.2　Genealogies of the Hani-Akha

Most Hani-Akha groups❶, and some other current Tibeto-Burman groups such as the Yi (or Lolo), use a patronymic linkage system to record their genealogies, which is called *tseevq* in Hani-Akha language. This patronymic linkage system is a social device for showing generational order and affiliation whereby the name of a son always contains an element from the name of his father. The common form of this system as used by Hani-Akha is that the first syllable or two of the son's name is always identical with the last syllable or two of his father's name. For instance, if the father's name is A _ B _ C then the son's name could be B _ C _ D (two identical syllables) and grandson's name could be D_E_F (one identical syllable), and so on. In this way, the majority of contemporary Hani-Akha groups can trace their ancestry back more than 60 – 70 generations to a common apical ancestor referred to as *Mq-ma* (pronounced "um-ma").

It is generally agreed that these genealogies are composed of four parts: mythical genealogy (*naevq-tseevq* in Akha), national genealogy (*Dzoeq-tseevq-tavq* in Akha), chiefdom genealogy (*dzoeq-tseevq*), and patrilineal genealogy (*da-tseevq* in Akha), which correspond to the four major historical periods mentioned above. The lengths of mythical genealogies vary among

---

❶　Among the Hani Nationality, Ha-Ya and Hao-Bai dialect groups possess genealogies, while the Bi-Ka dialect groups do not. In terms of populations, Ha-Ya and Hao-Bai groups take up more than three quarters of the total population of the Hani Nationality. Ya in Ha-Ya is an abbreviation of Yani, which is a general term used to refer to the Akha people, who actually refer themselves as *Zaq-niq*, *Yaq-niq*, *Aq-niq*, or *Haq-niq*, dialectic variations of various Akha subgroups. Yani is from *Yaq-niq*, the version is pronounced by villagers of Suhu, Gelanghe Township, Menghai County, Yunnan, which was chosen as a speech standard of Akha dialects by Chinese linguists in the early 1980s to develop Akha (Yani) dialect writing system based on Hani writing system created in 1957.

different subgroups, ranging from 7 generations up to 65 generations, but the commonest version has 12 generations, as documented in Table 2 below (Wang and Huang, 2008). The mythical genealogy is believed to consist of the names of mythic or legendary heroes/heroines of tribes or great chiefs of chiefdoms of the Hani-Akha ancestors in the North Country *Nya-mir*. The Hani-Akha genealogies have been conventionally believed to be patronymic linkage systems, but recent studies reveal that it contains some female or maternal names, particularly in the mythical part; at least the first figure *Mq-ma* (*Aoq-ma*) is believed a female (Yang, 2010).

Table 2 Mythical Genealogy of the Hani-Akha (the commonest version)

Generation No.	Commonest names	Variations	Notes
1	Mq-ma	Mq-mavq, Aoq-ma	1. *Mq-ma* (*Aoq-ma*) is regarded as the apical ancestor of all Hani-Akha groups. 2. *Tor-ma* is the First Master of Hani-Akha *pirma* (priest). 3. Yaer-daevq (*Yawr-daevq*) is believed to be Yan Di, the chief of the first know chiefdom recorded in Chinese history (Zhe, 2010).
2	Mq-ghanr		
3	Ghanr-naevq	Ghanr-neiq	
4	Naevq-zawvq	Neiq-zawq, Naevqghawq	
5	Zawvq-zev	Ghawq-ghev	
6	Zev-tor	Ghev-tor	
7	Tor-ma	Tor-ma	
8	Ma-cawr	Ma-caw	
9	Cawr-yawr	Caw-yaer	
10	Yawr-daevq	Yaer-daevq	
11	Daevq-bae		
12	Bae-smr		

The national genealogy is composed of fourteen generations shared by almost all Hani-Akha groups possessing genealogies with some dialect variations. And it is commonly agreed that the real Hani-Akha genealogies as a patronymic linkage system starting from *Smr-mir-or* (Yang, 2005; Wang and Huang, 2008; Kukaewkasem, 2008; Yang, 2010). The commonest version of these fourteen generations is listed in Table 3. These fourteen generations are believed to be the rulers of ancient federated chiefdoms or states of the Hani-Akha ancestors in the Middle Country *Ghanr-mir* (Wang and Huang, 2008; Kukaewkasem, 2008; Zhe, 2010).

Table 3   National genealogy of the Hani-Akha

Generation No.	Commonest names	Variations	Notes
13	*Smr-mir-or*	*Smr-mir-ir*	This version is almost uniformly ubiquitous in almost all Akha subgroups, while there are variations among other Hani subgroups in the form of either dialect variations or missing one or two generations. The latter was most likely caused by the mistakes in the process of passing down orally (Wang and Huang, 2008).
14	*Or-toeqloe*	*Ir-toeqloe*	
15	*Toeqloe-dzm*		
16	*Dzm-mawqyaer*	*Dzm-miqyaer*	
17	*Mawqyaer-ca*	*Miqyaer-ca*	
18	*Ca-tiqsiq*		
19	*Tiqsiq-lir*		
20	*Lir-pawqbaev*	*Lir-puqbaev*	
21	*Pawqbaev-uv*	*Puqbaev-uv*	
22	*Uv-nyoqzaq*	*Uv-hawqzaq*	
23	*Nyoqzaq-tsawr*	*Hawqza-tsawr*	
24	*Tsawr-mawqoer*		
25	*Mawqoer-dzoeq*		
26	*Dzoeq-tanqpanq*	*Dzoeq-taqpoq*	

After the 27th generation, the genealogies of the Hani-Akha diverge into seven major branches (*Tanqpanq xivq mae aqnmr* in Akha) and numerous minor branches. It is believed that the Hani-Akha polity split into seven chiefdoms after the death of the 26th great ruler *Dzoeq-Tanqpanq*, reflected in the seven branches of the genealogies since the 27th generation. Numerous genealogies of six out of these seven major branches have been documented (Yang, 2005). They are from *Tanqpanq-manr*, *Tanqpanq-jm*, *Tanqpanq-xav*, *Tanqpanq-dzuq*, *Tanqpanq-bur*, and *Tanqpanq-meeq* branches respectively (Wang and Huang, 2008). Among today's populations, members of the Ha-Ya dialect groups are descendents mainly from the first four branches, while those of the Hao-Bai dialect groups are from the last two branches. More specifically, majority members of the Akha are from *Tanqpanq-manr* branch with some from *Tanqpanq-jm* and *Tanqpanq-xav* branches, while the members of the Hani subgroups are from *Tanqpanq-dzuq*, *Tanqpanq-jm*, and *Tanqpanq-xav* branches. Besides these major branches, there are numerous minor branches. These minor branches are called *Paq-dawvq* in Akha, meaning "grafted lineages". They are developed by tribes and/or families with other ethnic origins who became members of the Hani-Akha nationality through creating and grafting their own lineages onto the last common chief/king *Dzoeq-Tanqpanq*. The lengths of these grafted genealogies from minor branches are shorter than 50 generations in total, while those from major branches are usually longer than 65 generations. The explanation for this is that the cultural tradition of creating and grafting new lineages was developed for those with other ethnic origins who were assimilated into *Jadae* polity during the period ruled by great chief *Jawr-ban* (Wang and Huang, 2008).

The Hani-Akha genealogies diverge from the 27th generation and develop into hundreds of patrilineal lineages. An example of a genealogical lineage from *Tanqpanq-manr* major branch is listed in Table 4. Names with three syllables (from 27th through 39th in Table 4) are believed to be the genealogy of chiefs (*Dzoeq-tseevq* in Akha), while those names with only two syllables are believed to be patrilineal lineage (*Da-tseevq*); this switch indicates a historical period when traditional Hani-Akha chiefdoms were dissolved (Wang and Huang 2008). The lengths of both *Dzoeq-tseevq* and *Da-tseevq* vary among different branches and patrilineal lineages.

Table 4 An example of Akha genealogies from *Tanqpanq-manr* branch

Generation No.	Commonest names	Variations	Notes
27	Tanqpanq-manr	Tanqpanq-mawr	This is the genealogy of the rulers of the *Jadae* chiefdoms in the South Country *Gee-mir*. *Ban-jeev* is believed the last ruler of *Jadae* polity who was killed in an invasion war by outsiders, and his son *Jeev-lmq* was the leader who led Akha people migrated out of their last home country *Jadae*.
28	Manr-khawqtan	Mawr-khaeqtan	
29	Khawqtan-jeiq	Khaeqtan-jeiq	
30	Jeiq-lei-nyawr	Jeiq-li-nyawr	
31	Nyawr-cir-laq		
32	Laq-tanrboeq		
33	Tanr-boeqsoev		
34	Boeqsoev-laev		
35	Laev-lmr-bor		
36	Bor-manqpov	Bor-mawqpov	
37	Manqpov-tir	Mawqpov-teir	
38	Tir-sar-byev	Teir-sar-byov	
39	Byev-ma-dzanr	Byov-ma-dzanr	This is the genealogy of the rulers of the *Jadae* chiefdoms in the South Country *Gee-mir*. *Ban-jeev* is believed the last ruler of *Jadae* polity who was killed in an invasion war by outsiders, and his son *Jeev-lmq* was the leader who led Akha people migrated out of their last home country *Jadae*.
40	Dzanr-jeq		
41	Jeq-jawr		
42	Jawr-ban		
43	Ban-jeev		
44	Jeev-lmq		
.	.		
.	.		
.	.		

2.3 People of the Sky in North Country *Nya-mir*

According to Akha oral texts, the North Country Nya-mir is described as a desert, phrased as *Nya-mir xavmaw aqmir* in Akha. It is divided into two major phases: *Tmq-lanr* and *Yaer-lanr*.

Tmq-lanr is usually the starting place when Akha recite their migratory history, phrased as *Zaqniq* (or *Haqniq*) *ga bae Tmq-lanr dzanr*. It is described as a big lake surrounded by mountains. It is believed the homeland of the Sky Mother or Sky Goddess *Mq-ma* ❶, the apical ancestor of all Hani-Akha people. This is phrased in Akha as *Aqpoeq Mq-ma tsanqbae laerymr*, literally meaning "homeland governed by Great Ancestor Mq-ma". It is a place where the Sky Mother lifted three huge stones to keep the sky from falling down, referred as *Mq ga lo nyoer smr siq* . It is the place where the Sky mother planted the holy evergreen spruce trees on the mountains, phrased as *Aqpoeq Mq-ma ka xu xuqlir* , and three bunches of grasses at the foot of the mountains, phrased as *Mir ga daqghawq* (or *daqzawq*) *smq ji* . The mountains (or its peaks) have glaciers (*xoeqmq* in Akha), from which streams are flowing down to form a big lake. The lake itself becomes headwaters of a river❷ that flow over a rocky mountain down to a basin, from whence the river flow into underground world. Therefore, it is believed the place on the earth that connects to both the sky world (*mq-tav*) and the underground world (*mir-ov*). The ancestors of the Akha are described as hunters and gatherers in this phase, who did not know how to grow crops nor raise animals. This land is also described as a home place of leopards (*sanqtaw zeeqlaq* in Akha) and huge eagles (*mqtaw sanqdzeir* or *xawqdzeir* in Akha), who helped the Akha ancestors finding or competed over foods with them.

I suspect that *Tmq-lanr* refers to Tianchi (meaning Sky Lake in Chinese) in the eastern Tianshan (meaning Sky Mountain in Chinese) range, east of Urumqi, Xinjiang Province, Northwest China (see Figure 4 and Picture 1).

---

❶ *Mq-ma* is also pronounced as *Mq-mavq* in the Akha oral texts, while other Hani subgroups usually pronounce it as *Aoq-ma*, *Woq-ma*, or *Hoq-ma*. *Mq*, *Aoq*, *Woq*, *Hoq* all mean sky in their dialects respectively, while *ma* means mother or goddess.

❷ The name of the river is called *Aqdiqgolyei* in the Hani migratory epic Ha Ni A Pei Cong Po Po (Yunnan Provincial Office of Publication and Plan for Ethnic Minorities' Archaic Texts, 1986).

Chapter 2　Dynamic Politics of Akha Identities

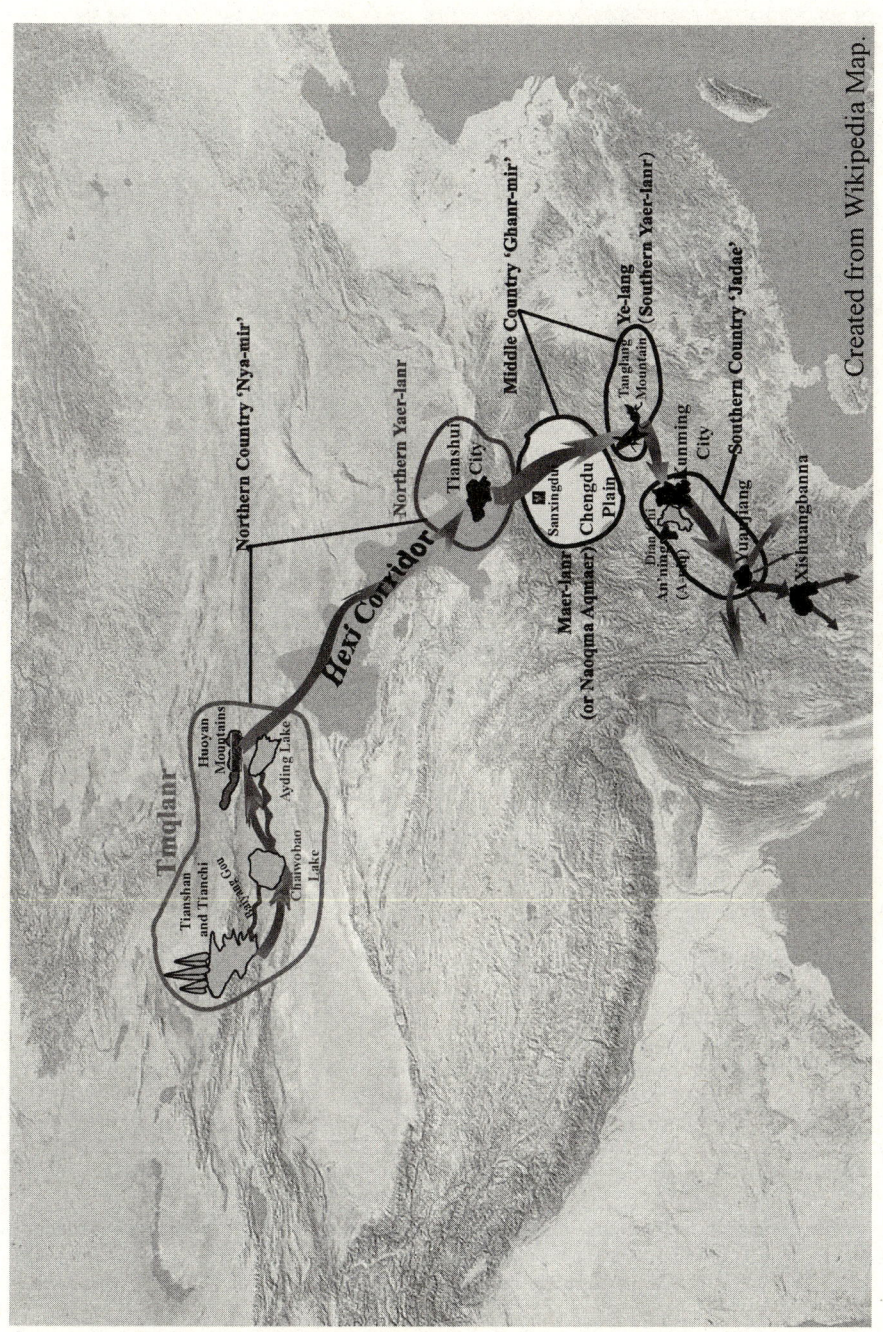

Figure 4　A hypothesized route of the Hani-Akha migration

| Sacred and Contested Landscapes

Picture 1　Tianshan and Tianchi (Baidu Baike 2013a)

Tianchi is located at the foot of three holy snow peaks all named Bogda. According to Chinese legends, Tianchi (Sky Lake) is believed to be the summer palace of Tianmu❶(Sky Mother) where she used to take a bath in the lake and hold parties at her palace. A shrine temple of Tianmu titled Xiwangmu Miao is located at the lake bank. It is said that the holy spruce forests were converted from fairy servants by Tianmu because they were caught bathing in the forbidden lake. There are also three huge holy stones pointing to the sky. It is said that a black water monster was upset because he was not invited into Tianmu's party, and he was trying to destroy the sky but was subdued by Tianmu. Tianmu lifted the three huge stones to support the sky from falling down (Baidu Baike 2013a). All of these Chinese and local legends almost exactly match those of the Akha about *Tmq-lanr* and *Mq-ma*. Most of my informants (Akha priests/reciters or cultural specialists) who have provided Akha internal historical information/texts have never lived in China and only two of them speak Chinese. It means that it is impossible for the Akha cultural specialists to have learned these stories from Chinese recently. Rather, they were evidently passed down in parallel lines from the

---

❶　Tianmu is also known as Xi Wang Mu or Wang Mu Niang Niang in Chinese. She is believed the Queen of Yu Huang Da Di, the Heaven Emperor by Chinese.

same legend over thousands of years, during which both versions could influence each other though. Therefore, I suspect that Akha's legendary apical ancestor *Mq-ma* and Tianmu of the Chinese version are the same figure, both means Sky Mother, or Mother of Sky-land or Sky Mountain. In addition, Tianshan (Sky Mountain) is famous for being home of snow leopards, eagles (goshawks *Accipiter gentilis*), which are parallel with Akha description of their original land being home to leopards (*sanqtaw zeeqlaq*) and huge eagles (*mqtaw sanqdzeir*). There is no need to mention the glaciers, the lake, the spruce forests, the grass, and the three holy stones (or peaks).

Other Hani groups usually state that their ancestors originated from a mountain called *Huqnir Huqnav* , from whence they migrated southeast along a river called *Aqdiqgol yei* that flow into a big lake called *Soexoe Eerma* (Yunnan Provincial Office of Publication and Plan for Ethnic Minorities' Archaic Texts, 1986). Some Akha also start their migratory history from a mountain called *Naqneir Naqnav* . Both *Huqnir Huqnav* and *Naqneir Naqnav* literally mean a high mountain where one can see the sun immediately when it first rises as well as the moon and stars as soon as it gets dark. Therefore, I also suspect both names refer to the same place by different Hani-Akha groups and the place is Tianshan, because a river (called Baiyang Gou in Chinese now) flows southward down from Tianchi (Sky Lake) and continues eastward into Lake Aydingol. The Hani-Akha name of the river *Aqdiqgol yei* and the name of the Lake Aydingol are almost identical. I suspect that the name of Lake Aydingol came from the name of its headwater river *Aqdiqgol yei* . Since Aydingol is a dead lake and no river flows out of it, the ancestors of the Hani-Akha thought it flowed into the underground. Though the name of the lake was called *Xoesoe Eerma* by the Hani-Akha ancestors, it seems that name of the end part of this river was gone along with migration, while the name of the whole water body, including the headwater river and the lake, remained as the name of the lake alone. It is further interesting to note that the reason mentioned in their migratory history why the Hani-Akha ancestors left the lake area is a big fire that not only destroyed forests and animals, but also caused the lake to shrink greatly and all fish to die out (Yunnan Provincial Office of Publication and Plan for Ethnic Minorities' Archaic Texts, 1986). It is evident that Lake Aydingol used to be one thousand times larger ten thousand years ago, and it was a fresh water lake then in which there were plenty of fish. But it gradually dried out and became a salty and dead lake with no fish, due to world climate change as well as extreme heat from Huoyanshan (see Picture 2), meaning "Flame Mountain", located roughly 50 – 60 kilometers north of Lake Aydingol. Its dried-out lake bottom has become the lowest terrace in China with an altitude of 155 meters below sea level, the world's second lowest terrace after the Dead Sea in Jordan (Baidu Baike, 2013b). Huoyanshan is the hottest place in China. As indicated in its name, Flame Mountain, this mountain has been burning underground historically, because of natural fire from burning coal underground. This burning mountain has been recorded in many Chinese documents and literature, including the famous Xi You Ji or The Pilgrimage to the West, a fairy tale that depicts a Chinese Buddhist monk's pilgrimage to the West in the Tang Dynasty. The last natural fire was extinguished only in 2008 (Baidu Baike, 2013c).

Furthermore, more than 40 cliff paintings are found on the rocks along the bank of Tianchi, depicting animals including but not limited to goats, deer and foxes, as well as ancient hunters with bows in hands, indicating ancient human activities, particularly hunting, in the Tianchi area (Baidu Baike, 2013d). Neolithic archaeological sites dated 6,000 – 10,000 years ago have been also

Chapter 2 Dynamic Politics of Akha Identities

Picture 2　Huoyanshan

(Courtesy of Yang Jiaxing, Department of Culture and Media,
Chongqing University of Arts and Sciences, Chongqing, China)

discovered on the banks of Lake Chaiwobao (Baidu Baike, 2013e). Chaiwobao is a fresh water lake located in the middle of Baiyang River between Tianchi (Sky Lake) and Lake Aydingol. Although more researches need to be done in order to make direct connections between these earlier human cites with the ancestors of the Hani-Akha, there is linguistic evidence to show ancestors of the Hani-Akha once lived in environments of high mountains and oases in deserts, besides the evidence of oral history discussed above. I will demonstrate this through linguistic analyses of two pairs of core notions in Hani-Akha culture, i.e., *yaw-khawr* versus *maq-khawr* and *nmq* versus xav[❶].

Yaw-khawr means awesome, sacred, and dangerous in Hani-Akha, while *maq-khawr* is opposite, meaning mundane and safe. The root of both *yawr-khawr* and *maq-khawr* is *khawr*, while *yaw* and *maq* are affixes. *Yaw* is a very common affix in Hani-Akha, indicating it is an adjective, such as in *yaw-neir* (red), *yaw-ba* (white), *yaw-khaq* (bitter), *yaw-coer* (sweet), etc. *Maq* is the commonest affix meaning "no" in Hani-Akha. The root *khawr* means not only awesome, sacred, and dangerous as in *yaw-khawr* and *maq-khawr*, but

---

[❶] Other Hani groups pronounce them as *naoq* and *sav*.

also high as in an Akha word *khawr-dmr* (high mountain or cold areas, *dmr* means cloud, so *khawr-dmr* literally means height to reach clouds) or a Hani word *khawr-gawq* (also means high mountain, *gawq* means mountain in Hani-Akha). I argue that "high" is the prime meaning of *khawr*, while the meanings of awesome, sacred and dangerous are derivative. It is a common feature of Akha language and culture that descriptions of notions of feeling are developed from those of topographies. For instance, as Dr. Deborah Tooker (1988, 2012) demonstrates well, *xaq* (written as *sà* by Tooker) means deep slope, while *yaw-xaq* (written as *jɔsà* by Tooker) means difficult and poor; *sar* (written as *sá*) means flat, while *yaw-sar* (written as *jɔsá* by Tooker) means healthy, happy and peaceful. The notions of *yaw-xaq* and *yaw-sar* indicate a history of the Akha society that experienced hardship in mountains as well as prosperous lives in flat lands. Similarly, the notion of *khawr* indicates that ancestors of the Hani-Akha once lived in or nearby very high mountains. High mountains, especially snow peaks, are not only dangerous but also awesome and sacred. Later, *yaw-khawr* is used by the Akha to describe any kind of awesome and sacred landscapes that are dangerous if no appropriate respect and/or observations are paid (see Chapter 3).

While the notion of *yaw-khawr* does not necessarily indicate that the ancestors of Hani-Akha came from Tianshan or any specific high mountains, the notions of *nmq* versus *xav* will provide stronger evidence that would point the ancestral land of Hani-Akha toward oases in the deserts of Xinjiang. *Nmq* is believed a path to the original ancestral homeland where ancestral spirits live happily forever, while *xav* is believed a path to a land of death with no hope of reincarnation and a world full of evil spirits who can not go back to their ancestral homeland. *Nmq* and *xav* are also used to describe a status of a death in Akha. If a person died normally at home, it is a death of *nmq*, called *nmq-xir* (*xir* means death in Akha). If a person died abnormally, for instance, from suicide, or killed by a wild animal such as a tiger or a leopard, or is drawn, or is shot, it is a death of *xav*, called *xav-xir* in Akha. A *nmq-xir* is qualified to travel back to the ancestral world to join his/her ancestral families. Of course, the spirits can not travel back to the ancestral land by themselves without guidance from *boermawq pirma*s reciting their migratory routes. Therefore, the whole purpose of culturally appropriate funeral ceremonies is to guide the spirit of a dead to travel through a path of *nmq* and do not get into a path of *xav*, in order for it to arrive at the ancestral world safely. Those ancestral spirits that have left male heirs can also travel reversely back to their earthly home at ancestral shrine where they are regularly offered❶ rice, chicken, rice cake, rice liquor, and tea. Some of these benevolent ancestral spirits can also reincarnate in the next generations of their family. Therefore, a *nmq-xir* (death of *nmq*) is not believed to be a real death. Instead, it is believed a transformation of a mundane person into a ancestral spirit who live immortally. On contrary, the spirits of *xav-xir* are not allowed to travel through the path of *nmq* ❷; instead they have to go through the path of *xav*, and will become homeless wandering evil spirits, also called *xav-xir*. They are not allowed to travel back to their earthly village and home either, nor will they be able to reincarnate in the future. Thus, envy and hatred make these evil spirits *xav -xir* angry, constantly looking for revenge against living persons. Therefore, Akha people always try best to

---

❶ There are usually 12 annual ancestor offerings in typical traditional Akha families and societies.

❷ Some of *xav-xir* (abnormal deaths) can be restored a status of *nmq-xir* through appropriate purifying ceremonies, which are required to sacrifice numerous livestock such as goats, pigs, chickens, etc. and thus are very costly.

avoid an abnormal death. In other words, *nmq* is a symbol of permanent life or life recycles while *xav* is a symbol of permanent death.

Let us now examine how these two notions were developed. The word *nmq* has two other meanings. One is used as a noun, referring to the tree species from Salicaceae family, particularly poplar and willow trees❶. Another is used as a verb, meaning sprout or regenerate. Poplar (*Populus euphratica*) is a dominant tree in central Asian deserts. Due to its great tolerance of cold, drought, salty soils, and windy environments, poplar trees are often regarded as "guardian gods of deserts" (see Picture 3) (Baidu Baike, 2013f). Similarly, Akha people also depict poplar trees (and willows as well) as a symbol of life, and regard them sacred. On contrary, *xav* also means deserts, as in the phrase *Nya-mir xavmaw aqmir* (the North Country is desert). Therefore, I argue that, like that of *khawr*, the cultural meaning of *nmq* as symbol of life derived from its strong regenerating capability of *nmq* trees (poplar and willow), while that of *xav* as symbol of death is derived from features of deserts.

Picture 3   Poplar Groves in Tarim Basin (© Baidu Baike 2013f)

According to Baidu Baike (ibid), an overwhelming majority of the world's trees of *populus euphratica* is growing in China, among which 90% of them are in Tarim Basin of Xinjiang. Tarim basin is located in south of Tianshan (Sky Mountain), within which both above mentioned Lake

---

❶   Willow is called *eer-nmq* in Akha and *eer-naoq* in Hani dialect, meaning water poplar. *Eer* means water in Hani-Akha.

Chaiwobao and Lake Aydingol located. Therefore, based on all the pieces of evidence discussed above, it is highly likely that ancestors of the Hani-Akha came from Tianshan (Sky Mountain) and oases of the Tarim basin, particularly in the Lake Chaiwobao and Lake Aydingol areas. I suspect that ancestors of the Hani-Akha referred themselves as *Mq-niq* or *Aoq-niq* back then, meaning people of the sky (or Sky Mountain), an ancient name that has been most frequently recorded as Ho Ni or Wo Ni in Chinese characters to refer to ancestral groups of Hani-Akha, and is still used by some of the Hani subgroups today (Jiang, 2007).

A great fire that destroyed forests and dried the lake *Soexoe Eerma* forced the ancestors of Hani-Akha to leave their homeland *Tmq-lanr*. They arrived in Yaer-lanr with some stops in between. *Yaer-lanr* is the homeland of Great Ancestor *Miq-Yaer*, who taught the Akha to grow crops and raise animals. It is the first place where ancestors of the Hani-Akha built permanent villages or residency, phrased as *Yaer-lanr Khanq* in Akha and *Yeirlanr Pu Tsov* in Hani dialect. Historical figures in this phrase are usually depicted as half-divine and half-humans who were able to travel between the earth world (*mir-tav*) and sky world or heaven (*mq-tav*) as well as between the earth world and the underground world (*mir-ov*). The First Master of Akha Reciter *Yaerpir Aqpoeq Torma* (the 7th figure on the mythical genealogy of Hani-Akha, see Table 2) is one of such figures. All Hani-Akha *boermawq pirma*s (priests/reciters) always recall the First Master's name and asks his permission to perform rituals under his name.

Through a thorough research, comparison, and analysis of relevant texts in Chinese, Yi, and Hani, Mr. Zhe He (2010) demonstrates that the legendary home country of Hani-Akha, *Yaer-lanr khanq* or *Yeirlanr Putsov* is recorded as Hu Ren Guo❶ (or Country of Hu People) in the first Chinese geographic classic Shan Hai Jing, the Classic of Mountains and Rivers, compiled in pre-Qin, and that the tenth figure on the mythical genealogy of Hani-Akha, *Yaer-daevq* and Chinese legendary greater chief Yan Di are the same figure. Like *Yaer-daevq* in Akha myth, Yan Di is depicted as the father of agriculture called Nong Huang who taught people how to grow crops and raise animals, in Chinese legendary history, Shan Hai Jing. Yan Di is also regarded as Master of Fire, who mastered using fire in clearing lands for farming. This is the reason why his name Yan is written as double fire "炎" in Chinese character (Zhe 2010). This is also the reason why he is titled as *Miq* ❷ *Yaer* in Hani-Akha, meaning Fire Master *Yaer*, and this land is called by Hani-Akha people "the homeland governed by the Fire Master *Yaer*, *Yaer-lanr Khanq* or *Yeirlanr Putsov*". Due to his great merits, *Miq-Yaer* is deified as the supreme ancestor God by Hani-Akha people, referred as *Aqpoeq Miq-Yaer*.

It is speculated that Yan Di was the founder and chief of the Qiang chiefdom — the first known chiefdom in the speculative ancient history of China. The first Chinese states later grew out of the Yan Di chiefdom and its successor, Huang Di chiefdom (Tian, 2001). This is why Chinese people today regard themselves as descendants of the Yan and Huang or *Yan Huang Zi Sun* in Chinese. The reputed founder of the Xia Dynasty, Great Yu, is said to be descendant of Yan Di, and thus of Qiang people (Sima Qian 145 – 90 BC). The earliest "Chinese" scripts found on oracle-bones dated ca. 1200 BC from the Shang Dynasty (1600 BC – 1045 BC) contain many descriptions of

---

❶ Hu Ren Guo is written as 互人国 in Chinese. According to Mr. Zhe He (2010), 互 should be pronounced Huo. I suspect that Hu Ren or Huo Ren is a Chinese translation of Hani word *Hoq-niq*, derived from the original self-denomination *Mq-niq* or *Aoq-niq*. Here *niq* means people, the same meaning as Ren in Chinese.

❷ *Miq* means fire in Hani-Akha here.

the Qiang (Yang, 2010). Some historical linguists have even hypothesized that an early form of Tibeto-Burman language was used by the Yangshao culture of the Shang states, or at least in the middle and upper reaches of the Yellow River (Wilkinson, 2000). Archaeological evidence also sheds light on the development of Paleolithic culture by the ancient Qiang people at the upper streams of the Yellow River in the eastern Tibetan plateau of this region. By about 7,000 − 8,000 years ago, they had entered into the Neolithic age and started migrating in three directions — to the east where they later occupied the middle Yellow River; to the west where they eventually reached the central Tibetan plateau;and to the south where they later populated the Sichuan plain. Ancient Qiang people later merged with various indigenous groups in these respective areas and developed into many new groups. Those groups residing in the Sichuan Plain are called Di Qiang[1](Liang et al., 1985). Most historians agree that Hani-Akha groups are descended from the Di Qiang (ibid). Internally, Hani-Akha history enters into the Middle Country Ghanr-mir period from here. It is said a serious plague of diseases forced ancestors of Hani-Akha left *Yeirlanr Putsov* and migrated south into the Middle Country Ghanr-mir (see Figure 4).

2.4 People of the Bamboo Kingdom in the Middle Country *Ghanr-mir*

The Middle Country *Ghanr-mir* is described as flat lands where the ancestors of the Akha (and the other Hani groups as well) built big towns, phrased as *Ghanr-mir tevqlevq puma* . This period is also divided into two

---

[1] Some speculate that Di Qiang are from the Eastern Tibetan Plateau, while others have argued that the Sichuan plains would have been a more likely place of origin (see Wiens 1967 and Bradley 1979). It is more likely, however, that Di Qiang represent a mixture of both local populations and populations migrating from the north.

major phases: *Maer-lanr* and *Gee Yaer-lanr Khanq* .

Maer-lanr is called as *Naoqma Aqmaer* in other Hani subgroups. It is described as a flat and fertile land, where ancestors of the Hani built a polity called *Naoqma Aqmaer* that governed four towns, whose economy was based on irrigated rice cultivation (Yunnan Provincial Office of Publication and Plan for Ethnic Minorities' Archaic Texts, 1986). According to Mr. Zhe He (2010), Naoqma Aqmaer is the legendary ancient Shu states (ca. 3,000 BC – 676 BC) in Chengdu Plain. Zhe further argues that the four figures on the Hani-Akha genealogy from *Smr-mir-or* through *Dzm-Mawq-Yaer* (see Table 3, 13th – 16th generations) correspond to four phases of the ancient Shu State. These four figures are also shared by the Yi genealogies (ibid). Recent archaeological discoveries at Sanxingdui, north of Chengdu have proved the existence of the ancient Shu State dated roughly from 2,800 BC to 800 BC, and this ancient civilization is highly likely created by Tibeto-Burman groups, including ancestors of Yi and Hani peoples (Loloish groups) (Ma, 2002; Zhe, 2012).

I suspect that formation of Loloish groups or at least proto-Loloish groups has to do with the ancient Shu States. It seemed that this historical phase shaped the basic ethno-linguistic commonalities among the Loloish groups and it is still difficult to make clear-cut ethnic boundaries between some of these groups today. For instance, members of Bi-Ka dialectic groups within the Hani Nationality feel that some of their cultural traditions or vocabularies are more similar to those of the Lahu or the Lisu nationalities, and yet they are identified as branches of the Hani Nationality due to two facts: first, their current geographic locations are proximate to or overlapping with those of other Hani groups; second, it is undeniable that they also share numerous cultural traditions, some of which are actually pan-Loloish, such as similar lunar calendar. However, the genealogies of Loloish and/or Hanoish style composed of patronymic linkage systems had not developed in this phase yet, instead, it was developed in the next phase, which I will elaborate shortly.

Hani-Akha internal history states that their flat and fertile homeland *Naoqma Aqmaer* was invaded and conquered by *Laq-beeq* people coming from the east, which forced the ancestors of Hani-Akha left their homeland. The majority of them migrated southward along the *Naoma Lawrbaq* , i. e. the Minjiang River (Zhe, 2010), while the rest migrated toward southwest into the Yalong River area. The southward-migrating groups were led by one of their greatest ancestor heroes, *Dzm-Mawq-Yaer* or *Dzm-Miq-Yaer* , and established another state also called *Yaer-lanr-Khanq*. This state is usually referred as *Gee-Yaer-Khanq* , meaning South Country governed by *Dzm-Miq-Yaer* , in order to distinguish it from the *Yaer-lanr-Khanq* in the North Country, which is accordingly referred as *Nya-Yaer-Khanq* , meaning North Country Governed by *Miq-Yaer* . *Dzm-Miq-Yaer* is a shamanistic leader who (self-)claimed as the reincarnated greatest ancestor *Miq-yaer* . Since *Yaer* could be, and, often than not is, understood as God in Hani-Akha, *Yaer-lanr-Khanq* could also be translated as the country governed by God. Many succeeding rulers of *Dzm-Miq-Yaer* are also claimed as reincarnated great ancestors. *Dzoeq-Tanq-panq* , for instance, another one of the greatest ancestor heroes, is (self)claimed as the reincarnated common ancestral mother *Tanq-panq-Aqma* , who is believed a great mother of not only human beings but also of spirits. This is one of the main characteristics of this historical phase. It is described that *Dzoeq-Tanq-Panq* was a great ruler who governed numerous tribes, not only of the Hani-Akha people but also of many other peoples particularly *Na* people. It is said that cultural tradition of sacrificing a water buffalo to honor a death of a respectful elder started at the funeral ceremony of *Dzoeq-Tanq-panq*.

It is speculated that the ancient Shu State was conquered by Kaiming people from the east in 676 BC (Tong, 1979). Kaiming is also known as Ba or Bo people, worshipers of tigers or whose totem is tiger. Accordingly, the new state is referred as Ba-Shu from then on in Chinese records. It is generally agreed by historians, particularly those of Hani Nationality, that Kaiming or Ba/Bo people in Chinese source and *Laq-beeq* in the Hani-Akha oral history are the same people, because *Laq-beeq* ❶ also means tiger-worshiping people *Beeq* (Yunnan Provincial Office of Publication and Plan for Ethnic Minorities' Archaic Texts, 1986). Conquer of Ba/Bo people forced the last king of the ancient Shu State Du Yu (also recorded as Zhong Mou-you) fled to Zhuti, i. e. today's Zhaotong, northeast Yunnan, and he is believed to be *Dzm-Mawq-Yaer*, the 16th figure on the national genealogy of the Hani-Akha (Zhe, 2010).

The famous Chinese historian Sima Qian (145/135 BC – 90/87 BC) recorded in *Shiji* (Records of the Grand Historian) that Southwest People Ni❷ established a state called Yelang Guo❸ roughly in today's northwest Guizhou and northeast Yunnan. It is generally agreed by historians and scholars of Yelang Guo studies that it is a shamanistic state whose shamanistic ruler (s) governed numerous tribes/chiefdoms of various peoples, including but not limited to ancestors of Buyi, Ge-lao, Dong, and Yi, but scholars are still debating on such issues as origin and meaning of Yelang, ethnic belonging of the main body of its subjects and its rulers, and location

---

❶ *Laq* means tiger in Loloish languages.

❷ It was written as 西南夷 in Chinese characters, literally meaning southwestern hunting people, or southwest barbarian. The character 夷 implies "hunting people", and should be pronounced "ni" in ancient Chinese (see Zhe 2010).

❸ Written as 夜郎国 in Chinese characters.

of the center of the state (Qin, 2005). It is recorded in Han Shu (the Book of Former Han Dynasty) that Yelang State was conquered by the Western Han Dynasty between 28 BC and 25 BC (You, 1994: 61-62), but historians are still debating on the date of its establishment, and the earliest establishing date is in 651 BC (Wu, 2013).

  I suspect that Yelang Guo (Yelang State) was first established by the last king of the ancient Shu State Du Yu, who is also known as Zhong Mouyou in Chinese or Du Mu in Yi or *Dzm-Mawq-Yaer/Dzm-Miq-Yaer* in Hani-Akha. I argue that the name Yelang Guo is a Chinese transliteration of the Hani-Akha term *Yaer-lanr khanq* , meaning the country governed by *Dzm-Mawq-Yaer* , both Guo in Chinese and *khanq* in Hani-Akha mean "state, country". Scholars of ethnic nationalities from this region try to explain the origins and meanings of Yelang from their own languages and culture, but there are no vocabularies that pronounced the same as Yelang in their languages nor are the meanings explained by them convincing each other. For instance, Duan Shuqiao (2011) of Yi Nationality claims that Yelang is derived from Yi word Yi-na meaning (a country by) deep water; while Wang Hui (2011) of Buyi Nationality argues that Ye is from Yue, the ancient self denomination of Buyi ancestors, and lang is from "langz" (meaning legging in Bu-yi) and "laangh" (meaning vast), thus Yelang means a vast country of legging Buyi people. On the contrary, though Yelang and *Yaer-lanr* are written differently in different writing systems, their pronunciations are almost identical. My argument could be supported by the Chinese records stating that the king of the ancient Shu State Du Yu (also known as Zhong Mouyou or Zhu Ming in various sources) fled to Zhuti (today's Zhaotong, northeast Yunnan) and later settled in Tanglang Mountain (Zhe, 2010). I suspect that the name Tanglang is also a Chinese transliteration of the Hani-Akha name

Tmq-lanr, a place name that migrated with its people, which is a very common cultural practice of the Hani-Akha people, and this place name actually continued migrating further south in other two places which I will address later. Du Yu, known as Du Mu in Yi, is also regarded a great ancestor of almost all Yi people and Tanglang Mountain as their ancestral land where their ancestors migrated out to various directions, and thus Yi scholars (Wang, 2009; Duan, 2011) claim that Yelang State was established by their ancestors. But they usually ignore the fact that Du Yu (or Du Mu or Zhong Mouyou) is also ancestor of the Hani-Akha people, or it would be more accurately to say that he was a shamanistic ruler of a shamanistic state composed of various tribes and/or chiefdoms of different people.

The main feature of this historical phase, according to the Hani-Akha oral texts, is that the ancestors of the Hani-Akha lived side by side with other peoples under the same leaders. The dominant other people is recorded as *Na,* which should be the ancestors of the Yi because Na is also a very common self denomination of Yi people both in ancient time and today, meaning black (worshiping) people. In Akha oral literature, the *Na* people are also often depicted as *Naevq*, meaning either evil spirits or others. As a side note, Akha people also refer this land as *Guoluo Aqmir*, meaning land of Guoluo; and a branch of Yi people living in this area still call themselves Guoluo today. I suspect that the genealogies of Loloish and/or Hanoish style composed of patronymic linkage systems were created during this historical phase. It is the reason why some of the Loloish groups particularly the Yi and the Hani possess genealogies but the others do not. It also explains why not all Hani subgroups possess the genealogies either. It seems that the ancestors of the Bi-Ka dialectic groups are the ones who migrated southwest to Yalong River area from *Naoqma Aqmaer,* and those of the Ha-Ya and

Hao-Bai followed their great leader *Dzm-Mawq-Yaer* and established another state *Gee Yaer-lanr Khanq* .

I also argue that another key notion of the Hani-Akha cultural concept *Geeqlanq* was developed during this historical phase. The term *Geeqlanq* has been variously translated as "well being ""good fortune" (Tooker, 1988: 54, 133), "blessing" (Kammerer, 1986: 66), "blessing, luck, grace (religious sense)" (Lewis, 1989: 179), "potency""the life force" (Tooker 2012: 24, 40), among others. But *Geeqlanq* also has other two meanings that are missed by these scholars. *Geeq* means "copper or bronze" in Hani-Akha, and *Lanq* has various meanings including but not limited to dragon, water container such as basin and pot as a noun, or to increase as a verb. Together it means either bronze basin, or accumulating/increasing bronze. But how could a word mean both a bronze basin and blessing/good fortune? According to Sun and Chen (2009), Tanglang Mountain had been famous historically for its high-purity copper ore, which had been extracted by local people since at least 4,000 years ago, and it is proved to be the main source of bronze for the Sanxingdui civilization and ancient Shu State. Numerous Tanglang Tongxi, a particular kind of bronze basin that characterizes Tanglang bronze civilization, have been excavated in Tanglang area. And the bronze basin is used as a symbol of wealth, power and high social status by the ruling class of the Loloish people (ibid). Since ancestors of the Hani-Akha participated in building this civilization, it could explain why they use the phrase *geeqlanq heeq* (lit. meaning big bronze basin) to refer to blessing, good fortune, and well being.

Another distinguished feature of Yelang culture is bamboo worship and the rulers of Yelang states often claim themselves as the King of Bamboo Kingdom, as it is recorded both in Hou Han Shu (History of Later Han

Dynasty) by historian Fan Ye (AD 398 – AD 445) and Huayang Guo Zhi (Chronology of Huayang Country) by historian Chang Qu (AD291 – AD 361) that the King of Yelang was son of bamboo god, thus was regarded as Zhu Wang, i. e. Bamboo King or King of Bamboo Kingdom. Therefore, I argue that the ancient self denomination of the Hani-Akha people *Haq-niq* , *Aq-niq* , *Yaq-niq* , or *Zaq-niq* was adopted during this historical phase as they became subjects of Yelang state, because *Haq* , *Aq* , *Yaq* (or *Yavq*), or *Zaq* (or *Zavq*) all mean bamboo in their respective dialect. Therefore, *Haq-niq* , *Aq-niq* , *Yaq-niq* , or *Zaq-niq* all mean people of the bamboo country, or subjects of the Bamboo Kingdom. Here, *niq* means people. As a matter of fact, the Hani-Akha people share many cultural traditions with those ethic groups still living in Guizhou, such as the Yi, Buyi, Ge-lao, and Dong Nationalities, even though they belong to different linguistic families. These common cultural traditions include but are not limited to ancestor worship, shamanistic beliefs and rituals, sacrificing water buffalo for funeral ceremonies, offering to the Earth Goddess/Sky God/Village Lord, wedding ceremonies, chasing evil spirits out of village rituals, eating colorful sticky rice in spring festivals, legging, etc. A possible explanation for these cultural commonalities is that their ancestors were subjects of the same shamanistic state Yelang Kingdom, as all of these groups claim Yelang State were established by their ancestors, though some of these commonalities could also be resulted from cultural diffusion.

However, inter-tribal tensions over natural resources had been developed between the Hani-Akha ancestors and other peoples, particularly the *Na* people, which had been mitigated by the mighty ruler. Intertribal conflicts became inevitable immediately upon the death of *Dzoeq Tanqpanq* , which caused emigration of some Hani-Akha tribes out of *Yaer-lanr Khanq* . They immigrated south into the South Country *Gee-mir* (see Figure 4). The Hani-Akha describe this historical event as "splitting from *Na* people" or portrait it as "breaking family with evil spirits *Naevq* " in oral literature. The Hani-Akha ancestors also split into seven major chiefdoms or the seven major chiefdoms existed already but now migrated into different directions upon the death of their common shamanistic leader *Dzoeq-Tanqpanq* , which reflects in the seven major branches of the genealogies after it. It is interesting to note that ancestors of the Yi people also split into six branches at Tanglang Mountain and migrated into different directions during this period of time due to a big flood (Sun and Chen 2009). It seems that emigrations of the ancestors of the Hani-Akha and the Yi (or Lolo) did not cause the collapse of Yelang shamanistic state(s). Instead, it continued to be ruled by ancestors of other ethnic groups, such as Buyi, Gelao, and Dong. It also seems that the political centers of the state(s) switched many times along with alternations of the rulers from various ethnic groups at its different historical phases. Almost all known Chinese records of Yelang kingdom(s) were done during the Han Dynasty or later and apparently covered the latter phases of it only. It is the reason why it is very difficult to know the date of its establishment. Fortunately, the earlier phases of Yelang State are numerously recorded in Yi texts as well as the Hani-Akha oral texts. Therefore, studies of these non-Chinese texts are equally and maybe even more important for particular historical contexts.

2.5 *Jadae* polities and formation of Akha identity in the South Country *Gee-mir*

The South Country *Gee-mir* is also called *Jadae* in Akha. It is divided into three major phases: Earlier, Middle, and Latter. Akha oral history states that ancestors of the Akha left *Yaer-lanr Khanq* and arrived in the vast flat land of *Jadae* , following their leader *Tanqpanq-manr* . As he became the first ruler of *Jadae* country, *Tanqpanq-manr* is also called *Dae-manr* in Akha oral texts. I suspect that *Jadae* refers to Lake Dian area. There is a city named Anning at the south bank of Lake Dian. The name Chinese Anning comes from A-ni, ancestors of the Hani-Akha who lived in this place historically (Ma et al., 2008). Historian Sima Qian also recorded, in his Shiji, that the King Qingxiang (ruled 298 BC – 263 BC) of Chu State (1,042 BC – 223 BC) dispatched General Zhuang Qiao on a military expedition westward in order to expand its territory in 279 BC. General Zhuang conquered some small states and/or chiefdoms on the way to Dian Country. But, meanwhile, the Qin army conquered Ba State and Qianzhong Jun (Qianzhong Prefecture in today middle Guizhou Province) of Chu State in 277 BC, which cut the path of General Zhuang and prevented his going back to Chu State. Therefore, he had no choice but to stay and marry a local woman, and later declared himself King of Dian. And the Chu General Zhuan Qiao is the first King of the ancient Dian State (s) recorded in Chinese source. This event is also recorded in the Akha oral texts, stating that one day an *Aq-cmq* ❶ (also pronounced *Aq-cuq*) man from the downstream came to *Jadae* Country, asking the Akha chief *Aqbawr Jadae* for a place to stay because he got lost. The chief *Aqbawr Jadae* built a small house beside his own mansion and let the man stay in the

---

❶ *Aqcmq* or *Aqcuq* , is a general Hani-Akha term referring to Tai speaking peoples. They are also called *Biq-cmq* , meaning *Cmq* people from downstream, here biq means downstream. I suspect that this term was adopted to refer to Chu people in ancient time when they were first met by the ancestors of the Hani-Akha because the pronunciation of the Hani-Akha term *cmq* or *cuq* is very similar to that of the Chinese word Chu. Chu is also called Chu Yue in ancient time, regarded as a branch of Yue, and are regarded as among the ancestors of today's Tai speaking peoples. The Chu State is located in the middle Yangtze River, which is the downstream of Lake Dian because water of Lake Dian flows into Yangtze River via Tanglang River, and thus Lake Dian is one of headwaters of Yangtze River.

small house. *Dae-yur* , the daughter of the Akha chief fell in love with the man soon, and they were granted the marriage. But later, the man took over most lands of the *Jadae* country and ruled it with support from his own people. Since then, *Aqbawr Jadae* set up a rule that forbids a son-in-law coming to live with the bride's natal family. This is reason to explain an Akha marriage tradition that Akha women always need to marry out.

Both Mr. Zhe He (2010) and Dr. Bai Yongfang (2013) also demonstrate with evidence that the ancestors of the Hani participated in building the ancient Dian State roughly from the fourth century BC to 109 BC. According to the Hani migratory epic (Yunnan Provincial Office of Publication and Plan for Ethnic Minorities' Archaic Texts, 1986), several Hani chiefdoms allied to declare a war against the ruling Pu-ni King of the ancient Dian State, but they were defeated because the Pu-ni King got military aid from outsiders. Loss in this war forced ancestors of the Hani people migrated further south into the Red River (or *La-sav/xav* in Hani-Akha) area. The war was also recorded in both Shiji (Sima 145/135 BC? - 90/87 BC?) and Huayang Guo Zhi (Chang AD 291 - 361), stating that in 109 BC, Sou[1] people rebelled in Dian State and the Han Dynasty dispatched General Guo Chang to assist the King of Dian State to suppress it. In doing so, the King of Dian surrendered and was willing to become affiliated with the Han Dynasty, and thus he was granted the title of King of the Dian Country and an official seal of the title by the Han emperor.

The rise of Han Dynasty and its conquest of the Dian State were depicted metaphorically as a giant tree invading *Jadae* country, in the Akha migratory epic Ya Ni Ya Ga Zan Ga (Shida and Ahai, 1992). It is described

---

[1] Sou is a name to refer to ancestral people of Southern Loloish groups including the Hani-Akha (see You 1985: 59 - 60).

that the tree grew up to sky in three days and blocked the sun, so the whole *Jadae* country became dark. The ancestors of *Laqbeeq* (Bo people), *Arboer* (Pu people), and Akha were gathered to cut the tree. But the majority populations of them were killed when the tree finally fell down, and they were forced to move out of their homeland because of the event. Akha ancestors survived from protection under a *Boeqsoev* tree (*Eurya groffii*). It is the reason why Akha people always insert three branches of *Boeqsoev* tree at their ancestor shrine. But this is another metaphor in which *Boeqsoev* tree is used to memorize one of the Akha greatest ancestors *Boeqsoev-laev*, the 34th figure on the Akha genealogy from *Tanqpanq-manr* major branch (see Table 4). Based on this account, I suspect that the leader who led the ancestors of the Akha people left Lake Dian area is *Boeqsoev-laev*. It means that the ancestors of the Akha had lived in the Lake Dian area for seven generations from *Tanqpanq-manr* through *Boeqsoev-laev* (see Table 4). The Hani version of the migratory epic also indicates that the ancestors of the Hani also had lived in Lake Dian area for seven generations, which was about 200 years from the fourth century BC to 109 BC (see Bai 2013). This phrase is called *Jadae nyamir* in Akha, literally meaning North *Jadae* land, which I call the Earlier Phase of *Jadae* Period in the Hani-Akha history here.

Then ancestors of the Hani-Akha people migrated into the Red River area and gradually occupied valleys along the river and its tributaries (see Figure 4). The collapse of a united Chinese empire at the end of the Han dynasty led China and its frontier regions into a historical period during which numerous independent local states and chiefdoms developed. During this period of historical time, numerous Tibeto-Burman polities, particularly the Nanzhong Great Chiefdoms (*Nanzhong Da Xing* in Chinese) in eastern/northeastern Yunnan, southeastern Sichuan and northwestern Guizhou had risen since the fourth century AD (Yang, 2003) and the Six Kingdoms had formed in western Yunnan since the seventh century AD (Backus, 1981). It is generally agreed by Chinese historians and scholars that it was during this historical period that self-conscious political entities more or less related to current ethnic nationalities of China were formed (You, 1982, Tian, 2001). Ancestors of the Hani-Akha also established seven chiefdoms in their territories along the Red River and its tributaries during this period of time. These seven chiefdoms are recorded as Yinyuan, Situo, Xichu, Luokong, Weimo, Qiangxian, and Wangnong in Manshu (Huang, 2007: 47). It seems that the proto-Hani Nationality was also formed during this historical period of time, because these seven chiefdoms are recorded as the same people under the same name Ho Man❶ or Honi Man in Chinese sources during Tang Dynasty (Fan AD 863). I suspect that the seven major *Tanqpanq* branches of the Hani-Akha genealogies are the genealogies of the rulers of these seven chiefdoms. It is evident that at least four of the seven major branches correspond to four of the Honi Man chiefdoms reported to be in the Ailao mountain area, that is, the *Tanqpanq-manr* branch corresponds to the Yinyuan chiefdom, the *Tanqpanq-dzuq* branch to the Situo chiefdom, the *Tanqpanq-jm* branch to the Xichu chiefdom and the *Tanqpanq-xav* branch to the Luokong chiefdom (Wang and Huang, 2008). In addition, it was recorded that a Ho Man great chief named Wang Luoqi from the Red River area paid tribute to the Tang court in AD 656, and another Ho Man great chief named Meng Guwu also paid tributes to the Tang court in AD 734 (Bai, 2013). Wang Luoqi and Meng Guwu are apparently chiefs of two of those seven chiefdoms respectively.

---

❶ Man is written as "蛮" in Chinese character, literally meaning "barbarian", which is referred to non-Chinese people in its southern frontier by Chinese.

The Yinyuan chiefdom was apparently established by the ancestors of the Akha. Akha oral history states that their ancestors arrived at a flat valley along the *La-sav/xav* or the Red River after they left Lake Dian. The Akha call this valley as *Hoerlanr Dae*, meaning hot valley. *Hoerlanr Dae* is generally agreed to refer to Yuanjiang valley because the latter is also first recorded as Huilong Dian in earlier Chinese sources (Jiang, 2007: 7). These two terms look different as they are written in different writing systems, but their pronunciations are almost identical. Later, Yuanjiang valley was recorded as Yinyuan (Jiang, 2007: 7).

It is recorded that by AD 765 one of the six kingdoms in western Yunnan, Nanzhao (AD 653 – AD 902), had conquered five other small states in the west and Nanzhong great chiefdoms in the east and ruled over the area known as Yunnan today (Backus, 1981). Nanzhao was a federated state that had allied with numerous smaller chiefdoms. Those allied chiefdoms located in today's southern, southeastern and northeastern parts of Yunnan were referred to as *Dongfang Wu Man 37 Bu*, meaning the 37 Eastern Chiefdoms of Black Barbarians[1]. Those seven Honi Man chiefdoms are among these 37 chiefdoms (Huang, 2007: 47). These 37 chiefdoms were maintained as important polities in this region throughout the period of the Nanzhao dynasty as well as its three immediately following short-lived dynasties (AD 902 – AD 937)[2]. These polities also served as major military forces that aided Duan Siping in establishing the kingdom of Dali (AD 937 – AD 1253) later (Huang, 2007). It seems, however, that the military campaign led by Duan

---

[1] Since the capital of Nanzhao was located in the city of Dali in western Yunnan, the southern, southeastern and northeastern parts of today's Yunnan were all located east of the Nanzhao.

[2] These short-lived states are the Ta-ch'ang-he kingdom (AD 902 – AD 928), Ta-t'ien-hsing kingdom (AD 928 – AD 929) and Ta-i-ning kingdom (AD 929 – AD 937) respectively (Backus, 1981: 162).

Siping and the subsequent establishment of Dali Kingdom led to the dissolution of the traditional boundaries of these 37 chiefdoms. Some of these chiefdoms grew significantly while others were either fragmented or completely dissolved during the reign of the Dali Dynasty. Yinyuan chiefdom was one of these chiefdoms that gradually expanded and eventually became the leading chiefdom and the center of a federated Hani-Akha polity.

It is recorded in Ming Shi (History of the Ming Dynasty) that in 1053, a Zhuang uprising leader Nong Zhigao❶ fled to Yuanjiang valley, which forced the Honi people moved to the south bank of Yuanjiang River and established the Luopan Dian Guo there (see Jiang 2007: 7; Huang 2007: 47). The term Luopan is said to refer to Luopan Mountain which is located to the northeast of Yuanjiang town (Pu, 2008), while the term Dian means "flat valley" in Chinese and corresponds to the term *dae* in Akha. Luopan Mountain was probably the location of ancient cemetery of the Hani-Yani tribes, because in Hani-Akha language, cemetery is called *lawq-bymr* or *Lmq-bymr*, to which the Chinese word *Luo-pan* presents one of the closest transliterations. Another opinion is that, since the Hani-Akha call the Red river *La-sav* or *La-xav* (pronounced as "*la-sha*") *Lawrbaq*, the term *Luopan* could also be a Chinese transliteration of *Lawrbaq*. Whichever the case is, historians usually agree that Luopan Dian Guo is a federated polity established by the Hani-Akha people (Huang, 2007: 47).

According to the famous migratory epic of the Akha, Ya Ni Ya Ga Zan Ga (Shida and Ahai, 1992), *Jadae* polity was seated at *Jadae Lanr*, meaning a

---

❶ Nong Zhigao (AD 1025–1055) is a famous Zhuang hero who established a Zhuang state called Dali Guo in today's Guangxi Zhuang Aotonomous Region in 1041 and later renamed as Danan Kingdom in 1052. Rise of Nongzhi Gao was suppressed by the Song Dynasty, which forced him to flee into Yunnan area in 1053 (Huang, 1983).

walled Jadae town and it reached its highest height of power and splendor when it was ruled by the great King *Jawrban*, who ruled over 12 regions. The King *Jawrban* seated at the capital town *Jadae Lanr*, while the other eleven regions are governed by eleven appointed *Sanqpaq* or governors[1]. In the central court there were also appointed ministers of water/irrigation, population, finance, information/communication, food, and military (ibid: 58-59). *Aqkaqzanr* or the elaborate system of Akha customary laws that governs all Akha cultural traditions including annual festivals, ancestral services (*aqpoeq lawr-e*) and the Akha calendar (*khovqtovlatovq*) was standardized during this period. In addition, during the early stages of the Jadae polity, Akha societies experienced great economic prosperity and a flowering of their cultural identity (ibid: 59-85). However, as time went by, King Jawrban grew to become a severe tax/tribute collector who even used military force to extract taxes/tributes. It is recorded that many other ethnic groups such as *Laqbeeq* (Bai people), *Biqcmq* (Dai or Tai people), and *Arboer* (Mon-khmer people) also paid tributes to the *Jadae* court. These practices were decried by the people, which eventually culminated in a conspiracy to assassinate King Jawrban by several super lineages of the Akha within Jadae[2]. Following Jawrban's death, however, Jadae polity was not dissolved. Jawrban's wife, Queen *Kertiv Arber* (who was pregnant with Jawrban's only male heir at the time), ruled over Jadae until their son *Banjeev* was crowned at the age of fifteen. Jadae polity continued to prosper during the reigns of *Kertiv Arber*

---

[1] These eleven governors are recorded as *Sanqpaq Kertiv Arber* (the wife of Jawrban, from the *Mawqtavq* lineage), *Sanqpaq Byanlaeq Laeqjaq*, *Sanqpa Jeqjawr Jawrovq* (the sister of Jawrban), *Sanqpaq Jawrbaeq Baeqjur*, *Sanqpaq Marzoe Zoekan*, *Sanqpaq Xawqdan Danjawr*, *Sanqpaq Oerkanr Kanrhan*, *Sanqpaq Oerlo Loyo*, *Sanqpaq Khavjiq Jiqma*, *Sanqpaq Aqnanq Khanqjae* and *Sanqpaq Naqgaq Jaehaw* (Jinghong County Bureau of Ethnic Affairs, 1992: 58).

[2] It is generally accepted that the leaders of the *Mazev*, *Ghoeqlanq* and *Mawqtavq* lineages all conspired together in assassinating King Jawrban.

and *Banjeev*. Eventually, however, Jadae polity was conquered following its siege by a foreign military (ibid: 112-149).

According to *Yuanshi* (The History of the Yuan Dynasty) (Song et al. 1310 – 1381), following their conquest of Dali Kingdom in 1253, the Mongols encountered fierce resistance from Honi Man soldiers belonging to Luopan Guo or Luopan Kingdom. The Mongols attacked the fortified Luopan city located on the south bank of the Red River many times but failed to conquer it until 1274 when Sai Dianci, the Mongol general and governor of the newly established Yunnan Province under the Yuan Dynasty, led a Mongol army to successfully besiege and persuade the Luopan leader Ahobi to surrender (see Jin et al 2007: 165). I suspect that the recorded Honi leader Ahobi is the Queen Kertiv Arber because she was called *Aqhoqber* (pronounced as *A-ho-be*) by the Akha. Two years later, the Mongols renamed the Lishe River, an ancient name of the Red River transliterated from the Hani-Akha name *La-sav* or *La-xav*, as Yuan Jiang, meaning "the river of the Yuan Dynasty", and established Yuanjiang Wan Hu Fu, the second highest level of administration and military forces under Yunnan Province, in Luopan city (Bai, 2008). In the same year, another Woni/Hani fortified town, Talang (today's Mojiang city), fell to the Mongols (Xinhuanet Yunnan Channel 2007, also see Alting von Geusau, 2000: 140). Later in 1284 another Mongol army led by General Meng Gudai attacked the important fortified Honi town, Luobi Dian, in Yinyuan basin, south of Yuanjiang valley and Luopan city, and massacred the city's soldiers and people (Pu, 2008).

As a side note, it is well-known among the Akha that two of the oldest Akha lineages, the *Mazev* and *Civqmavq*, had never acknowledged the centralized authority of *Jawrban* and refused to pay him any tributes. They actually migrated south right after they assassinated King Jawrban, and they are the pioneers of southward migrating Akha group who first entered in Laos, Myanmar and ultimately Thailand among any other Akha subgroups. Alting von Geusau mainly worked with the Ulo Akha subgroup, who is dominated by the Mazev lineage. It is not surprising, therefore, that Alting von Geusau (2000) concluded that Akha never had their own regular state system, considering that his primary sources are from members of the *Mazev* lineage (Mazeu/Mayev in his spelling). Instead, he regards the Jawrban Dynasty (Dzjawbang in his spelling) as a short-lived shamanic chiefdom. Alting von Geusau further claims that Jawrban (Dzjawbang) and his clan *Arjawr* (Adzjhaw in his spelling) are Hani rather than Akha. As a result he concludes that "he Akha name derives from their being 'refugees of war' in a Hani dominated, class-based corvée system" (ibid: 140).

In contrast to Alting von Geusau, however, I argue that the Jadae polity was a federated state ruled by the Akha and it is recorded as Luopan Dian Guo in Chinese historical documents. Chinese records show that the Ho(ni) Man people in this area had long been cultivators of irrigated rice since Tang Dynasty (Fan AD 863). Akha internal historical texts (Shida and Ahai, 1992) also inform us that Akha practiced irrigated rice farming in the context of Jadae. In addition, numerous contemporary Akha ceremonial traditions and cosmological views can only be explained by the earlier practices of Akha as irrigated rice farmers in Jadae (Tooker, 1996). Irrigated rice farming provides a strong economic basis for supporting the elite ruling class and state administrative affairs. Moreover, according to Akha internal historical texts as described earlier, Jadae polity exhibited several key characteristics of a state. These characteristics include but are not limited to: 1) a hierarchical political structure with a hereditary apical ruler, 2) a centralized court and military, 3) a sovereign territory with a fortified capital city and several fortified defensive towns, and 4) compulsory taxation. Another piece of evidence to support my argument is found in a semantic analysis of the title of the rulers of Jadae. In Hani-Akha languages, *dzoeqma* is used to refer to chiefs or village heads. But Jawrban and the other eleven rulers of Jadae polity were all given the title of *Sanqpaq*. The Akha term *Sanqpaq* refers to a ruler of a state or a state-like polity such as an emperor, king, prince or the like in the past. In the present day *Sanqpaq* is also used to refer to governors at various administrative levels within modern nation-states.

I further hold that the formation of the Akha identity that distinguishes them from other Hani subgroups is a direct result of the state building projects of Jadae. There are four pieces of evidence — from oral histories, genealogies, ethnographies and linguistics — to support my argument. First, the possession of oral texts referring to Jadae or Jadae polity is *the* ultimate criterion that distinguishes the Akha from other Hani subgroups. All *Zaq-niq/Yaq-niq/Aq-niq/Haq-niq* groups who call themselves "Akha" regard Jadae as their homeland and possess a rich body of oral texts relating to Jadae and Jadae polity. In contrast, all other Hani groups that do not refer to themselves as "Akha" have little such knowledge about Jadae or the Jadae polity. I attribute this distinction to asymmetric political positions of the Akha groups and the other Hani groups. The Akha groups are apparently at the political center of the Jadae polity, that is, the Luopan Dian or Yuanjiang Valley, while the other Hani groups are located at peripheries of the Jadae polity, both geographically and politically. This could be supported by a famous story called *Durma Jeiseq* (meaning Lady Jeiseq) which has strongly contrasting versions in Hani and Akha groups. In Akha version, *Jeiseq* was a bad princess who was always drunk and married many men from different ethnic groups one after another. But in Hani version, *Jeiseq* was a knowledgeable lady and loyal lover who refused to marry to a man arranged by her parents because she had her own lover already. So, she escaped from the arranged marriage with her lover, and traveled through the Hani lands to teach them knowledge such as the calendar. However, these two seemingly contrasting versions of the same story could be harmonized if we read it in the following way. *Jeiseq* was a princess of the Jadae Kingdom, who was arranged for a political marriage. But she refused to obey this order because she had her lover already. So, she escaped from the arranged marriage with her lover to and kept hiding in the Hani lands, peripheries of the Jadae polity. Therefore, from the ruling class's perspective, *Jeiseq* was a bad princess; but from the perspectives of the commoners in peripheries, she was appraised by the virtue of her loyalty to her love and her rich knowledge. As a matter of fact, the Akha standardized a calendar (which I will introduce in Chapter 3) during the historical phase of the Jadae polity; and it is stilled completely preserved and practiced by most Akha populations today. On the contrary, the Hani versions of the calendar are usually incomplete and have much Chinese influence which occurred later.

So far as genealogy is concerned, the majority of today's Akha are descendants of the *Tanqpanq-manr* major branch, while the majority of the Hani in Honghe area of China are descendants of the *Tanqpanq-jm*, *Tanqpanq-xav* and *Tanqpanq-dzuq* major branches. However, some Akha subgroups such as *Mawqtavq* in China and *Nuqghoeq*, *Peerxaw* and *Awrma* in Laos descend from *Tanqpanq-jm* major branch, the same genealogical branch as many Hani from Honghe area. These Akha subgroups are actually more similar to the Hani groups in terms of their dress and dialects. For instance, like Hani women, the Akha women descended from *Tanqpanq-jm* major branch wear trousers and long jackets down to the knees, unlike the majority Akha women descended from the *Tanqpanq-manr* major branch who wear skirts and shorter jackets. My own fieldwork in Zomia also confirms that these Akha subgroups speak a dialect that is closer to that of the Hani groups in Honghe area than to that of the Akha subgroups in Thailand. And yet they regard themselves as Akha as a result of the fact that their ancestors lived in Jadae under King Jawrban and his successors. In contrast, the Hani groups in Honghe have little knowledge of Jadae polity and thus never regard themselves as Akha. Their ignorance about Jadae polity either resulted from their unwillingness to pass down the knowledge on purpose, which could be understood as a form of resistance against the ruling center, or otherwise they were too peripheral to involve in the state building.

Similarly, the *Ghoeqlanq* lineage of Akha are descendants of the *Tanqpanq-xav* major branch who later became Akha by virtue of their integration into Jadae polity, while the majority of this genealogical branch's descendants remain as Hani residing in Luchun and Jinping counties of Yunnan. Considering the fact that members of the *Ghoeqlanq* lineage were completely assimilated as Akha, it is highly likely that their ancestors were brought as soldiers into the territory of the then *Tanqpanq-manr* chiefdom as a result of the military campaigns by Duan Siping in AD 937 as mentioned earlier. On the other hand, it is possible that the Akhanization of the *Mawqtavq*, *Nughoeq* and *Peerxaw* subgroups may have resulted from their closer proximity to the center of the Jadae polity, either geographically or politically or both, than the other Hani subgroups were.

Secondly, not all of today's Akha subgroups are descendants of ancient *Zaq-niq/Yaq-niq/Aq-niq/Haq-niq* groups. For instance, members of the *Bawrcaeq* lineage, also known as Kopien in Laos, refer themselves and are called by other Akha subgroups *Haqboer* Akha because their ancestors were

Mon-Khmer speaking people. *Haqboer* is a general term used by Akha to refer to Mon-Khmer speaking groups. It seems likely that the Jadae polity did in fact conquer and assimilate a number of smaller groups with different cultural-linguistic-racial-kin backgrounds. The *Bawrcaeq* lineage, for example, presents such a case of a Mon-Khmer group that was assimilated to the Akha way of life by the way of forming their own genealogy and grafting it onto the last common ancestor of the Hani-Akha people *Dzoeq-tanqpanq* ❶ . I have recorded some genealogies of members of the *Bawrcaeq* lineage from the Muang Sing District of Laos in 2002 and discovered that their ancestors became Akha roughly 23–25 generations ago. This number corresponds perfectly with the chronology of Jadae polity, as the genealogies of the present-day descendants of King Jawrban have a similar number of generations following Jawrban as those of the *Bawrcaeq* lineage. In addition, members of the *Bawrcaeq* clan in Laos today still retain some traditions from their Mon-Khmer ancestors, particularly those related to funerary rites, and have their own distinctive dress as well. Apart from this, however, they are indistinguishable from other Akha in Zomia. Finally, their Akhanization or assimilation is more complete in China, Burma, and Thailand where current

---

❶ In order to integrate people from different ethnic origins, Jadae State developed a rule that every one could become an Akha as long as he/she could follow *Aqkaqzanr* (customary laws and guides to Akha way of life particularly ancestor worship) and carry out ancestor offerings. I call this process Akhanization. In order to carry out ancestor offerings, they need to create their own patrilineal genealogies, in case they do not have own before, which graft/start from *Dzoeqtanq-panq* , the last generation of the Hani-Akha national genealogy. This is called *Paqdawvq* in Akha, meaning "genealogy grafting". For people from other ethnic origins who want to become Akha, genealogy grafting to *Dzoe-tanqpanq* is the key step. This explains the reason why there are numerous minor branches of the Hani-Akha genealogies after *Dzoe-tanqpanq* . Since this cultural tradition developed in Jadae, when most Akha's genealogies had reached 42 generations or more, all grafted genealogies are much shorter than the authentic Akha genealogies in number of generations. From the number of generations of their grafted genealogies, we could roughly reckon when they became/joined Akha. Other Hani groups do not practice this cultural tradition of genealogy grafting due to the fact that their ancestors were not at the political center of Jadae, if they were involved in it at all.

members of the *Bawrcaeq* lineage have no distinguishing features from other Akha apart from their lineage name. It is evident that Mon-Khmer-speaking groups have long lived in close proximity with the ancestors of today's Hani-Akha (Song et al., 1310 − 1381; Yang, 2010:311 − 312).

Thirdly, a semantic analysis of the term *Akha* reveals that Akha were the dominant group or ruling class of Jadae. The etymon "Kha" (low tone) in "Akha" literally means "between " "middle " "center " or "distance". The affix "a" is used to refer to the names of people, animals, plants, and so on, and indicates that the word is a noun. Therefore, the term *Akha* can be semantically translated as "people in-between " "people of the middle" "people of the center "and/or "people from the distance". These meanings are quite simple to explain in reference to the history of Jadae polity. The people of *Jadae* clearly did not want to be subjects of either the Dali Kingdom to their west and north or the Tai State❶ to their south;rather, they wanted to be an independent people living in their own territory. In addition, the people of Jadae were composed of various tribes and clans with different names and even different ethnic origins. As a newly formed group of people they needed a new name by which to label their unified collectivity.

The term *Akha* aptly applies to their political and geographical positions. Therefore, the Akha as "people in-between" refers to a politically independent group of people who were geographically juxtaposed between other (stronger) states. The Akha as "people of the middle" in turn reflects their cosmological view of being at the "center" of the universe. The concept of the geographic center has long been a symbol of power in Akha cosmology. For example, the house of the traditional leader of an Akha Village, the

---

❶ A Tai State, *Sipsongpanna*, began to develop since AD 1180 in regions that cover today's Xishuangbanna in southwest Yunnan and neighboring parts of northern Laos (Hsieh, 1995).

Dzoeqma, needs to be built at the village's center (Tooker 1988). Similarly, "people of the center" indicates their geopolitical position at the center of Jadae. This could be supported by a cultural tradition that came to distinguish the Akha from the other Hani groups. It is required that all Akha men should have a top-knot on the top-center of their heads, referred to in Akha as *dzanbawq*. In Akha language, the sky *mq* (which usually pronounced as *uq*) and head *uq* are symbolically interchangeable. So are the center of sky and center-top of the head. Therefore, like genealogies connect the Akha people to the Sky Mother who descended from the center of the sky, the *dzanbawq* growing down from the center-top of the head is a symbol of both an individual's manhood and their Akha identity of being people of the center. In this sense, *dzanbawq* is a representation of one's own genealogy. On the contrary, other Hani groups usually do not have this tradition.

The collapse of Jadae in turn forced the Akha to leave their beloved homeland and begin their centuries-long migrations south into the mountains of Zomia. The demise of Jadae and subsequent migrations of Akha are well depicted in their famous migratory epic (Shida and Ahai, 1992). The term Akha was further reinforced as a term of self-reference as a result of the demise of Jadae and migrations of Akha to areas far from their original homeland; hence the fourth semantic meaning of Akha as "people from the distance", or people residing a great distance from their lost homeland. In other words, Akha refers to "the diaspora of Jadae" and as such embodies a strong nostalgic sentiment towards the Jadae polity, the common homeland of all the Akha. During their centuries-long migrations and settlement in the mid-slopes of mountainous Zomia, the Akha as a "people of the middle" gained yet another meaning referring to their newly acquired ecological niche at middle altitudes between other ethnic groups, as interpreted by Alting von

Geusau (2000). I have noticed that many young Akha in Thailand who lack knowledge of their history tend to give the meaning of the term Akha as "a people of distance from the lowlands" or the political, economic and cultural centers of modern nation-states. This new connotation reflects the marginalized positions of Akha people in Thailand and Zomia today. Therefore, I call the post-Jadae polity period as Diasporic Period of Hani-Akha history (see next section), while I call the historical time of Jadae polity (AD 1054 – 1284) the Latter Phase of the Jadae Period, and that of the seven chiefdoms from 109 BC through AD 1053 the Middle Phase of the Jadae Period.

The fourth and last piece of evidence comes from members of the Ake group. The Ake are a very small Tibeto-Burman-speaking people who tend to live in close proximity to Akha communities throughout Zomia. While their language and culture are very distinct from that of Akha, they nevertheless possess genealogies that are similar to and yet different from those of Akha. The Ake people share the mythical and national parts of the Hani-Akha genealogies as listed in Table 2 and Table 3 with some linguistic modifications. Ake genealogies after *Dzoeq-tanqpanq* are not only different from but also much shorter than those of Akha. The length of their genealogies is usually less than 20 generations after *Dzoeq-tanqpanq*, indicating that they have a non-*Zaq-niq/Yaq-niq/Aq-niq/Haq-niq* origin. I have been informed by some Ake that their language and cultural traditions are much closer to those of the Jinuo people in China and the Muji people in Laos than to those of the Akha[1]. All three of these groups, the Ake, Jinuo and Muji, follow a

---

[1] I once recorded Muji language and played it to Ake villagers in Thailand who claimed that it was their language. With the exception of a slight dialectic difference in pronunciation of the number 3, all other counting numbers are the same between these two groups. I was also informed by some Ake villagers in Mengsong that they can communicate with Jinuo people directly in their own languages.

patronymic naming system that can be reversed between the names of fathers and sons. For instance, if a father is named Ya-dzoeq, then his son could be named Dzoeq-ya. This practice, however, is forbidden among all Akha groups, for whom only the last syllable or two of a father's name may be used as the first syllable or two of his son and the ending syllable of the son's name may not repeat any of the syllables used earlier in the patrilineal ancestral genealogy. At the same time, Ake differ from both Jinuo and Muji in that the latter only memorize three generations of their ancestors and as such do not possess lengthy genealogies as the Ake (and Akha) do.

Another difference is that both Jinuo and Muji have no knowledge about Jadae and King Jawrban while Ake elders are generally knowledgeable about both. I was also informed by some knowledgeable Ake elders that their original homeland was located in today's Mojiang, Yunnan Province. Based on all of these bodies of evidence, it is reasonable to argue that the Ake people may have been a tribalized group residing along the periphery of the Jadae polity, as demonstrated via their adoption of Akha-style genealogies and their bilingualism in both Ake and Akha. These cultural features can not be explained simply on the basis of their proximity to Akha communities as both Jinuo and Muji groups also have lived in close proximity to the Akha for centuries.

2.6 Diasporic Period of Akha History[1]

The Akha's centuries-long southern migrations after the collapse of Jadae involved a process of political fragmentation or marginalization (Alting

---

[1] Since the Akha split off from the other Hani groups at this point and the Akha is my study subject, I only focus on the history of the Akha from this point.

von Geusau, 2000), by which Akha became a typical upland group in Zomia seeking to avoid "the oppression of state-making projects in the valleys — slavery, conscription, taxes, corvée labor, epidemics, and warfare" (Scott, 2009: ix). As such their shifting cultivation technology, relatively egalitarian social structure and even orality — both *post*- and *pre*-literate traditions[1] (Alting von Geusau, 2000: 130-131), are best understood as secondary adaptations allowing for them to avoid incorporation into various lowland states (Scott, 2009). This period also involved a process of re-tribalization (Harrel, 2001) or fragmentation, through which each village became integrated into a small independent chiefdom led by a dzoeqma or chief, and spread to occupy the yet-or less populated mountainous areas, as a consequence of the conflicts and fights with the more dominant Tai Lue societies in Sipsongpanna (Shida and Ahai, 1992). As a result, it is not surprising that various western scholars (Kammerer, 1989: 277; Tooker, 1988, 2004) describe Akha as a "tribal people" with no extra-village political organization. Their descriptions are drawn from observations of Akha villages in contemporary Thailand, where most Akha arrived only after the turn of the twentieth century. In much older Akha settlements in Xishuangbanna, China, however, numerous Akha chiefdoms covering a cluster of villages were well developed and/or maintained until the onset of the Peoples Republic of China. The most famous great Akha chief in Sipsongpanna was *Pyavqlo Hobym* from *Byevho* lineage. He was titled as the greatest Akha chief whose power was granted to rule all the Akha chiefdoms within the territory or periphery of the

---

[1] Alting von Geusau (2000:. 130-131) describes Akha society as both post- and pre-literate society, arguing that "Akha and Hani societies are 'post-literate' in the sense that they stem from highly developed Yi groups which possessed a script, as their histories tell us. They are "pre-literate" in that they had "lost" their script;they say "they ate their books of buffalo-hide when they were hungry [during their migratory journey]" (Lewis, 1969, vol. 1:35;Yang, 1991).

Sipsongpanna, by its Tai *cao phaendin* (overlord), roughly in 1696. As an anecdote, *Pyavqlo Hobym* was also selected as the Godfather of the crowned prince of the Tai King. As such, he was granted certain privilege that other eleven princes of the Sipsongpanna State did not have. His chieftain position had been passed down through nine generations to *Pyavqlo Tserlov*, who was served at the deputy chair of the Consultative Council of Nanqiao County, Republic of China, when it was established in 1936, and later was appointed as the first Akha deputy governor of Xishuangbanna Dai Autonomous Prefecture when it was established in 1953, and he had served that position for four terms until he passed away in 1972 (Xishuangbanna Bureau of Ethnic and Religious Affairs, 2006: 274 – 275). Smaller supra-village polities also developed in both my research sites Mengsong and Baka (which will be discussed in Chapter 3, Chapter 4 and Chapter 5). Henri Roux (2011: 23 – 24 [Orig. 1924]) also describe a similar supra-village political organization among the Nu Quay Akha in northern Laos in the 1920s (also see Roux and Tran, 1954 [cited by Tooker[1], 2012: 33]). I am also informed that such polities existed in eastern Shan States until the early 1980s (*Saeduqguq Aqbawrhaq* 2012, personal comm.). While an additional full-length paper would be required to adequately describe the post-Jadae period of Akha history in Zomia, it is worth noting here briefly that the history of Akha migrations and settlement in northern Laos and eastern

---

[1] Tooker tends to deny such supra-village polities existing in Akha societies despite of noting the existence of a supra-village chief called *sam-p'a* among the Nu Quây Akha, because she believes that the term *sam-pha* comes from the term for Shan princes *sawbwa* (Leach 1954: 34) and is related to the Thai terms *cao* (Lord) and *caofa* (Lord of the Sky), based on Lehman's (1967: 99) account: "The sawbwa system is a Shan political system, which derived its jural authority mainly from the old Burmese kingdoms." (Tooker, 2012: 33). But Tooker fails to recognize that the term "sawbwa" is a Burmese title in Burmese language for the princes in the Shan States and also in Sipsongpana (see Giersch 1998: 50, also cited by Sturgeon 2005: 69), which is the same term as *sanqpaq* in Hani-Akha or *sam-pha* in Roux and Tran's account.

Myanmar can be traced back roughly 700 and 500 years ago respectively, which could be reckoned based on the historical facts as noted in Akha migratory epics (Shida and Ahai, 1992).

The Diasporic Period of Akha history can be further divided into three phases: traditional, modern, and post-modern. I call this period of time, ranging from the collapse of Jadae to the earliest conversions of Akha to Christianity in Myanmar in the 1920s or to onset of the People's Republic of China, the traditional phase. During this phase, the Akha ethnic/cultural identity was shaped by their shared worldview and embodied in their replicated landscapes. Tooker (1988), for example, describes how an Akha village and its surrounding territory represent a replicated micro-cosmos of the world for Akha. In terms of worldview Akha are "animists" and ancestor worshipers. They speak the same language, even though they may have different dialects. Their economy and polity were still relatively independent. Chapter 3 will document the traditional way of natural resource management by the Akha people under this social-political environments.

During the twentieth century, however, Akha ethnic/cultural identity began to change drastically with the arrival of Christian missionaries and the emergence of modern nation-states throughout Zomia. In Myanmar, for example, since the 1920s, Christian missionaries started converting Akha into Christians during the period of British colonial rule. Christian Akha came to regard themselves as the "new Akha", salvaged by God and superior to traditional Akha whom they came to regard as "dirty" and "backwards demon-worshipers" following the teachings of western missionaries in reference to their animist and ancestral beliefs and practices. For example, see the historical novel of Jean Nightingale, one of the earliest missionaries to work with Akha in northern Thailand during the 1950s, wherein she refers to traditionalist Akha as "demon-worshipers" living in constant fear within the "demon gates" of their villages (1990: 2, 147). Christian missionaries such as Nightingale and other Akha and non-Akha church leaders have brought about drastic changes in the worldview and cultural identity of their Akha converts. Ironically, Akha belonging to different Christian denominations (e. g. Baptist and Catholic) also tend to look down on each other and see members of the other denomination as inferior to themselves. Other Akha in Myanmar have adopted the dominant Shan culture and become Buddhists. Yet the rest of the Akha have retained their traditional practices. As a result, religion has become a major factor dividing Akha in Myanmar into four main groups. Akha belonging to each of these groups are often reluctant to even converse with Akha belonging to other groups. Another social issue in Myanmar stems from the long-term civil strife and economic deprivation that has plagued the country since the rise of a military dictatorship in 1962. Conflicts and economic deprivation in Myanmar have pushed various Akha communities (as well as other ethnic groups) to migrate across the border to either China or Laos where they have since become Chinese and Lao citizens respectively or Thailand where many of them are still treated as "illegal" migrants and denied citizenship status.

In Thailand, religious divisions have similarly developed among Akha and are as complicated as in the case of Myanmar. In China, various communist campaigns such as "Great Leap Forward" and "the Great Proletarian Cultural Revolution" had forced the Akha to abandon many of their cultural traditions. Their traditional belief system was labeled as "superstition" and Akha were forced to abandon it. Under the influence of an enforced belief in atheism, Akha began to perceive of communist Chinese Han as *naevq* or spirits whose power surpassed that of all of the natural spirits that Akha traditionally believed in. In order to avoid any harmful punishment from these new *naevq* , Akha came to believe that they had to listen to and obey the commands of Chinese Han officials. Akha were not even allowed to wear their traditional costumes because they were viewed as an impediment to agricultural production.

In Laos, Akha did not experience the same degree of dramatic social and cultural changes as their counterparts did in other countries. They were able to maintain a relatively traditional way of life until about two decades ago. However, the cultural identity of Akha is invisible in Laos until recently because the government had only categorized its national populations into three kinds: lowlanders, mid-landers, and highlanders. In Laos, Akha were classified as highlanders alongside numerous other unrelated ethnic groups.

Yet all Akha in these modern nation-states have one thing in common — they have all lost their political independence and become registered peasants living in separate villages. They have all become the targets of various government assimilation efforts. They are required to be educated in the national educational system and to learn the dominant, national culture and language. As a result, younger generations of Akha are losing their own cultural traditions. I have witnessed, in my own fieldwork within Akha communities throughout the region in last 20 years as well as my own life experiences in last four decades, that many Akha youths who were born and/or raised in towns and cities are no longer learning how to speak the Akha language. They are no longer told traditional Akha stories. They have begun to think of themselves as Burmese, Chinese, Laotian or Thai first and Akha second, if at all. When Akha from the younger generations come into contact with Akha from other countries in this region they often cannot communicate with each other and no longer feel a sense of connectedness with each other. They no longer feel a sense of belonging to the larger Akha community in Zomia. In many cases they often try to hide their Akha identity in order to avoid real and/or potential discrimination from the majority populations of the countries wherein they reside, as shown by Toyota (1999). These individuals have become yet another kind of "Akha" — people of the distance without any sense of nostalgia and who are too distant to know their roots. Thus Akha history has entered a period of deconstruction, loss and decomposition of their cultural identity under the powerful political, economic, and cultural influences of modern nation-states and Western colonialism and cultural imperialism (most notably Western Christian missionaries). I call this period of Akha history "the Modern Phase". In this phase, Akha people have been ethnicized and divided into different peoples residing in different countries of Zomia.

Yet the Akha spirit still lives on. The stories of their ancestors still echo in the minds and hearts of many Akha today — including the old and young, men and women. The spirits and memory of Jadae polity are calling their souls back to their long-lost homeland. Akha are beginning to search for their long-lost roots. A sense of pride in being Akha is reemerging. In China, Akha have started to revive traditional festivals such as their New Year Festival (*Kartanrpar*) and Swing Festival (*Yaerkuqdzaq*) with support from their local government since the 1980s. Along with its national "reform and open" policy since 1978 after the end of "the Great Proletarian Cultural Revolution", Chinese governments encourage to revitalize cultural traditions of all the ethnic groups in its country through legislation and financial supports. For instance, the Akha New Year Festival *Kartanrpar* was legislated as a local official holiday by Xishuangbanna prefecture government in 1987. In Myanmar and Thailand, Akha have also begun to revive these traditions, and interestingly Akha from different religious backgrounds have begun to celebrate these traditional festivals collectively as one united group. When I visited Kengtung, Myanmar in 2001 I was shown an Akha school, an orchard garden and a restaurant all named after *Jadae*, in order to cherish the memory of their lost homeland. There is a coffee brandname and a drinking water brandname is also named as *Jadae* in Doichang village, Chiang Rai of Thailand.

There are now a growing number of indigenous Hani-Akha scholars in Zomia, especially in China and Thailand, which is bringing about a new phase in Hani-Akha history, the post-modern phase. This new phase in Hani-Akha history was marked by the First International Conference on Hani/Akha Culture held in Kunming, Yunnan, China in 1993. Since that time six additional conferences have been held every three years in various parts of Zomia[1]. At the same time, Akha from Zomia are organizing international meetings and working groups in order to develop a new common Akha writing system and promote literacy in Akha throughout Zomia (Morton 2010). Another new development is the formation of Mekong Akha Network called NADA, abbreviation from *Naqkaw Aqkaq Dzoeqcawq Armavq*, in 2009. The main vision and mission of NADA is to reaffirm Akha identity through revitalizing Akha cultural traditions. A striking result of NADA's recent work is that more than 400 Christian Akha families have reconverted back to Akha traditional belief and practices.

All of these activities are bringing about a sense of solidarity and belonging among many Akha, if not all, in Zomia once again. This

---

[1] The second conference was held in Chiang Mai, Thailand in 1996; the third in Jinghong, Yunnan in 1999/2000; the fourth in Honghe, Yunnan in 2002; the fifth in Mojiang, Yunnan in 2005; the sixth in Luchun, Yunnan in 2008; and the seventh in Yuanjiang, Yunnan in 2012.

reemerging sense of solidarity is expressed in the popular Akha saying *Aqkaq tseir kaq tiq kaq*, literally meaning "ten Akha are as one". After all, all Akha in Zomia today have a common origin in Jadae. While Akha today may speak different languages, follow different religions, hold different national citizenship and have different livelihoods, they are all "Akha" and not Chinese, Burmese, Laotian or Thai in terms of ethnicity. All Akha have their roots in the homeland of Jadae and as such are part of the Akha diaspora of Jadae. It is in the latter sense alone that all of the various meanings of being "Akha", that is, "people of the middle" "people in-between" "people of the center" and "people of distance", are coalesced (or united). Akha oral historical texts, particularly those related to Jadae, remain as fundamental sources that Akha use to (re-)negotiate and (re-)construct their collective identity today.

2.7 Discussion

Until recently, in cultural anthropology, the study of a culture has traditionally focused on that culture's economy, politics, language, kinship, ritual, arts and symbolism and less on place as such. There is no doubt that knowledge of each of these aspects is very important in understanding a people and their culture. However, more recent ethnographic studies show the importance of place-related identities to various groups such as the Pintupi Aborigines in Australia (Myers, 1991), Lambee of North Carolina (Blu, 1996), Wamirans in Papua New Guinea (Kahn, 1996), and various ethnic groups in China (Swain, 2001).

It is not the place itself, however, but what a group of people experienced together in a particular place that leads them to develop a strong sense of solidarity, belongingness or relatedness — in short a feeling of *collectivity*. In this chapter I have shown that what quintessentially "make" or have "made" the Akha as a people are their collective experiences in cultivating and transforming their homeland Jadae—particularly their collective experiences in building, defending and eventually losing the Jadae polity. The Akha collectivity as such has not simply evolved from a cultural-linguistic-kin-racial collectivity, but has rather been constructed and negotiated through the inclusion and exclusion of various groups of people through time and space.

The Akha ethnic identity has been constructed, deconstructed and reconstructed under certain socio-political circumstances through time and space. At the same time, however, their shared history, especially during the classic period of the Jadae polity, has remained as the ultimate source for Akha to negotiate their identity and maintain their collectivity. For Akha, Jadae is like a "place-world" (Basso, 1996), wherein portions of the past are brought into being. Jadae and the Akha "inter-animate (d)" each other, "[a]s places animate the ideas and feelings of persons who attend to them, these same ideas and feelings animate the places on which attention has been bestowed" (Basso, 1996:107).

This inter-animation is articulated in the very term "Akha", simultaneously meaning "people in-between" "people of the middle" "people at the center" and "people of distance". The first three meanings indicate that the Akha built Jadae and that Jadae in turn "made" the Akha, or to put it in another way, Jadae and the Akha (were) inter-animated and inter-belonged. The last meaning indicates the sense of both "inter-lost" and "sense of connection"; the distance comes from a sense of loss, on the one hand, and yet on the other, without a sense of connection, the distance (from Jadae) is meaningless. Whenever we call an Akha "Akha", such an inter-animation is articulated. The very meaning of the term "Akha" is thus an articulated landscape in which the distant homeland of Jadae (distant in both time and space), is the background or horizon, while the Akha people are the foreground. Their narrative stories about their collective history in Jadae in turn make connections between the background and foreground. In other words, the term *Akha* itself articulates inter-relations between the Akha people and Jadae — the Akha people as a diaspora of Jadae in the sense of being both a place of belonging and loss.

Chapter 3

Ecology of Sacred Landscape:
Natural Resource Management of
Akha People in China Prior to 1950

3.1 Introduction

In Chapter 1, I have defined landscape as a perceived and culturally presented environment, natural or modified or created by people. People may know little about their bio-physical environment, but by definition, they see, know, and interact with the landscape. Therefore, recognition of a distinction between landscape and bio-physical environment is fundamental to the study of human-environmental interactions. Any natural resource management procedure always involves two interdependent processes: 1) a cultural presentation or mental transformation of their bio-physical environments into natural landscapes; and 2) a physical and/or ritual management of natural landscapes. The purpose of the second process is either to maintain the natural landscapes through rituals or to modify/transform them for the benefits of the people. The latter will result in modified, transformed, or even created landscapes. In other words, landscape is both the *medium* and the *outcome* of human-environmental interactions. Following the idea of Berkes'

Sacred Ecology (1999), I am using the term *sacred landscape* to refer to the perceived and culturally presented/transformed environments by traditional societies like the Akha according to their worldview and/or belief systems. I use the term *ecology of sacred landscape* to refer to study of natural resource management through sacred landscapes. In this chapter, I will demonstrate the ecology of sacred landscapes of the Akha people in China prior to 1950. This will be exemplified by an intensive case study of Mengsong Akha community, supplemented by extensive comparisons with other Akha communities in China and Southeast Asia.

Administratively speaking, Mengsong Akha community belongs to Mengsong Administrative Village, Damenglong Township, Jinghong Municipality, Xishuangbanna Prefecture, Yunnan Province, southwest China. Located at the southern tip of Jinghong City, Damenglong Township borders with Myanmar at its east and south. It is the biggest township within the municipality both in terms of area and population (Yunnan Provincial Government, 2006). Topographically, Damenglong Township comprises two basins (Damenglong and Mengsong) and surrounded mountains. Damenglong Basin is the third biggest basin in Xishuangbanna Prefecture; while Mengsong Basin is the highest one with an altitude of 1,557 meters at its lowest point. Damenglong town is 60 km south to Jinghong City.

Damenglong Township governs twenty Administrative Villages. Mengsong is one of them. The name "Mengsong" is from a Dai (Tai Lue) word "Muang song," meaning "high basin." Mengsong Administrative Village is located at the southwestern tip of Damenglong Township (see Figure 2). It comprises eleven natural villages — 8 Akha (Xianfeng, Dazhai, Hongqi, Dongfanghong, Hongxing, Guangming, Buba, and Chala), 2 Ake (Yakou and Ake), and 1 Lahu (Lahu), with 2,851 people in 2017. About three quarters of

Chapter 3　Ecology of Sacred Landscape

Mengsong population are living in six Akha villages (i. e., Dazhai, Xianfeng, Hongqi, Dongfanghong, Hongxing, and Guangming) around Mengsong Basin (see Figure 5), the center of Mengsong area. As they represent the core

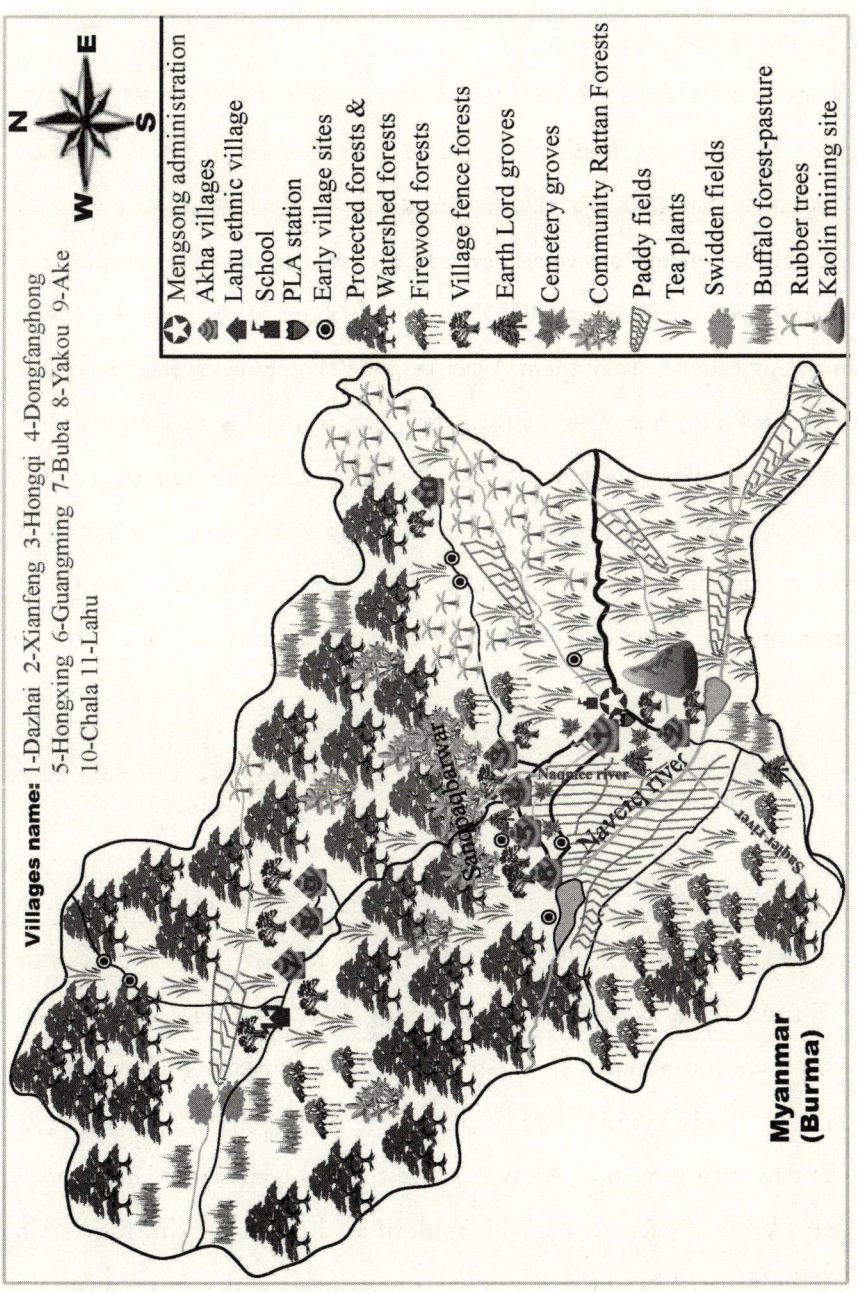

Figure 5　Mengsong Administrative Village

community of Mengsong Akha, these six villages will be my major research sites in Mengsong, while others will be mentioned for comparison. Mengsong is about 37 km away from Damenglong Town and 97 km away from Jinghong City (see Figure 2).

Located between 21°27′−21°34′east latitude and 100°25′−100°35′north longitude, Mengsong Administrative Village covers an area of 100 km^2, which altitudes range from 800 to 2,000 meters above sea level. Mengsong Basin is located at 1,557 meters above sea level. It is mountainous area, in which the flat Mengsong Basin takes up only 3% of its total area. It is under the typical mountainous climate of Southern Asian tropics. The annual average rainfall is 1,600 − 1,800mm, but 80% of them happens from May to October. The average atmosphere moisture is over 80% , and the annual average temperature is 18 ℃. There is light frost during the winter. The types of vegetation include tropical mountain rain forest, mountain monsoon evergreen broad leaf forest, and needle and broad leaf mixture forest (Wang, 1998).

3.2 Akha Belief System

Traditionally, Akha are animists (a term coined by Tylor 1871, and well defined by Hunn 1990, Harvey 2006) who believe that any living organism or physical entity (such as earth, sky, rock, spring, lake, etc.) has a spiritual lord called *yaw-sanr* (pronounced "yaw-song"). The literal meaning of *yaw-sanr* is "owner" or "lord". A *yaw-sanr* could be either worldly or spiritual. It is believed that an organism or entity is possessed and governed by its spiritual *yaw-sanr*. When it refers to a specific spirit of an organism or entity, the affix *yaw* will be replaced by the name of the organism or entity. For instance, a spiritual lord of earth, sky, spring, or village is called *mir-sanr* (pronounced "me-song"), *mq-sanr* (pronounced "um-song"), *cuq-sanr* (pronounced "chu-song"), *pu-sanr* respectively, while *mir*, *mq*, *cuq*, and *pu* mean "earth", "sky", "spring", and "village" respectively. All *yaw-sanr* are believed agents whose powers vary greatly from one to another. Many of these spiritual lords have the status of deities. For instance, *mq-sanr*, *mir-sanr* and *cuq-sanr* could be translated as deities of sky, earth and spring respectively. Offering to these deities is conducted annually in any traditional Akha village. For instance, a ritual called *Mir-sanr lawr-e*, meaning "offering to the earth deity/lord" is conducted annually by every traditional Akha village. This ritual also includes offering to the Sky God and Water God, though this is not reflected in its name.

Besides *yaw-sanr*, another category of spirits in Akha belief system is *naevq* (pronounced "neh", creaky voice with low tone). *Naevq* are free spirits who act as the watchful lawmen of the world. Akha people believe that a person would become a *naevq* when she/he dies. According to the pre-death status of the person as well as the way the person died, three different kinds of *naevq* she/he would become: *aqpoeq aqpiq* (pronounced as "aa-poe aa-pi"), *naevq* and *xavxir* (pronounced as "sha-shi"). *Aqpoeq aqpiq* are spirits of one's ancestors who died normally, or *nmqxir* (see Chapter 2); *aqpoeq* are male ancestors while *aqpiq* are female; and they are believed sources of blessings and protectors of its descendants. Only those who were married with male offspring would become *aqpoeq aqpiq*, whose names will be recorded and memorized in one's genealogy. Those spirits of immediate ancestors — usually within seven generations — are termed as *poeqpiq jmma*. Twelve offerings are given to these immediate ancestors annually at the ancestor shrine located at the middle post of each house called *jmgher* or *jmzer*, by each family during nine annual religious festivals/rituals in traditional Akha societies. These offerings are called *aqpoeq lawr-e*, meaning "offering to ancestors". Thus, Akha people are described as ancestor worshipers. The greatest ancestral spirit *Aqpoeq Miqyaer* is regarded as the Supreme God who governs all other deities and spirits as well as the universal that is, physical entities and living organisms including humans, through various deities and spirits.

Those, single or married without any male offspring, who die naturally (from illness or diseases) at any ages, simply become *naevq*. This type of death is also identified as of *nmqxir*, which means these spirits or *naevq* are allowed to travel back to the ancestral land, but their status in ancestor world be lower and not allowed to travel back to be seated and take offerings at one's ancestor shrine. In other words, they are not regarded as one's ancestors because their names can not be recorded in one's patrilineage. Those who die abnormally — killed, drowned, hanged, etc. — at any age would become *xavxir*, as explained in Chapter 2. Unlike *aqpoeq* who are believed benevolent, or ordinary *naevq* who are believed neutral towards people, *xavxir* are believed malevolent. Therefore, *xavxir* could be translated as demons or evil spirits.

3.3 Akha Worldview and Sacred Landscapes

Akha divide the universe into three worlds vertically: Heavenly World (*Mqtav Khanq*, pronounced "um-ta hong"), Earthly World (*Mirtav Khanq*, pronounced "me-ta hong") and Underground World (*Miro Khanq*, pronounced "me-o hong"). It is believed that the Supreme God *Aqpoeq Miqyaer* and his assistant *Jabi Aqlanq* (pronounced "jabi a-long"), Sky God (*mqsanr*), and all Akha's ancestral spirits❶, along with sun, moon and all stars, live in Heaven;and that the Underground is full of *aqcawq-e zaq* or "other beings" who are governed by serpents *eerlanq* (also known as *byavyanq*), the God of Water;while the Earthly World is not only composed of human beings, animals, plants, water/rivers, and any other natural entities, but also full of various supernatural spirits (*naevq* and *yaw-sanr*) who are immortal and maintain the natural order.

According to Akha worldview, the Earthly World is further divided into two domains: the Inside or *lavqkhoer* (pronounced "la-hoe") and the Outside *lavqnyir* (pronounced "la-nyi"). The Inside is people's domain where it is supposedly free of *naevq* , while the Outside is *naevq*'s domain. Villages and agricultural fields are the Inside, people's domain; while the rest of world is the Outside/*naevq*'s domain. Villages are the centers of the Inside domain, while sacred places, where *naevq* are believed to live, are the centers of the Outside domain. These centers are the core territories exclusive to one another, while the peripheries of each domain allow other side to reach. A well-known Akha myth❷ narrated below explains how this division came to be:

Once upon a time, people and *naevq* were brothers and sisters;they were children of *Tanqpanq Aqma* (Mother Tanqpanq) who had two breasts in front feeding human babies and seven breasts in back feeding *naevq* babies. In *Tanqpanq Aqma*'s huge house Tanqpanq Ymrma, people and *naevq* were living harmoniously together. All animals also lived harmoniously together, as

---

❶ As the Hani-Akha's first ancestor *Mq-ma* or *Aoq-ma* (i. e. Sky Mother) is believed descent from the sky as explained in Chapter 2, the Hani-Akha people believe their original homeland is in the sky or a place that is connected to the sky.

❷ There are many versions of the myth. Here I am citing the one collected from Mengsong area, Damenglong Township, Jinghong Municipality, Xishuangbanna Prefecture, Yunnan Province, China.

buffaloes and tigers were penned together; chicken and eagles stayed together; while sheep and wolves were good friends. As *Tanqpanq Aqma* was getting old and sick, people and *naevq* started a contest for the privilege of taking care of their sick mother. People requested *naevq* to leave, saying "*Tanqpanq* is people's mother". *Naevq* also requested people to leave and persisted that *Tanqpanq* was *naevq*'s mother. As no side could persuade another to leave, *Tanqpanq Aqma*'s huge house became crowded of people and *naevq*. In order to pacify both people and *naevq*, *Tanqpanq Aqma* announced that when she died, if her face were turned toward the front, she would be the people's mother and they should conduct the funeral for her; but if her face were turned toward the back, then she would be the *naevq*'s mother and they should be responsible for her funeral❶. Then, people and *naevq* looked after *Tanqpanq Aqma* in turn with the former by day and the latter by night. When people were looking after her, they promised to *Tanqpanq Aqma* that they would give her a water buffalo, a pig, a horse, and a goat when she went back to the ancestor's world if she would choose to be the people's mother. When *Naevq* were looking after her, they promised to *Tanqpanq Aqma* that they would give her a tiger, an eagle, a deer, and a bear if she became the *naevq*'s mother. *Tanqpanq Aqma* died when people were taking care of her, and she faced back. People could not turn her face to the front forcefully. But the smarter people released all tigers, eagles, deer and bears into the forests so that the *naevq* could not sacrifice these animals for the *Tanqpanq Aqma*'s funeral. Since *Tanqpanq Aqma* wanted to be buried gloriously she then turned her face to the front. Thus, *Tanqpanq Aqma* became the people's mother;

---

❶ It is Akha cultural tradition that it is his/her legitimate heirs who are responsible for funeral of a dead. In return, it is also the case that the one who carries out a funeral inherits the property of the dead person.

people fulfilled their promise and sacrificed water buffaloes for their mother's funeral ceremony❶.

However, tension between people and *naevq* grew sharply from then on. They went to the fields in turn. When *naevq* were at home, people complained that chicken eggs disappeared. At the same time, *naevq* also complained that cucumbers disappeared when people worked in the fields. They could not live together any longer and had to break up. On the night before they broke apart, *naevq* gathered together to discuss how to divide the world between people and *naevq*. They said that "when roosters start crowing❷, we will declare that *cuqya* (springs and wetlands), *lanyaq* (swamps), *loganq logur* (rocky mountains), *yawxaq ghovkhanr* (steep slopes), and *tsaeqseq miseq tsaeqxmr mixmr maq ka nya mir* (any un-arable lands) will be people's, while the rest of world will be *naevq*'s." However, people eavesdropped on *naevq*'s discussion and kept awake that night. When roosters started crowing, people declared prior to the *naevq* that "all springs, wetlands, swamps, rocky mountains, *nyirdzanr* (various fig trees), steep slopes, and any other un-arable lands will be *naevq*'s domains, while the flat, fertile and/or any arable lands will be people's." Since it was a common rule in Akha traditions that, for the common properties such as lands, who claimed first had the privileged use rights over it, *naevq* could not dispute the announcement. In other words, they had to accept this division. Accordingly, they agreed that they should not trespass each other's territories; otherwise the lawbreaking side will get punished. They further decided that day time was people's, while night time was *naevq*'s.

---

❶ Sacrificing water buffaloes is still a highest honor in a funeral for traditional Akha today.

❷ In Akha time calculation, when a rooster starts crowing first time in the early morning, it marks the start point of a day.

This is how people and *naevq* divided the world into two parts. Since people buried *Tanqpanq Aqma*, they stayed in the house and thus in villages; while *naevq* had to leave the house and village to live at the above mentioned locations in the dark forests. As a result, all domestic animals and cultivated crops also belonged to people, while those released wild animals belong to *naevq*. When the *naevq* left the house, people covered their eyes with winnowing baskets and swore that they did not want to see *naevq* anymore. Thus people can not see *naevq* today, while *naevq* can still see people because they covered their eyes with sifters when they walked out the house. Because of the small deception people did when *Tanqpanq* died, the people should always be very careful to treat *naevq* since *naevq* are always looking for chances to take revenge on people whenever they break the law.

This myth is also shared by other Hani groups. It has been pointed out that ancestral Tibeto-Burman groups developed agriculture 7,000 – 8,000 years ago, which allowed them to spread out and took over most of Eastern Asia (Liang et al., 1985; Van Driem, 1999, 2002). I suggest that the Hani-Akha's animist belief in spirits *naevq* was well developed when their ancestors were hunter-gatherers; and the myth was their way to record the long historical period of their ancestors when they gradually switched from hunter-gatherers into agriculturalists 7,000 – 8,000 years ago, as it emphasizes that "flat, fertile and arable lands are the people's (i. e. ancestors of the Hani-Akha)". This type of representation of their history conforms to their animist beliefs and worldview. Acquiring growing crops and raising animals, no matter whether it was achieved independently or learned from others or a combination of both, is a significant achievement of the ancestors of the Hani-Akha that made them different from nature and from their hunting-gathering past and/or other hunting-gathering peoples at that time. It seems to me that nature along with their hunting-gathering past, and/or other hunting-gathering peoples, are all represented as wild spirits *naevq* in the narration, because this text is used again and again in the Hani-Akha oral history to describe and/or justify their separation from other peoples such as *Laqbeeq* in *Naoqma Aqmaer* (Yunnan Provincial Office of Publication and Plan for Ethnic Minorities' Archaic Texts, 1986) and *Na* in *Yaer-lanr* (Shida and Ahai, 1992). Thus, separation from *naevq* means separation from wild nature, from their hunting-gathering past, and also maybe from other hunting-gathering peoples. However, separation does not mean "to sever" here, instead, it means "to divide" "to distribute" which implies "to share." This is the main theme of the myth and core concept of the Akha worldview.

As implied in the myth, Akha people believe that *naevq* live in the following places: 1) *cuqya* (springs and wetlands), 2) lanyaq (swamps), 3) *danrlan* (natural water ponds and/or springs on the mountains), 4) *lanma* (lakes), 5) *mirdzmr* (a place where a stream flows through under it, like an earth bridge), 6) *eerpanq* (a place where a stream disappears under the ground), 7) *loqkawv* trees (*Terminalia myriocarpa* Heurck), 8) *eernmq* trees (*Salix tetrasperma* and *S. araeostachys*), 9) *nyirdzanr* (many fig tree species that are characterized by their capability to parasitize other trees and eventually kill the host, such as *Ficus curtipes*, *F. virens*, *F. hookeriana, F. altissima Bl.,* and *F. religiosa*), 10) *xirsav nyoerdawvq* (when *Schima argentea* or *S. wallichii* trees are colonized by epiphytes or parasitized by other plants), 11) *tseevqganq nyoerdawvq* (*Betula alnoides var. pyrifolia* trees colonized by epiphytes or parasitized by other plants), 12) *loganq logur* (rocky mountains), 13) *mirboe* (caves), 14) *yawxaq ghovkhanr* (steep slopes), and 15) *mir-byav* (places where a landslide occurred❶). These places are regarded as the centers of the Outside/*naevq*'s domain and forbidden for any human activities. I call these places "forbidden ecotopes". Other forbidden ecotopes are habitats of sacred animals and birds, including, but not limited to, lorises (*myovq-lanr*), wild buffaloes (*naevq-nyoq*), rhinoceri (*naevq-ya*), pangolins (*tanq-keeq*), elephants (*ya-ma*), peacocks (*xmr-doeq*), eagles (*haq-dzeir*), hornbills (*khanq-byavq*), crows (*awvq-avq*), and wild geese (*haq-tsanr*). These animals and birds are believed to belong to *naevq* and/or have powerful spiritual lords, *yaw-sanr*.

There are other sacred places where only certain prescribed human activities are allowed. These places include, but are not limited to: 1) *putsanq* (village fence forest, home of the spiritual lord of a village, *pu-sanr*); 2) *lawq-bymr* or *lmq-bymr* (village cemetery), also called *nyirpu dzanrzar* (literally meaning "outside village"); 3) *mirsanr sanqcu* (Earth Lord grove); 4) *eerxawr lawrkhawvq* ❷ (holy water well); 5) *khmqmaer gawvmaer* (watershed forests); 6) *aqnanq tsaqkhanq* (places where people particularly pregnant women take holy dirt for eating); 7) *cuq* (places where wild animals drink and bath); 8) *tsaqdzaq* (special places where wild animals eat salty dirt or clay); 9) *myovq yavq* (habitats of monkeys); and 10) *siqdzaq arbaw* (wild trees that bear fruits edible by people and/or wild animals). I call these places "restricted ecotopes." These are the buffering zones of the Outside domain where people could reach and conduct certain prescribed activities such as offering rituals. All these sacred places, including both forbidden and restricted ecotopes, are regarded as *yaw-khawr*, literally meaning "awesome," "sacred", and/or

---

❶ Akha people believe that a landslide is caused by serpents, *eer-lanq*. It is the reason why *eer-lanq* is also called *byav-yanq*, the god of landslides.

❷ It was also called *dzoeqpir lawrkhawvq*, literally meaning "holy water of the chief and priest".

"dangerous", a key concept that is mentioned in Chapter 2, and will be more elaborated in this chapter.

In the rest of the Outside domain more human activities are allowed such as hunting, fishing, collecting (timbers, firewood, vegetables, fruits, and medicines), and horticulture (growing economic plants such as bamboo, indigo, tea, and rattan), but not farming. These places are subject to human modifications through above mentioned activities. Therefore, I call these places "modified ecotopes". These are the peripheries of the Outside domain.

On the other hand, traditional Akha villages, the centers of the Inside domain, are believed free of *naevq*. I call villages "created ecotopes". A typical Akha village is always surrounded by a shelter forest called *putsanq*. *Putsanq* is believed the home of the spiritual lord of the village, *pu-sanr*. It is the physical as well as symbolic "fence" that protects people from vicious *naevq*.

Other places of the Inside domain are fenced gardens (*yarkmr*) and agricultural fields (*yar*). Fenced gardens (*yarkmr*) are usually built at flat or slightly sloped areas along streams or near water sources surrounding village. Sometimes they can be built at the back yards of family houses where irrigation is allowed. Agricultural fields include permanent irrigated paddy fields and temporary swidden fields. As both the fenced gardens and irrigated paddy fields need to be maintained through constant human inputs and care, I call them "domesticated ecotopes". But, since swidden fields are subject to constant switches between farming and fallow phases, and are not "domesticated" permanently as fenced gardens and irrigated paddy fields, I call swidden fields as "transformed ecotopes".

Wild animals are outside of all the categories described above. I call them "mobile ecotopes". As they move across over space and time, their statuses could change. For instance, some animals/birds such as eagles and hornbills are sacred at their habitats and cannot be killed, but they can be killed if they enter into villages, the Inside domain. A pangolin is a taboo when it is seen at day time, but it is acceptable to kill it at night. Many game animals also become sacred and forbidden to be killed during mating season. This will be elaborated in following sections.

Therefore, Akha people perceive the world according to their worldview and represent their environment into a sacred landscape composed of various ecotopes with various degrees of sacredness, which are determined by their distances to both centers of the Inside and the Outside domains on their mental map (see Figure 6). Humans are safe at the center of the Inside domain, i. e. within villages, because they are believed free of *naevq*. The degree of safety of human activities decreases as one moves from the center of the Inside domain toward the center of the Outside domain, which culminates in forbidding any human activities at all at the other pole. This mental distance of ecotopes to the centers of the Inside and the Outside domains, however, does not correspond to the physical distance in reality. In a reality, some of the ecotopes, particularly forbidden and domesticated ones, could be sporadically distributed wherever they are applicable all over the territory of a village or community. Therefore, more practically, a typical Akha village always divided its homeland/territory into six zones of land use: 1) *pu*, residence; 2) *putsanq*, village fence forest; 3) *ghaqtsanq*, protected forests; 4) *miqkhaevqlavqghaw aqganq*, firewood forests; 5) *nyoqjawr kmrteev aqganq*, fenced buffalo forests or pasture; and 6) *yarmr jawqxmq aqdae*, agricultural lands (see Figure 7). And outside of a village's territory is called *mirma tseirganq*, or wilderness (No. VII in Figure 7).

Those seven types of ecotopes, including wild animals, do not completely correspond to these seven zones of land uses (including the

Chapter 3 Ecology of Sacred Landscape

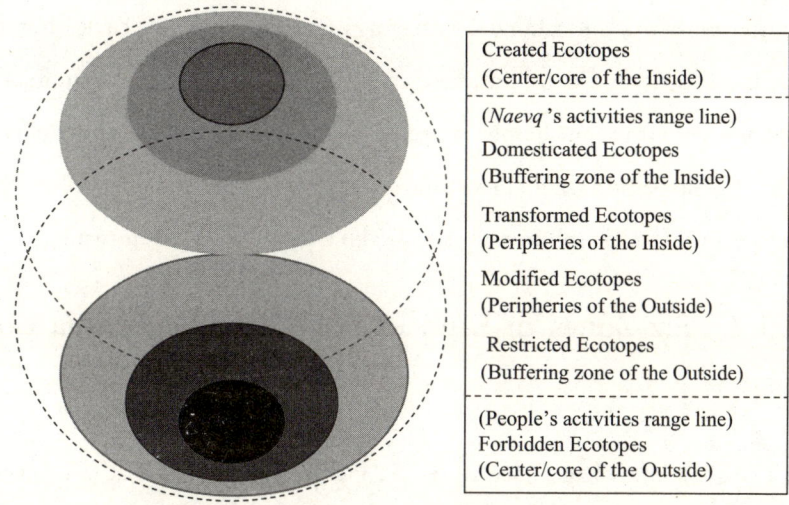

Figure 6 A Mentalmap of Akha Sacred Landscapes

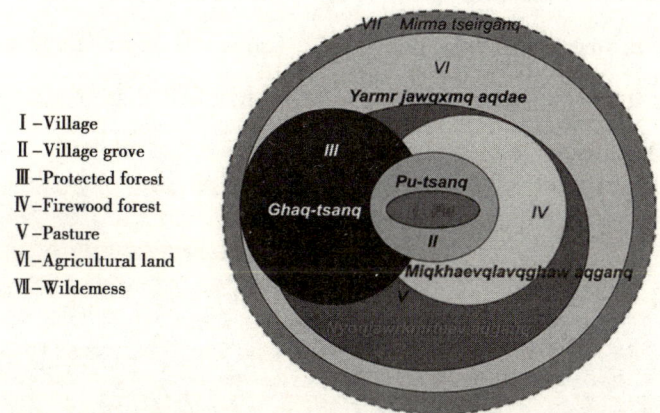

I – Village
II – Village grove
III – Protected forest
IV – Firewood forest
V – Pasture
VI – Agricultural land
VII – Wildemess

Figure 7 Six Zones of Land Use in a Traditional Akha Village

wilderness area) except the village residence, mainly because sacred (forbidden) ecotopes could appear in any of these zones outside of the village. Besides, domesticated ecotopes could be in zone No. VI or No. IV or even in No. I (in the case of homegardens); wild animals/birds (mobile ecotopes) will be found in various zones, including wilderness outside of a village's territory. Ideally the village is the center of its homeland, while other zones radiate from the center with the agricultural lands lying outermost of the circles; but in a reality, these zones need to be arranged practically according to landform of the terrain, and thus are hardly expected to be symmetric. In the following section, I will demonstrate how these zones are allocated as well as how those ecotopes are distributed in a real Akha community, Mengsong.

3.4 Six Zones of Land Uses in Mengsong Akha Community

The six Akha villages (see zone I in Picture 4) are located at hill feet with an altitude roughly about 1,600 meters above sea level, surrounding Mengsong Basin. Each village is partially or completely surrounded by its own village fence forest, *putsanq* (zone II). These village fence forests are adjacent to either protected forests *ghaqtsanq* (zone III) or firewood forests *miqkhaevq lavqghaw aqganq* (zone IV). Each village has its own firewood forest and protected forest, which cannot be seen completely in Picture 4;

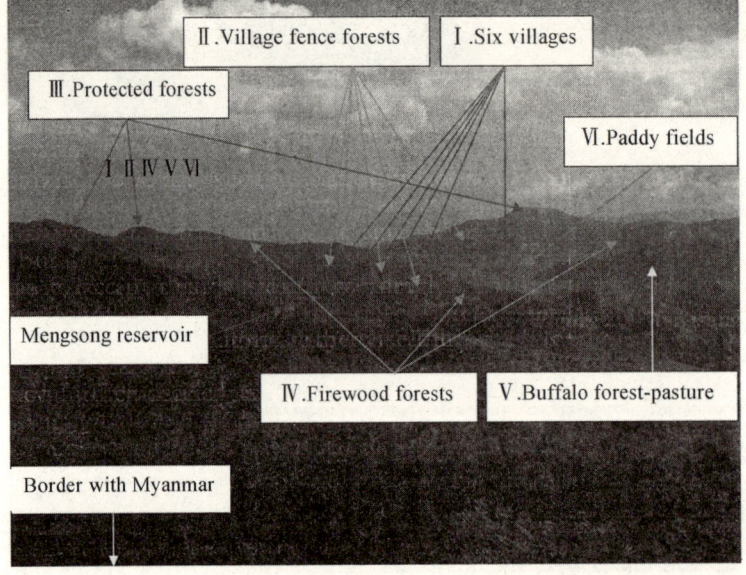

Picture 4 Six Zones of Land Uses in Mengsong Akha Community (Partial)

while there are also some communally protected forests, such as *Sanqpaqbarwar* (community rattan forest) and *Gaovmaer-sanqkhav* (watershed forests). Next to the firewood forests are either pastures called *nyoqjawr kmrteev aqganq* (literally meaning "fenced buffalo forest") or agricultural lands, *yarmr jawqxmq aqdae* (swidden fields or irrigated rice terraces). One of the pastures can be seen in Figure 8 (zone V). Mengsong Basin has been developed as irrigated paddy fields divided by these six villages (zone VI). A simplified transect map of Mengsong land use zones is illustrated in the Figure 8 below. In the following sections, I will demonstrate how various ecotopes are distributed in different zones and how Mengsong Akha manage them.

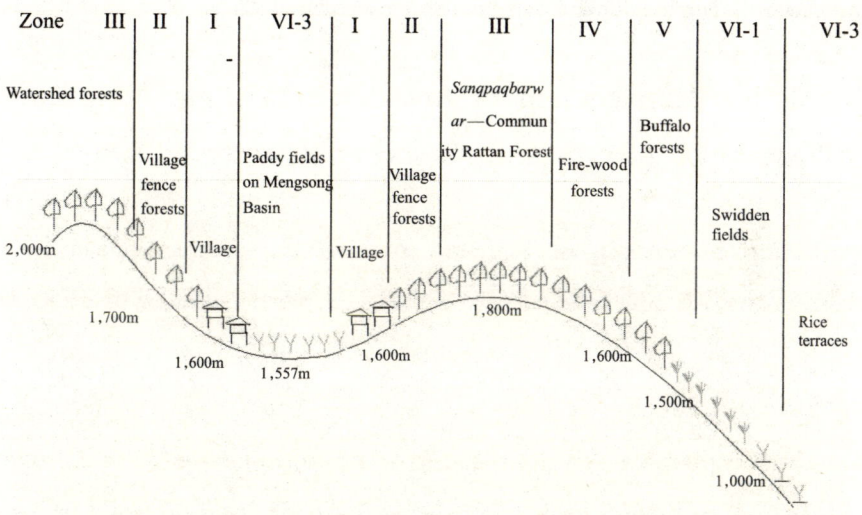

Figure 8 Mengsong Land Use Transect Map (Simplified for Better Illustration)

3.5 Management of Forbidden Ecotopes

As we mentioned earlier, forbidden ecotopes are believed centers of *naevq*'s domain. Therefore, it is a taboo to enter into and/or conduct any human activities in forbidden ecotopes. "Leave them alone" is the strategy that Akha people to "manage" the forbidden ecotopes. The concept is equivalent to "the core of natural reserves" in modern conservation practices. Since they could be distributed irregularly all over the terrains outside of a village residency, a typical Akha village does not assign any particular zone for them. But wherever a forbidden ecotope occurs in any those identified zones, the avoidance attitude and policy will be restrictively observed by individuals and communities. The existence of forbidden ecotopes, therefore, would affect the way different zones are managed, particularly in the agricultural zone. It means that a large scale "slash-and-burn" type of agriculture is almost impossible in a traditional Akha community, which will be more discussed in the section of management of transformed ecotopes later.

3. 6 Management of Restricted Ecotopes —*putsanq* (village fence forest) and *ghaqtsanq* (protected forests)

Restricted ecotopes are buffering zones of the Outside domain where people can reach and conduct very limited and prescribed activities, such as offering rituals and in some cases hunting and gathering. They are quite similar to the concept of "buffering zone of natural reserves" in modern conservation practices. Among the ten types of identified restricted ecotopes, *putsanq* (village fence forest) is assigned as a separate land use zone (II), due to its cultural significance of being not only the home of the spiritual lord of a village, but also the physical and symbolic boundary between the Inside of the village and the Outside domain. Both the ecotope and the land use zone take the same *putsanq* because they are identical in terms of area. The next three types of restricted ecotopes *lawq-bymr* or *lmq-bymr* (cemetery), *mirsanr sanqcu* (Earth Lord grove), and *eerxawr lawrkhawvq* (holy water well) could be located within either village fence forest *putsanq* (zone II) or protected forests *ghaqtsanq* (zone III); while *khmqmaer gawvmaer* (watershed forest) is always located within protected forests. *Aqnanq tsaqkhanq* (holy dirt hole) are usually located at the upper side of the paths to agricultural fields and/or to the holy water well. The rest four types, i. e. *cuq* (places where wild animals drink and bathe), *tsaqdzaq* (special places where wild animals eat salty dirt or clay), *myovq yavq* (habitats of monkeys), and *siqdzaq arbawr* (wild trees that bear fruits edible by people and/or wild animals) are also usually located within the protected forests, though some of them (particularly those of the last type) could be distributed anywhere.

In Mengsong, each natural village has its own village fence forest, cemetery, the Earth Lord grove, holy water well, and protected forests. In the meanwhile, the Mengsong Akha community as a whole (even beyond those six natural villages surrounding the basin) also has its own Earth Lord grove and protected forests. The latter includes watershed forests and community rattan forest (known as *Sanqpaqbarwar*). Picture 5 below shows locations of some of these landscapes.

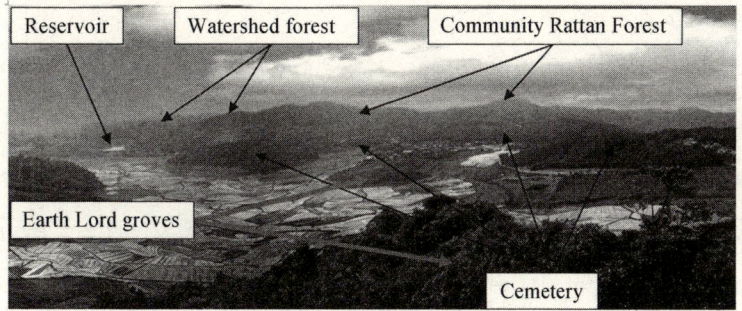

Picture 5   Restricted Ecotopes of Mengsong (Partial)

3. 6. 1 *Putsanq* (village fence forest)

The purpose of setting up and managing *putsanq* is to build and maintain a boundary between the Inside and the Outside domains. Usually four major paths (*garma*) are built across *putsanq* at four directions: *dzanrhuq* (upper slope), *dzanrdanq* (lower slope), *dovkhaeq* (east-ward), and *gakhaeq* (west-ward). These four paths connect a village with various significant cultural places outside the village; the upper path (*dzanrhuq garma*) connects to the *daekhanq* (the traditional dancing/singing square), the *lavqceq* (the village swing), and the *nyoqsaevq aqgher bawrdaw* (the holy post of sacrificing water buffalo); the east path (*dovkhaeq garma*) connects to the *eerxawr lawrkhawvq* (the holy water well); the west path connects to the *nyirpu dzanzar* or *lawqbymr* (the cemetery); and the lower path (*dzanrdanq garma*) connects to the *ghavqsaevq loma siqpyaer* (the holy stone of sacrificing pigs). The lower path also usually connects to the *garjawq* (the main road connecting to other communities, particularly those of in lowlands). Four village gates, *lanrkanq* , are built over these four paths. These gates are called *dzanrhuq lanrkanq* , *eerxawr lawrkhawvq lanrkanq* , lawqbymr lanrkanq, and *dzanrdanq lanrkanq* (also called *garjawq lanrganq*), respectively.

The main purpose of these gates is to prevent vicious *naevq* , bad people, diseases, and wild animals from entering the village, while (good) people and livestock are free to pass. A couple of sculptured wooden human figures (one man and one woman), *tanqpanq mawrkawr* , are raised outside of two major gates (usually the upper gate and lower gate), next to the up-slope side post (if both are raised together) or to each post. These figures are guardians of the gates. Besides, nine figures, including wooden birds *arjir mawrkawr* (usually believed crows) and various weapons, are fixed on the top of the gate beam. The Akha word *ghoeq* means both the number "nine" and "to be covered/closed/protected completely", thus, using the number of nine implies full protection here. Similarly, nine layers of *darlaer* , a bamboo stick weaving in a shape of hexagon or octagon or round, are tied on the posts and beam of the gate, to warn the evil spirits or *naevq* off from entering the gate (see Picture 6).

These gates are annually renewed in spring after the Akha spring festival (*Khmqxeevq aqpoeq lawr-e*). An adult man from each household is required to participate in the village gate renewal, called *lanrkanq mr-e* in Akha. The purpose of the village gate anewal ritual is to honor the village spiritual lord, *pusanr*. The traditional greater village chief *dzoeqma* initiates the renewal ceremony. Traditionally, a new village gate would be lifted outside of and next to the previous one. The wooden human figures, birds, weapons and *darlaer* need to be re-made. But nowadays, a permanent cement concrete village gate and cement human figures are usually made, so only the bamboo weaving *darlaer* are replaced annually, while the gate posts and human figures are "renewed" by being washed/purified with holy water.

Picture 6   An Akha Village Gate*Lanrkanq* at Doichang, Chiang Rai, Thailand❶

Outside of the upper village gate (*dzanrhuq lanrkanq*), a flat square called *daekhanq* is made, within the village fence forest. It is the place where

---

❶   Since a traditional village gate was no longer to be built in China since in the late 1950s, I use a photo taken from Thailand to show it here. This will be the reason for other cases using photos taken from elsewhere.

Akha youth villagers socialize with each other in the evenings. It is conventionally portrayed as Akha courting square and/or dancing square by outsiders, but it is much more than that. It is the place where Akha youths to learn traditional dances and songs, as well as traditional knowledge and wisdom recorded in these songs. It is usually the married knowledgeable middle-aged men and women who are responsible to teach these dances, songs and knowledge. It is also the place to hold parties to receive guests from other villages. Therefore, it would be more appropriate to translate *daekhanq* as "village cultural center", a center of education (like a school), entertainment, and socializing. *Daekhanq* is also renewed annually on the same day the village gates are renewed, and it is maintained by the youths on voluntary basis between the renewal intervals.

3.6.2 *Lawq-bymr* or *Lmq-bymr* (cemetery)

The village cemetery is also called "*nyirpu dzanrghar*", meaning "the village of ancestral spirits". The cemetery grove is sacred in which any human activities other than funeral ceremonies are forbidden. Each village has its own cemetery, which is divided into two parts; one is for burying *nmq-xir* (those who died in good terms), while another is for burying *xav-xir* (those who died in bad deaths) and children with still birth or died before he or she is named. The cemetery is usually located west or lower side of the village. In Mengsong, and in *Arghoeq* ❶ Akha subgroups in general, people are buried parallel in a same vertical line from upper to downhill regardless his/her lineages; while in villages of *Arjawr* Akha subgroups, each lineage has its own line. When the line reaches the bottom of the cemetery, new burials will

---

❶ *Arghoeq* and *Arjawr* are two major Akha subgroups, led by the super-lineage *Jeqghoeq* and *Jeqjawr* respectively. *Jeqjawr* is the lineage of rulers of Jadae polity.

be buried at a new parallel line at the other side of the previous line away from the village, from upper to downhill again. A corpse is buried in a whole-wood carved boat-shaped coffin. The tradition is believed to be developed in the *Gee Yaerlanr Khanq*, a flooding homeland. Burying in boat-shaped coffins is regarded an old tradition of ancient people of Bashu states and still widely practiced by various people in Southeast Sichuan, Chongqing, and Guizhou today (Baidu Baike, 2013g).

Traditionally, Akha people do not leave any permanent mark on the tombs, which eventually become unrecognizable when time goes by. When a group of Akha people split from their mother village to establish their own village, or the whole village moves to a new location, a new cemetery needs to be established accordingly. They can no longer use the old cemetery, no matter how close the new location is to the old one. An abandoned cemetery becomes a forbidden ecotope immediately, not only to the Akha people, but also to the other neighboring peoples such as Dai (Tai Lue). As Mengsong Akha villages have been relocated many times in their settlement history from northwest to southeast (which will be more elaborated in Chapter 4), numerous old cemeteries have been left and still exist as forbidden ecotopes in Mengsong today.

3.6.3 *Mirsanr sanqqu* (Earth Lord grove)

Each village chooses a big tree as the home of *mirsanr*, the Earth Lord. The trees are usually dominant species in local environment. For instance, the holy tree of the Mengsong communal Earth Lord grove used to be a *tseevqkav* tree (*Castanopsis mekongensis*); while those of individual villages such as Xianfeng, Hongqi, and Hongxing are *xirsav neir* (*Schima wallichii*), *nyirdzanr* (*Ficus religiosa*), and *xirsav ba* (*Schima argeatea*), respectively (see

Picture 7). A lifted square altar, *lawrgeer*, is built under the holy tree. The altar has a ladder with nine stairs connecting to the ground. Each village sacrifices a pig and two chickens (one rooster and one hen) annually to *mqsanr* (the Sky Lord or God), mirsanr (the Earth Lord or Goddess), and *cuqsanr* (the Water God) at the altar. Although this offering ritual is called *mirsanr lawr-e*, literally means "offering to the Earth Lord", it is meant to offer three deities listed above, as three paper figures will be made to represent them during the offering ceremonies (see Picture 8). The grove in which the altar is built is also called *mirsanr sanqcu* (the Earth Lord grove) accordingly. The altar could be built more permanently or annually. In case of the former, the Earth Lord grove is usually fenced, while it is not in case of the latter.

Picture 7　The Earth Lord Grove of Hongxing Village

3.6.4 *Eerxawr lawrkhawvq* (holy water well)

Eerxawr lawrkhawvq (literally meaning "holy water well"), is also called *dzoeqpir lawrkhawvq*, literally meaning "water used by the greater village chief and priests", because all the holy food offering ancestors need to be purified and cooked using water from the well, and all the holy rice liquor and ginger tea also need to be made from the water. It is holy because it is believed to

Chapter 3 Ecology of Sacred Landscape

Picture 8 An Altar in a Earth Lord grove, Doi Chang Village, Chiang Rai, Thailand❶

flow from the *Aqpoeq Miqyaer Lawrgawv*, the Supreme Ancestor God *Miqyaer*'s stream, which is guaranteed by *cuqsanr*, the Water God. A couple of chickens (a black and a white one, regardless of sex) need to be offered to the Water God for his governing the holiness of the water. This holy water could be a natural spring or a man-made well. It needs to be located opposite side of the village from the cemetery, or upper stream to the cemetery. Each village has its own holy water spring/well. It is cleaned annually before it is offered of the two chickens by the greater village chief *dzoeqma* and a few other respectable male elders. The *dzoeqma* will clean his holy rice seeds with the holy water and initiate the "rice sowing ceremony", opening up a new rice sowing season for the whole villagers, when the raining season starts in May.

---

❶ Again, since *mirsanr lawr-e* ceremonies have been forbidden since the late 1950s in Mengsong and other places in China, I use a photo taken from Doi Chang Village, Chiang Rai Province, Thailand, for illustration purpose only. It is unusual to choose such a small tree as holy tree for mirsanr in other places, but Doi Chang villagers have to choose it because there was no other tree available at this location and no other appropriate place available for them when they moved into this area around 30 years ago.

3.6.5 *Aqnanq tsaqkhanq* (holy dirt hole)

Akha people, particularly pregnant women, eat a particular kind of reddish earth, called *aqnanq* in Akha. It is believed that *aqnanq* is necessary to make a strong and healthy baby for pregnant women. Therefore, it is necessary to find this kind of dirt and make at least one and usually several *aqnanq tsaqkhanq* (holy dirt holes) along the convenient paths to agricultural fields and/or to the holy water well. A woman usually digs a basket of the fresh holy dirt and smokes it in a bamboo basket above the cooking fire place in her house. The dirt is smoked and ready for eating when it is dried completely and the color turns darker from smoke. It smells very good and tastes a little bit bitter from the smoke. Not only pregnant women eat *aqnanq*; Akha people in general, women and men, old and young, eat it. People can get addicted to it and some will eat it throughout their lives, while some other people may want to eat it at a certain period of time, for example, during pregnancy. I myself got addicted to *aqnanq* when I was a child and throughout my puberty; and I was diagnosed anemic. I did not know that my addiction to *aqnanq* had to do with my anemia at that time. I just remember that I was starving for *aqnanq* when I was living in the boarding secondary and high schools in Xiaojie Town and Jinghong City away from my village. So, I would take a bag of *aqnanq* with me to school when I traveled back to my home village during weekends and vacations. But there were always periods of time when I ran out of *aqnanq* before I could travel back to home. Fortunately I overcame my addiction to *aqnanq* after I entered into college and when I was cured from anemia. Now I believe that the reddish dirt *aqnanq* is rich of mineral nutrients, particularly iron, necessary for human health. Today, Akha people take much less *aqnanq* than before, due to improvement of nutrients in their diets; and pregnant women are usually given iron pills with other necessary nutrients today.

The holy dirt holes are usually located on a steep slope where animals particularly pigs and dogs cannot reach. They are also located upside of paths so that people never walk through above them. It is also a taboo to relieve nature near by a holy dirt hole.

3.6.6 *Ghaqtsanq* (protected forests)

Each Akha village also sets up a big area of protected forests *ghaqtsanq* (zone III) for headwaters and timbers. In some places, protected forests could set up for other particular resources such as rattan. This is the case of *Sanqpaqbarwar* in Mengsong. These protected forests could take up to half of a village/ community's territory, as in the case of Mengsong. Usually, most of the other types of restricted ecotopes, such as *khmqmaer gawvmaer* (watershed forests), *cuq* (places where wild animals drink and bathe), *tsaqdzaq* (special places where wild animals eat dirt or clay or salt), *myovq yavq* (habitats of monkeys), and *siqdzaq arbawr* (wild fruit trees) are located within this zone. These restricted ecotopes are sacred; tree cutting is not allowed at these locations. But hunting is allowed during certain seasons (this will be elaborated in the management of mobile ecotapes later).

In Mengsong, the watershed forests are protected collectively by the six villages and beyond. There are three major brooks (*lawrgawv*) that feed Mengsong Akha community and their paddy fields on the basin: *Naqmee*, *Navciq*, and *Saqler*. Accordingly, the watershed forests of these three brooks are called *Naqmee sanqkhav*, *Navciq gawvmaer sanqkhav*, and *Saqler gawvmaer sanqkhav*. These three forests formed the main body of Mengsong communal protected forest zone (III). Except hunting and fishing, collecting

NTFPs (Non-Timber Forest Products including medicinal plants, fruits and vegetable), and collecting coffin woods, no other trees can be cut in these areas, nor other human activities are allowed. As *Naqmee sanqkhav* grows many rattans, it was declared a community rattan forest, also known as *Sanqpaqbarwar* in Akha. Although rattan is a common natural resource found in Akha area, establishing a named community rattan forest is rare in other places. Management of it is treated in a separate subsection below.

3.6.7 Sanqpaqbarwar (Community Rattan Forest)

The term *Sanqpaqbarwar* is a combination of Akha and Dai (Tai Lue) words—*Sanqpaq* means *"ruler"* in Akha *(referring to lowland Tai Lue rulers)*, *bar* from *pa* means *"forest"* and *war* is from *wai* meaning *"rattan"* in Dai. Therefore, *Sanqpaqbarwar* literally means *"royal rattan forest"*. But, it should be understood as a "community" rattan forest for the royal family, because there is no evidence to show that the Dai State was ever involved in managing the forest in any form, except for receiving rattan as tribute from the chiefs of Mengsong. Instead, it is evident that it is the Mengsong Akha community that established the community rattan forest in order to protect rattan, a highly valued and yet scarce natural resource in the region. Though it grew abundantly in *Naqmee sanqkhav*, it could be depleted very easily without an appropriate protection measure, because the growth cycle is very long for rattan. It takes at least 15 years before rattan canes could be harvested in Mengsong, and many of them only grow one vine out of one seed and cannot regenerate or sprout after being harvested. Thus the Mengsong Akha community established protected rattan forest in order to meet both demands of self-consumption and requirements of the lowland Tai State. It was indeed a required tribute item by the lowland Dai rulers (Wang, 1998). Mengsong

Elders' Council decided to enhance their management over rattan through adopting the name *Sanqpaqbarwar*, emphasizing that they needed to protect rattan in partially to avoid troubles from the lowland Dai State by paying them required tribute. Therefore, the adoption of the term *Sanqpaqbarwar* provides a hint on the political and economic relationship between upland Akha societies and the lowland Dai State, Sipsongpanna, in the past. However, I decided to translate it into a more general term "community rattan forest" because another term "royal rattan forest" is prone to being misread semantically without knowing historical contexts.

Before *Sanqpaqbarwar* was established, the forest had been called *Naqmee sanqkhav*, which is still used more commonly than *Sanqpaqbarwar* is. The term *Sanqpaqbarwar* is actually only known by knowledgeable elders today. The name *Naqmee sanqkhav* literally means "watershed forest of *Naqmee* brook". *Naqmee* brook is source of drinking water for five out the six Mengsong Akha villages, and it is also one of two major brooks❶ that irrigate the paddy fields on Mengsong Basin. Therefore, *Naqmee sanqkhav* had been protected as watershed forest even before *Sanqpaqbarwar* was established. At the same time, it happens that there are abundant sources of rattan in the forest. There are four species and five varieties of rattan well preserved in *Sanqpaqbarwar* by Mengsong Akha community. These species and varieties are, respectively, *Calamus nambriensis*, *C. nambriensis var. alpinus*, *C. nambriensis var. Damenglongensis*, *C. nambriensis sishuangbannaensis* (all varieties of *Calamus nambriensis* species are called *darhmr* in Akha), *C. obovoideus* (*xawqlawr* in Akha), *Plectocomia himalayana* (*haqciv* in Akha), *C. yunanensis* (*laev-laevnyoer* in Akha), *C. yunanensis var. densiflora* (*laev-*

---

❶ Another major brook is *Navciq*, while the third brook *Saqler* is minor and irrigates much smaller portion of the paddy fields on Mengsong Basin.

laevxeer in Akha), *C. yunanensis var. intermedius* (*laev-bawlaev* in Akha) (Wang et al., 1999). As a necessary material for not only making many productive and living tools, for instance, it is used as track-ropes for water buffalo-driven plowing tools, and it is also used to make round tables, stools, chairs, and other items. It also has been the most important materials to make ropes of the Akha swing, *lavqceq*, without which one of the three most important Akha festivals, the Swing Festival (*Yaerkuq dzaq-e*) cannot be performed. Thus, rattan has been one of most valuable natural resources to Mengsong Akha community.

In the past, the chief of Mengsong paid tribute to the rulers of lowland Dai State, in order to avoid political and military conflicts. Rattan was required as one of the major tribute items from Mengsong by the Dai Sanqpaq (i. e. rulers). Rattan grows slowly and cannot be harvested until after at least 15 years of growing. Besides those uses mentioned above, its young stem and leaves are a very delicious vegetable; and its fruit is rich in nutrition too. But the ability of rattan to sprout is very low. For instance, laev cannot sprout at all if its top is cut; *darhmr* can only sprout from roots, so a stem will stop growing if the top of the stem is cut; only *haqciv* can sprout from stems, but this species has the poorest quality as weaving material. In short, the resource of rattan is very easily depleted without good management. Because of its economic and political importance, about 150 years ago, the Mengsong community established *Sanqpaqbarwar* to protect rattan. Six regulation rules were set up to manage *Sanqpaqbarwar*. These regulations were known to all the population of the six villages (Wang, 1998), and they are listed below:

1) Nobody can cut any trees in the forest, but wild fruits and medicines can be collected.

2) From the three parts of a rattan plant nobody can collect the tender

rattan leaves for vegetable. The stem is also forbidden to be used individually. Only the fruit can be collected for private cultivation and food.

3) However, before the plowing, rattan is collectively harvested and distributed among families; usually, each household gets one stem of rattan approximately 15 *lmr* ❶ long, which is used in making tools for plowing.

4) Every year in late July or early August, Akha people celebrate the Swing Festival, *Yaerkuq dzaq-e* . Each village can harvest several stems (2 to 4) for making the rope of the swing. It is an opportunity to show the beauty and the best knowledge of the Akha people. This festival takes place right after the tedious farming work of transplanting rice seedlings. There is a folktale to explain the origin of the festival. It tells that all the spirits of animals and insects killed during rice cultivation accused the Akha of these crimes to the supreme God *Aqpoeq Miqyaer* . The God promised to punish the Akha by hanging them one by one. However, because of his preference of Akha people over the animals, the God cheated the spirits by asking Akha people to swing one by one instead of hanging one by one. Swinging looked like hanging from a distance, so all the spirits of the killed animals were happy with the "punishment". This story reveals an Akha philosophy that cultivation requires "destruction" but within the extent that harmony with nature and the supernatural beings can be restored.

5) When a family prepare to build a house, they can harvest about 50 *ji* ❷ of rattan as binding stuff during building.

6) If a villager breaks one of these rules, the family are punished by being required to sacrifice a big pig and offer a bottle of rice wine to the

---

❶ *Lmr* is an arm-span or a length between tips of two hands when two arms spread to form a line. It is usually used as a unit of length in Akha societies. One *lmr* is about 1. 6 – 1. 7 meters.

❷ *Ji* is Chinese unit of weight. One *ji* equals to half kilogram. Therefore, 50 *ji* = 25 kilograms.

community (usually consumed by the Elders' Council).

The regulations were discussed among all villagers, and approved by the Community Elders' Council (which was a loose political organization composed of the general chief, greater village chiefs and elders from each patrilineage). Every villager is responsible for keeping his or her eyes on rattan and *Sanqpaqbarwar*. The punishment for the law-breaker is a serious matter in the community. The economic loss may not be important, but loss of face is serious in Akha society. I have witnessed that some Akha have committed suicide because of losing face. So, the rules are not only environmental laws, but also, and maybe more to the point, social morals. The power of the laws involves cultural value, social morals, and social institutions which ensure effective implementation. Because of its importance and scarcity, Mengsong Akha started domesticating and planting rattan about 150 years ago. Most of the families have their own rattan bushes now, either in natural forests or homegardens or both. Similar process of domesticating and planting rattan has been documented in East and South Kalimantan in swidden fallows roughly in the last 150 years (Dove, 2011: 86).

3.7 Management of Modified Ecotopes — *miqkhaevq lavqghaw aqganq* (firewood forest) and *nyoqjawr kmrteev aqganq* (fenced buffalo forest)

The next two zones of Akha traditional land uses are *miqhaevq lavqghaw aqganq* (literally meaning "firewood forests", zone IV) and *nyoqjawr kmrteev aqganq* (literally meaning "fenced buffalo forest", zone V) respectively. These areas are regarded as peripheries of the Outside domain, where humans can conduct more activities such as collecting firewood and timber, clearing the understoreys and planting economic plants (such as tea trees, rattan bushes, bamboos and indigo), or fencing and grazing livestock (such as water buffaloes, cattle, and goats), but no total clearing and farming are allowed. These human activities have modified local environments, so I call them modified ecotopes.

3.7.1 *Miqkhaevq lavqghaw aqganq* (firewood forest)

As indicated in the name, *miqkhaevq lavqghaw aqganq* is the main place where Akha people collect their firewood (*miqdzaq miqkawq*). In general, Akha people collect three types of firewood: *miqdovq* (flammable firewood), *miqkawq* (stick firewood), and *miqger* (big pieces of firewood). *Miqdovq* is easily ignited but does not last long. Akha people prefer *miqger* to hard wood so that it will produce clean and long-burning charcoal. Such wood is hard to ignite, and *miqdovq* is usually not able to ignite the hardwood *miqger*. A medium type of firewood is necessary. The stick firewood *miqkawq* falls into this category. So, Akha always use these three types of firewood together. *Miqdovq* is used to ignite *miqkawq*, which in turn will ignite hardwood *miqger*.

In Mengsong, each village traditionally had its own firewood forest. Mengsong villagers prefer bamboo, particularly species from genus *Dendrocalamus*, as flammable firewood *miqdovq*. Bamboo from this genus is actually the commonest source for *miqdovq* in Akha communities in Mengkong River region. Mengsong villagers get their *miqkawq* from dead branches of any flammable trees, though *tseevqnyaevq* trees (*Machilus rufipes*) are preferred; while hardwood from *Fagaceae* family is preferred source for *miqger*. I have also noticed that trees of *Fagaceae* family are actually most preferred source for hardwood firewood in Akha communities in Mekong River region. But since some species of *Fagaceae* trees (particularly from genus *Castanopsis*) are not only preferred hardwood timbers for house construction but also produce edible acorns which are consumed in Akha society, they only cut trees of other species and small twisted/sick individual trees of *Castanopsis spp.* for firewood, and leave fruit-bearing and/or straight individuals for acorns and timbers.

Even though it is conventionally called a firewood forest, *miqkhaevq lavqghaw aqganq* is also the main place where Akha people get their timbers for house construction. Twenty species of trees are identified as preferred sources of timbers in Mengsong, and most of them are preferred in Akha society in general (see Appendix I). Please note that *boeqsoev* tree (*Eurya groffii*) is a must material, necessary for building an Akha house, not because of the quality of its wood, but because it bears the name of one of Akha greatest ancestor leaders *Tanr-boeqsoev* who led the Akha ancestors fighting against one dynasty of Chinese empire's rule (most likely the Han Dynasty as explained in Chapter 2). It is said Akha tribes survived from the protection of *Tanr-boeqsoev* . Therefore, *boeqsoev* has been used as a symbol of Akha ancestors, and two wood sticks of *boeqsoev* tree need to be put on the roof above the ancestor altar in every traditional Akha house. Three small branches of *boeqsoev* tree with nine leaves on each are put in the ancestor shrine to represent one's ancestors.

Besides collecting firewood and timbers, Mengsong villagers also constantly take care of some special plants with high economic value in the zone of *miqkhaevq lavqghaw aqganq* . These plants include, but are not limited to, wild tea tree *lawrbawq* (*Camellia sinensis var. assamica*), various bamboo bushes *haq* ❶ bawq (usually *Denbrocalamus spp.*), rattan bushes, and indigo plants *myanq* (*Baphicacanthus cusia*), and claim them as their individual family's gardens. Of course, they often build private "gardens" by planting more of these plants at the sites where they already grow wild, or at any suitable places even where there are no such plants growing naturally. It is such a common practice that almost all families in Mengsong have developed their own "gardens" in the forests in this way. Each family had at least one "tea garden" before, though not every family had bamboo or rattan or indigo gardens. Tea is more emphasized here because it is more essential to Akha in their way of life. It is not only the daily drinks of Akha people, but also one of six sacred items❷ that need to be offered to one's ancestors 12 times per year. It is actually regarded as a holy crop. The original/ancient name of tea is *laqpaer*, which is used in ancient texts; but it is no longer used in daily communications because it is not respectable to call it in its real name. Instead, it is called by its holy name *lawrbawq* , literally meaning "offering plant" or "offering drink". As a side note, the other Hani groups still call tea *laqpaer*. I suspect the holy name *lawrbawq* was adopted by the elite Akha ancestors during the historical period of Jadae polity, and it represents a higher version/dialect of Hani-Akha language spoken by the Akha ruling class; the other Hani groups did not pick it up and still use the original term, as they were living in the peripheries of the state.

While the forests were still owned by the village/community collectively,

---

❶ The name of bamboo is pronounced variously by different Hani-Akha subgroups. These variations include *haq, ghaq, aq, yavq, and zavq* . But all of these variations seem to derive from haq because bamboo worm is called unitarily as haq-boeq by all Hani-Akha subgroups. The suffix *boeq* means "insect" "worm".

❷ The other five items are chicken, cooked rice, sticky rice cake, rice liquor, and ginger. Since three of them are made of rice, tea is actually one of four ingredients (chicken, rice, ginger, and tea) to make holy food to offer one's ancestors.

the plants (tea, bamboo, rattan, indigo, among others) became private properties. This dual tenure system works well in traditional Akha society, but become sources of conflicts later in the 1990s and onward (see Chapter 4). Since only understorey bushes are cleared and no canopy trees are cut when these plants are planted, Mengsong Akha community has transformed huge areas of *miqkhaevq lavqghaw aqganq* into agroforests. This kind of horticulture, particularly tea agro-forestry, is a common cultural practice among indigenous peoples, particularly the Akha, the Bulang, and the Jinuo, in Xishuangbanna. Dozens of such tea gardens under forests, up to eight hundred years old, can be found in Akha villages in Mengsong, Nannuo, Bulang, and Daheishan Mountains in Xishuangbanna. These Akha tea gardens along with those of the Bulang and the Jinuo ethnic groups are among the oldest agroforests in the world that are maintained very well and still under good use today. These groups have been the major producers of famous Puer tea in this region, historically and contemporaneously (Long et al. 1997). An interesting parallel case is that yerba mate trees (*Ilex paraguariensis*) had been also planted under forests by indigenous Guaraní people in Paragua prior to the European colonization (Reed, 1997).

3.7.2 *Nyoqjawr kmrteev aqganq* (fenced buffalo forest)

Water buffaloes have been the most valuable livestock in Akha societies. Not only are water buffaloes employed as the sole plowing animals in irrigated paddy fields, but more importantly the most honorable funeral ceremony for an elder who died a good death, i.e., *nmqxir*, is to sacrifice three water buffaloes for him/her. Each village also sacrifices a water buffalo collectively for their ancestors at a festival called *Ghola aqpoeq lawr-e* in summer every year. So, no matter whether there are irrigated paddy fields that need water buffaloes, Akha people love to raise water buffaloes whenever their economic and environmental conditions allow. Traditionally, each village will set aside a hill with pastures and bushes to keep their water buffaloes together. The hill is fenced in order to keep the animals from entering agricultural fields and eating crops. This fenced hill is termed as *nyoqjawr kmrteev aqganq* (zone V) in Akha.

Besides water buffaloes, Akha people also love to raise other livestock such as cattle and goats. Cattle are raised for meat only. Akha people do not produce milk from the cattle, nor do they use them for plowing land. Akha people plow their irrigated paddy fields by using water buffaloes, but they usually do not plow upland fields. Cattle cannot be used to plow irrigated paddy fields as they avoid water. Cattle are also kept in *nyoqjawr kmrteev aqganq* along with water buffaloes; but the practice of keeping cattle in the fenced grazing pasture does not change the name, because water buffaloes are essential while cattle are dispensable in Akha culture. In addition, goats are raised because two goats need to be sacrificed for an honorable funeral with three water buffaloes. But since goats cannot be fenced in the way water like buffaloes and cattle, as the goats can climb over almost anything, goats need constant attention. They are grazed by individual families separately.

Though the water buffaloes and cattle are owned privately by individual families, the buffalo forest is owned and fenced by the village collectively. A *nyoqjawr kmrteev aqganq* is usually set up on the fallow lands of previous swidden fields, particularly when they start growing grasses instead of trees. When buffaloes and cattle are grazed on these grassed fallow lands, they will not only eat up the grasses but also fertilize the lands with their manure; therefore, it will accelerate the succession of vegetation from grass pasture to forests with trees and bushes. When there are no more grasses, a new *nyoqjawr kmrteev aqganq* will be established on newer fallow lands with grasses again. In the meanwhile, the abandoned *nyoqjawr kmrteev aqganq* will be available for swidden agriculture again. In other words, *nyoqjawr kmrteev aqganq* is actually an organic part of Akha swidden agricultural cycle, in which the livestock are used to accelerate the regeneration/successions of the forests.

3.8 Management of transformed ecotopes —*yarmr jawqxmq aqdae* (swidden fields)

The agricultural zone (VI), *yarmr jawqxmq aqdae*, particularly swidden fields, is usually located at the outermost areas from the residence in a village's territory. In other words, a traditional territory of an Akha village is usually demarcated by their agricultural lands, although not all agricultural lands are located at the furthest locations. The reason for this is very practical. It is not only an effective strategy to protect their villages from the fire used in clearing the swidden fields, but also an effective strategy to expand and protect their territory because the *de facto* use of the land was the most effective way of establishing a legitimacy of the ownership in the traditional land tenure system in this region in the past.

Even though this area is classified as agricultural, this does not mean that every single place can be cleared for farming in this area, because all those sacred ecotopes could be located in this zone, as often as they would occur in other zones. Since they are regarded as home of *naevq*, these forbidden ecotopes are always kept as primitive as possible in the agricultural zone, and farming activities are only allowed on the lands outside these forbidden locations. Picture 9 below shows a grove of sacred tree *loqkawv* (*Terminalia myriocarpa*) along a stream at valley and watershed forests are reserved in agricultural zone.

Chapter 3 Ecology of Sacred Landscape

Picture 9 Forest Reserved in Agricultural Zone

All the lands out of these forbidden ecotopes in *yarmr jawqxmq aqdae* zone are allowed for farming. Traditionally, these lands do not belong to individuals, but are owned by the village collectively. More accurately, these lands are believed to be owned by the spiritual lords, *yar-sanr*, by the animist Akha. In this sense, everything is sacred in Akha world. Therefore, even in a place out of these forbidden locations where swidden agricultural activities are allowed, Akha people cannot do anything without paying respect to the spiritual lord of the land. Anyone willing to farm the lands should ask permission from the *yar-sanr* first. Akha people then "sign a lease" and pay "rent" symbolically by sacrificing animals such as chickens to the spiritual lord, called *yarpoeq gaw-e* or *yarlawr lawr-e* in Akha. By doing so, the land temporarily becomes of the Inside domain, and thus safe for agricultural activities. After having harvested, they perform another ceremony (which is called *banqyoe pyaev-e* in Akha) to return the land back to the *yar-sanr*; thus it becomes a part of the Outside world again. The "lease" is valid only for one year. If a field needs to be used for more than one year, the "lease" needs to be renewed annually, and the ceremonies need to be repeated annually.

Since an appropriate "lease" from the spiritual lord has been made, a swidden field temporarily becomes the Inside domain, physically and symbolically, which is regarded as a "temporary village", called *yarkhanq* in Akha, literally meaning "field village". Every family builds a *yarcmr* (field house/shed) in each swidden field. Part of the family stays in this shed seasonally particularly when intensive labor is needed in the field, such as during weeding and harvesting time. In some cases, some family members go to live in the fields during the whole season of crop growing, or even year-round if there are enough people in the family who can take care of other activities both in their village and other fields. Although *yarkhanq* are temporary "field villages", some of them could become bases for permanent residence, especially when the population in the mother village becomes too large and/or their swidden fields become too far from the village. This is one of the commonest patterns for developing a new Akha hamlet or village. It illustrates the way the Akha people migrated through the highlands of Mainland Southeast Asia until a few decades ago.

Rice was the main crop cultivated in swidden fields of Mengsong. Traditionally Mengsong Akha identified eight steps of cultivating rice in swidden fields: 1) *yarghar xar* (selecting a land plot), 2) *yarmyaq myaq* (cutting trees), 3) *yar keq-e* (burning), 4) *yarcmr tsov-e* (building a field shed/house), 5) *yarjiv jiv-e* (clearing the field), 6) *yarka ka-e* (sowing), 7) *yarmovq movq-e* (weeding), and 8) *caeryaeq caeryur* (harvesting).

3. 8. 1 *Yarghar xar* (selecting a land plot)

Selecting a land plot was performed solely by male adults in a family, in the first Akha lunar month *Ghaeqla* (also called *khovqxeevq*), which is roughly in late December and early January. Having avoided all those forbidden ecotopes, Mengsong Akha use three criteria to select a good land plot. The first criterion is soil quality, determined by fertility and drainage capability. Soil can be classified into three kinds in terms of color: *mirnav* (black soil), *mirneir* (red soil), and *mirxeer* (yellowish soil). The fertility of three kinds of soil decreases in the order from black to yellow. Soil is also identified as two kinds in terms of texture: *mirmar* (clay soil) and *mirpoq* (loose soil). The fertility of the former is better than the latter. Soil is yet classified into another three kinds in terms of humidity: *mirdmq* (wet soil), *mirsawq* (intermediate dry soil), and *mirgee* (very dry soil). The black, clay, wet soil is regarded as fertile soil (*mirtsur*) or good soil (*mirmeeq*) and yellowish, loose, and dry soil is regarded as infertile soil (*mirkov*) or bad soil (*mirdoer*). Combinations of other features are in between.

The second criterion is location of the land plot. A land plot could be located at *gawqdur* (mountain ridge), *baqgha* (hillside), or *daekhawvq* (cove). A land plot could also be located as *nanrghovq* (shady slope), *nanrse* (semi-shady slope), or *nanrdaeq* (sunny slope). A land plot yet can be located at different altitudes: *khawrdmr* (cold land, usually higher than 1,500 meters above sea level), *jawqkaq* (warm land, usually between 1,200 – 1,500 meters above sea level), or *jawqba* (hot land, usually below 1,200 meters above sea level). Semi-shady cove at *jawqkaq* (warm land) is preferred land plot for Mengsong Akha.

The third criterion is vegetation covering on the land. Bamboo or *lmqpyar* (*Macaranga spp.*) forests are preferred land plots. Both plants are good indicators for fertile soil. If a *savlav* tree (*Dalbergia spp.*) grows, the taller the tree is, the more fertile the land is. A place where *uvqjir* grass (*Imperata cylindrica*), or *yarkajeiqdawvq* grass (*Artemisia austro-yunnanensis*), *Caevqpartsawq* (*Eupatorium coelesticum*) grow is the least preferred place for swidden field. These plants are indicators of degraded soil.

Based on these three criteria, three categories of swidden lands were identified by Hongqi villagers in their agricultural zone: *mirma* (solid land), *mirpawvq* (porous land), and *mirpeq* (worn-out land). The first category *mirma* has black, thick, wet, clay soil, and is usually located at slight slopes or coves. It can be cultivated continuously for usually 6 – 7 years. When it is fallowed, the first plants come to occupy are *yaqyirkawv* (*Eupatorium odoratum*), which will be replaced by *lmqpyar* (*Macaranga indica*) in a few years. By the time of 7 years of fallow, it will be *lmqpyar* forest with *iqtseevq* grass (*Digitaria violascens*) growing understorey. And it is ready for next cycle of farming. Examples of *mirma* kind of swiden lands are those located at *Lawrbymr daekhanq* , *Davsaer* , *Borhor* , and *Caerpanq* areas. Almost any kinds of rice varieties can be planted here; but the soil needs to be turned over with hoes before rice is sowed, which requires a lot of labor. The second category *mirpawvq* has loose and dry soil, and is usually located at mountain ridge or deep slopes. But it is usually covered by good vegetation of tree species. Therefore, rice and other crops can be sowed without soil being turned over in a field on *mirpawvq* lands. Despite of the poor soil, the crops usually grow very well in the first year because the soil is fertilized by the ashes of burned thick vegetation. Weeds are minimized in such a field, because weed seeds are usually killed by thorough burning, guaranteed by the good vegetation. Therefore, such land requires the least labor input. This kind of swidden field is called *yarnav* , literally meaning "black field" , referring to the color of the field covered by dark thick ashes from the burning. However, the fertility of such a field is depleted very quickly. It is either fallowed immediately after the first year cropping, or planted with more infertile-soil-tolerant crops such as maize or beans for a second year, being fallowed thereafter. *Yaqyirkawv* (*Eupatorium odoratum*) bushes will cover the terrain immediately after the field is fallowed, which will be replaced by fast-growing small trees *lawrtawq*

(*Trema orientalis*) by the fourth year of fallow. The sprouts from the old tree stocks will surpass and take over *lawrtawq* populations later; and the previous vegetation will be restored by the 13th year of the fallow, when the field is ready again for the next farming cycle. Examples of *mirpawvq* lands are those located at *Argo*, *Tseevqganq aqnaq*, *Borhor gawqdur*, and *Lawrbymr daekhanq-e gawqdur* in Mengsong.

The soil quality of the third type of land *mirpeq* is in the between of *mirma* and *mirpawvq*. It is usually covered by *uvqjir* grass (*Imperata cylindrica*) and *yarkajeiqdawvq* grass (*Artemisia austro-yunnanensis*), along with other small bushes. This type of vegetation is an indicator of soil degradation, as implied in its name *mirpeq*, literally meaning "worn-out land". It becomes a good place for setting up a pasture. In case of land shortage, this area could be cropped for 2-3 years before it is fallowed. The soil needs to be turned before rice is sowed each year. Infertile-soil-tolerant varieties are also required on this type of land. Usually the *uvqjir* grass (*Imperata cylindrica*) will cover the terrain again immediately after it is fallowed.

A family chooses a land plot based on their preference and availability of the land within the traditional agricultural zone *yarmr jawqxmq aqdae* of the village. After a land plot is selected, it is marked by four marks called *byavq* ❶ (see Picture 10) at the four sides of the land plot boundary respectively, so that other

Picture 10 An Akha Mark *byavq*

---

❶ The *byavq* mark is used to claim exclusive use privilege over common natural resources in Akha society. For instance, if a person sees a wild bee hive, he/she would claim his/her exclusive use over it by putting a *byavq* mark nearby. So, "first claim first use" is the general rule to regulate general common natural resources in Akha society.

Sacred and Contested Landscapes

people would know this plot has been chosen by somebody. As the person marks the land plot, he must ask permission from the spiritual Land Lord, *yarsanr*, orally saying that "please come to tell us if you do not allow my family to farm your land; if you do allow us, we will pay you the "rent" appropriately later." If any family member has a bad dream during the following three nights, it is believed a warning sign from *yarsanr*; therefore the land cannot be farmed and new land will be selected. If nobody in the family has a bad dream during the following three nights, then the land selection is finalized. The size of a land plot enough for a family is about 3 *mu* per person, which is about one-fifth hectare.

3.8.2 *Yarmyaq myaq-e* (cutting trees)

Trees are cut in the third Akha lunar month *Boeqzoq* (or *Boeqyuvq*), roughly in late February and early March. Cutting starts from the bottom (lower parts) of the field. The cutting needs to be stopped and the field needs to be given up under one of the following three circumstances, 1) if a loris (sloth monkey) is encountered; 2) if a cut tree slides all the way down to the bottom of the slope, which is called *sanqpyawr* in Akha; or 3) if a cut tree falls upside down with the bottom up, pointing to the sky, which is called *sanqghur* in Akha. The first circumstance is discussed before; the loris is regarded as an animal of *naevq* and its habitat cannot be disturbed, therefore the field will be given up unconditionally in this case. The latter two phenomena are also read as warning signs from *yarsanr* or some upset spirits, and a field is usually given up in these cases too. But if no other suitable lands can be found and the field has to be farmed in the two latter cases, an offering ceremony to the *yarsanr* and upset spirits with two chickens (a black and a white, regardless of sex) needs to be performed later, after the field is sowed, to ask for forgiveness. This ceremony is called *yarcavq cavq-e* . A square altar called *lawrgeer* (see Picture 11) is built for this offering.

Fruit trees, particularly fig trees such as *siqpuv* (*Ficus racemosa*), *siqguq* (*Ficus semicordata*), and *siqguq levtev* (*Ficus hirta*), are not

Picture 11 An Offering Altar *lawrgeer*

cut in the field. In addition, some other plants particularly *savlav* trees (*Dalbergia spp.*) are not cut either. There are three reasons for not cutting *savlav* trees; first, they increase soil fertility; second, they provide necessary shade for crops; third, if a *savlav* tree is cut, numerous small *savlav* trees will sprout from its roots and become annoying weeds in the field. Furthermore, preferred tree stocks about 50 – 60 centimeters high are left when trees are cut down, so that the forest regeneration would be faster when the field is fallowed. Both men and women are responsible for cutting trees, although men usually cut big trees, while women cut bushes and small trees. Individual families cut their own field (s) separately.

3.8.3 *Yarkeq-e* (buring)

The field is usually burned 33 days after the trees were cut, in the fourth Akha lunar month, *Khmqxeevq* , roughly in late March and early April. A fire belt wide 5 *lmr* (roughly 8 meters) is cleared usually at the upper side of the field or any necessary sides, before the fire is set. The fire is set from the upper side in the early afternoon of a peaceful sunny day. A fire is also set from the bottom side but only after the upper side fire burns to safety area. The burning of a field will be finished before it gets dark. Both men and

Sacred and Contested Landscapes

women participate in burning. Usually extended families and close friends all come to help in burning a field. A lot of people are needed in case a fire needs to be stamped out from expanding to excepted areas.

3.8.4 *Yarcmr tsov-e* (building a field shed)

A *yarcmr* (field shed) will be built soon after the field was burned. It is built at a flat place in the middle of the field where it is close to water source. The shed is usually made of wood and bamboo and thatched by grasses. It will be finished in a few hours. Both men and women participate in building the shed. A vegetable garden will be set up surrounding the shed after it is built.

3.8.5 *Yarjiv jiv-e* (clearing the field)

After the field shed is built, the field needs to be cleared for sowing. All the unburnt stuff from the previous fire needs to be piled up and burned again. If it is *yarnav*, the soil does not need to be turned over, otherwise the soil is usually turned over before it is sowed.

3.8.6 *Yarka ka-e* (sowing)

As a staple food of the Akha, rice is the main crop planted in the swidden fields. Rice is a sacred crop and needs to be treated respectfully with delicate care at any place and any time. Every family builds a small house, elevated about 1.5 meters from the ground to protect from pigs, goats, and chidren's reach, for the Rice Goddess, *caersanr* or *karsanr*, who looks after holy rice seeds. This house is called *caerjir siqma uqghmq*, meaning "holy rice house", within which holy rice seeds were kept. A rice sowing initiation ceremony, *caer kadawvq-e*, was performed by the greater village chief *dzoeqma* to declare the beginning of rice sowing season, in the fifth Akha lunar month, *Tsaqngawq . Dzoeqma* would take out the holy rice seeds reserved in the holy rice house and perform a rice seed purifying ceremony, caer siqyoeq bu-e, at the holy water well, before the seeds were planted. In some villages of Mengsong such as Hongqi, this rice seed purifying ceremony was performed by a selected "holy woman", *tsawrxawr nyawqxawr*. This woman should be a married woman with at least a son and a daughter. She should be sexually abstinent with her husband during the rest of the year in which she performs as a "holy woman". She was regarded as a representative of the Rice Goddess, *karsanr aqma*, and thus would be able to bring good fortune and blessings to her family by performing it. After the holy rice seeds were purified, *dzoeqma* would take them to his cleared swidden field. Before these holy seeds were planted, a hut needed to be built for the Rice Goddess, *Khmqpiq aqtsanq* ;and the holy rice seeds would be planted in nine bushes at three parallel rows, three bushes in each row (see Picture 12). In the following days, each family also chose an auspicious day of the family to build *khmqpiq aqtsanq* (the Rice Goddess Hut) in each of their fields

Picture 12 *Khmqpiq aqtsanq* (Rice Goddess Hut)

and plant the nine bushes of holy rice above it, in the same way as the greater village chief did, before they started sowing rice in the field. Usually, extended family members and close friends came to help and finish the rice sowing in the one field in one day.

Two offering ceremonies would be performed;one is for the God of Fire and another is for the Rice Goddess. One chicken for each God/Goddess was sacrificed. The offering to the God of Fire is called *Joemiqsaevq*, meaning "pacifying the fire god". It was to thank the Fire God for helping clearing the field with his might power, and in the meanwhile to tell him that it is time for him to rest. A chicken was killed above an ash mound (*jaevbymr*) burned from the piled branches during *yarjiv jiv-e* (clearing the field), and then cooked in the field shed. After offering three pieces of chicken meat, the rest of it was eaten by people. Then a burning fire stick was taken out from the fire place in the shed and then extinguished above the ash mound (*jaevbymr*) by holy water thatched with wild banana stem. When the water was pouring on the burning sticker, the performer articulate that "*miq miv dei!*" meaning "Fire, please be quenched!" The offering to the Rice Goddess was called *ghaciv peevlmr-e*, meaning "hut warming ceremony". It was performed for the Rice Goddess hut so that the Goddess felt home to live in the hut and looked after the rice/crops.

As staple food for the Akha, rice is the main crop in swidden field. More than 100 varieties of rice have been planted in Mengsong (Xu et al., 1997); among which 32 varieties were stilled planted in 1998 (Wang, 1998). These rice varieties are planted in different soils at various locations and also used in rotation for multiple years of cropping. Rice is usually inter-cropped with taro, chilli pepper, ginger, sorghum, sunflower, pumpkin, wax gourd, cucumber, muskmelon, Job's-tears, sugar canes, egg plants, banana trees, and many other crops. During my field research in 1996 – 1998, I identified 156 species and varieties of crops and plants used for food, medicine, entertainment, and religious purposes in Mengsong swidden fields, and many of them are planted in a small garden surrounding the field house, similar to home gardens in villages (see Appendix II). Rice is usually rotated with cotton, maize, peanut, and soybean, too. After a field is not good for cropping, then it will be fallowed, ideally for 13 years❶.

3.8.7 *Yarmovq movq-e* (weeding)

Weeds start growing along with or even before rice does, particularly bamboo shoots, which sprout and grow quickly when the raining season starts in May. The first round of weeding would begin a few days after rice sowed. This first round of weeding is called *arban jaevq-e*, literally meaning "removing bamboo shoots". After the first weeding was finished, the Akha villagers would hold the annual offering to the Earth Lord collectively. In a following Akha week❷ after it, each family would perform two offering ceremonies in their swidden rice fields: *Khmqpiq lawr-e* (offering to the Rice Goddess) and *Yarlawr lawr-e* (offering to the Field Lord). A red rooster was sacrificed for the Rice Goddess in *Khmqpiq lawr-e*; while two chickens (one black and one white, regardless of sex) were offered to the spiritual lord of the field. The former is to ask the Rice Goddess to take good care of rice and other crops in the field; while the purpose of the latter is to pay "rent" to the spiritual lord of the field, *yarsanr*. Therefore, *Yarlawr lawr-e* is also called *mirpoeq xawq-e* or *mirpoeq gaw-e*, both literally meaning "paying the land

---

❶ Thirteen is a culturally lucky and meaningful number for the Akha. There are twelve animals naming different years and every single day. When it goes around a circle and comes back to the beginning animal (year or day), it is 13. The Akha call such a circle as *yei* (for instance, *nan-yei* is a day circle; *khoq-yei* is a year circle). Akha people use it as a unit for calculating ages such as one *yei*, two *yei*s, and so on. On the 13th day after a baby born, there is a big celebration in the family: the new parents will bring their baby to the mother's side of the family, asking for blessings to the baby from his/her uncle. When he/she comes in his/her 13th year, he/she will be treated as an adult by the society. In sum, the number is associated with an adult, mature being, who can protect him/her from *naevq* and other evil spirits. In the same way, the fallow land was believed to become "mature" to be cultivated again after 13 years, and should start another life circle. So, 13 years is an ideal period of fallow for any fields if allowed. However, in reality, lands are short, and people need to recycle their lands before full regeneration, which causes degradation eventually. This would be the case of *mirpeq*, literally meaning "worn-out lands".

❷ An Akha week comprises 12 days, with each day named after one of the 12 animals.

rent". A swidden field "officially" becomes the Inside domain temporarily after the *Yarlawr lawr-e* ritual, which in turn establishes the family's the exclusive use right over the field within the "lease term".

Another ceremony called *yarcavq cavq-e* needs to be performed before these two offerings on the same day or a prior date, if *sanqpyawr* or *sanqghur* or both occurred during cutting trees of the field, as we mentioned earlier. This ceremony would be conducted outside of the field. After these two or three ceremonies, the second round of weeding would begin soon. When the second round of weeding is accomplished, the villagers would celebrate their annual Swing Festival (*Yaerkuq dzaq-e*) and Buffalo Festival (*Ghawla aqpoeq lawr-e*), after which a third and last round of weeding would start.

3.8.8 *Caeryaeq caeryur* (harvesting)

After three rounds of weeding, the rice would be ready for harvesting. But before harvesting, the First Rice Festival, called *Odov ghawrdzaq-e* or *Hawqxeevq dzaq-e*, literally meaning "eating new rice", would be celebrated. Three pieces of rice ears (heads) would be picked from the nine holy rice bushes and given to one's ancestors by putting them under the ancestor shrine. At the same time, new rice is slipped off by hands, taken home and stir-dried in an iron pan above a fire place, husked, cooked, and offered to one's ancestors along with sticky rice cakes, rice liquor, and ginger tea. Then Akha people start celebrating the First Rice Festival, in which delicious Akha foods are prepared, shared by extended family and villagers. Pigs are usually killed to celebrate this festival.

After harvest, each family would perform another ceremony called *Banqyoe pyaev-e* in their major swidden field. Only male adults are allowed to perform the ceremony. This ceremony is performed for three purposes; the first is to harvest the nine holy rice bushes kept in the Rice Goddess House; the second is to invite the Rice Goddess to go back to her house in the village; the third is to return the field to the Spiritual Lord *yarsanr*. After this ceremony, the field becomes the Outside domain again. If the family decides to farm the same field again in the following year(s), all the ceremonies mentioned above need to be performed again annually, in order to make sure that the field would appropriately switch between the Outside and the Inside domains. Because of its transitional feature, I call a swidden field "transformed ecotope", but not a "domesticated ecotope", The latter is a permanently transformed ecotope, as I will address shortly in the following section.

After a swidden is fallowed, it becomes not just the Outside, but also accessible publicly to other villagers; and it could be farmed by any other families in the next farming cycle. But sometimes perennial plants such as tea, rattan, and bamboo are inter-cropped or rotated with rice. Such a swidden field will become an agroforest as it fallows. In this way, the family can establish more permanent access to this land in general and ownership over these plants in particular.

3.9 Management of Domesticated Ecotopes —*daema* (paddy fields) and *yark mr* (fenced gardens)

As being demonstrated above, the most intensive interactions between the Akha people and their environments (swidden lands here), physically and spiritually, occur in their practices of swidden agriculture, through constant switches between the Outside and the Inside. Since they believe that any improper conduct in the Outside domain may get a punishment from the *naevq* (representative of nature here), which could cause a disaster, Akha people try to avoid any human activities in the Outside domain as much as possible. A strategy to achieve it is to "domesticate" the Outside domain and transform it into Inside domain permanently. *Daema* (irrigated paddy fields) and *yarkmr* (fenced gardens) are two examples of such attempts. *Daema* is an attempt to domesticate the lands; while *yarkmr* is an attempt to domesticate wild plants.

Akha people prefer to develop their arable lands into irrigated paddy fields wherever it is possible—environmentally and economically, and in order to avoid or reduce any unnecessary interactions with the spirits. Being permanent farming lands, these paddy fields are regarded almost completely domesticated, and thus are part of the Inside. Study of early settlement history of Mengsong Akha community shows that the main reason why they moved to Mengsong from Nannuo Mountain in Menghai County about 200 – 300 years ago was to develop irrigated paddy fields in the Mengsong Basin, because they knew from their history that irrigated rice cultivation would provide them a more stable economic basis. Their original goal of moving into Mengsong was to build an economy on wet rice cultivation in the basin and tea on the mountains. But they became substantially dependent on swidden agriculture because the Mengsong Basin is too cold and too small to produce enough rice for growing population (Wang 1988). And yet, Mengsong Akha have tried their best to turn their arable lands into irrigated paddy fields wherever it is possible, not only in the Mengsong Basin, but also in many small valleys such as *Tsaqla* and *Navciq* (see Figure 9).

Another way to "domesticate" the Outside domain is to establish fenced gardens, *yarkmr*. In Mengsong, almost every family has a homegarden or two at the back yard of their house or its lower side; at least 227 species and varieties of crops and useful plants are planted in Mengsong's homegardens (see Appendix III). Many of these plants are introduced by the villagers, women and men, from the local forests and are still under process of domestication. Some of the plants, such as rattan, are introduced because they become scarce or less available in natural forests. Therefore, Mengsong homegardens are not only important places for folk experiment of domesticating plants, but also effective locations for ex-situ conservation of local important economic plants (Wang et al., 1999). Growing homegardens is a long tradition of Akha people. It is recorded in Akha oral history that homegardens were popularly practiced by Akha families in the *Jadae* country (Shida and Ahai 1992). Of course, fenced gardens are not limited to homegardens; Mengsong families also tend to have at least one vegetable garden outside of village.

As both *daema* (irrigated paddy fields) and *yarkmr* (fenced gardens) become domesticated, they not only become part of the Inside domain, but also become private properties. Therefore, the Outside domain corresponds to common domain and/or properties, while the Inside domain corresponds to private domain and/or properties, in Akha concept. A swidden field becomes a "property" of the family temporarily only after it has become the Inside domain through the *Yarlawr lawr-e* ritual, but it becomes a common property again after it is returned back to the spiritual lord and the Outside domain. Similarly, the dual tenure system of the agroforests could be explained in this logic; those planted and/or domesticated plants (tea trees, bamboo, rattan, and indigo) are private properties, while the land and wild plants of the agroforests still belong to the common. These permanent private properties, particularly irrigated paddy fields and tea gardens, became commodities for sale or being used to pay off debts after opium poppy was introduced in Akha society in general and in Mengsong in particular in the late 19th century

(Sturgeon, 2005).

3.10　Management of Mobile Ecotopes —*bawrtsanq jeiqzaq* (wild animals)

Like other living creatures and natural entities, all animals and birds are believed to have their own spiritual lords, *yawsanr*. In this sense, all animals and birds are part of sacred landscapes. Animals and birds are sorted into two categories, *lanq* and *dawr*, by the Akha people according to the magnitudes of the spiritual power they possess and/or access. If an animal or bird possesses and/or accesses to spiritual power beyond the Akha's capability to manipulate, it is a *dawr* animal or bird; otherwise, it is a *lanq* animal or bird. The source of a *dawr* animal/bird is either from its own powerful *yawsanr* or its affiliation with *naevq* or both. For instance, elephants, tigers, leopards, lynxes, peacocks, eagles, hornbills, wild geese, crows, swallows, among others, are *dawr* animals and birds that have their own powerful *yawsanr*; while lorises, pangolins, wild cats, turtles, wild buffaloes, rhinoceroi, among others, are *dawr* animals that belong to *naevq*, and the latter two are also believed to have their own powerful *yawsanr*.

We need to exlain more about these two terms *lanq* and *dawr*. As a verb, *lanq* means "increase, add, accumulate"; and as a noun, it could be translated to "good luck, good future, blessing", or even "life force or potency" (following Tooker 2012). In Akha society, if some individuals or families increase their wealth, population (particularly number of sons), among others, it is a good sign of *lanq*; and it is called *geeqlanq heeq-e*, "a big blessing", or "a big copper basin", as discussed in Chapter 2. On the contrary, as a verb, *dawr* means "drink, drain", implying "decrease"; and as a noun, it could be translated to "bad luck" or "drainage of luck" or "decrease of luck". Since such a thing of "bad luck" or "drainage of luck" or "decrease of luck" is something needs to be avoided as much as possible in Akha society, a *dawr* means a taboo in Akha culture. Therefore, it is a *dawr* or a taboo to see those animals and birds affiliated with *naevq* or to kill those have powerful *yawsanr*, because both could cause bad luck to the doer and drainage of his/her family's blessings. There are two kinds of *dawr* animals/birds here;one is affiliated with *naevq* and the other is not. It is a taboo to see/encounter the first type of *dawr* animals/birds;while it is a taboo to kill the second type. If a *dawr* animal/bird of the first type is seen/encountered or a *dawr* animal/bird of the second type is killed accidentally in a trap, a particular ceremony needs to be performed to prevent the doer's family from draining their blessings. This ceremony is called *dawr jaw-e*, literally meaning "avoiding *dawr* ".

The notion of *lanq* versus *dawr* impacts all aspects of the Akha way of life, some parts of these (i. e. *geeqlanq* related issues) have been well studied by Dr. Deborah E. Tooker (2012). In this section, I only talk about how these notions impact and/or guide Akha hunting practices in general and hunting ethics in particular. These hunting practices and ethics include: 1) limiting certain animals and birds for hunting; 2) treating games with respect; 3) sharing; 4) limiting numbers of killings; 5) limiting hunting seasons and time; and 6) other taboos.

3. 10. 1 Choosing game

It is said that there are 64 *dawr* and 46 *lanq* animals and birds. I was not able to collect all the information on these animals and birds during my fieldwork. It is apparent, however, from the limited information I have collected, that all known/identified *lanq* or *dawr* animals and birds are significant to Akha culture, economically and/or culturally; while the rest seem to be out of these two polar categories and are regarded more or less neutral in terms of "luck". Those *dawr* animals and birds are never hunted, though some of them may be killed accidentally by traps (as mentioned above), or for the purpose of protecting people's life and property, such as in case a tiger or a leopard enters into a village and preys on livestock or people. All Akha preferred game animals fall into *lanq* category. These game animals include, but are not limited to, *ghavqteiq* (wild boars or *Sus scrofa*), *haqtsaev* (red deer *Cervus unicolor*), *haqhmr* (bears *Selenarctos thibetanus*), *yaq* (serow *Capricornis sumatraensis*), *cirhaq* (barking deer *Muntiacus muntjac*), *pyaqiq* (civet *Paguma larvata*), *ho* (various rodents), *hopur* (porcupine, *Hystrix hodgsoni*), gevq (silver pheasant *Lophura nythemera*), *gha'nyiq* (red junglefowl *Gallus gallus*), *ngacaer* (fracolin *Arborophila rufogularis*), *hawqkhoeq* (wild pigeon *Streptopelia spp* .), *haqguq* (turtledove, *Treron spp* .), among others. Most of them had large populations in this region in the past, and some of them (such as bears, hedgehogs, rodents, wild pigeons, among others) liked to eat crops in the swidden fields.

The first four game animals were usually hunted collectively with crossbows (*kav*) and/or bows (*tsavqoeq*) in the past and with guns (*miqbev naqpa*) more recently. Others were hunted individually. Besides crossbows, bows, and guns, other hunting methods were various traps, including, but not limited to, 1) *saeqtov* , 2) *eerniq* , 3) *lanrju* , 4) *pyavtaeq* , 5) *ghadmq* , 6) *dzaeqbev* , and 7) *xaqduq* . These traps were set up to catch from small birds to large animals like bears. Detailed description of these methods is documented by me elsewhere (Wang, 1998).

As a side note, the Akha word for game is *xaq* . While the Akha use only one term *ma* to refer to "female" of various game animals, they use various terms to refer to "male" for different games. For instance, a male deer is called *tsaev laq* ; a male barking deer is called *cir poer* ; a male serow is called *yaq buq* ; a wild boar is called *ghavqteiq tanr* . Here, *laq* , *poer* , *buq* , and *tanr* all mean "male". This detailed linguistic richness about game indicates that Akha society not only possesses rich hunting knowledge resulted from their long hunting history but also prefers to hunt male game animals.

3. 10. 2 Treating game with respect

Game animals were treated with great deal of respect, *tagheeq -e* . A ceremony would be conducted in the village, to ask permission to kill game from their spiritual lords the day or night before hunting, especially a collective hunting, was planned. It is an augury, the reading of which would decide whether the hunting was to be conducted or not during the next day(s). In addition, it is believed that each hunter has a hunting spiritual lord, *xaqsanr* , whose guidance is fundamental for a successful kill. This hunting lord is living in a tree selected by the hunter. This tree is called *loema arbawr* , and usually located in the jungle of *putsanq* or *ghaqtsanq* . A hunter needs sexual abstinence the night before he goes out for hunting because sex is regarded unclean and thus is not respectable to the hunting lord and spiritual lords of game. The hunter's wife, if he had one, also needed to stay at home as long as her husband was gone. She was not allowed to go out to visit other people, nor to spin threads or weave cloth. The purpose of all this abstinence was to pay respect (*taqheeq-e* in Akha) to the spiritual lords. Moreover, after a big game animal (e. g. the first five preferred game animals) was successfully killed, three pieces of fresh meat of the game needed to be offered to the killer's hunting lord at his *loema arbawr* . This offering is called *loema toeq-e* or *xaquq ceq-e* . The game would also be burned symbolically with three leaves from the *loema arbawr* before it was taken back to the village. This burning was read as an offering to the spiritual lord of the game. Furthermore, the spiritual lord of the game would be offered with three slices of raw meat and three slices of cooked meat before it allowed to be eaten by people. The last, the killer should keep sexual abstinence for 7 days after he killed a *khawqhe* game (see explanation in the following section — Sharing), or for 3 days after he killed a barking deer, without which the spiritual lord of the game would not be pacified completely.

If a kind of trap called *dzaeqbev* did not kill a game in a few days after it was set up, a ritual called *dzaeqbev cavq cavq-e* needed to be performed. In the ritual, a boiled egg would be offered to spiritual lords of the game at a lifted bamboo altar on four posts with a nine-stair ladder, called *lawrgeer* , the same as that was built for a swidden field lord (see Figure 17). When the egg was offered, the performer would articulate, saying "*Dzoeqxaq mawqxaq xar lar leiq-ei. Xaq xar-awq cawq baw;xaq pyav-awq cawq baw. Xa ma maq miv-awq xaq zaq bi miv lavq;xaq cur tiq mawr maq miv-awq yawjae tiq mawr gha lawq!* " which literally means "We come to beg a game animal for our elders; we come as a group and the game will be shared collectively. We are not asking for big game but please give us small ones;we are not asking for a fat game animal but please give us a skinny one!" From these texts, we can see how humble the Akha people put their own positions comparing with the respectable and awesome spiritual lords of the game. If a wild buffalo was killed accidentally by the *dzaeqbev* trap, its meat could not be eaten; instead, its corpse should be covered by rice husks. When this was performed, the performer would say "*caer dzaq khoeq mirnae iqbavr navqleir-awr xir nga!*" literally "it was sentenced because it ate our rice without permission!" The Akha people wish that this ritual along with respectable behavior (such as burying the corpse with rice husks) would pacify the powerful spirits❶ of the buffalo who would in turn forgive the trap owner (s).

3.10.3 Sharing

Big games such as *ghavqteiq* (wild boar), *haqtsaev* (red deer), *haqhmr* (bear), *yaq* (serow), and *cirhaq* (barking deer) are identified as *puxaq*, literally meaning "village game". A successful kill of village games needed to be announced and celebrated in public by certain musical instruments before entering to the village. For instance, a kill of a wild boar or a red deer or a bear or a serow should be announced and celebrated by playing *khawqkhe*, a specific bamboo musical instrument made after the game was killed. Accordingly these animals are called *khawqkhe xaq*, or *khawqkhe* games. Similarly, a kill of a muntjac deer would be announced and celebrated by blowing a *laejaq* (a clarion made of water buffalo's horn). Meat of a village game needed to be distributed among the killer, other accompanied hunters, the village chief *dzoeqma*, the village blacksmith *bajiq*, a priest *boermawq*, and the village duty group *lanxanr* ❷. The killer would get the head and the whole skin as bonus. The village chief would get a front leg. The blacksmith would get a piece of rib. The priest, who was invited to conduct a ceremony to pacify the spirits of the game, would get half of the game's waist part. The village duty group would get three pieces of ribs, called *pubyar* (lit. meaning "village ribs") or *lanxanr jaev* (lit. meaning "village duty ribs"). The rest of

---

❶ It is believed that a wild buffalo has nine powerful spirits.

❷ A typical Akha village usually divided their households into several groups; each group took in turn the village duty, called *lanxanr dan-e*, for a specified period of time. Their duties include: 1) patrolling the whole village to check each house to see whether the fire was controlled, especially during the dry and windy season; 2) taking care of any public guests visiting their villages; and 3) making sure there was no theft in the village.

the meat was divided equally among the involved hunters including the killer[1]. The killer would also share the meat with his ancestors by hanging the head at the ancestor altar. A chicken would also be sacrificed for the ancestors for their blessings without which the kill would not be possible. A rooster would be sacrificed if a female game was killed, and a hen if a male game was killed.

Wasps were also regarded as *pubyaq*, village insects. Therefore, if a wasp nest was found by any individual villager, the larvae should be shared by all families of the village. I believe that this might be one of oldest sharing practice and ethics developed when the Akha ancestors were hunters-and-gatherers many millennia ago. It is amazing to see an old tradition passed down for such a long historical time. I was also informed that legs of silver pheasants needed to be shared among the killer's married sister(s). I also believe that sharing legs of pheasants with one's sisters is also an old tradition developed during the hunting-gathering period of time. Akha people believe legs of pheasants and chickens always belong to sisters, as in an Akha phrase saying "*zaqmiq bawrdur*", literally meaning "daughter/sister's legs". Therefore, whenever a married daughter/sister visits her natal family, legs of a killed chicken are always given to her. It is also strikingly interesting to note that a leg of a pig sacrificed in many ceremonies also needs to be given to married daughter/sister(s). In Akha culture, collecting is women's domain, while hunting is men's domain. In the famous Akha migratory epic *Za Ni Za Ga Dzan Ga* (Shida and Ahai, 1992), it is said that the technology of collecting wasp larvae was taught by a widow. It is also speculated that the

---

[1] Formulas for dividing up large animals, especially buffaloes, are very common in upland Southeast Asia—Zomia and Indonesia. Similar division formulas exist among northern North American native people and other groups worldwide. Usually the division is along kinship lines — particular categories of kin get particular cuts — but division by status and occupation is also found widely; see Richard Lando (1979).

Akha ancestors were living in a matrilineal society when they were hunters-and-gatherers (Yang, 2010). Apparently, collecting and sharing wasp larvae was done by a gathering mother and then shared with her band members. This is why wasp larvae are regarded as *pubyaq* , village insects, because a village evolves from a band. Similarly, a man shared his killings with his sisters, which was the origin of the cultural practice of sister's legs of the pheasants and of chickens/pigs.

Last, but not least, Akha people share their game not only with various spirits, and with family and human members of the community, but also with the animal members of the community, as they left those accidentally killed *dawr* animals, these corpses would be consumed by the wild predators, scavengers, and micro-decomposers.

3. 10. 4 Limiting numbers of killings

A successful kill was believed a sign of good luck *lanq* . It was also believed, however, excessive *lanq* could turn into *dawr* . Therefore, a hunter should not kill more than nine *khawqkhe* game animals in any given single year, including game animals killed in traps. This was especially effective in preventing from killing pregnant animals since all the unborn fetuses were counted as separated individuals for this regulation. It was even said that a hunter should not kill more than three *khawqkhe* animals in one year. An old lady in Mengsong told me that three red deer were killed in her husband's traps *Dzaeqbev* in 13 days one year. They were afraid of excessive *lanq* turning into *dawr* . So, the third deer was not taken home and all traps were unset in order to prevent from more kills. It turned out that her husband was never able to kill any game for the rest of his life. "So, if a hunter killed three *khawqkhe* game animals in a year, an Inside-and-Outside purification ceremony[1] with one hog and one sow needs to be conducted in order to re-establish the flow of *lanq* . " She complained that bad luck of her husband was due to not conducting such a ceremony. It is also a *dawr* to kill two big game animals by the same person in a single day for a similar logical reason[2].

3. 10. 5 Limiting hunting seasons and time

It is a *dawr* or taboo to see wild animals in mating[3] in Akha culture. It is also a taboo to kill a pregnant game. In other words, a *lanq* or a neutral animal would become *dawr* temporarily when it is mating or pregnant. So, usually Akha people do not arrange any collective hunting during animal breeding season, in order to avoid *dawr*. Akha hunters also have accumulated rich knowledge to distinguish not only between male and female game animals, but also between pregnant and non-pregnant female game. For instance, if a *ganqho* (a kind of big rodent) is seen holding leaves in her mouth, it is pregnant. Another example is that a pregnant monkey would cover her belly with leaves when it is seen by people. If a pregnant game was killed accidentally, the meat of the game could not be eaten; a *dawr jaw-e* ceremony would be performed by a priest *boermawq* for the killer, in order to prevent the blessings and luck of his family from being drained. The killer would also be barred from hunting for three years in order to pacify the spirits of the killed game.

---

[1] This kind of ceremony is performed whenever a family feels its flow of *geeqlanq* or blessing is not functioning due to various reasons;see Deborah Tooker (2012).

[2] As a side note, the similar beliefs — that a successful killing is a sign of good luck but excessive killings would lead to bad luck, therefore the number of killings by a hunter should be limited — exist among the Maya in Southeast Mexico (see Anderson and Tzuc, 2005).

[3] It is also a *dawr* if one sees two persons having sexual intercourse. Therefore, Akha culture does not allow to have sex during day time in order to avoid being seen.

Collective hunting was usually organized in the dry season, or *Jawrla yamq*, literally meaning "non-farming season", roughly from January through April; while individual hunting could be year-round as long as avoiding particular mating season for particular animals. Some traps were set year around, while others were limited to particular seasons.

3. 10. 6   Other hunting taboos

A killed game animal cannot be taken/eaten by people if it dies standing, or four legs pointing up to the sky, or with its head looking back over its body, because all of these situations are read as a sign that they were not supposed to die. The last case is called *xaqma nanrghovq*, and usually a sign of pregnancy if it is a female game. In addition, a hunter also abstains from hunting for a year after one or two of his parents passed away, because Akha people believe that their spirits could transform into various animals traveling the places they stepped before, particularly for the purpose of picking up all of their foot marks. The spirits could also transform into mushrooms, bamboo shoots, or fish. This is the reason why a woman/daughter does not collect mushrooms and bamboo shoots, nor does she fish in a month after her parent(s) pass(es) away.

In a summary, these hunting practices, ethics and taboos together assured that wild animals and birds were managed sustainably by Mengsong Akha community, as an elder *Aqbawr Dzawrtev* stated, "the big wild animal populations were at least five times more than that of Mengsong community 50 years ago" (Wang, 1998: 50). Similarly, fish and aquatic animals had been managed sustainably prior to 1950 (Wang et al., 1999).

3.11 Management of Created Ecotope—*pu* (village)

3.11.1 *Putsov oeq coer oeq pyawq jaq*

A typical Ahka phrase describing a village is "*putsov oeq coer oeq pyawq jaq*", literally "a good village has four good corners and four good sides". Here, the four sides refer to the four village gates over the four paths at four directions; while the four corners refer to four official positions in Akha society: *dzoeq*, *pir*, *civq*, and *khav* ❶. *Dzoeq* is an inherited political/ruling position in Akha society. The person who takes this position is called *dzoeqma* (the greater chief). Only males from ruling lineages (*dzoeqca*) could take this position. A traditional Akha village must have one and only one *dzoeqma* (the greater chief). His position has to be inherited by his eldest son after he dies, and then by the eldest grandson. If the eldest son dies without a male heir, then the second son would inherit the position. If a *dzoeqma* decides to join another village, the newly joined *dzoeqma* would become a *dzoeqzaq* (the lesser or deputy chief). The *dzoeqma* is responsible to initiate all village ceremonies/rituals that are related to the wellbeing of the whole village. The house of *dzoeqma* is usually located at the center of a village, and it must be built first when a new village is established or when a village is relocated (Tooker, 2012).

Pir are religious clergy, including *boermawq* and *nyirpaq*. *Boermawq* are solely men and they are Akha priests who have been trained in their whole lives to perform life cycle ceremonies including funeral ceremonies as well as

---

● The commoners are called *mavq* in Akha.

all kinds of purifying ceremonies. It is the responsibility of *boermawq* to memorize all the migratory routes and genealogies of all the patrilineages of the villagers. They are also trained to memorize various kinds of oral texts related to different kinds of rituals, ranging from calling a lost soul to a funeral. A *boermawq*'s position cannot be inherited. A *boermawq* needs to be trained from early age as an apprentice (*pirzaq*) of a *boermawq pirma* master. An apprentice (*pirzaq*) cannot conduct any rituals independently until he is titled *boermawq* by his master (pirma). This entitlement is called *boermawq tsov-e*, similar to a graduation with a certain degree in a modern educational system. *Nyirpaq* are usually women although occasionally could be men. They are shamans who can travel into the underground world, communicate with all kinds of spirits there, and thus diagnose causes of illness through a ceremonial trance, called *Nyirpaq xir -e* in Akha. Many illnesses caused by minor offenses to the spirits could be cured by a *nyirpaq* through appropriate ceremonies and medical treatments, but some illnesses caused by major offenses to spirits need to be cured by *boermawq* through purification ceremonies. Like that of a *boermawq*, a *nyirpaq*'s position cannot be inherited. And a person cannot decide to become a *nyirpaq* as her will. Only those who are called by her spiritual lord, *yawsanr*, living in the underground world, could become a *nyirpaq*. But calling from her *yawsanr* is insufficient to become a *nyirpaq*; she must choose a *nyirpaq pirma* (master *nyirpaq*) as her master, who will teach her the necessary sacred texts and knowledge for conducting a *nyirpaq* trance ritual. A new *nyirpaq* also needs to be entitled by her master, without which she could not perform any rituals independently.

Civq are technicians, particularly the blacksmith, called *bajiq*. The *Bajiq* are always men, who are not only responsible for making all iron tools, such as machete, hoes, etc., needed by the whole village, but also all iron paraphernalia for *dzoeqma*, *boermawq*, and *nyirpaq*. *Dzoeqma* and *nyirpaq*'s iron paraphernalia are special knives, called *lavqyaeq*, which are used to kill the animals for various rituals. A *Boermawq*'s iron paraphernalia include a *lavqyaeq* and a *ganq* (a spear, used to kill water buffalo in funerals). A village must have at least a *bajiq*. A *bajiq*'s position has to be inherited by one of his sons.

Khav used to be military force and *khavma* be military generals in Jadae polity. But any knowledgeable and influential persons are called *khavma* in traditional Akha society. *Khavma* include *paqmawq* (the leader of each patrilineage) of all patrilineages and other knowledgeable/influential persons in a village.

A traditional Akha village is ruled by the *Pulanr tsawrmawq* (the Village Elders Council), comprising the *dzoeqma* (chair), *bawrmawq pirma*, *bajiq*, and *khavma*. As stated in the Akha phrase at the beginning of this section, these four kinds of personnel are regarded as "four supporting posts of the village". They manage every aspect of the villagers' lives through practicing a set of *ghanr-sanr-khovq*.

3.11.2 Ghanr-sanr-khovq

Ghanr sanr khovq is also written as *zanrsanrkhovq*, or simply *zanr* (or *zang* in English). Although it is usually used and defined as a general term by western scholars (Lewis, 1969; Alting von Geusau, 1983)[1], it comprises of three parts: *ghanr*, *sanr*, and *khovq*.

Ghanr is a set of behavioral codes or customary law that regulates

---

[1] Paul Lewis (1969) defines *zang* as "religion, custom, way of doing things"; while Leo Alting von Geusau (1983: 249) defines it as "religion, way of life, customs, etiquette, and ceremonies."

interpersonal relationships, including kinship and Akha cultural membership, in Akha society. The kinship further includes that of among the living populations and between the living populations and their ancestors. Since the ancestors are regarded as inside spirits, *ghanr* could be translated to "a set of customary law that regulates interpersonal relationships within the Inside domain in Akha society". The core principle of the *ghanr* is to maintain the continuity of patrilineages (*tseevq*) and Akha cultural membership (or Akha identity or Akhaness, *Aqkaq tsawrjeq*) through practicing ancestor offerings. The idea that Akha *Ghanr* is central to Akha ethnic identity, or "Akhaness", has been noticed by many scholars (Alting von Geusau, 1983; Kammerer, 1989; Toyota, 2003; Li, 2012). Recall how a Mon-khmer group became Akha in Jadae polity through creating their own patrilieages and practicing ancestor-offering centered Akha *ghanr*. I have collected evidence that many families of Lahu, Wa, and Yunnanese Chinese ethnic groups have become Akha in the same way in the last 100 years or so. This tradition still continues today.

Because Akha people believe that *Geeqlanq*, blessing or life force flows from the ancestors through both one's patrilineage and mother's natal patrilineage (Tooker, 2012), a baby will be given a name that connects to his/her patrilieage so that he/she would grow healthily and get continuous flow of life force and blessing throughout his/her life. As a person grows old and dies eventually, his mother's or her husband's patrilineage would be cited in reversal order so that his/her spirits could travel back to the ancestral lands along the ladder/path of the lineage. In order to maintain the flow of *geeqlanq*, the Akha conduct twelve offerings to their ancestors annually, called *Aqpoeq lawr-e* in Akha (see Appendix IV).

Besides the twelve annual ancestor offerings, Akha *ghanr* also includes a series of rituals pertaining to a life cycle of individuals. These rituals include, but are not limited to, 1) A Naming Ceremony for a newborn (*Zaqmyanr Myanr-e*), 2) Wedding Ceremonies (*Oermr Bar-e*), 3) Paying Bride Price (*Yaerdanr Xawq-e*), 4) White-skirted Woman Initiation (*Yayaer Aqma Mr-e* ❶), and 5) Funeral Ceremonies (*Xirghanr Mr-e*). If a married couple want to separate their own household from their parents, they need to build their own house, install their own ancestor altar, and perform house warming ceremony (*Ymrdav dav-e*) and an extra ancestor offering ceremony (*Ymrdav Aqpoeq Lawr-e*). Various kinds of Inside and/or Outside purification ceremonies (*LavqkhoerLavqnyir Mr-e*) are also performed by the *boermawq* (priests) for families whose members are sick due to offenses to spirits or ancestors. All of these rituals are prescribed by Akha *ghanr*.

The second part of the behavior codes is *sanr*, "spiritual lords". Therefore, it is a set of customary law that regulates human's relationships with various outside spirits, or spiritual lords of the nature. There are seven annual rituals paying respects to various Gods/Goddesses and spiritual lords, or suppressing certain vicious spirits. These rituals include, 1) Village Gate Renewal (*Lanrkanq mr-e*); 2) Offering to the God of Sky, Goddess of Earth, and God of Water (*Mirsanr lawr-e*); 3) Curing Earth Worm Day (*Beeqdeir beeqtsaev lan-e*); 4) Catching Earth Grubs (*Boeqovq nyaevq-e*); 5) Offering to Lord of Rice Field and Rice Goddess (*Yarlawr lawr-e* and *Khmqpiq lawr-e*); 6) Catching Grasshoppers (*Nyaerbanr nyaevq-e*), and 7) Fetching Rice Goddess Back Home (*Banqyoe pyaev-e*). Four of these rituals (e. g. No. 1, 2, 5 & 7) have been described in earlier sections. The Curing Earth Worm Day (No. 4) is observed right after all families have finished their rice sowing, in

---

❶ A white skirted woman is regarded as a representative of the Rice Goddess. It is the highest honor to a senior married woman with at least a son and a daughter.

order to "cure" the wounded earth worms during the clearing, soil turning over, and sowing, and pacify their spirits. On the contrary, earth grubs and grasshoppers are pests and need to be controlled. That is the purpose of the rituals of No. 4 and 6.

The third part *khovq* is an abbreviation of *khovqtovq latovq*, meaning "calendar". The Village Elders' Council control/regulate the villagers' behaviors in natural resource management and social lives through implementing two sets of customary laws/behavioral codes *ghanr* (for the Inside domain) and *sanr* (for the Outside domain) according to the calendar *khovqtovq latovq* (see Appendix V). They regulate the villagers' activities at four levels of time scale: daily, weekly, seasonally, and annually. First, at the daily level, Akha *ghanrsanrkhovq* proscribes certain activities on certain days. For instance, any rituals done by a family, such as rice sowing or offering to the Field Lord, or for a family, such as a purifying ceremony or an inside chanting, Tooker, 2012) need to be performed on an auspicious day of the family, *nan meeq*. The day of the animal on which one was born is not regarded as an auspicious day for him/her. Accordingly, all the days of the animals of the household members are not auspicious for that household. The days of the animals on which any immediate members of the household die are not auspicious days either. Therefore, the number of auspicious days available for a household is usually very limited. However, if all the days of the animals are occupied either by births or deaths of the household members, then all days would become auspicious for that household. Second, at the weekly level, the days of tiger and sheep are set as off-farming days. But people can use those days to do other work, such as gardening or fishing.

Third, at the seasonal level, the Akha divides a year into two periods: one is the Inside and the other is the Outside. Certain activities are allowed only in the Inside period, while the others are in the Outside period. For instance, traditionally, new house building and wedding ceremonies are allowed in the Inside period. The marks that divide the Inside and Outside period are the Rice Sowing Initiating Ceremony (*Caerka aqpoeq*) and the Rice Flowering Festival (*Karyaev aqpoeq*); the Outside period is from the Rice Sowing Initiating Ceremony to the Rice Flowering Festival, while the Inside period is the other part of the year. In other words, the Akha's binary division of the world into the Inside and the Outside is not only spatial but also temporal. The rice planting marks the start of a farming season along with the arrival of raining season. All living beings resume a new season of growing and proliferating along with the rain. Akha people term it *aqcawq-e aryamq*, which means "time of other beings' breeding". Therefore, human beings should not be allowed to do the same, which means that they should not get married after the rice sowing is initiated. It is a code to regulate people (especially unmarried youths)'s time and energy, directing them into productive activities rather than reproductive ones. Since the productive activities are not done until all the crops, particularly rice, have been harvested, dried appropriately, and stored safely, the complete sense of the Inside period will not start until after the Akha New Year Festival, which is the celebration of good harvest of the whole year farming and mark of the end of the farming season. Therefore, wedding ceremonies are prescribed (and preferred by parents) after the New Year Festival. It is a taboo for a girl to get pregnant before she is appropriately married in Akha culture[1]. And yet, youths cannot always control their behaviors completely according to the prescribed codes, and a marriage becomes necessary when a girl gets pregnant and a wedding

---

[1] It is believed that if a girl gets pregnant before she is married, it will decrease or drain the blessings of her natal patrilineage.

ceremony should be held before her pregnancy becomes noticeable. Therefore, Akha society makes a channel to deal with this situation. After the last round of weeding is finished, the rice starts flowering, and it will be ready for harvest in one month. Akha people hold the Rice Flowering Festival to celebrate the most tedious farming work being accomplished. In this festival, all evil spirits will be chased away out of houses and villages. The Inside domain is cleaned again. Therefore, the festival is also called *khovqzaq*, "the Minor New Year", after which a wedding ceremony is allowed, though not preferred yet. So, strictly speaking, the time between the Rice Flowering Festival and the New Year Festival (*Kartanrpar-e*) is a transition period from the absolute outside domain to the absolute inside domain.

Fourth, at the annual level, all those annual rituals are prescribed by the *ghanrsanrkhovq* and the specific date of each village level ritual and of all twelve annual ancestor offerings is decided by the Village Elders' Council according to the calendar; the dates of other household rituals are usually framed by the village level rituals. For instance, all households have to perform their offering to the Field Lord and the Rice Goddess rituals in an Akha week following the village level ritual *Mirsanr lawr-e*, offering to the deities of the sky, earth, and water. Similarly, the First Rice Festival needs to be initiated by the village chief *dzoeqma* on his auspicious day, called *yawqpu nanmeeq tseir-e*, literally meaning "selecting an auspicious day for the village", and each household should conduct their first rice ceremony on their own auspicious day in the following Akha week. Besides, Akha society also maintains certain days of rat, pig, and termite as annual holidays, for the purpose of paying respect or suppressing their spirits.

3.12 Conclusion and Discussion: Ecology of Sacred Landscapes of the Akha

In summary, the Mengsong Akha community managed their natural resources through religious representation, both in space and in time. The Akha people divide the whole world into two domains, the Inside (*lavqkhoer*) and the Outside (*lavqnyir*), both in space and time, according to their animist beliefs; the Inside space is of humans, while the Outside space is of spirits; day time is of humans, while the night time is of spirits; the dry season is of humans (in terms of reproductive activities), while the raining season is of spirits. They transformed their environment into a landscape with six types of ecotopes — forbidden, restricted, modified, transformed, domesticated, and created — with the forbidden (*yawrkhawr*) and created (*pu*) ecotopes being centers of the Outside and the Inside domains respectively, according to their worldview. These two centers of the Outside and Inside domain are at polar opposites, while the other four types of ecotopes are positioned with various distances from both centers, on a mental map. The distances are not physical, but instead are identified in terms of intensity and frequencies of human activities, ranging from a taboo on human activities in the forbidden ecotopes to culturally appropriate activities being allowed and safe in the created ecotope. The wild animals and birds are identified as yet another type of ecotope — mobile ecotope, which are moving across the other six ecotopes spatially. In reality, Mengsong Akha community divided their territory into six land use zones — *pu* (village), *putsanq* (village fence forest), *ghanqtsanq* (protected forests), *miqkhaevq lavqghaw aqganq* (firewood forests), *nyoqjawr kmrteev aqganq* (fenced buffalo forests), *yarmr jawqxmq aqganq* (agricultural lands), and the outside of it as the seventh zone *mirma tseirganq* (vast wilderness). These seven land use zones (including the wilderness) more or less correspond to the seven types of landscapes—village as created ecotope, village fence forest as restricted ecotopes, protected forests as forbidden ecotopes (roughly as they may occur in other zones too), both firewood forests and fenced buffalo forests as modified ecotopes, agricultural lands as transformed ecotopes (swidden fields) or domesticated ecotopes (irrigated paddy fields and fenced gardens), vast wilderness as home of mobile ecotopes (roughly so because wild animals and birds are also moving across other ecotopes). The Village Elders' Council control or regulate the villagers' behaviors in their social lives in general and in natural resource management through implementing two sets of customary laws/behavioral codes *ghanr* (for the Inside domain) and *sanr* (for the Outside domain) according to the calendar *khovqtovq latovq*. This regulation institution is termed *ghanrsanrkhovq* in Akha.

Though it is demonstrated through a case study of Mengsong, the natural resource management system presented here was prevailing in most Akha villages in China prior to 1950, and in other countries of Mekong region as well (Sturgeon, 2005)[1]. This was discussed with and confirmed by numerous Akha elders and cultural experts at a workshop on this topic organized by me at Mengsong, from February 20th to 25th, 2008[2], as well as

---

[1] The exception would be the Christian Akha villages in Eastern Shan State of Myanmar, who were converted by Christian missionaries since the 1920s. There have been more and more Akha communities converting into Christians (either Baptists or Catholics) in Myanmar and Northern Thailand since then. Since they regard Akha traditional beliefs as evil religion, we should expect changes of natural resource management by the Christian Akha. But questions on how these changes would occur and what the ecological consequences of these changes are beyond the scope of this study, though they remain as a very interesting topic for future studies.

[2] Forty-three knowledgeable Akha elders (both male and female) and cultural experts from 14 Akha villages participated in the workshop. Half of the participants are from seven villages outside of Mengsong area, representing various Akha subgroups in Damenglong Township.

at several other focus group discussion meetings held in various Akha villages in Damenglong Township, and in numerous key informants' interviews in various Akha villages throughout Mekong region. Though variations might exist in different villages according to their locations, all of those ecotopes should be expected in all traditional Akha villages. This is further confirmed by many Akha classic poetic songs in which a landscape of Akha homelands are always portrayed exactly as I described above. For instance, a classic song in a wedding ceremony depicts a journey passing the groom's village's *putsanq* (village fence forest), *ghaqtsanq* (protected forests), *miqhaevqlavqghaw aqganq* (firewood forests), *nyoqjawr kmrteev aqganq* (water buffalo forests), *yarmr jawqxmq aqdae* (arable lands with paddy fields), and *mirma cerganq* (vast wild forests), then entering the same landscape of the bride's village's homeland with the same ecotopes in reverse order. This kind of landscape can still be seen in some old Akha communities in Xishuangbanna, besides Mengsong, Nanpen in Jinghong City, and Nannuo, Bulangshan, and Bada in Menghai County, as well as in traditional Akha villages in Eastern Shan State of Myanmar, in Phongsaly Province of Northern Laos, and in Northern Thailand (e. g. Saenjalurn Village) (personal observations). The sacred landscape and its management system, however, have been disappeared or are disappearing in most Akha villages in Mekong region due to various reasons. The Chinese versions of these changes will be addressed in the following Chapter 4 and Chapter 5.

 I argue that the Akha natural resource management, regulated by the *ghanrsanrkhovq*, is an adaptive management (Holling, 1986; Lee, 1993; Gunderson et al., 1995; Berkes, 1999), which acknowledges that environmental conditions will always change, thus requiring management institutions to respond to feedback by adjusting and evolving. As I argued earlier, the animist belief and the community-of-beings worldview were well developed when the Akha ancestors were hunter-gathers. As they became agriculturalists, the binary worldview was developed as the Akha society adapted to new way of life, agriculture and more or less permanent residency, etc, which made them separate from nature (spirits), their past hunting-gathering life, and/or other hunters-gathers. However, separation does not mean "to sever" here, instead, it means "to divide" "to distribute", which implies "to share". Therefore, the new form of binary worldview still conforms to their old animist belief and the community-of-beings worldview. Notwithstanding agricultural development in Akha society, the hunting-and-gathering has been remained, as a supplementary economic activity and a cultural tradition, along with its ethics throughout the Akha history.

It seems that the framework of the *ghanrsanrkhovq* was also developed along with the binary worldview in a process through which the Akha ancestors moved from being hunters-gathers to agriculturalists — a process evolved and enriched as the Akha society became involved in various ancient states, and standardized during the historical period of Jadae polity when the Akha ancestors practiced irrigated rice cultivation. It is evident that the Akha ethnic and political identity was also formed in the historical process of building, defending and eventually losing the Jadae polity. Accordingly, the Akha traditional standardized land uses system also seemed to be developed during the Jadae polity period. The last argument can be supported by the following evidence. The word *aqdae* in the term for the agricultural zone *yarmr jawqxmq aqdae* actually means "irrigated paddy fields", while the Akha call swidden fields *danryar*, literally meaning "upland fields". When I asked Akha elders why they still refer the Akha agricultural lands as irrigated paddy fields when they describe the landscape they see in a journey song to fetch the bride during a wedding ceremony, they answered that the song was developed when their ancestors practiced irrigated rice cultivation in *Jadae* and it was not supposed to be changed. Some Akha subgroups, particularly *Arjawr* Akha (the subgroup dominated by the ruling lineage of Jadae polity) made a rice seedling nursery bed, called *ocaev caev-e*, above the swidden field shed, used before rice was sowed. I was told that they did this because their ancestors grew wet rice which needed transplanted from seedlings and they continued this tradition in a form of ritual, to memorize the history. This tradition, labeled as "superstition", was forced to be abandoned in China during the Great-Leap-Forward movement in the late 1950s. Similarly, entire traditional Akha families of Doichang Village in Northern Thailand still make miniature rice fields for ritual purposes even though they have become coffee farmers and no longer grow rice. Deborah Tooker (1996, 2012) has also noticed that Akha people perform a lot of rituals related to irrigation water and channel in order to restore the flow of the blessings or life potency/force for one's family. Therefore, I argue that the system of the six land use zones is a legacy of the Jadae polity; the village fenced forests are equivalent to defensive walls of Jadae city and other Akha towns in the Jadae polity; four village gates are also the legacy of the four gates at the four sides of the city and towns in Jadae (Shida and Ahai, 1992).

Apparently, the Akha people have accumulated a rich body of ecological knowledge regarding natural resource management as they become swidden agriculturalists in Zomia. As an oral culture without writing scripts, their Traditional Ecological Knowledge (TEK) was vividly recorded and presented in proverbs and a phenomenological calendar, and was represented in a lot of stories (including fairy tales) and myths. Through reciting those proverbs and the calendar and retelling those stories and myths constantly, the Akha TEK had been taught and transmitted from generation to generation for centuries. More importantly, their TEK had been efficiently applied in their practices of natural resource management (such as forest management, agricultural activities, home gardening, collecting plants, hunting and fishing, among others) through embedding them in landscapes. This efficiency had been not only guaranteed by the Village Elders' Council, an internal government led by a chief *dzoeqma* who monitored and enforced their customary laws (*Ghanrsanrkhovq* which included environmental rules of natural resource uses) but also, and more importantly, enhanced through the religious representations and moral transactions of their natural resource management. In other words, besides being embedded in landscape, Akha TEK was also represented in their belief system and worldview as environmental taboos and rules, and integrated into their moral system as environmental ethics. Those taboos and rules are observed in their practices of natural resource management and enforced as religious rituals which are repeatedly conducted. Almost all forbidden and restricted ecotopes of the Akha are ecologically significant locations that are vital to maintain healthy local ecosystems. For instance, fig species in the ecosystem of tropical rain forests play key roles in maintenance and re-establishment of the ecosystem when it is disturbed (Xu, 1994), and the Akha forbidden ecotopes protect these fig species. Another protected species loqkawv tree (*Terminalia myriocarpa*) in Akha forbidden ecotopes is a dominant and representative species in tropical rain forests (Wang et al., 1999). Akha forbidden ecotopes tend to protect water sources, which are vital for the health of tropical/subtropical forests. Furthermore, forbidden and/restricted ecotopes are not only animal-friendly, but in particular many sacred animals and birds (e. g. hornbills, loris) are protected by the Akha only found in primitive forests (Wang, 1997). And last, but not least, some forbidden ecotopes contain ecologically fragile locations, such as landslides, rocky areas, water springs and/or ponds on the mountains. These taboos were effective measures that would minimize any possible harmful damages of Akha swidden agriculture to the ecosystem. Observation of these taboos guaranteed that practices of swidden agriculture could only open limited dispersed plots in the jungle—which was the case prior to 1950.

It is strikingly interesting to note the parallel between the Akha landscape and concept of a modern natural reserve. For instance, the forbidden ecotopes (*yawkhawr*) are equivalent to cores of natural reserves; the restricted ecotopes are equivalent to buffering zones of natural reserves; and modified ecotopes are similar to peripheries of natural reserves. The difference between the two systems is that the Akha use terms that conform to their worldview to describe their ecological knowledge, while the ecologists use scientific terms to describe it. For instance, a fig tree (*Ficus religiosa*) is called *nyirdzanr* in Akha, literally meaning "village of the outside beings". The name reflects their knowledge gained from their observation that the fig trees are important to a lot of other beings (plants and animals), and so, they should be respected and protected. But Akha do not say this directly, instead they classify it in a religious term, *yawkhawr*, "awesome, sacred, and dangerous". The purpose of doing this is to protect fig trees by using emotionally powerful symbol of "*yawkhawr*". Therefore, I use the term "ecology of sacred landscape", following Berkes' (1999) "sacred ecology", to describe natural resource management system by traditional societies through religious representation. And I think the term "ecology of sacred landscape" is better than "sacred ecology", because people interact with their environment through landscape, as I discussed in Chapter 1. Furthermore, I argue that the widely used definition of Traditional Ecological Knowledge by

Berkes (1999) confuses knowledge with its practice and representation. Alternatively, I suggest that Traditional Ecological Knowledge should be redefined as *a cumulative body of knowledge of a people, evolving by adaptive processes in practices, represented in their belief system and/or worldview, embedded in their landscape, and handed down through generations by cultural transmission, about the relationship of living beings (including humans) with one another and with their environment.*

I conclude that the Mengsong Akha community managed their natural resources sustainably in history through successful embedding their traditional ecological knowledge into their landscape and religious representation of their management system.

Chapter 4

From Swidden Agriculture to Cash Crop Monoculture: A Case Study of Mengsong Community

4.1 Introduction

As mentioned in Chapter 2, Akha societies experienced political fragmentation or re-tribalization (Harrell, 2001) in which most Akha populations ended up living in a village *pu*, a small chiefdom governed by the *dzoeqma* (the village chief)-led Village Elders' Council, in Zomia, after fall of the Jadae polity. When conditions were allowed, this process was reversible (Harrell, 2001), and a bigger chiefdom covering a cluster of Akha villages could develop, as in the case of the Sam pa of the Nu Quay Akha in northern Laos [Roux, 2011: 23-24 (Orig. Roux, 1924)]. Usually, a wealthier and influential *khavma*, particularly a successful trader from a ruling/leading lineage (*dzoeqca* in Akha), became the leader of such a supra-village polity. He usually had outside support from lowland Tai (Dai) lords. During the traditional phase of Akha history after fall of Jadae polity, *khavma* played very important roles in the Akha society, particularly because a *dzoeqma* could die before his heir was old enough to lead a village, which apparently was common in their centuries-long southward migration to and within Zomia. In that case, it is usually the *khavmá s* responsibility to help the minor *dzoeqma* to run the village affairs through the Village Elders Council. Especially as Akha society integrated into the *Sipsongpanna* Tai (Dai) State, it was usually a rich and influential *khavma* with Tai language skill who was appointed as a village official, *jawrbavr* (derived from a Tai word, *cao ban*), with main duty to collect taxes/tributes for the lowland rulers. *Jawrbavr* was classified into four ranks: *lawqsae, laqjaq , pyavq* and *pyavqlo* , whose ranks increased in this order. A *lawsae* was appointed to take care of one small village; while a *laqjaq* took care of a big one; a *pyavq* (derived from a Tai word *paya* , meaning "chief") was appointed to run more than one village or hamlet; and a *pyavqlo* (derived from the Tai word *paya luang* , "a great chief ") was like a mayor of a mountainous municipality, a counterpart of a lowland Tai (Dai) *cao muang* (prince or land lord) in *Sipsongpanna* . The official paraphernalia of a *pyavqlo* included a golden umbrella, a red hat, a horse with a saddle covered by red cloth, an iron chain (right to arrest offenders), and a sword (right to sentence a criminal). Each *jawrbavr* was also appointed one or two assistants as treasurers, *naqngeq* (from the Tai word *nai ngeu*).

The Akha started to settle in Mengsong area in the middle eighteenth century, and a *jawrbavr* and a *naqngeq* were appointed by the prince of Damenglong (*cao muang long*) to collect taxes/tributes for the ruler of Sipsongpanna. By the middle of nineteenth century, the Mengsong community grew bigger backed up from the cultivation of wet rice on the Mengsong Basin and tea in their forests, and split into two villages[1]; in the meanwhile, the community (or royal) rattan forest, *Sanqpaqbarwar* , was established to enhance the management of rattan. A greater chief *Haeqovq* from one of the leading lineage Dancan emerged and was titled as *pyavq* by

---

[1] The big village was *Tsaqlaq puma* ; while the small one was *Maercaer pu* (also called *Naqdar*).

the lowland Dai lord of Damenglong. Introduction of opium poppies and planting of them brought an economic boom and great population growth through immigration in the late nineteenth century and early twentieth century. The Mengsong Akha community split into six villages ❶ (see Figure 9); and another greater chief *Marzoe* emerged from another leading lineage *Jeirbeeq*, whose family became wealthier from opium plantation and tea trading. *Marzoe* was granted the title of *pyavqlo*, who was granted the official right to govern all the Akha communities surrounding Damenglong Basin by the Lord of Sipsongpanna. *Pyavqlo Marzoe*'s position was inherited by his son *Zoesar* in 1930, like that of a traditional chief *dzoeqma*. Since then, *Zoesar* held his position as *pyavqlo* from 1930 to 1957, through the Nationalist period, the Communist revolution, and up to the onset of the Collective period (Wang, 1998; Sturgeon, 2005❷).

In the meanwhile, a lower ranked official village head *jawrbavr* and a treasurer *naqngeq* were also appointed in each village by the lowland lords to help the *pyavqlo* to collect taxes. More often than not, the official village head *jawrbavr* was not the traditional village chief *dzoeqma*; the former

---

❶ These six villages included *Navciq* (later was named Xianfeng by the Chinese), *Almar* (i. e. Hongxing), *Khaeqxawq* (i. e. Hongqi), *Zmrdanr puma* (predecessor of Dazhai), *Haqpaq pucoeq* and *Naqdar*. They were not the current six villages yet; the last two were dissolved into other villages in the 1930s and 1980s. In the meanwhile, an *Uqcae* Akha group from Myanmar and a *Baja* Akha group from Bulang Mountain joined Mengsong community and formed *Laeqovq* and *Yaevqneir* (today's Dongfanghong and Guangming) villages respectively.

❷ *Marzoe* is recorded as *Sadyer* by Sturgeon (2005: 81, 127, 131). But I believe that she must have confused *Marzoe* with his grandson *Sardzer* (1930-2006), who was never granted the title of *pyavqlo*. As a matter of fact, *Zoesar* was the last great chief *pyavqlo* in Mengsong, whose position could not be passed down to his son *Sardzer* due to the liberation of Mengsong by the People's Liberation Army in 1950. Nevertheless, *Sardzer*, being the son of the last great chief, was appointed as a member of the National Work Team of Xishuangbanna in 1953, and all the way up to the deputy chairperson of the People's Congress of Jinghong County until he was retired.

required a linguistic skill in Tai, while the latter usually lacks it for various reasons, such as being too young when he had to inherit the position, or being constrained very much within the village performing a lot of rituals. In this way, a dual political system was formed in Akha society in Sipsongpanna❶: the *dzoeqma* -led Village Elders' Council and the *jawrbavr-naqngeq* system. All the inner affairs were still dealt by the former system; while the outside affaires related to lowland polity were dealt by the latter system. The *jawrbavr-naqngeq* system is a Tai (Dai) version of Tusi system, learned from Chinese empires. ❷

Scholars usually agree that premodern Southeast Asian states were galactic polities, in which the king's power radiates from a center and diminishes with distance from the monarch, like the light of a candle (Tambiah, 1976: 123; Steinberg, 1987: 60). The capital city of the kingdom, such as Bangkok in Siam, is the center, where the king resides. Circling the capital are provinces under princes or governors appointed by the king. Beyond the provinces, at a greater distance from the king, are "independent 'tributary' polities" over whom the king holds "indirect overlordship" (Tambiah, 1976: 112 – 113). The image is not of a bureaucracy with descending rankings; rather, each succeeding ring outside the capital replicates tributary relations with smaller entities. Not only princes, but also independent tributary polities, might be surrounded by chiefs paying them tribute. Sturgeon (2005) identifies the state of Sipsongpanna as such an

---

❶ Similar kind of a dual political system was also developed when the Akha societies were integrated into modern nation-states in Laos, Myanmar, and Thailand, where the traditional village chief *dzoeqma* has become a spiritual leader, while a newly appointed one by the state has become the village head in a real sense.

❷ Sipsongpanna started to employ this system to rule over ethnic minorities through local rulers, traditionaly or newly appointed, as we see in the case of *Pyavqlo Hobym* in Chapter 2. In the same way, *cao phaendin* (overlord) of Sipsongpanna also appointed local rulers in Jinuo Mountain since 1735 (Liu, et al. , 1990: 148, 158).

Sacred and Contested Landscapes

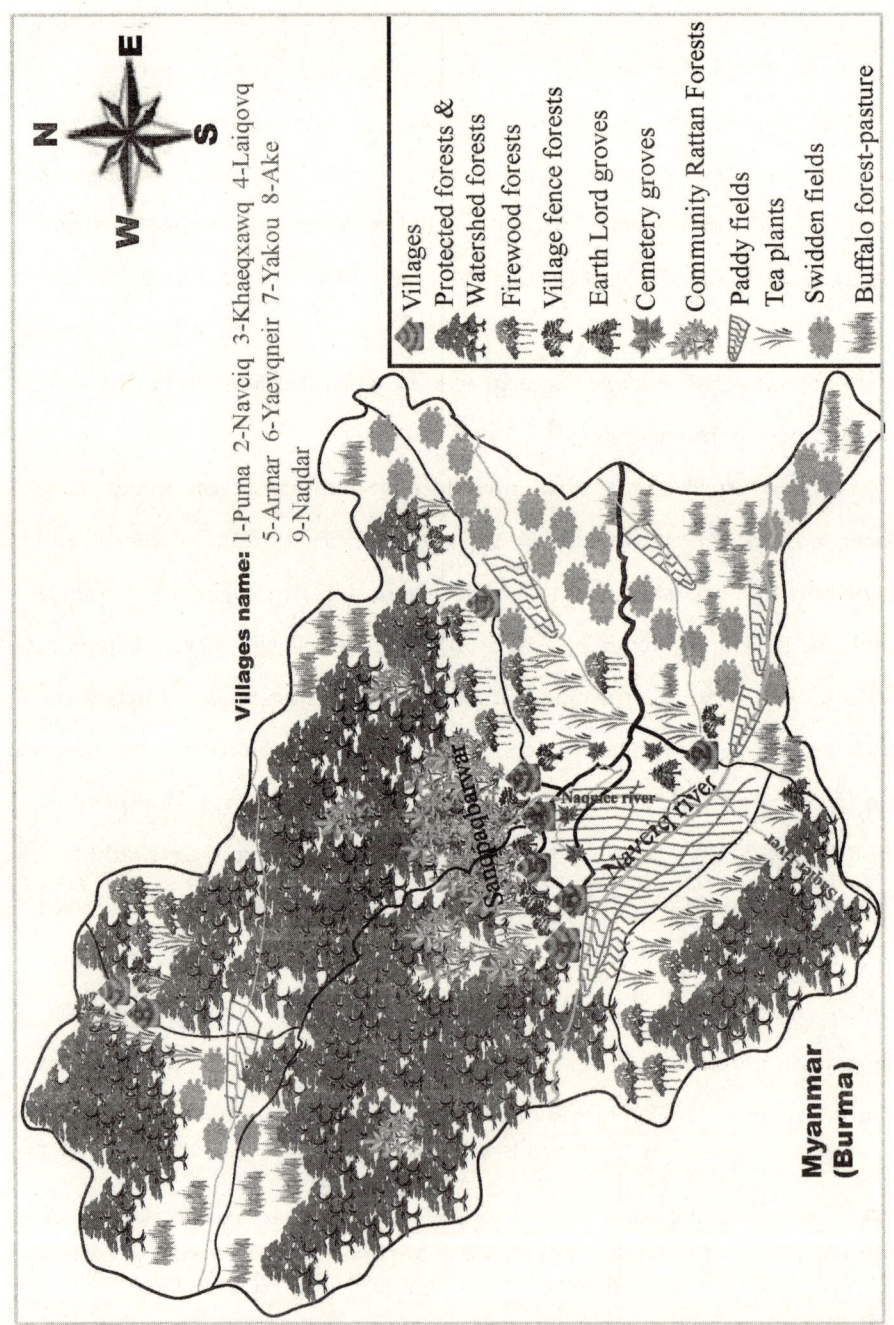

Figure 9 Mengsong Community and Land Use Map Prior to 1950

independent tributary polity participating in some form of galactic polities, particularly during the nineteenth century (65-66). The *pyavqlo* of Mengsong was such an Akha chief who paid tribute to the *cao phaendin* (overlord) of *Sipsongpanna* via the local lord of Damenglong. As long as paying the requested taxes (silver coins) and tributes (in the form of rattan and tea) as well as corvée labor once a year, they were autonomous in the sense that they could decide how to manage their natural resources in the way laid out in Chapter 3. The taxes were moderate and labor was only needed to build and maintain the major road connecting the valley of Sipsongpanna through mountains to the Shan States once a year. But the lord of Sipsongpanna was not the only recipient of tribute and taxies;the Mengsong Akha also needed to offer a bottle of homemade rice liquor to the head of Bulang❶ village, located at lower elevation between Mengsong and Damenglong, because the Bulang villagers were regarded the first dwellers in this area and thus "owners" of the lands where Mengsong villagers conducted their swidden agriculture❷(Sturgeon, 2005: 81-82).

But Mengsong community and their normal lives were changed dramatically when two Chinese Nationalist Army (GMT) companies took over Mengsong in 1937, as Sturgeon (2005) described,

---

❶ The Bulang is a Mon-Khmer speaking group, believed to be one of the earliest dwellers in this region, even before the arrival of the Tai speaking group (s).

❷ When the first ancestors of current Mengong Akha populations arrived at this place, it was a territory of Mansan Bulang village, located roughly 600 meters below Mengsong Basin. They got permission from the Bulang chief to settle down and farm in his territory;in return they had to pay tributes to the Bulang chief to acknowledge this patron-client relationship. Only after the Mengsong Akha community grew substantially and had their own big chief, the lowland Tai lords of Sipsongpanna started to collect taxes and tributes from Mengsong Akha community directly. But, this did not sever the patron-client relationship between the Mansan Bulang and the Mengsong Akha, at least it was maintained symbolically by offering a bottle of homemade liquor by the Mongsong chief to the Bulang chief.

"Nationalist soldiers enlisted Akha farmers as forced laborers to produce grain and vegetables for them...The soldiers also confiscated and slaughtered all Mengsong livestock...The troops further increased local production of opium, which they sold to support themselves."(130)

As a result, a pan-Akha uprising against the Nationalist Army, called *saese se -e* or *aqpoeq se -e* (literally meaning "ancestral renascence" or "ancestors revival"), erupted along the today's Sino-Burman border, in 1942, which caused all Mengsong villagers fled into the jungle to fight. The uprising was suppressed by the Nationalist Army with support from Tai forces the next year. Mengsong villagers returned to their villages gradually by 1945 (Sturgeon, 2005: 130)[1]. These unpleasant experiences with the Nationalist Army (called *Laqbeeq xeer*, "Yellow Chinese", referring to the yellow-green uniform worn by them) paved out a smooth path to welcome the Communist guerrilla, who came to chase the Nationalist Army away from Mengsong in 1950. In this way, Mengsong, along with other parts of Sipsongpanna, which was transliterated as Xishuangbanna in Chinese, was liberated and integrated to the newly established People's Republic of China. The Communist cadres eradicated opium cultivation by 1954 and posted a People's Liberation Army (PLA) company in Mengsong to keep the Nationalists and opium out. The PLA company has been stationed in Mengsong since then and up to the present (Sturgeon, 2005).

Mao Zedong, in a view adopted from the Soviet Union, believed that societies evolve from primitive to slave, feudal, capitalist, and socialist modes of production (Gladney, 1997: 72). All ethnic groups in China were sorted

---

[1] Sturgeon (2005) mentioned Mengsong Akha fled into hiding in the nearby forest, without explaining the reason behind this.

into the various ladderstages according to this evolutionary theory of modes of production. The Akha (as a branch of the Hani Minority Nationality), with their shifting cultivation, were rated at a primitive mode of production; they were seriously "behind" and backward in their social development. Therefore, "[t]he state project, dominated by Han, was then to help Akha farmers learn to be productive and advance into socialist modernity" (Sturgeon, 2005: 27-28).

In this chapter, I will examine how these two sets of landscapes confronted each other; and what are the social, cultural, and ecological consequences of these contests. More specifically, I will do these through examining impacts of some national and local milestone policies from 1950 up to the present. The major policies that will be examined here include the Land Reform Act of P. R. China in 1950, the Commune System under centralized plan in 1957 – 1977 (impacts of two outstanding social and political movements, i. e. , "Great Leap Forward" in 1958 – 1960 and "Great Proletariat Cultural Revolution" in 1966 – 1976, will be discussed here), the Economic System Reform in 1978, the Household Contract Responsibility System in the early 1980s, the Natural Forest Protection Project (also known as "Logging Ban") in 1998, and the Land Conversion Project (also known as "Grain for Green") in 1999. These can be roughly put into three major historical periods of People's Republic of China: period I—Planned Economy Period (1949 – 1977); period II— Reform and Open Stage I (1978 – 1998); and period III—Reform and Open Stage II (1998 – up to today). In terms of rural economic (agricultural) policy, the first period was characterized by the Commune System under the centralized-plan-oriented economy; while the second and third periods are characterized by the Household Contract Responsibility System based on the market-oriented economy. But the difference between the last two is that economic development is the first priority of the national policy in the second period while ecological concerns are put into the agenda of the national development policy in the third period.

4.2　Period I (1949 – 1977)

People's Republic of China passed the Land Reform Act on June 28, 1950[1], according to the evolutionary theory of modes of production. The purpose of the act was to abolish the feudal ownership of land (or means of production) through confiscating arable lands, agricultural tools, labor animals, and even surplus foodstuff from the land lords "*dizhu*" and kulaks "*funong*" and then redistributing them among all farmers ideally within each township. A land reform was accomplished according to the act in most parts of China by 1953. In the meanwhile, China was undertaking a nation-wide Socialist Reform (i.e. Collectivization) of Private Ownership of Means of Production in industries, which was accomplished by 1956. The collectivization of means of production was the fundamental achievement of the "First Five-Year Plan" (1953 – 1957) of P. R. China. As a result, the state and collective economy contributed to 92.9% of the total national income in 1957, compared to 21.3% in 1952[2]. This achievement had paved a path for the Chinese socialist economy under centralized plans. The combination of the exigent desire for changing the poverty-driven China with the ideology of belief in the superiority of socialist mode of production over capitalist and

---

[1] The act is available on the webpage of the Ministry of Agriculture of People's Republic of China's website at http://www.agri.gov.cn/zcfg/t20030624_94255.htm.

[2] Sources come from Xinhua News Agency at http://www.xinhuanet.com/report/16j5zqh/index.htm.

other modes of production, Mao-led new Chinese government launched the "Great Leap Forward" in 1958, claiming that the economy of China would surpass that of the United Kingdom in five years and would catch up with that of the United States in ten years. It was believed by Chairman Mao and some other leaders of China that the nation would accomplish its socialist development in five years before it would move to a communist society. In rural China, Collectivization occurred soon after the Land Reform was finished; and by 1958 most parts of rural China were organized under Commune System, in which all the means of production (e. g. , lands, crops, livestock, fish ponds, forests, etc.), agricultural production activities, and even consumption of the products (e. g. food) were all collectivized in large scale. "The larger the scale was, the greater the commune economy would contribute to the construction of socialist-communist society!" as a slogan says.

With no exception, all the Akha communities in China also became parts of the people's commune system by 1958. Ironically, contrary to the intention to leading the national economy to a take-off, the "Great Leap Forward" movement under the commune system triggered the biggest famine in the history of P. R. China in 1959. Deteriorating situations forced the Chinese government to abort the movement in 1960, but the famine continued until 1962. The famine is referred as the "Great Famine" in China, which caused numerous deaths. it is impossible to know the exact number of the death in the famine as the official data have not been available up to today. The last national disaster during the Planned Economy Period was the "Great Proletariat Cultural Revolution" (1966 – 1976), which destroyed a lot of cultural heritages and traditions of both the majority Han and minority nationalities. It was launched by the central government under the name of "protection of the proletariat government."

The Akha traditional natural resource management system including their swidden agriculture was not significantly affected by the Land Reform as the means of production controlled by those a few rich families were not significant for the Akha economy as a whole[1]. However, the management system was totally dissolved during the "Great Leap Forward" and the "Great Proletariat Cultural Revolution" movements under the commune system. First of all, the Akha traditional land tenure system and ownership system of other resources were abolished. Most natural resources (i. e. swidden lands, forests, etc.) were common properties in traditional Akha communities, while other certain properties such as permanent paddy fields, livestock, tea gardens, bamboo and rattan bushes, and other crops were owned by individual families. All those common and most private properties (e. g. , paddy fields, tea gardens, and big livestock such as water buffaloes, cattle, horses, goats, or even bamboo and rattan bushes) were confiscated and became communal properties in 1958. There is an essential difference between the common and the communal properties. As it is showed in Chapter 3, the common properties (e. g. swidden lands, forests, etc.) were co-managed by the whole community, in which households had the rights to choose where and how much to farm in the allowed swidden lands;and individuals had the rights to choose when and where to hunt and fish, as long as they observe

---

[1] Here I am referring Akha societies in general, where collective ownership of means of production especially arable lands and forests were still prevailing in most Akha communities. There were some Akha areas in which "feudal" economy had been well established and substantial portion of arable lands (particularly irrigated paddy fields) were private properties of a few landlord families such as in Xiding Township where the greatest Akha chief *Pyavqlo Hobym* and his successors resided. In the latter cases, the Land Reform did bring significant impacts on local Akha communities, which forced some of the rich families to flee into Myanmar or even into Thailand during that period of time.

those taboos and regulations agreed by the whole community; and the products generated from those activities still belonged to the households and individuals. On contrary, in the commune system, the political and economic independence of households was totally killed and freedom of individuals was extremely restricted;decisions were made at the central government and orders were sent out from top to down; the whole commune carried out their activities according to the orders from the above; products generated also belonged to the commune, subjected to redistribution of the state. In other words, a commune was a working unit of the state, which was under total control of the state. Therefore, the commune properties were more like the state properties than anything else. Moreover, the Akha land use system based on their sacred ecology was abandoned. As an alternative, "slash-and-burn" agriculture❶ at large scale without observing those Akha land use taboos and regulations was promoted, under the slogan "Requiring Foodstuff from the Uplands" during the "Great Leap Forward" movement. Furthermore, the traditional governing body of the *Dzoeqma* -led Village Elders' Council was replaced with the people's government led by the Communist Party and commune leaders who had no concerns about the environment but cared only about the production.

The whole commune system with the collectivization followed by the "Great Leap Forward" and "Great Proletariat Cultural Revolution" caused

---

❶ Though many people (including scholars) use the terms "swidden agriculture" "shifting cultivation" and "slash-and-burn" interchangeably, I do want to distinguish them in my own way as demonstrated in this dissertation. I use "swidden agriculture" as not only a technological term, but also a cultural term, which refers to a rotational farming (technologically)—rotations of both crops and lands—that is a part of the ecology of sacred landscapes (culturally) with those taboos and rituals described in the Chapter 3. Though "shifting cultivation" is also a both technological and cultural term, it doesnot automatically imply the cyclic nature of the system, and it also often implies "migrating along with their fields". "Slash-and-burn" is just a simple technological term to me.

serious ecological, socio-economic, and cultural consequences to the Akha societies in Xishuangbanna. Ecologically, the local ecosystem was destroyed and local bio-diversity was threatened along with huge deforestations in Xishuangbanna. The large scale "slash-and-burn" agriculture not only destroyed most forbidden ecotopes in the traditional swidden areas, but also extended into the traditional non-farming protected forest areas (i. e. restricted ecotopes). Since the forbidden ecotopes (sacred forests/sites) were regarded "superstitious" and labeled as parts of "Four Olds" (Old Thoughts, Old Culture, Old Traditions, and Old Habits) that needed to be eradicated during the "Great Proletariat Cultural Revolution," many other Akha sacred forests and sites (including cemetery groves, watershed forests, the Earth Lord groves, springs reserved for animals, among others) were destroyed either for agriculture where it was suitable or just for the sake of the movement if the sites were not suitable for agriculture. In fact, all indigenous groups in Xishuangbanna practiced ecology of sacred landscapes and each had their own holy hills or sacred forests. For instance, there were more than 1,000 holy hills/forests preserved by the Dai people in Xishuangbanna, which took up about 5% of its total lands. Similarly, most of these holy hills and sacred forests were destroyed by the "slash-and-burn" agriculture under the revolutionary slogan "launch a battle against ghost mountains (i. e. holy hills);ask foodstuff from sacred forests" during the same time (Gao, 1999; Pei, 1984). Moreover, immeasurable areas of forests in Xishuangbanna and in all over the country were also cut down for the nation-wide movement of steel-making during the "Great Leap Forward," which marks as the most severe deforestation in the history of P. R. China. As a result, big predators like tigers and leopards began coming to prey livestock in the villages at a very high frequency, or even attacking people more often in Xishuangbanna in the

1950s and 1960s since their habitats and natural food chains were destroyed. Baka❶ village unprecedentedly caught eight tigers and leopards in their traps around the village during that period of time. According to the Akha informants I interviewed, most big wild animals such as tigers, leopards, bears, monkeys, deer (except muntjac), and serows had disappeared in most Xishuangbanna areas except in those natural reserves by the end of 1970s. They attribute this to two major reasons: on one hand, a substantial amount of wild animals were killed by the workers of the state farms❷ in their organized hunting; on the other hand, the rest populations had fled to neighboring Burma and Laos as a result of loss of their habitats, destruction of their natural food chains, and threats of human predators in some areas of China.

Socio-economically, Akha people in Xishuangbanna experienced the most serious and longest famine in their history — as far as their cultural memory could remember — during the "Great Leap Forward" in particular and the whole commune period in general. A lot of Akha informants from Mengsong, Baka, and other communities have told me that they dug all possible edible tuberous roots of plants such as *Dioscorea spp.* (or wild yam, *manq* or *arziv* in Akha) and peeled off all barks of certain plants such as *Phyllanthus emblica* (*ciqcaq* in Akha) that they could find in the forests for food during the famine time. In some places like Mengsong, the famine was simply resulted from their failure of producing enough food during the commune period. There were three major reasons. First, too many laborers were sent to build the Mengsong reservoir and the road to Damenglong,

---

❶ Baka is another research site of mine, which will be more elaborated in Chapter 5.

❷ Numerous state farms aiming at rubber tree plantations have been established in Xishuangbanna since 1956, which will be more elaborated in Chapter 5.

which left too few people for agricultural activities. Second, the commune economy did not motivate people to do their best. When people worked and ate together, the reward did not respond to the effort. Third, as the large scale "slash-and-burn" agriculture did not follow the well established ecological rules embedded in those Akha landscapes, it resulted in low yields. In other places like Baka, however, the famine was simply resulted from the failure of redistribution of the commune economy. It happened that there were large areas of fertile forested lands in Baka as it was located at much lower altitude. This allowed the large scale "slash-and-burn" agriculture had very good yields in short terms. Baka commune indeed produced much more grain (rice) than they could consume, and yet most families were starving due to the principle of "allocation according to one's labor❶" (an lao fen pei in Chinese). As most families had more children than adult laborers, they were not redistributed enough food. For instance, there were six children and only two adults (parents) in my family. My family could get foodstuff (mainly rice) only according to two laborers' work, and the food was only enough for half of a year. My father was endlessly weaving baskets during evenings and had been exchanging some rice from some better-off Dai people with the baskets throughout the whole period. My father had made some life-long good Dai friends through these exchanges. My mother of course also dug wild yams off working time from the commune farming, even evenings. I was told that when I was still a baby, my mother was cooking a vegetable soup while holding me. I peed into the cocked soup, but the soup was eaten by my whole family without wasting a drop, because the soup was the only dish

---

❶ Every worker got work points (called *gong fen* in Chinese) according to the work hours and/or amount of work done. Food (rice here) was allocated based on the total work points one made in a year; see detailed description of this system in Janet Sturgeon (2005: 148, 151).

going with rice. I myself remembered this hungry time continuing until 1979 when private farming was allowed again. Ridiculously, most grain produced by the Baka production team (i. e. Baka village) was not redistributed within the team, but expropriated by the state via commune or sent out to other communes like Damenglong where they needed to support brigades with food shortage like Mengsong. Many Mengsong elders told me that they went to transport rice on cattle's back from Baka. It took two whole days by foot one way.

Culturally, almost all Akha cultural traditions or the *ghanrsanrkhovq* were forced to be abandoned for more than two decades and have not been recovered completely since then. The Akha were forbidden to carry out all their traditional cultural festivals, religious practices and agricultural rituals, and even to wear their traditional costumes, because all of these were regarded as time wasting and burdens for the production activities during the "Great Proletariat Great Leap Forward." These were further labeled as parts of "Four Olds" that needed to be eradicated during the "Cultural Revolution". Those who dared to carry on any bit of it would get a severe punishment. Village gates were destroyed and religious apparatus including the ancestor shrines and altars were burned. As a result, the cultural identity (except the language) was erased and the cultural value was suppressed. Though most of the bans have been lifted since the middle 1980s, only one cultural festival among a dozen has been recognized by the local government. When I asked the villagers if they were scared of getting punishment from the ancestral or natural spirits as they were forced to burn the ancestral paraphernalia and destroy those sacred forests and sites. They answered by saying that "of course, we were scared dearly, but if we did not do that, we would get more serious punishment from the Red Guards immediately". But when further asked them that the Communists have taught you there were no spirits in the world and do you believe that, they answered immediately saying that "well, the communist Han Chinese were stronger than the *naevq* (evil spirits); even the *naevq* had surrendered to the communists, we should also obey to them in order to avoid punishment from them". This reminds how the Akha ancestors also represented *Na* and other strong people as *naevq* in the past. Instead of changing it, the Akha explained the new situations according to their existed belief system.

Another effort to increase agricultural yields during commune period was to create more irrigated fields. In Xishuangbanna, this was done through creating a lot of irrigated paddy fields in numerous not-yet-cultivated small valleys or making terraces on hillsides. In order to irrigate these new fields as well as to generate hydropower at some places in mountainous areas of Xishuangbanna, many reservoirs were constructed during commune period. In the meanwhile, a lot of mountain-dwelling villages were ordered to be relocated closer to valleys in order to make and cultivate paddy fields. Many of smaller villages were also ordered to settle down together in order to form larger productive brigades. In Mengsong, besides expanding the existed paddy fields on Mengsong Basin, a lot of terraces were made on hillsides, though many of them were abandoned as the soil was not suitable for irrigation (the soil was too loose to hold water and landslides could not be prevented if irrigation was applied). The road connected Mengsong and Damenglong was completed in 1964. A small hydropower station was established in Mengsong in 1965. But soon Mengsong decided to build a bigger one, so Mengsong Reservoir started to be built in 1970 and finished in 1978 with a new hydropower station. In Baka, another research site of mine, many paddy fields were made at three valleys along three rivulets in lowlands: *Saergevr*,

Khaqsaer, and *Ngaqbovq* in the 1950s and 1960s. According to the resettlement policy, Baka village was ordered to be relocated and to form Baka production team with *Gawqghor Nyadzanq* village at *Baqnor* by *Saergevr* River in 1967. The resettlement forced Baka village to abandon their paddy fields created along *Ngaqbovq* River because the distance was too far away from the new location. In order to make more paddy fields, a decision was made to build a dam across *Saerge* vr River and the work started in 1968. Since Bayi Reservoir (Baka was renamed as Bayi in 1958 until the end of commune system) was going to flood some parts of *Baqnor*, Bayi production team moved to today's location in 1971. *Bayi* Reservoir flooded 70 *mu* of Baka's paddy fields along *Saetgevr* Village when the dam was completed in 1976. It was intended to irrigate 50 *mu* ● Baka paddy fields at *Dawqgee* and 100 *mu* at *Laersaq Dzanrtav*, but the latter was, more often than not, out of irrigation due to lack of water. Therefore, it is ironical that Baka Village actually lost 20 *mu* of irrigated paddy fields due to the construction of the reservoir. Though ecological impacts of the dam need to be evaluated through more studies, it is sure that the migratory route of the biggest fish (called *Ngaqbolo* in Akha) in *Saergevr* River has been blocked by the dam. The fish needs migrating upward for the purpose of reproduction. Since it was impossible for Baka Village to choose a culturally and ecologically appropriate place for its new location, Baka Village has been unrooted from its cultural landscapes of sacred ecology through the resettlement. A long term consequence of the resettlement, therefore, is that loss of traditional ecological knowledge, cultural identity and value attached to sacred landscapes is more serious among the Akha in resettled communities like Baka than the ones in old settlements like Mengsong.

● *Mu* is a unit of area in China. 15 *mu* equals to one hectare.

4.3　Period II (1978–1998)

Failure of the commune/collective economic system under the centralized plan has forced the Deng Xiaoping-led Chinese government to carry out a series of reform and opening policy since 1978, particularly the Economic System Reform in 1978. The purpose of the reform is to gradually replace the planned economy with marke-toriented economy. Even though China's rural reform did not start until the early 1980s, the wind of the reform and opening policy did flow into rural areas immediately, allowing commune members to carry out some private economic activities since 1979. Because of this milieu, besides accomplishing the assigned commune productive activities, most Akha commune members in Xishuangbanna were also allowed to cultivate private rice plots on the so called "Zi liu di" (free-holding fields) or "waste uplands" if there was no "Zi liu di" in 1979. Thanks to these private cultivations, most Akha people in Xishuangbanna liberated from the two-decade long starvation in that year. This kind of experiment was nationwide and its positive result encouraged the Deng-led second generation of Chinese Communist leaders to carry out a nationwide rural reform in the early 1980s. The purpose of this rural reform was to liberate the force of production in agricultural sector of China without jeopardizing collective ownership of means of production (particularly lands). It was achieved through allocation of commune farming lands and other means of production (e. g., livestock, etc.) among its member households proportionally according to its population size under a contract system called "Jiating Lianchan Chengbao Zeren Zhi, that is, the Household Contract Responsibility System. A dual tenure system is practiced here, in which the ownership and use rights of the lands are separated. The ownership is till collective, the lands cannot be sold. However, the households were granted the free use rights of the contracted lands including leasing out during the contract period. In return, the households need to pay annual taxes to the state in a form of grains and in a form of cash proportionally to the community (the land owner) according to the size of the contracted lands. The contract period was set for 15 years in 1984, but was amended for 30 years in 1993.

Not only agricultural but also forestry lands were allocated among households in a commune under the Household Contract Responsibility System. In China, forestry lands are classified into two categories: forested lands (called "you lin di" in Chinese) that are covered by trees (forests) and waste uplands (called "huang shan"❶ in Chinese) that are covered by bushes and grasses. According to Chinese forestry policy, there are only two kinds of ownership: the state and the community (or collective). But during the commune period, the demarcation was not clear, nor the tenure system and responsibility. Therefore, the purpose of the forestry reform was to stabilize ("Wen Ding" in Chinese) forest tenure system; demarcate ("Hua Ding" in Chinese) state and collective forestry lands; and clarify ("Que Ding" or "Ming Que" in Chinese) the forestry responsibility system. In other words, the purpose of the forestry reform was to clarify the rights (ownership and use right), responsibilities, and benefits of the state, communities, and households in the management of national forestry. Therefore, the forestry reform is also

---

❶ In Chinese, "shan" literally means "mountain" or "hill". Since most China's forests exist on mountains, in Chinese forestry vocabulary, the term "shan" is often used to refer to forestry lands, including forested lands and waste uplands (bush or grass lands). Since a dual tenure system is practiced in China, in which ownership of the land and that of the trees are separated, the land ownership is termed "shan quan" while the trees ownership is termed "lin quan".

known as "Lin Ye San Ding". Here "Lin Ye" means "forestry"; "San" means "three" and "San Ding" refers to "stabilizing" "demarcating", and "clarifying". Another part of the forestry reform was to distribute or contract out a substantial portion of community-owned forestry lands to each household according to their population size within each community or commune. These forestry lands are identified in three categories: "Zi liu shan" (i. e., freehold forested lands, allocated), "Ze ren shan" (i. e., responsible waste uplands, contracted), and "Lun xie di" (i. e., rotational farming lands, contracted). So, this part of the forestry reform is also often referred as "Liang Shan Yi Di"❶. First, the rotational farming lands (i. e. lun xie di) are sorted out as agricultural lands from forestry lands❷; second, "Ze ren shan" was designed to develop household-based forestry, but in Xishuangbanna's mountainous areas where its traditional economy was based on swidden agriculture, almost all "Ze ren shan" was identified and/or used as "Lun xie di". The total contracted area of "Lun xie di" (i. e., rotational farming lands) in Xishuangbanna was 1,447,800 mu (equals to 96,520 hectares) in the early 1980s, which took up 5% of its total lands (Forestry Bureau of Xishuangbanna Prefecture, 2000).

Let us examine the impacts of this rural reform on the Akha natural resource management in Mengsong community (please see dynamics of land

---

❶ "Liang" means two, "Yi" means one, "Shan" refers to the forestry lands, "Di" refers to the rotational farming lands.

❷ This will be reconverted back to forestry lands later by the "Land Conversion Project" (i. e., "tui geng huan lin" in Chinese, literally meaning "returning farming lands back to forests") in 1998.

uses in Mengsong in Appendix VI). In Mengsong[1], *Sangpaqbarwar* (the community rattan forest) and other watershed forests became state forests, while the rest forests particularly those traditional tea forests were allocated as collective forests ("Ji ti lin" in Chinese) and household forests ("Zi liu shan" in Chinese) among those six Akha villages around the Mengsong Basin. Each village was allocated a collective forest, which would produce house construction timbers for the villagers. Each household was also allocated a 5 *mu* [2] forests as self-held forests (Zi liu shan) which would provide firewood for the household. Each village's traditional tea trees were also allocated among its households according to its population size. However, a very complicated forestry tenure system was established by the forestry reform. Remember that all these forests belonged to the whole community (including those six villages) as common properties, while traditional tea trees were dispersed in the forests as households' private properties prior to the Commune System. During the commune period, a production team was formed based on a natural village as a basic productive unit, called "Shengchan xiao dui", while the whole Mengsong community formed a production brigade called "Shengchan da dui". Accordingly, all these private properties of a natural village were pooled together to form the common properties of the production team; while those community common properties became the brigade's properties. Therefore, when it came to the

---

[1] Here, I will particularly talk about the six traditional Akha villages around Mengsong Basin. As a side note, a proportion of Mengsong populations split to form another six new hamlets in 1980, just after the commune was dissolved but before the lands were allocated among households. More specifically, *Tsaqla* split from *Hongqi*, *Burbar* split from *Guangming*, *Huida* split from *Hongxing*, *Buqjaq* split from *Dazhai*, *Naqyoq* and *Longqiu* split from *Dongfanghong*. All of these new hamlets were relocated outside of Mengsong Basin at lower elevations. The first two still belong to Mengsong Administrative Village, while the other four belong to Mansan Administrative Village today.

[2] 5 *mu* = 0.33 hectare.

forestry and agricultural reform in the early 1980s, each natural village allocated its collective forests and household forests according to its population and regardless of the traditional boundary of natural Villages; but tea trees were allocated among the households within a natural village, more or less according to traditional tenure system. This resulted in that a household's tea trees could be located in other villages' collective and households' forests as well as state forests. For instance, Dongfanghong village's tea trees are dispersed in all those six villages' collective and households' forests as well as the state forests. Because of this complicated situation, while the collective and households' forests were granted land and forest titles, the traditional tea trees were not. In other words, the new forestry tenure system has overwritten the traditional one *de jure* where the latter is still practiced *de facto*. This has not only caused a lot of conflicts between households and households, households and villages (may be own or other village) in management of the forests and the tea trees, but also made these conflicts unsolvable in both theory and practice. For instance, tea trees of 21 households from Xianfeng Village are located in Dazhai Village's household freeholding forests. Among which nine Xianfeng households have conflicts with those of Dazhai due to the reason that the former's tea trees were cut by the latter when they (the latter) cut firewood in their own forests. None of these conflicts have been satisfactorily settled because mediation within the community respects traditional tenure system while those of outside the community (including the Damenglong Township Government as well as Damenglong Court) tend to respect only the official tenure system and neglect the traditional one. These conflicts have become sharpened since 2004 when the market price of the tea soared up to sky, which culminated in an arson on October 2, 2007.

Moreover, allotment of tea trees as well as paddy fields among households within the production team (i. e. a natural village) confirmed the economic differentiation among the six villages created from uneven poppy opium cultivation and trade as mentioned in Chapter 3 (see Table 5). For instance, households from Dongfanghong Village got about two times of tea trees per capita and about three times of irrigated paddy fields per capita than those of Hongqi Village. As a general rule that lack of irrigated paddy fields should be compensated by uplands (i. e. , lun xie di, or rotational farming lands, or swidden lands here), villagers from Hongqi got the biggest proportion of swidden lands per capita among these six villages. Since it requires more labor input for rice cultivation in upland and swidden fields than for irrigated paddy fields (Wang, 1998), swidden agriculture dominated Hongqi villagers are more bound by subsistence activities; plus lack of capital accumulation, partially resulted from their lesser possession of major cash crop tea trees, makes them restricted from other business investments. All these factors have put Hongqi villagers in a very disadvantaged position under the market-oriented economy. Therefore, Hongqi is still the poorest village as it was in the 1940s among the six villages. In contrast, due to their special locations, both Dazhai and Xianfeng have gained a lot of cash income from mining operation and management since the late 1980s (Sturgeon, 2005), though they have fewer tea trees in terms of per capita than any other villages. Also, Dazhai is located at the political (administrative office), commercial (market and shop), educational (school), serving (hotel and restaurant), and entertaining (Karaoke, etc.) center of Mengsong area, which provides a lot of business to its villagers. These have allowed Dazhai and Xianfeng to catch up with Dongfanghong in terms of wealth accumulation and become among the richest villages with their new money in Mengsong.

Table 5 Forest and Land Distribution among Households in Mengsong under the Household Contract Responsibility System in the Early 1980s

Village name	Household forest (mu/household)	Tea trees (mu/capita)	Irrigated paddy fields (mu/capita)	Swidden lands (mu/capita)
Guangming	5	1.2	1.2	6
Hongxing	5	1.1	1.6	6
Dongfanghong	5	1.6	2.2	3
Hongqi	5	0.8	0.9	9
Dazhai	5	0.2	1.4	6
Xianfeng	5	0.6	1.1	6

Note:

1. The number of tea tree is calculated based on data from Mengsong Annual Statistical Book (2007). The absolute number of tea trees is not correct. According to Mr. Lao Er, the official head of Mengsong Administrative Village in 2008, there were about 5,000 mu old tea trees but the whole population of Mengsong was less than 2,500 in the early 1980s, which should give us average tea trees of over 2 mu per capita. It was not only because that it was very difficult to measure, but also because that the tea trees were not granted official title of ownership, in order to reduce any real or potential taxes, the official data tend to be lower. But the proportion is relatively reliable.

2. Since the paddy fields could be more accurately measured and land title was granted, the data was more accurate.

3. Different key informants (community leaders as well as village heads) gave me different data on swidden lands. This number was based on a rule of thumb in allocatement of swidden lands (i.e., lun xie di) that in a village where there was less than 1 mu of irrigated paddy fields per capita, it should be given about 9 mu of swidden lands per capita; if there was more than 2 mu of paddy fields per capita, the number of swidden lands should be no more than 3 mu per capita; if the paddy fields was between 1 and 2 mu per capita, the number of swidden lands should be about 6 mu per capita. In reality, most households in all these villages got more swidden lands than this quota.

Furthermore, land distribution pattern under the Household Contract Responsibility System — alongwith the market-oriented economy — has accelerated the pace of ending swidden agriculture in Mengsong (and in Xishuangbanna), because the system has not only demarcated swidden lands (i.e., lun xie di) within limited areas, but also frozen the fluidity of the lands within and beyond the community. Population growth is often regarded as a key factor that leads swidden agriculture to its end at historical stage; however, this is not the case in Mengsong. First, about 25,000 mu lands (mostly traditional swidden lands) were identified as "guoyou huangshan" or state wastelands (part of forestry lands), which is bigger than the total area of contracted lun xie di or rotational farming lands❶ in Mengsong. This has limited swidden agriculture in a much smaller area, though it should be enough to have a healthy rotation (ecologically) for swidden agriculture if it would have allocated more lands reasonably. According to our previous studies (Wang, 1998), an ecologically healthy rotational period is about 10 – 12 years in Xishuangbanna if the lands are cropped no longer than two continuous years, which allows about 8 – 10 years of fallow. If there is no irrigated paddy field, it usually requires about 3 – 4 mu upland to produce enough food (particularly rice) for one person each year. If each plot is cultivated for 2 years averagely, a 10-year rotation requires about 15 – 20 mu uplands per capita. However, since there are irrigated paddy fields, Mengsong does not require that amount of uplands for their swidden agriculture being in a healthy rotation. In fact, Dongfanghong villagers do not need to cultivate upland rice at all. Xianfeng villagers also converted parts of their swidden lands into irrigated paddy fields through terracing, and gradually stopped swidden agriculture by the mid 1990s (Sturgeon, 2005). Because of economical benefits from other activities including mining, most Dazhai villagers also gradually stopped swidden agriculture. This led to the abandonment of much of their swidden lands and thus, by the late 1990s, it was estimated that there were about 3,000 mu of swidden lands and regenerated forests. In contrast, paddy-field-deficient Hongqi Village had been experiencing shortage of uplands

---

❶ If we calculate the total area of Mengsong *lun xie di* using 9 mu per capita times by 2,500 (population), we get 22,500 *mu*.

while their economy was still based on swidden agriculture. It is evident that most Hongqi swidden lands had been operated with a fallow period shorter than 8 years by the late 1990s (Wang, 1998). Shortage of uplands is also a key factor for Baka villagers to abandon swidden agriculture in the 1990s (which will be elaborated in Chapter 5). However, the vital policy that ends swidden agriculture in Mengsong and Xishuangbanna is the Logging Ban in 1998, which will be discussed in the following section.

4.4　Period Ⅲ (1998—up to date)

The great flood of Yangtze River (and other major rivers of China) in summer of 1998 urged China to enact a nationwide logging ban. Shifting cultivation or swidden agriculture was banned along with the logging ban because the ban forbids cutting any natural trees including the fallow fields of the swidden lands. In order to help both loggers as well as upland farmers become forest curators without jeopardizing their economic benefits from it, two twin projects were initiated: Natural Forest Protection Project ("Tianranlin Baohu Gongcheng" in Chinese) and Land Conversion Project ("Tui Geng Huan Lin Gongcheng" in Chinese) in late 1998. The purpose of the Natural Forest Protection Project is to protect the national natural forests through logging ban as well as to increase forest coverage through reforestation. This project has been conducted in upstream of Yangtze River [covering Hubei, Chongqi, Guichou, Yunnan, Sichuan, and Xizang (Tibet) provinces and regions], middle-and-up-stream of Yellow River (covering Henan, Neimeng/Inner Mongol, Shanxi, Shaanxi, Ningxia, Gansu, and Qinghai provinces and regions), and other state natural forest located areas (including Xinjiang, Northeastern Inner Mongol, Heilongjiang, Jilin, and Hainan provinces and regions) since 1999. It covers 69% of the national natural forests, that is, 1.1 billion mu (about 73.3 million hectares) out of 1.7

billion mu (about 113.3 million hectares). All commercial logging of natural forests have been banned in these areas as those previous logging companies and workers were compensated for their loss from the ban by the state funding (80% from the central government and 20% from its corresponding provincial governments) (State Forestry Bureau of China, 1998; Zhou, 2000).

The purpose of the Land Conversion Project is to decrease soil erosion through converting deeper sloping farming lands into forests or grasslands with compensation/subsidy from government. The lands can be converted to either ecological or economic forests. For 1 mu of reforestation on farming lands, it is said to be compensated with 150kg husked grain (particularly rice) in southern parts of China, or with 100kg husked grain (such as wheat) in northern China per year, and subsidized with another 30 − 50 Chinese Yuan per year as educational and healthy welfare. It is said to be compensated/subsidized continuously for 8 years for ecological forests or 5 years for economic forests. Thus, this project is also known as "Grain for Green" project. In case the grain is given to the farmers in a form of cash, the change rate is based on the equation of 1 kg grain equals to 0.7 Chinese Yuan (i.e., the average market price of grain in 2000) (State Office of Land Conversion Project, 2000), which gives 210 Chinese Yuan per mu per year. This project has been conducted in 25 provinces and regions (including Yunnan) since 2000.

Though it is not in the Yangtze River region, Xishuangbanna is still identified as a key target area for these two projects in Yunnan due to its ecological significance mentioned in chapter 1. The Natural Forest Protect Project was started in Xishuangbanna in 1998. It is reported that in its first eight years phase, the project had successfully protected 17 million mu (about 1.13 million ha) of existing natural forests as well as regenerated about 1.79 million mu (about 119,285 ha) forests through various reforestation activities (see Table 6 and Figure 10), which make up 59.3% and 6.2% of its total

Table 6 Xishuangbanna Natural Forest Protect Project (1998 – 2006)

Project Activities / Counties		Mengla County	Jinghong City	Menghai County	Total area (mu)
Reforestation (mu)	Plantation (mu)	35,950.0	26,600.0	86,017.5	148,567.5
	Broadcast sowing by aircrafts (mu)	21,000.0	35,999.0	26,012.0	83,011.0
	Promoted natural regeneration (mu)	46,200.0	52,704.5	53,556.0	152,460.5
	Managed natural reforestation (mu)	15,075.0	18,240.0	16,324.5	49,639.5
	Natural reforestation (mu)	379,930.0	319,920.0	655,739.5	1,355,589.5
	Subtotal (mu)	498,155.0	453,463.5	837,649.5	1,789,268.0
Protected natural forests (mu)		6,690,000.0	5,830,000.0	4,480,000.0	17,000,000.0
Total area (mu)		7,188,155.0	6,283,463.5	5,317,649.5	18,789,268.0

Data sources for Table 6 and Table 7:

1. Data of Mengla County are from Forestry Bureau of Mengla County, available at its official website: http://www. mlly. gov. cn/.

2. Data of Jinghong Municipality are from Forestry Bureau of Jinghong Municipality, available at its official website: http://www. jhsly. gov. cn/.

3. Data of Menghai County are from official website of Yunnan Digital Rural at http://ynszxc. gov. cn/szxc/.

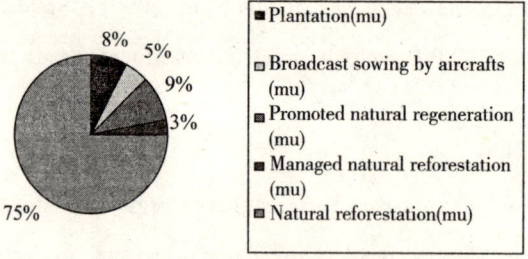

Figure 10 Xishuangbanna Reforestarion in the Natural Forest Protect Project (1998 – 2006)

lands in Xishuangbanna respectively. If what had been claimed were true, the project should have increased Xishuangbanna's forest coverage by about 6.2%. Plus 59.3% existed natural forests and about 12% plantations (conservative estimation of rubber, tea and other plantation areas),

Xishuangbanna's forest coverage should be about 77.5% by now. However, it is reported that the figure is about 67.69% ❶ in 2008 (State Forestry Administration, P. R. China, 2008). The same report also says that the net increased forests area in Xishuangbanna through reforestation of the project is about 970,000 mu (about 64,667 ha), which has increased its forest coverage by 4%, and is less than what they had claimed earlier. Therefore, though achievement of the project is positive, the amount of the reforestation as well as its ecological benefits may not be as great as have been claimed. Part of the reason is that, in reality, the same areas may be claimed by different projects, as in a case in Mengsong, a site set up for natural reforestation area in the project was picked up as a site for the land conversion project too (see Picture 13).

Picture 13   A Site of the Natural Forest Protect Project at Mengsong, Damenglong Township, Jinghong City.

---

❶   This number includes all mono-cultural plantations of rubber, tea, Chinese fir, etc.

The sign reads: "Jinghong City 2002 Natural Forest Protect Project: Natural Reforestation Area". But later, the area also became the Land Conversion Project target area, under which tea plantation has been conducted since 2004.

Though the Land Conversion Project was initiated in 1998, it was not carried out in Xishuangbanna until 2002. Since shifting cultivation was banned, the project was designed to convert 1,337,943 *mu* (89,196 ha) sloping uplands into forests in Xishuangbanna, which took up 92.4% of its total swidden lands (Forestry Bureau of Xishuangbanna Prefecture, 2000). However, due to the limited budget, there were only 90,000 mu of converted farming lands plus 89,000 mu of reforested wastelands which had been subsidized in the project from 2002 through 2006 (see Table 7). Similarly, though almost all wastelands in Mengsong (about 25,000 *mu*) and 80% swidden lands of Mengsong (about 18,000 *mu*) were cultivated with tea under the influence of the land conversion project, only 4,940 mu of tea plantations were identified and subsidized by the project.

Table 7 Xishuangbanna Land Conversion Project (2002—2006)

	Reforestation on farming lands (mu)	Reforestation on wastelands (mu)	Ecological forests (mu)	Economic forests (mu)	Total areas (mu)
Mengla County	33000	22000	54000	1000	55000
Jinghong City	25000	25000	47000	3000	50000
Menghai County	32000	42000	61325.8	12674.2	74000
Total area (mu)	90000	89000	162325.8	16674.2	179000
Percentage (%)	50.28	49.72	90.68	9.32	

Notes: Major species include
In Mengla:rubber, tea, teak, Neolamarckia cadamba, Chinese fir (Cunninghamia lanceolata), Betula alnoides, Simao pine (Pinus kesiya), and bamboo
In Jinghong:tea, Chinese fir, Neolamarckia cadamba, and Simao pine
In Menghai:tea, rubber, Chinese fir, bamboo, among others

(Data source see Table 6)

The initial purpose of these two projects along with the logging ban was to achieve ecological goals in the targeted areas, but in their implementations, they became market-economy oriented, which was reflected in the species used for reforestation (or plantation) in the projects (see Table 7). Main species used in the plantations of the Land Conversion Project are rubber, tea, and Chinese fir, which are economic species. Yet about 90.7% of the plantations are identified as ecological forests. Though in theory the ecological and economic forests should be defined according to 1) the species of plants used in reforestation; 2) planting density; 3) planting techniques; and 4) its purpose (ecology-oriented or economy-oriented) (State Forestry Administration of P. R. China, 2001), in practice only the planting density is applied to identify them. I was told by the project personnel from Forestry Bureau of Xishuangbanna Prefecture that ecological forests require to plant 100 trees or more per *mu*. In case of rubber plantations, since one *mu* land can be planted only less than 40 trees, a leguminous species *Cajanus cajan* are intercropped in order to meet the ecological criterion (see Picture 14). *Cajanus cajan* plants are leguminous bushes that will die out naturally in a few years. However, the ecological benefits of the project have been jeopardized by the way it was conducted. For instance, there were already 3,000 mu naturally reforested swidden lands in Mengsong prior to the project. These lands should be regarded as "converted" forests and the owners should be compensated for the loss of their farming lands or rewarded for their contribution to nurturing ecological forests, but in practice, the only way for them to get benefits from the project was to follow the standardized procedure, which includes cleaning the fields and planting tea trees (or other identified species) with standardized techniques (see Picture 15). When I asked the reason from the project authorities and personnel, they answered that

Sacred and Contested Landscapes

people's livelihood and economic development (here refers to cash income) should be put at first priority in the government's agenda, therefore, economic species should be used in the reforestation and the best result in terms of production should be guaranteed by the standardized techniques (i. e., clearing, burning, ditching, etc.). But what we faced was an ecological crisis, ecological measures should be our first priorities, or at least needed to be balanced with economic and social concerns. These standardized techniques may optimize economic benefits of the reforestation, but would minimize its ecological benefits, because the best ecological benefits of afforestation and reforestation could be achieved on degraded lands with natural regeneration and native species, and minimal clearing of pre-existing vegetation (cf. Murray, 2006). Since the Land Conversion Project in particular and the government in general favor economic benefits over ecological ones, the natural vegetation of almost all "wastelands" and understory of most state, collective and households' forests in Mengsong have been or are going to be replaced with tea plantations (see Picture 16, Picture 17 and Picture 18).

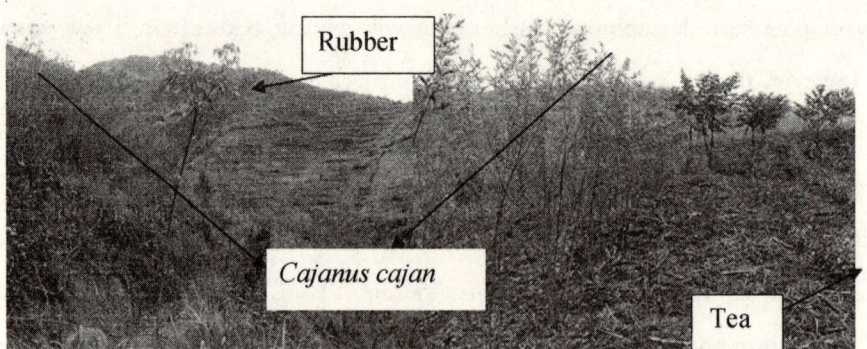

Picture 14　Both Rubber (Above Left) and Tea (Above Right) Plantations are Identified as Ecological Forests Since They are Intercropped with*Cajanus cajan* .

Chapter 4 From Swidden Agriculture to Cash Crop Monoculture

Picture 15 The Land Conversion Project in Mengsong I (Above Left)
(Naturally Reforested Fallow Lands were Cleaned for Tea Plantation in order to Get Subsidy)
Picture 16 The Land Conversion Project in Mengsong II (Above Right)
(Naturally Vegetated Wastelands were Cleaned for Tea and
Chinese Fir Plantations in order to Get Subsidy)

Picture 17 Freehold Household Forests were Cleaned for Tea Plantation under
the Influence of Land Conversion Project in Mengsong (Above Left)
Picture 18 Understorey of the State Forests in Mengsong Cleaned
for Tea Plantation (Above Right)

4.5 Other Activities in Mengsong

Besides the policies discussed above, there are several government sponsored or approved activities that have social, economic, and ecological impacts on Mengsong. These activities include, but are not limited to, dam construction, mining, a rattan weaving factory, and logging. Mengsong is one of several key water sources to irrigate lowland paddy fields on Damenglong

Basin. Therefore, Jinghong City government decided to build a dam on *Navciq* River in Mengsong (Picture 19 and Picture 20). Long term ecological and economic consequences of the dam construction to local community were not clear. What was sure is that the reservoir was going to submerge 130 *mu* (about 8.7 hectares) of paddy fields, over 3000 *mu* (200 hectares) of collective forests, and about 15,000 tea trees in the forests[1] (Picture 21 and Picture 22). Though the government promised that all of the loss would be compensated and that the project would not start until all of the investigation and estimation of the loss (especially the tea trees) and agreement on the compensation by all stakeholders were accomplished, still, the government started the project before all of those conditions were fulfilled in 2007. This led to tensions between the local community and the government/project. Since the collective forests were titled, compensation for them seemed to be more secure; but those tea trees had not been granted titles, therefore, compensation for these tea trees was not secure. As mentioned earlier, ownership of these tea trees were not acknowledged by the government officially, so the government usually favors the forest owners over tea tree owners when a dispute between them needs to be mediated. Negotiation on the compensation between the community and local government continued up to 2008 when I finished my field work[2].

Another environmental threatening factor in Mengsong is mining activities. Tin and manganese mining had destroyed some paddy fields and forests in the 1980s and 1990s (also see Sturgeon, 2005). Both of these are forbidden now. But kaolin mining is under operation (Picture 23 and Picture 24). Since strip mining technique has been adopted, not only all trees as well as topsoil of mining sites have been stripped, but also have downstream paddy fields been threatened

---

[1] These figures were provided by Mr. *Lawqer*, the official head of Mengsong Administrative Village in 2008.
[2] I was informed that the reservoir was finished on June 28, 2012.

Chapter 4　From Swidden Agriculture to Cash Crop Monoculture

Picture 19　Mengsong Dam Construction Site (Above Left)
Picture 20　Navciq River on Which Mengsong Dam will be Built (Above Right)

Picture 21　150 *mu* of Paddy Fields and 3000mu Forests will Be Submerged by the New Mengsong Reservoir (Above left)
Picture 22　It is Estimated that about 15,000 Tea Trees in the Forests will Be Submerged Too (Above Right)

Picture 23　A Kaolin Mining Factory in Mengsong (Above Left)
Picture 24　A Kaolin Mining Site Used to be Covered by Forests. The Trees and Topsoil were All Striped in order to Mine Kaolin (Above Right)

(Picture 25 and Picture 26). Though the kaolin mining company had obtained permission from the Environmental Protection Bureau (EPB) of Jinghong City, Mengsong leaders and villagers have doubted the company's and the bureau's de

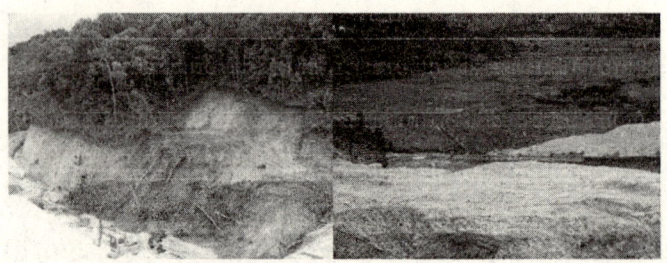

Picture 25 A Land Slide Occurred at a Kaolin Mining Site (Above left)
Picture 26 Kaolin Mining is Threatening Paddy Fields (Above Right)

facto measures for protecting Mengsong's environment/forests and arable lands. Mengsong leaders also think the mining company should pay its environment protection fee to Mengsong community, not to the EPB, because it is not the EPB but Mengsong community who protected its environments and who will also suffer from the degradation caused by the mining.

Local governments, particularly Damenglong Township Government, are also responsible for depletion of bio-resources (particularly rattan) and degradation of forests in Mengsong. In order to promote enterprises in rural areas, Damenglong Township Government established a rattan weaving factory in Mengsong in 1986. However, since profits in market economy were emphasized, rattan sources in *Sangpaqbarwar* that had been conserved by Mengsong community for over 150 years were depleted in six years of mismanagement by the government sponsored factory after it was established. The rattan weaving factory was forced to move out of Mengsong in 1992. Many outsiders (mostly Dai people from lowlands) also came to log in Mengsong forests with logging permission granted by the Damenglong Forestry Station, as they were identified as state forests in the early 1980s and therefore were subject to regulation of the forestry agency. It was stopped for a few years after the logging ban in 1998, but resumed in recent years. These logging activities have degraded the quality of the state forests in Mengsong. Mengsong villagers think it is unfair to allow outsiders to log in Mengsong without any compensation for them. Though they were identified as state forests in the early 1980s, the forests have been conserved by Mengsong community for centuries.

4.6　Conclusion

The Mengsong Akha community has never lived in an isolated milieu since its first forebears settled down in the area. Mengsong Akha acknowledged the patronage of the Mansan Bulang chief by paying tribute to him; and this initial relationship had been maintained even after the Mengsong Akha chief's territory surpassed that of the Mansan chief and the former was requested to pay tributes to the lowland Tai lords. This more or less harmonious or peaceful inter-tribal or inter-chieftain relationship was possible because they had occupied different environmental niches of the area; in other words, they did not really compete over the resources, at least in the early stage of Mengsong Akha settlement and development. The Mansan Bulang chief even regarded the Mengsong Akha chief as a potential ally in case of need to defend against the stronger lowland Tai lords. Both the Mansan and the Mengsong should be understood as more or less independent chiefdoms that participated in the network of larger galactic polities through paying tributes to the lords of Sipsongpanna. The specific location of Mengsong, with a 300 hectare flat basin at very high altitude (about 1,600 meters above sea level) was the material basis for the formation of a supra-village polity for the Akha in Mengsong. It was regarded too high and too cold for agriculture by both the Bulang and the Tai people. In addition, Mengsong Basin was covered by very dense, almost primitive forests when the first Mengsong forebears arrived. Both conditions combined created an ideal peripheral space to both the Bulang and the Tai, which allowed the Akha to create an ideal homeland according to their worldview and manage it according to their ancestor's tradition *ghanrsanrkhovq*, without much external intervention prior to 1937. Therefore, the Mengsong Akha community and their traditional resource management system described in Chapter 3 presents a typical and yet an untypical case of a traditional Akha society; it is typical in the sense that it was created and managed according to the ancestral traditions *ghanrsanrkhovq* shared by all the traditional Akha societies, and same type of society and landscapes were prescribed by the cultural traditions (Tooker, 1988, 2012; Sturgeon, 2005); at the same time, it is untypical because the environments, bio-physical and social-political, in which the type of society and its landscapes created in a reality, were contingent historically and not common if not unique geographically throughout the Akha villages in Zomia[1]. Internally, Mengsong needed a supra-village chief to regulate some vital common resources such as rattan in *Sanqpaqbarwar* and water to irrigate the paddy fields as well as to conduct communal level ceremonies[2], particularly after the community split into several independent villages with its own *dzoeqma*. Externally, the lowland Tai lords needed a big chief to supervise the appointed village heads who could be the old *dzoeqma*s or different figures, to collect and submit taxes and tributes for them. Therefore, I argue that the emergence of the Mengsong great chief, who was granted the title of *pyavqlo* by the Tai lords of Sipsongpanna, was a result from need to regulate a dual political system comprised of the *dzoeqma*-led Village Elders' Council and the *jawrbavr-naqngeq* system.

The invasion of the Nationalist Army in 1937, however, had forcefully

---

[1] A similar case should be the supra-village chief *Sam pa* described by Sir Henri Roux (1924) in Northern Laos. I was also informed by elders from Doichang Village, Chiang Rai, Thailand, that a similar big chiefdom was established on Loimi Mountain in Eastern Shan State.

[2] An example was the annual offering to the Earth Goddess, Sky God, and Water God at communal level at their communal Earth Lord grove, *Jeiqjeiqma*.

intervened the established social structure and its productive system through extreme extractions and exploitation (Sturgeon, 2005); and it led to a strong response by a pan-Akha uprising under the name of ancestor revival or resurgence (*aqpoeq se-e*) in this region from 1942 to 1943. These extremely unpleasant experiences with the Nationalist Army paved the path to welcome the Communist guerrillas who chased the former out of Mengsong first, and the Communist cadres who eradicated opium cultivation by 1954 and posted a People's Liberation Army (PLA) company in Mengsong to keep the Nationalists and opium out.

In the meanwhile, their ancestor's ways of life had been changed substantially afterward. Their ancestor offering and agricultural rituals as well as any other cultural traditions and ceremonies were forced to be abandoned. Their ancestor shrines and altars were forcefully burned during the movements of Great Leap Forward and Cultural Revolution. The traditional village chief *dzoeqma* was replaced by the head of the production team❶, shengchan duizhang; and the Village Elder's Council was replaced by the revolutionary committee, geming weiyuanhui. The head of production team controlled the rhythm of the villagers' productive activities, which was the same role that a traditional village chief *dzoeqma* would fulfill. The difference is that the former regulated the villagers activities according to the order and quota given from the above, the head of production brigade (shengchan daduizhang), who got his order from the above commune (renmin gongshe); while *dzoeqma* regulated the villagers activities according to the shared customary law *ghanrsanrkhovq* under the name of ancestors and various spiritual lords. The revolutionary committee was responsible for teaching the doctrines of Marxism and Maoism as well as socialist

---

❶ The head of the production team was usually the *jawrbavr*.

and communist ideology and atheism to the villagers, as the Village Elders' Council was responsible for educating the villagers about *ghanrsanrkhovq*. The difference is that the former inspected, monitored, and guaranteed the villagers to confirm to the new way of thinking and new rules of behaviors at political meetings and criticism and self-criticism sessions held every night until midnight; while the latter would perform their duty through guiding the villagers to follow the rhythm of annual rituals. In order to educate the "backward" Akha people and increase the productivity, the revolutionary committee also ordered them to cut trees or open farming lands in the forbidden or restricted areas. For instance, the communal Earth Lord grove, *jeiqjeiqma* was cleared for farming. Mengsong lanyaq, a forbidden swamp located in a small valley between the *Dazhai*'s cemetery grove and the communal Earth Lord grove hill, was also opened for paddy fields. Sturgeon also recorded a case that a militia person (Yah Teh) ordered the Xianfeng villagers to clear the village fence forest in order to plant fruit trees (2005: 152). Hongqi villagers were also ordered to cut a huge fig tree that was reserved at a forbidden site in *Tsaqla* to open for farming land. The fig tree stretched over hundreds square meters with numerous stems developed from aerial roots. It took the whole male villagers three days to cut this fig tree down alone. The persons who participated in this cutting still feel guilty today. In this way, the state imposed its landscapes of productivity and control over the sacred landscapes of the Akha (and of other ethnic groups as well[1]).

During the Planned Economy Period, the state announced that forests were an inefficient land use; trees were either to be exploited for steel-making to

---

[1] For instance, there were more than 1,000 holy hills/forests preserved by the Tai (Dai) people in Xishuangbanna, which took up about 5% of its total lands. Similarly, most of these holy hills and sacred forests were destroyed by the "slash-and-burn" agriculture under the revolutionary slogan "launch a battle against ghost mountains (refer to holy hills);ask foodstuff from sacred forests" during the same time (Gao, 1999; Pei, 1984).

support for industrialization of the nation, or simply moved out of the way for the production of both grain and economic crops, such as fruit trees (Sturgeon, 2005). It is evident that the forest coverage rate in Xishuangbanna was over 60% in 1953 (Forestry Bureau of Xishuangbanna Prefecture 1998: 49); but the figure dropped down to 36. 2 % in 1963 (ibid: 50) and further to 29. 6% in 1980 (ibid: 53). Assuming that the local land use patterns did not change significantly before the rubber plantations at the state farms (started in 1956), it is reasonable to conclude that over half of the forests in Xishuangbanna was destroyed during the commune period.

Through all of these various ideological campaigns, political movements, social measures and other assimilation efforts such as national education[1], Akha cultural traditions, particularly those related to ritual practices, have been seriously damaged. However, the Mengsong traditional social-political structure and sacred landscapes framework have endured the destructive interference, and survived in the new form that conforms to both the state rules and the traditional structure in the Reform and Open Period, particularly after introduction of rural election at natural village level in the early 1980s and at the communal (or Administrative Village, equivalent to sub-district administrative unit in urban) in 2000[2]. Except those destroyed during the "Great Leap Forward" and "Great Proletarian Cultural Revolution", most forbidden and restricted ecotopes (*ghatsanq*) were restored in the early 1980s (see Appendix Ⅵ), with different names and under the state protection though;both the watershed forests and *Sanqpaqbarwar* became state forests. The cemetery forests remained. The village fence forest (*putsanq* became the village scenic forest (fengjing lin in Chinese). The firewood forests (*miqkhaevq*

---

[1] Mengsong School was opened in 1955. It was one of the earliest schools opened by the Communist Government in Xishuangbanna.

[2] The rural election at the Administrative Village level was carried in most parts of China in 1998.

lavqghaw aqganq) became the village collective forest (jiti lin in Chinese) for house construction timbers and also were allocated to each household with 5mu (0.3 ha) as freehold forest/hill (Ziliu shan in Chinese) for firewood collection;tea gardens were also allocated among households. The fenced water buffalo forests (*nyoqjawr kmrteev aqganq*) were partially converted into fruit orchids during commune period and remained thereafter;some of them were also allocated as swidden lands for some households;and the rest of them remained as pastures. Most of the agricultural lands (*yarmr jawqxmq aqganq*) were declared as the state wastelands or waste mountains❶(guoyou huangshan in Chinese); the rest of them were allocated as swidden fields (*lunxie di* in Chinese) among the households according to the population sizes of the households; and paddy fields were also allocated among the households (see Table 5). Moreover, the allotment of tea trees as well as paddy fields among households within the production team (i.e. a natural village) confirmed the economic differentiation among the six villages created from uneven poppy opium cultivation and trade as mentioned in Chapter 3.

　　The fact that Akha people did not get punished from the spirits for destroying those sacred forests and sites as well as not offering to their ancestors and various spiritual lords, as they used to believe before, did not stop them from believing in spirits;instead they interpreted it that the forest spirits were suppressed by and/or escaped from the Han Chinese (which is interchangeable with the state to the Akha people), who were more powerful *naevq* — could be understood as either "spirits" or "the stronger others" as I explained in Chapter 2 — with whom the Akha people had to deal. One would get punished if she/he did not listen to them, just as one could get

---

❶　Most of them were cleared by the slash-and-burn farming during the commune period.

punished by offended spirits. Therefore, Akha people started believing that they would be blessed and not be punished as long as they followed Chairman Mao and the Communists. This is an instance of "the internalization of rule by villagers" (Agrawal, 2001: 14) in the process of state formation. This process of internalization of rule was further enhanced by the ensuring forestry reform in the early 1980s, in which the forestry staff and local village leaders designated areas for forest protection together. The traditional village fence forests (*putsanq*) became a scenic forest (fengjing lin in Chinese), where nothing could be cut, the same function but under different names; the existing cemetery forest was remained the same; the traditionally protected watershed forests including *Sanqpaqbarwar* were also acknowledged by the team but designated as state forests (guoyou lin in Chinese) and thus under the protection of the state law. The state was effectively co-opting the Ahka way of protecting forests under the name of spirits. The difference is that "[r]ules and enforcement now came from the state forestry station rather than from village elders, and indeed villagers look to the forestry station for punishment of infractions" (Sturgeon, 2005: 156); being ethnic minority, the Mengsong Akha were still regarded "backward" and were not qualified to manage the state properties (i. e. state forests here). Nevertheless, the traditional landscapes were more or less restored, albeit some of them were in different forms; and this led to improvement of forests from the early 1980s through the late 1990s (see Figure 11). The forest coverage reached 49% in Mengsong by 1998 (Wang et al. , 1999).

In the meanwhile, the head of a natural village (cunzhang in Chinese) was elected by its whole adult villagers (18 years old and above) since the early 1980s;and they usually chose a person from a traditional ruling/leading lineage (*dzoeqca*) because the villagers still held the belief that only the ruling/

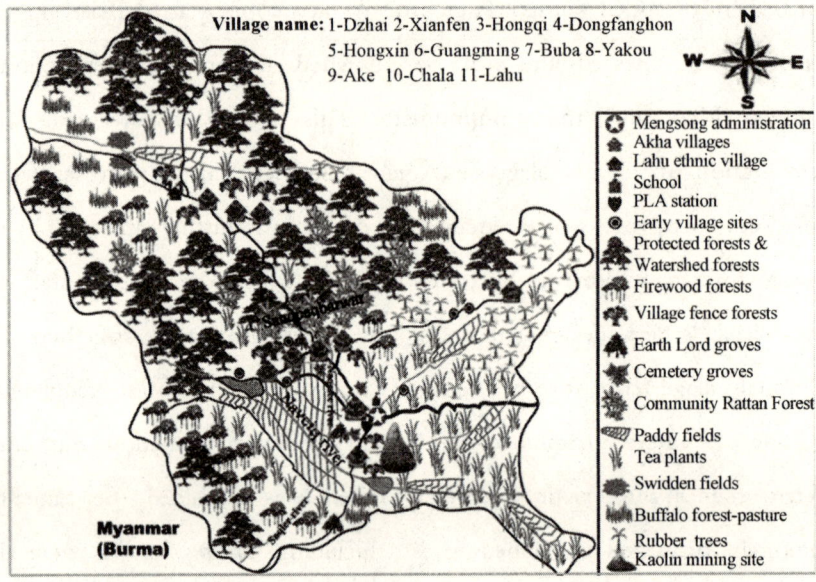

Figure 11 Mengsong Community and Current Land Use Map

leading lineages are appropriate to rule/lead. If they were not satisfied with the cunzhang they chose, the villagers would choose another person from the same or the other ruling/leading lineage in the next election which was run every three years. A person from a non-traditional ruling/leading lineage could be elected if there was no an appropriate candidate from the ruling/leading lineages; it was usually temporary and he would be replaced by a more appropriate person when the latter appeared in next election. Besides, the cunzhang was assisted and monitored by a village council (cun gugan in Chinese) comprised of representatives from each lineage and respectable elders. The cunzhang set up a set of village regulations and rules (cungui minyue in Chinese) with help from the village council. A lot of village affairs including but not limited to disputes, adultery, theft, and accidents were all settled by the village council. For instance, during my fieldwork, a case of adultery between a married woman and an unmarried young man was discovered; it was settled by the village council through fining both sides according to the village regulations and rules. The young man committed suicide because of losing face. In another case, a young man was killed accidentally in a group hunting trip. This was also settled by the village council secretly and peacefully without reporting to police. In this case, both owning a gun and hunting were illegal, and yet many villagers had guns and conducted hunting covertly; release of such an accident to the government agencies would cause huge trouble to the whole village or even to the whole community. Unfortunately, this case was reported to the police later by someone who remained unknown, and all the hunters were arrested. Nevertheless, cunzhang and the village council functioned today in the same way as dzoeqma and Village Elders' Council did in the past. The former system was the legacy of the latter in new forms. The difference is that the former used cungui minyue, a set of secular customary law written down in Chinese, to rule the villagers;while the latter used *ghanrsanrkhovq* , a set of sacred customary law passed down orally from their ancestors.

The restoration of the traditional social-political structure was not only at the natural village level, but also at the communal level. The chairman of Mengsong Administrative Committee (called cunweihui zhuren in Chinese, that governs 11 natural villages in Mengsong), "a small border chief Akheu" called by Sturgeon (2005), was also from the same ruling lineage *Jeirbeeq* of those great Mengsong chiefs acknowledged as *pyavqlo* by the Tai lords. But his rule was also monitored by the whole community and constantly contested by the heads of natural villages (cunzhang). As the communal discontent accumulated very high, Akheu resigned from his position in 1997 (just after Sturgeon finished her fieldwork); but his replacement was also from the same lineage, and the new one was also appointed by the above township government with content from all heads of the natural villages.

This lineage has been dominant politically in Mengsong through building and nurturing strong political connections with accumulated wealth from controlling over the access to or flow of highly valued resources (tea, opium, tin, manganese, game animals, etc.), both in the traditional Tai and modern Chinese states, over a century started from the great chief *Pyavqlo Marzoe*, to *Pyavqlo Zoesar*, to *Sardzer*, and to Akheu, with a season of dormancy during the commune period. Though *Sardzer* was not able to inherit the *pyavqlo* position from his father due to the Communist liberation, he nevertheless was appointed as a member of the National Work Team (minzhu gongzuodui) in 1953 to guide the national work among Akha communities all over Jinghong City and had held a senior office in the government of Jinghong City until he passed away in 1976. In the meanwhile, Akheu was enlisted in the PLA (People's Liberation Army) and posted as a communications officer in Myanmar, just across the border from Mengsong in 1974—1978, and then promoted as the security officer for the Mengsong production brigade in 1978. He maintained this official position from the end of the commune system through the rural reform, until he was appointed chairman of Mengsong Administrative Committee in 1993, after the sudden death of the previous chairman passed down from the previous head of Mengsong production brigade. Even though the leading position of *Jeirbeeq* lineage seemed to be "absent" in Mengsong during the commune period, its political influence and network were actually expanded beyond Mengsong, which paved the road for Akheu and his successors of this lineage to restore their traditional leading role. This was not challenged until the introduction of rural election at the Administrative Village level to Mengsong in 2000, when a new leader yet of another traditional leading lineage *Dancan* from Xianfeng Village was elected. But the new leader's powerful negotiation with the governmental agents over the compensation issues risen from the construction of new Mengsong Reservoir❶, made local authorities unhappy. *Jeirbeeq* lineage took this opportunity to help a young man in his late twenties from a non-traditional ruling/leading lineage to win an election in 2010, and finally restored its leading position again in 2013 election❷. From all of these pieces of evidence, we can conclude that leading lineages tend to stay leading lineages, which was also observed by Sturgeon (2005: 86 – 87).

Restoration of the traditional social-political structure albeit in the new forms guaranteed the improvement of forest management and regeneration of forests in Mengsong since the 1980s, which is also confirmed by other relevant studies (Sturgeon, 2005). However, this good developing trend in natural resource management was interrupted again by the new state policy of natural forest protection and the land conversion program introduced in Mengsong in the early 2000s. These new policies not only banned shifting cultivation legally, but also transformed Mengsong villagers into tea farmers, through converting their agricultural lands (both swidden fields and forested fallow lands) to tea plantations. This new wave of tea plantation not only covered agricultural lands, but also expanded to cover almost all "state wastelands" and most freehold forests, and further encroached into the "state protected forests". A crop (tea here) employed by the state as a technology of control was equipped by the Akha villagers as "weapons of the weak" (following Scott 1985) to resist against the state rule. The implication of these contested landscapes will be discussed more in Chapter 6.

---

❶ The new Mengsong Reservoir was constructed by the City of Jinghong, which would submerge many paddy fields, and collective forests containing old tea tree gardens, mostly of Xianfeng village.

❷ In 2010 election,*Jeirbeeq* lineage did not have a competitive candidate yet, but they successfully managed to elect a vice-chairman from its lineage through supporting the chairman's election. With accumulated political capital and experience, this vice-chairman eventually won in 2013 election.

Chapter 5

Rubber Plantations and Transformations of Akha Society in Xishuangbanna, Southwest China: A Case Study of Baka Village

5.1 Introduction

Development of rubber plantations in China could be roughly sorted into three historical phases: Period I (1904 − 1950), Period II (1951 − 1984), and Period III (post 1984). The first phase is characterized as private enterprise with slow development, while the second phase is of large scale plantations predominated by state rubber farms and the third is highlighted by the private small holders' rubber boom.

A Dai Lord, Mr. Dao Anren, bought 8,000 rubber seedlings from Singapore and planted them at Fenghuang Mountain, in today's Xincheng Township, Yingjiang County, Yunnan Province, in 1904. This was the first plantation of the Amazonian rubber trees *Hevea brasiliensis* in China. In the following few years, more rubber plantations were established in Hainan Island by some oversea Chinese from Southeast Asia, and later in Guangdong Province. However, large scale rubber plantations in China did not start until the establishment of state farms in the 1950s. Rubber was embargoed to China by the United States-led capitalist countries in 1950 as a direct result of

China's decision to get involved in the American-Korean war. In order to break the US-led economic blockade and embargo policies, the central government of China made a decision in 1951 to expand rubber plantations at any possible places within its territories, to meet a huge demand for national industrialization and defense building (Yunnan Agricultural Reclamation Cooperation Ltd. and Yunnan Association of Tropical Crops, 2005).

As the two largest national tropical frontiers, Hainan Island and Xishuangbanna were the main foci for the China's efforts in achieving self-sufficiency in rubber, where numerous state farms were established in the 1950s. In Xishuangbanna, these state farms were coalesced into ten county-level state farms in the early 1980s. Since these mountainous areas, particularly in Xishuangbanna, were dominated by ethnic minorities whose economy was based on swidden agriculture, rubber trees were also perceived as a perfect crop by which the state could gain control over the local resources and people, through transforming "primitive" (unproductive in term of taxability) traditional swidden agriculture into "modern" (productive in term of taxability) rubber plantations. The latter were regarded as "legible" (accountable), controllable (taxable), and thus, "legitimate" landscapes by the state (Xu, 2006). However, it had taken the state almost a half century to eliminate shifting cultivation through various policies and projects including the shifting cultivation ban in 1998, and in doing so, the local ethnic farmers were transformed into modern cash cropping farmers, particularly rubber farmers, in Xishuangbanna. These local ethnic minorities are so successful in rubber plantations that the total area of these small holdings surpassed that of the state farms by 2004 (Statistic Bureau of Xishuangbanna Prefecture 2005). Some of these small holders, particularly Dai (or Tai Leu) and Akha in

Mengla County along Sino-Laotian border, have even become successful private entrepreneurs and invested to develop more rubber plantations across the border in Laos after China entered the WTO in 2001 (Shi, 2008; Sturgeon, 2010). The same phenomenon could also be observed in Xishuangbanna along the Sino-Burmese border, where some successful local Dai and Akha farmers expanded outside China to develop more rubber plantations in northeast corner of Eastern Shan State, Myanmar. Proliferations of these small holders' rubber plantations within Xishuangbanna and across borders have created "chaotic landscapes" that were not expected by the state and were not under the state's control (Sturgeon, 2010).

This chapter aims to examine the dynamic/dialectic process by which the Akha have become rubber farmers in Xishuangbanna through a case study of Baka Village. Social, cultural as well as ecological consequences following the economic transformation of Baka Village through rubber plantations are analyzed, in order to discuss the sustainability of these transformations. Using households as units of analysis, differentiations within the community are emphasized, which aspect was not well addressed in relevant previous studies (Sturgeon, 2010).

Although it is neither the first nor the most important place of rubber plantations in Southeast Asia, Xishuangbanna is a pioneering and prominent place for experiment, establishment, and expansion of rubber plantations in highlands of Greater Mekong Subregion (GMS), which serves as an appealing model for the current rubber boom in its neighboring highlands of Laos (Shi, 2008), Myanmar, and even Northern Thailand. Thus, it remains as a very interesting place for studying rubber plantations and their related social, cultural, political, economic and ecological/environmental issues in highlands of GMS.

Chapter 5 Rubber Plantations and Transformations of Akha Society in Xishuangbanna, Southwest China

Picture 27   Baka Village Surrounded by Rubber Plantations (Dry Season)

Like Mengsong, Baka Village also belongs to Damenglong Township, Jinghong Municipality (see Figure 2). Damenglong is the biggest township in the municipality; and one of the three biggest state rubber farms in China, Dongfeng State Farm, is located at the foot of mountains surrounding Damenglong Basin. Dongfeng town is located between Damenglong Town and Jinghong City. Being one of twenty Administrative Villages of Damenglong Township, Baka Administrative Village is consisted of eight natural villages— 4 Akha (Baka, Bohe, Pisha, Manhanhuang), 3 Han and Hani (Nasha Yidui, Nasha Erdui, Nasha Sandui), and 1 Buxia (Buxia Huixian). Baka natural village was my major research site here; and in this chapter I use "Baka Village" or "Baka" to refer to Baka natural village, not the Administrative Village comprising 8 natural villages. Baka Village is located at northeastern corner of Damenglong Basin at an altitude of 650 masl (see Picture 27). It has 549 people in 121 households in 2008. In terms of land use, Baka Village has

10,000 *mu* ❶ rubber plantations, 3,000 *mu* collective forest, 280 *mu* paddy fields, 70 *mu* tea garden, and 150 *mu* residency area. Baka Village is 5 km away from Dongfeng Town, 25 km away from Damenglong Town, and 45 km away from Jinghong City.

5.2　Rubber Plantations in Xishuangbanna: State *vs.* People

In China, all rubber plantations outside of state farms are called min ying xiang jiao, which could be translated as 'people-run rubber plantations'. These can be sorted into three categories: collective, joint-operating (with state farms), and individual (or private) plantations. If we look through the history of rubber plantations in China, the first phase was exclusively of private plantations. However, private plantations were halted and replaced by state rubber farms in the 1950s and early 1960s because rubber was regarded as a key strategic material for national security and defense industry, and rubber production needed to be under total control of the state. As such, all managers and workers in the state farms during this establishing period were either transferred soldiers or Han Chinese farmers from other parts of China, particularly from Hunan Province, Chairman Mao's home area. Local ethnic minorities were excluded in these state rubber farms, on the one hand, as they were regarded "backward" and not "qualified" for this kind of "advanced" work (Xu, 2006; Sturgeon, 2010), and on the other hand, local farmers — mostly ethnic minorities — were required to produce and provide food for newly established state enterprises in Xishuangbanna, particularly rubber plantations and steel-making.

---

❶ *mu* is a Chinese unit of area, 1 *mu* = 666.7 m², or 15 *mu* = 1 ha.

Chapter 5 Rubber Plantations and Transformations of Akha Society in Xishuangbanna, Southwest China

However, the state rubber farms could produce far less rubber than what the state needed, and yet they could not expand the plantations endlessly, due to lack of "advanced" Han labor. Also, most lands were still occupied by ethnic minorities, who practiced swidden agriculture, regarded as "primitive", "unproductive" "illegible" or "illegitimate" (Scott, 1998). In other worlds, from the state's point of view, local natural resources were "wasted" and local people (particularly ethnic minorities) were not "cultured", but which needed to be "utilized" and "mobilized" for the state building. For the state, the best way to solve these problems was to replace local swidden agriculture with rubber plantations, and in doing so, transform local ethnic minorities into rubber farmers. This would allow the state to kill two birds with one stone — on the one hand, to control local resources and people in advanle, and on the other hand, to produce more rubber with little or no state cost. Therefore, the Ministry of Agricultural Reclamation ordered the state farms in Yunnan (and in Xishuangbanna) to help local governments to develop min ying or people run rubber plantations in 1964. Consequently, the first collective rubber plantation was established at Jinglan Village, near Jinghong City in 1964, and more collective rubber plantations were established in other places of Xishuangbanna and other tropical areas of Yunnan Province in the following couple of years; although these efforts were interrupted by the "Great Proletarian Cultural Revolution" (1966 – 1976). Another order to develop more rubber plantations in Yunnan was sent by the central government again in 1980. Accordingly, Yunnan Provincial Government requested the state farms to allocate 6% of their total profits to help develop more min ying rubber plantations in various forms, including providing free loans to local farmers to develop private plantations (Li & Wang, 1989).

This new policy promoted development of two kinds of min ying rubber plantations: collective and joint-operation. The collective rubber plantations were called she ban qi ye (commune enterprise) and later were renamed zhong zhi chang (collective plantation farms). These collective enterprises were developed with free loan and technical supports from the state farms. Though they were put under the name of "people run rubber plantations", i. e. min ying xiang jiao, these collective plantations were actually run by local governments at county or township levels and functioned as extension of the state farms from the state's point of view. The only difference is that the state farms were run by the governments at higher levels, i. e. provincial and central governments. At the same time, the state farms were also encouraged or required to develop joint-operated (lianying) rubber plantations with local villages, in which state farms provided seedlings and technical supports while villagers provided lands and labor, and in return, they would share the profits under 30/70 or 40/60 schemes with the villagers taking the bigger portion.

The real private/individual rubber plantations were not developed until 1985 after agricultural lands were contracted out to individual households in 1982 and 1983 under a national policy called jiating lianchan chengbao zerenzhi, or Household Contract Responsibility System. Regarded as an alternative to traditional swidden agriculture. These private plantations were encouraged by the governments through providing free loans, because the state valued rubber plantations much more than swidden agriculture, according to their ideology that the former would not only produce higher economic values but also be more legible and controllable (Chen, 1979; Huang et al., 1984; Xu, 2006). However, the state did not intend that these small holders' plantations would outdo the state farms. Government agencies planned to maintain predominant role of the state farms in rubber production, supplemented by the collective and joint-operation plantations, while giving these small holdings the least priority and a trivial position in rubber production (Li & Wang, 1989). The state also did not expect that these small holders' plantations would edge out of the state's control. Notwithstanding the state's intention, the total area of min ying or people-run plantations soon surpassed that of the state farms in Xishuangbanna. Furthermore, almost all of the rubber plantations developed under the collective enterprise and joint-operation schemes have been privatized and distributed among the local households in Xishuangbanna by the 2000s.

5.3 State Efforts to Eliminate Shifting Cultivation in Xishuangbanna

Although rubber plantation was promoted as an alternative to swidden agriculture at lower slopes[1], it took several strategic steps to eliminate shifting cultivation in Xishuangbanna. First, many highland villages were relocated from higher slopes into lower slopes during the Commune Period (1958 – early 1980s). The purpose of the resettlement policy was to replace shifting cultivation with sedentary agriculture, particularly through creating a lot of irrigated paddy fields in not-yet-cultivated small valleys or making terraces on low slopes as well as building irrigation infrastructure such as reservoirs and irrigation ditches. Although shifting cultivation was not eliminated through resettlement due to the fact that only limited area of paddy fields could be created, it laid out the physical and economic basis needed for these downhill

---

[1] Since rubber trees are not recommended at higher slopes beyond 800 meters above sea level, tea plantations are promoted as major alternative to swidden agriculture at higher slopes in Xishuangbanna by the government, as in the case of Mengsong covered in Chapter 4.

relocated villages to develop rubber plantations later, because 1) rubber trees need to be planted ideally lower than 800 meters above sea level; and 2) these paddy fields could produce much more rice per unit of land through intensified cultivation than the uplands which also allowed freeing up some uplands for other purposes. All Akha villages with successful rubber plantations studied by Janet Sturgeon (2009) were relocated downhill during this period of time. Baka Village was also relocated downhill and merged with villagers relocated from another village *Gawqhor Geedzanq*, to form a production team at *Baqnor* in 1967. It was relocated again at current location in 1971 due to construction of a reservoir at *Baqnor*. All irrigated paddy fields in Baka Village were developed during the Commune Period before which their economy was exclusively based on swidden agriculture.

The second strategic step was to establish and expand rubber plantations in forms of state farms, collective enterprises, and joint-operation, which was developed mainly on the fallow lands of local swidden agriculture. One of the national biggest state rubber farms, Dongfeng State Farm, was established surrounding Damenglong Basin in 1958. Its fifteenth branch or battalion was set up later mainly within the traditional territory of Baka Village and on their most favorite and fertile swidden lands. According to the elder villagers, when they fallowed their swidden fields this year, the state farm immediately planted rubber trees on these fallow lands next year. In other words, development of the fifteenth branch of Dongfeng State Farm was positively correlated with retreat of Baka villagers'swidden agriculture to marginalized lands at higher elevations and steeper slopes. As Baka Village was relocated downhill, it also meant that the most of these marginal lands at middle and high slopes were further distanced, usually with a distance of 2 − 3 hours of walking from the new location of the village. Moreover, establishment of Xiaojie Plantation Farm, a collective enterprise belonged to Xiaojie Township❶, in the early 1980s, appropriated a lot of Baka Village's traditional swidden lands. Furthermore, about 300 mu (equals to 20 ha) of rubber plantations were developed in Baka from 1982 to 1984 under the lianying or "joint-operation" system with the fifteenth branch of Dongfeng State Farm. The area of swidden lands available to Baka villagers for expansion of these rubber plantations had greatly reduced.

Finally, swidden agriculture in Xishuangbanna (and in China) was further limited by the Household Contract Responsibility System (HCRS) in the early 1980s and eventually banned along with Logging Ban in 1998. All agrarian households in China were allocated certain amount of lands for farming under HCRS. Though it did not stop swidden agriculture in Xishuangbanna directly, this policy fixed swidden agriculture practices on very limited lands. According to Forestry Bureau of Xishuangbanna Prefecture (2000), the total area of lands allocated for swidden agriculture in Xishuangbanna under HCRS is 1, 447, 800mu (equals to 96, 520 hectares) in the early 1980s, which takes up 5% of its total land area. The non-Han and non-Dai population in Xishuangbanna was 245, 946 in 1982. If we assume that 90% of them were practicing swidden agriculture in the highlands, then average size of allocated swidden lands was 6. 5 mu per capita, which is far less that the amount needed to maintain a healthy rotation of swidden agriculture❷. These lands were not

---

❶ During the Commune System, Damenglong basin was divided into two communes, Da Damenglong and Xiaojie, which became two townships later when the communes were dissolved. Mengsong belonged to the former while Baka belonged to the latter. However, Xiaojie Township was merged into Da Damenglong, and formed Damenglong Township in 2004.

❷ As a local rule of thumb, the minimum required land size for healthy rotation of swidden agriculture is 15 mu or 1 ha per capita in Xishuangbanna highlands. Usually, it requires 3 mu per capita of upland to produce enough food each year, and 15 mu of lands could be divided into 5 plots. If each plot was cultivated for 2 years, 15 mu of lands would allow a rotation of 10 years with 8 years of fallow.

evenly distributed among villages. The majority villages experienced shortage of lands for continuing swidden agriculture under HCRS, and replaced it with cash cropping such as rubber plantations, even before the Shifting Cultivation Ban, as it was exemplified in Baka below.

Each Baka household was allocated with 11 *mu* swidden lands per capita under the HCRS policy in 1983. These lands were dispersed in four plots, which were allowed for rice cultivation in a rotational period of 6 years (see Table 8). Since this allowed only for 4 years of fallow period, which was not long enough for sustainable swidden agriculture with a healthy rotation, searching for alternatives to the swidden agriculture was inevitable under the HCRS policy in Baka Village. Rubber plantation was picked up by the villagers with assistance from its neighboring state farm.

Table 8   Rice Cultivations on Swidden Lands in Baka Village under the Household Contract Responsibility System

Plot Number	I	II	III	IV
Plot size (mu/capita)	2	3	2	4
Years of rice cultivations	1983, 1984	1984, 1985	1986, 1987	1987, 1988
	1989	—	—	—

5.4   Rubber Plantations in Baka Village

As mentioned above, the first rubber plantation was developed collectively with help from the state farm under the joint-operation scheme in Baka in the early 1980s. Table 9 shows all smallholders' rubber plantations in Baka Village from 1982 to 2006 while Figure 12 shows only the current possession of rubber plantations by the households. Since collective plantation at Bano was replanted with second round of rubber plantation in

2005, its first plantation was not shown in Figure 12.

Table 9   Smallholder's Rubber Plantations in Baka Village (1982 – 2006)

Years	Land plot name	Tenure of the lands	Numbers of rubber plantation plots	Area of rubber plantations (mu)	Total plots	Total area (mu)
1982-84	Bano	Collective	Replanted in 2005 (see below)			
1985	Lawjilawha	Collective	5	22	11	71
1986			6	49		
1987	Swidden Fields Plot No. I	Households	1	17	66	811
1988			9	125		
1989			26	349		
1990			20	207		
1991			7	78		
1992			3	35		
1993	Gawjaw	Collective	25	83	55	279
1994			20	112		
1995			10	84		
1996	Swidden Fields Plot No. II	Households	20	257	83	1307
1997			51	852		
1998			12	198		
1999	Swidden Fields Plot No. III	Households	26	508	47	741
2000			2	27		
2001			11	89		
2002			8	117		
2003	Swidden Fields Plot No. IV	Households	51	1242	83	1973
2004			32	731		
2005	Bano	Collective	108	918	108	918
2006	Bada	State forest	96	1080	96	1080
	Total area (mu)		549	7180	549	7180

Note:

1. These numbers are calculated based on data collected in a household survey covering all households in Baka Village in 2006.

2. Except 15 mu or 1 ha of collective rubber plantation, which was excluded here, all these rubber plantations are owned by individual households, including those planted on the collective and state lands which

Sacred and Contested Landscapes

were distributed among households.

3. The reported number during the survey tends to be lower than the real amount of planting. I was told by the village head that there were about at least 10,000 mu rubber plantations in Baka. If this information is reliable, the villagers did not report about 30% of their rubber plantations during my survey. Similarly, I have noticed that, local farmers, with no exceptions, always underreport of their rubber plantations (as well as income and any other economic activities) to any government survey in order to reduce and/or avoid real or potential taxation.

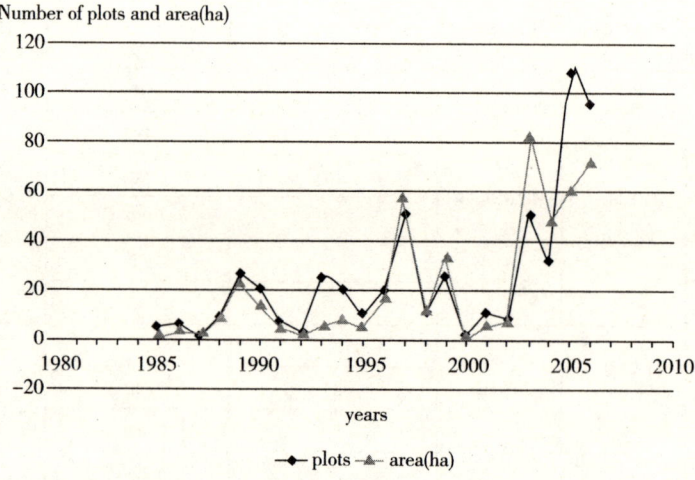

Figure 12　Smallholder's Rubber Plantations in Baka

Besides the collective plantations, each household was also encouraged to grow private rubber trees on a newly distributed small plot on Lawjilawha collective lands in 1985 and 1986 (first tip of the plantation waves on Figure 9). But this attempt was not very successful for three major reasons. First, the villagers were lack of confidence in this new crop; second, the villagers had not yet adequately acquired the techniques; and third, the plot was too small to be given enough input. However, the combination of two factors in the late 1980s—1) Baka villagers used out their swidden lands for first circle and the

Chapter 5 Rubber Plantations and Transformations of Akha Society in Xishuangbanna, Southwest China

previous fallow lands were not quite ready for its second circle of rice cultivation❶, and 2) those first planted and co-operated collective rubber trees started to be tapped and the profits were witnessed — pushed the real first wave of rubber plantations on their private lands in Baka Village in the late 1980s (second tip on Figure 9). Similar developing pattern of smallholder's rubber plantation is also observed in Northern Laos (Shi, 2008). This wave of plantation lasted the longest (1987 – 1992), as it took time for various households to initiate their first private rubber plantation due to financial and other reasons.

The next wave of rubber planting occurred on collective lands at Gawjaw during 1993 – 1995. Gawjaw was reserved as village fence forests, which was identified as Fengjing Lin (scenic forest) in the early 1980s. The forests were cleaned and distributed among households for the purpose of rubber plantating in 1993. As it required some investment, rubber plantation on the second plot of swidden lands did not occur until 1996 when the first plantations started to be tapped. With cash income from the first plantations, plantations on the third plot of swidden lands (those that were cleared before the logging ban was enacted in late 1998) started immediately after it was done on the second plots in 1999, but this was interrupted by the logging ban in 2000, and then continued with a new policy that allowed cutting trees under the Land Conversion Project in 2001 and 2002, though none of rubber plantations in Baka was subsidized by the project.

With capital accumulated from previous plantations, the fourth plot of swidden lands were quickly planted with rubber trees in 2003 and 2004. Thus,

---

❶ As a matter of fact, as they used out all their allocated swidden lands by the end of 1980s, Baka villagers went to starve. In order to solve this problem, there were allowed to cut their collective forests to grow rice in the early 1990s.

all swidden lands of Baka village were planted with rubber trees by 2004. The Bano collective rubber trees planted in early 1980s were cut down❶ and the lands were distributed among households in 2005. All of these lands were planted with rubber trees by the households in the same year. The last wave of rubber plantation in Baka occurred at Bada in 2006. Bada was Baka's traditional swidden land, but was identified as state forest during the national forestry and land reform in the early 1980s. In the meanwhile, a neighboring Dai village, Man Liangsan, wanted to plant rubber trees there, as they did not have much upland elsewhere. They applied for permission from the government to do so. In order to avoid all these lands being taken by the Dai village, Baka Village also submitted an application to claim it. It resulted in that each village got half of the Bada lands. These lands were planted with rubber trees in 2006.

  The state has been trying to stop uncontrolled development of private rubber plantations since 1999, partially due to environmental concerns. However, local governments were not able to stop villagers' expansion of rubber plantation not only on their own contracted lands, but also on state (waste or forest) lands. The villagers were able to use various reasons to justify their applications for permission to plant rubber trees on the state lands. This was the case of Bada just mentioned above. The reason Man Liangsan Village used was that they possessed too little rubber plantations compared with other villages in this area. But Baka Village claimed that these lands used to be their traditional swidden lands before. In order to avoid conflicts between these two villages, the government had to approve both applications and allow them to split the lands. Individual villagers were also

---

  ❶ Usually rubber trees can be tapped for 30 years, but these first trees were not tapped with skilled tappers at the beginning, which shortened the tapping span.

able to get permission to get a plot of land from state forest land through personal relations to governmental officials who were mostly from local villages. Many villagers also dared to encroach into the state forests for rubber plantations even without getting permission from local authorities. All of these situations could be observed in Baka. Because almost all cultivable lands of Baka Village (collective and households) had been planted with rubber trees by 2006, any villager who wanted to expand their rubber plantation has to do on state lands, legally or illegally. In my own observation, this happens not only in Baka, but also in many other villages wherever the conditions are allowed in Xishuangbanna. It is ironic to see that rubber trees, a new crop that was intentionally employed by the state to control over local resources and people, were unexpectedlyseized on by the local people like Akha, as "weapons of the weak" (Scott, 1985), to resist the state's total control.

5.5 Cultural Adaptations to Rubber Plantation in Baka

Rubber plantations have transformed natural landscapes as well as the whole society of Baka Village. Economic (in terms of cash income, rice production, pig husbandry, and fuel supply), socio-cultural (in terms of living standards, belief system, social status and cultural traditions), and ecological (in terms of biological resources) consequences of rubber plantations in Baka were examined in this study.

5.5.1 Rubber plantation and cash income

The first and direct economic benefit of rubber plantation is to bring unprecedented cash income to the households in Baka. This is the first reason why rubber trees have become the favorite cash crop in Baka and in most lowlands of Xishuangbanna. The per capita annual cash income was only hundreds yuan in the early 1990s, but it soared to 3801 yuan in 2005. Rubber contributed to about 92.4% of its total cash income in Baka in 2005. Since the villagers tended to underreport their cash income particularly from rubber in the survey, both the per capita cash income and rubber's contribution percentage should be higher than these numbers. According to the village head, Mr. *Nyirer*, per capita cash income from rubber reached 6,000 yuan in 2006.

However, the increased cash income is unevenly distributed among the households (see Table 10 and Figure 13). Most Baka households (91 out of 109, that is, 83.5%) earned less than 30,000 yuan, and the other 15.6% households (17 out of 109) earned between 30,000 and 50,000 yuan, while only one household (of the village head) had cash income more than 120,000 yuan in 2005. The median income was 60,600 yuan, while the average was 17,577.20 yuan. The huge difference between the median and the average is caused by the uneven distribution among households. This discrepancy is not only resulted from uneven possession of rubber plantations among the households (in terms of both total rubber trees and per capita, see Table 11 and Figure 14), but also reflects socio-economic differentiation in Baka Village.

There are two major reasons that caused the uneven possession of rubber plantations among the households. First was the uneven land distribution due to uneven power distribution. In theory, the Household Contract Responsibility System was meant to allot its lands among its member households within a production team (i.e. a natural village) equally according to household population size in the early 1980s. In practice, however, those with power in hand, being leaders or their relatives, grabbed much more lands disproportionally than the commoners, resulting in discrepancy in land possession among households, which laid a foundation for aforthcoming socio-economic differentiation under a market economy.

Uneven access to land and other resources was very common in mountainous communities all over Xishuangbanna after HRCS in the early 1980s, which was confirmed by other studies (Sturgeon, 2005). The Mengsong Village head as a border chief described by Sturgeon is from the lineage of the earlier great chiefs *Pyavqlo Marzoe* and *Pyavqlo Zoesar*. Similarly, the current village head of Baka is also from a leading lineage whose ancestors also used to be great *pyavqlo*; the village head has been of this lineage most of the time from Commune System up to the present in Baka Village. In addition, the forestry and agricultural reform in the early 1980s also left out a lot of uplands unidentified and un-allocated in mountainous communities all over Xishuangbanna (including Baka Village), which provided spaces for later village leaders with new power to possess as their own private property or to sell (contract out) on behalf of the communities and accumulate private capital from these conducts. With the capital, they could develop private rubber plantations on their own contracted and/or seized lands. Those commoners, especially the poorest, being lack of capital, had to sell (or lease out) some plots of their lands in order to plant rubber trees on their other lands. Those first rubber planters were able to purchase (or take lease of) those lands "sold" or leased out by the poor, with the capital generated from their earlier plantations. This is another reason that has further contributed to stratification between "the haves" and "the have nots". As rubber is the predominant source of cash income, it is clearly demonstrated that the amount of household cash income has a positive correlation with the number of rubber trees that have been under tapping in Baka (see Figure 15). Therefore, it can be concluded that rubber plantations have accelerated socio-economic stratification among households in Baka, and the village leaders, both previous and particularly current, are on the top of this stratum. This phenomenon was also observed in other Akha villages by Janet Sturgeon (2009).

Sacred and Contested Landscapes

Table 10 Distribution of Baka Household Cash Income in 2005

Unit No.	Cash income (yuan)	Number of households	Unit No.	Cash income (yuan)	Number of households
1	0-4,999	6	14	65,000-69,999	0
2	5,000-9,999	21	15	70,000-74,999	0
3	10,000-14,999	24	16	75,000-79,999	0
4	15,000-19,999	21	17	80,000-84,999	0
5	20,000-24,999	18	18	85,000-89,999	0
6	25,000-29,999	1	19	90,000-94,999	0
7	30,000-34,999	6	20	95,000-99,999	0
8	35,000-39,999	2	21	100,000-104,999	0
9	40,000-44,999	6	22	105,000-109,999	0
10	45,000-49,999	0	23	110,000-114,999	0
11	50,000-54,999	3	24	115,000-119,999	0
12	55,000-59,999	0	25	120,000-124,999	1
13	60,000-64,999	0	26	125,000-129,999	0
				Total	109

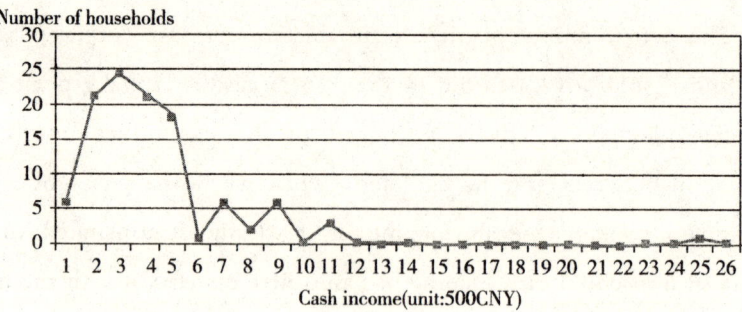

Figurs 13 Pattern of Baka Household's Cash income in 2005

Chapter 5 Rubber Plantations and Transformations of Akha Society in Xishuangbanna, Southwest China

Table 11 Distribution of Rubber Trees among Households in Baka in 2006

Unit No.	Rubber tree possession per household		Rubber plantation possession per capita	
	Total trees	Number of households	mu/capita	Number of households
1	0-699	7	0-4.9	4
2	700-1,399	28	5-9.9	31
3	1,400-2,099	30	10-14.9	28
4	2,100-2,799	24	15-19.9	26
5	2,800-3,499	10	20-24.9	13
6	3,500-4,199	7	25-29.9	4
7	4,200-4,899	1	30-34.9	2
8	4,900-5,599	1	35-39.9	1
9	5,600-6,299	1	40-44.9	0

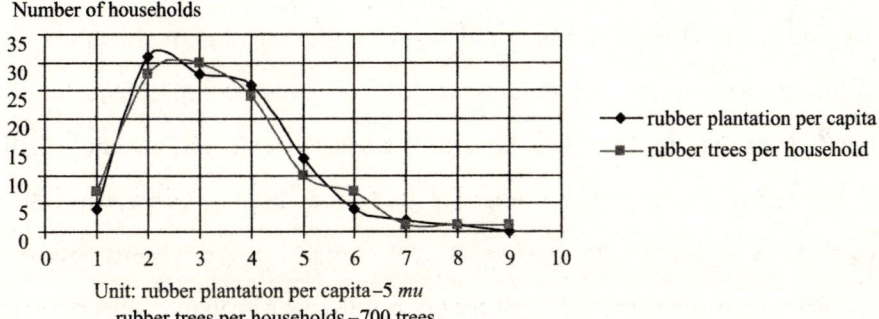

Figure 14 Distribution of Rubber Trees among Households in Baka in 2006

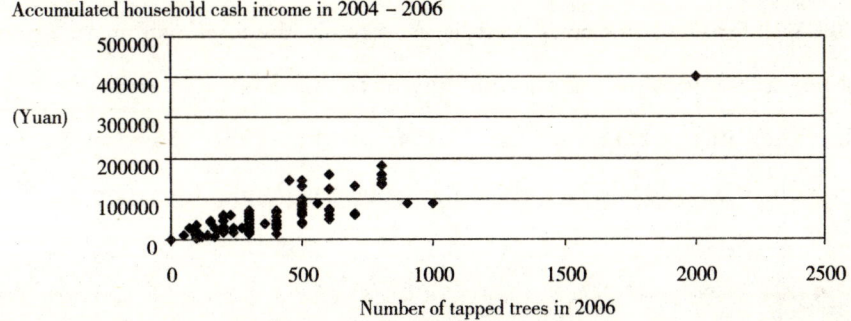

Figure 15 Tapped Rubber trees *vs.* Household Cash Income in Baka Village

· 229 ·

Even though the farmer's household cash income has been increased in many folds due to rubber plantations in last decade, an economy based on rubber plantations is very vulnerable in Xishuangbanna. First of all, rubber trees are very vulnerable to unfavorable weather conditions (such as cold winters and storms), pests, and diseases. A cold winter with a temperature that is lower by a few degrees than normal years could cause death of very many rubber trees in Xishuangbanna, as in the winters of 1973/1974 and 1975/1976 (Cold Injury Investigation Office of Agricultural Reclamation Bureau of Yunan Province, 2004). Rubber trees are also often killed by storms, pests, and diseases. Moreover, rubber production is often jeopardized by pests and diseases. For instance, all rubber trees in Xishuangbanna were infected by powdery mildew in early 2008. Experts estimated that this infection would decrease rubber production by 15,000 tons of dry rubber in Xishuangbanna, which would cause a loss of over 300,000,000 Chinese yuan[1]. According to 2008 Baka household survey, loss of cash income caused by the rubber powdery mildew infection was about 1,252,000 yuan in 2008, which takes up one third of last year's (2007) total cash income from rubber. Furthermore, market price of dried rubber has been fluctuating dramatically. It soared to 26 yuan/kg[2] for a few days in May, but then slumped continuously down to 7 yuan/kg for the rest of the year, which might be caused by the 2008 Wall Street's stock crisis partially. As a result, the total cash income from rubber in 2008 was only about one third of last year's income in Baka Village. Therefore, after taking out the loss from the rubber powdery mildew infection, Baka village's loss from the global economic depression in 2008

---

[1] Source is from Yunnan Branch of Xinhua Net at http://www.yn.xinhuanet.com/nets/2008-02/29/content_12582249.htm.

[2] This is the price that local farmers could sell their dried rubber to market.

was about one third of last year's total income.

What is more dangerous is that Baka villagers have not realized the vulnerability and high risk of their economy based on monoculture of a single crop rubber trees. In the 2008 household survey, most people could not relate the eruption of the disastrous epidemic to the large scale monoculture of rubber trees. Instead, they attributed it to either climate change or failure of the epidemic control (effective prevention and treatment of the disease) due to fake pesticide. Some people even believed that it was caused by malicious biological attacks by the West in order to breach the 2008 Beijing Olympic Games. Only three out of thirty respondents related it to the disappearance of local forests and worried that it would become worse year after year. When I asked what you and your household could do if a similar epidemic would occur next year, most of them did not know what to do, just hoping that it would not happen again, or they believe that the government will take some measures to prevent it from occurring again because state farms possess more plantations than the smallholders (these farmers have not realized that they, as a whole, possess more rubber plantations than the state farms now). If it would happen again, some said that they would go to look for some off-farm work in towns and cities. Two households said that they would raise more pigs, but worried about pig fodder since rubber seeds have been the main pig fodder and the rubber trees would not produce any significant amount of seeds if they got the disease. At the end, surprisingly, most of them answered me by saying that "the worst scenario would be that we will cut the rubber trees and pick up our shifting cultivation again if the rubber trees become really unprofitable".

5.5.2 Rubber plantation and rice production

Rice cultivation had traditionally been the major activity of subsistent economy of most Akha prior to the 1980s. Being staple food, rice had been the core crop of swidden agriculture in mountainous Akha villages of Xishuangbanna and beyond. When rubber trees were first introduced to Baka village, they were intercropped with rice on swidden fields. Intercropping rubber trees in their rice fields, however, decreased rice harvest, resulting in first food shortage in Baka village under the Household Contract Responsibility System in the late 1980s. This caused them to cut and clean their collective forests for rice cultivation in 1990 and 1991 with approval from the government. However, this could not solve food (rice) shortage problem in a long term. A better solution was to intensify their irrigated paddy fields, which previously were cultivated without much input and care. In doing so, Baka villagers have not only double cropped their paddy fields, but also started to adopt high-yielding hybrid rice varieties and modern cultivation techniques (including applying chemical pesticide, herbicide, and fertilizers) since middle 1990s. Despite of the fact that many villagers, particularly elders, were complaining about the taste of the hybrid rice, swidden agriculture along with its colorful and tasty upland rice and other traditional crops were gradually disappearing in Baka village before the shifting cultivation ban in 1998.

Intensification of rice cultivation on irrigated paddy fields, however, did not solve the rice production problem in Baka. According to 2006 Baka household survey, among 109 surveyed households, 22 households answered that they could not produce enough rice for themselves. Though the rest 78 households answered that they produced enough rice for themselves, 18 households bought or borrowed rice in 2005. Therefore, there were about 40 households out of 109, that is, 36.7% in Baka village that were not self-subsistent in rice production in 2005. It used to be shameful for Akha people as rice cultivators if they could not produce enough rice for their family. However, this did not matter much anymore economically as well as morally. On the one hand, economic role of rice cultivation has been marginalized by rubber plantations; on the other hand, it has become normal and acceptable morally to buy rice and any other available goods in market. Five households expressed that they were going to give up rice cultivation totally in the near future, as they would be too busy in rubber production. Not only those five households' fields, but all paddy fields of the whole village, were leased out for banana plantation in 2009. And no one has grown rice since then.

5.5.3 Rubber plantation and pig husbandry

Pig husbandry is the second important source of cash income in Baka Village. Total sale of pigs in Baka was about 74,416 yuan, which contributed to 3.9% of totalhousehold cash income in Baka in 2005 (see Table 12). The total number of hogs killed for self consumption was 130 head in Baka in 2005. If we use 800 yuan as an average price of a hog, it would save Baka village about 104,000 yuan, which would take up 5.4% of its total cash income in 2005. According to 2008 Baka household survey, total sale of pigs in 2007 increased 140% compared to that of in 2005, reached to 178,240 yuan in absolute value. Rubber seeds have become the main fodder for pigs in Baka and most lowland areas of Xishuangbanna. This is another reason why rubber trees have become the most favorite cash crop in this region. In Baka, a total of 77,160 kg of rubber seeds were fed to pigs in Baka in 2007, which valued 46,296 yuan[1]. Rubber seeds are free for anyone to pick. Except one household who bought some rubber seeds, all these rubber seeds were picked

---

[1] The market price of rubber seeds was 0.6 yuan per kilogram in 2007.

by the household members in the rubber fields.

Table 12 Household Cash Income of Baka Village in 2005

Source of cash income	Rubber	Pig	Tea	Others*	Total
Absolute value in CNY	1,770,300	75,478	13,040	57,100	1,902,878
Percentage (%)	92.4%	3.9%	0.7%	3.0%	100%

* Note: other cash income sources include labor wages, small occasional businesses, Amomum (a medicinal plant) and bamboo handicrafts.

5.5.4 Rubber plantation, fuel and timber

The third reason why rubber trees have become the most favorite cash crop is that rubber trees also provide firewood to local communities. Almost all firewood consumed in Baka is from dead branches of rubber trees. According to 2008 Bakahousehold survey, about 1,736 m^3 (cubic meters) of dead rubber tree branches were consumed in Baka in 2007. Traditionally, as explained in Chapter 3, there were three kinds of preferential firewood: *miqger* —hardwood, such as wood from *Castanopsis spp.*, *miqkawq*— small sticks, and *miqdovq* — flammable wood particularly bamboo. Hardwood would create charcoal when it burns, but it usually needs to be lit by flammable wood through small sticks. Rubber trees could produce these three kinds of materials perfectly;wasted rubber can be used as flammable material to light small dried sticks of rubber trees, which in turn light bigger rubber wood. Rubber wood is a perfect combination of both flammable and hard firewood;on the one hand, it is very easy to light;and on the other hand, it creates charcoal when it burns. Therefore, rubber wood has become most favorite and available firewood in Baka and in most lowlands of Xishuangbanna. In addition, rubber trees can be easily sold as timber to local timber/furniture factories when they are too old.

5.5.5 Rubber plantation and living standards

Living standards in Baka Village have been improved significantly by getting better shelters, better transportation, and better communications, among others along with the increased cash income from rubber plantations in recent years. Fifty-one households have built villa style houses in last few years. Almost all households have one or two motor bicycles; fifteen households have cars now. Almost all households have cable TV and telephone line. Most households had tractors. Rice cultivation had been mechanized before the paddy fields were leased out. Most teenager and adult villagers have mobile phones. Gravity-fed drinkable water has been piped to each household.

However, consumptionism is forming among the villagers along with the increased cash income from rubber plantations. Not only have traditional celebrations such as wedding and new house celebrations been revitalized at larger scales, but also some other new celebrations such as birthday celebrations (especially those of first and tenth birthday celebrations) have been adopted. These celebrations are lavish and competitive as they are regarded as the best way of showing the family's wealth and social status. Sacrificing a water buffalo and/or a hog is a must for such a celebration. A professional photographer must be invited to videotape the whole process and make a VCD or DVD for the celebration. Hundreds or even more than a thousand guests are invited to such celebrations. Invited guests should give a money gift to the holders, called "gua li" in Chinese. The amount of the money gift usually ranges from fifty to several hundred yuan. The more one gives, the more "face" one gains. All these gifts are recorded in a pre-prepared red book because these gifts should supposedly be paid back to the giver when he/she holds a celebration in the future. Such Acelebration usually costs tens of thousand Chinese yuan, but most of the cost is usually compensated by the money gifts. The higher a celebration cost, the more prestige would the holder gain. Though the cost would be somewhat offset by the money gifts, the high cost usually prevents poor families from holding as many and as grand celebrations as those of the better off. Therefore, although the gifts exchange in such celebrations seem to be reciprocal in theory, better off families usually get more benefits from this kind of social exchange than those poor ones. Expected money gifts for these frequent celebrations have become serious economic burdens to many households, especially poor ones. According to 2008 Baka household survey, the total money gifts given out by the villagers was about 416,000 Chinese yuan in 2007. It took up about 21.7% of whole village's total cash income in 2005. Even if the total cash income doubled in 2007 than that of 2005, the gifts would use up about 10.9% of its total cash income.

Moreover, though Baka villagers could get better health care and higher education with increased cash income, rubber plantations have caused them worse health conditions and discouraged more children to get higher educations. According to doctors from two local clinics, villagers from Baka have worse health conditions than those from Bohe, another Akha village which is only several hundreds meters away. They attribute this to the polluted water that Baka villagers drink. The drinking water of Baka Village is flowing from rubber plantations and has been polluted by pesticide and herbicide; that of Bohe is from reserved natural watershed forests. Four malformed babies have been born in Baka while there is none in Bohe in recent years. This may also be related to the polluted water. Teachers from local primary and secondary schools often complain that it is more difficult to

Chapter 5 Rubber Plantations and Transformations of Akha Society in Xishuangbanna, Southwest China

teach/discipline students today than ten years ago. They partially attribute this to the rubber plantation-based economy because tapping rubber does not need much education. Thanks to the family plan, each family usually has no more than two children in Baka and other Akha villages in Xishuangbanna. They hope at least one child would tap rubber when he/she grows up. Another reason is the fact that it is very difficult to find a job in cities and town even for people with college degrees in China now. Parents think it is wasteful to invest in their children's education for this reason.

Furthermore, though it is not the direct cause, a rubber plantation-based economy has also created conditions for some vicious life styles in Baka and other communities in this area. Rubber trees are usually tapped every other day in Xishuangbanna and a tapper could manage 300-600 trees a day depending on his/her skill. Since there are not many trees ready for tapping yet, most Baka villagers tap every other day. Therefore, the rubber tappers, particularly young generations who have nothing else to do rather than tapping rubber, have a lot of free time to kill. Even on the day they need to tap the trees, they are free in the afternoon because rubber tappers in Baka Village (and in this area) usually get up at 2 or 3 a.m. to start tapping and finish it at dawn because the early morning is the time of maximum latex production from the trees. Then they have a nap at the field shed for a couple of hours before they cook and eat brunch. They collect the latex around noon and transport it back to the village afterward. Along with the increase of cash income, gambling suddenly becomes a very popular game to kill the time for the villagers. Many people become addicted to gambling, and some not only lost all their rubber trees but also incur huge debts. Drinking is also a popular way of killing time. Many people become alcoholic. Five people died from alcoholism-related causes in Baka Village in recent years, among whom two were killed in motorcycle accidents when they were drunk, while the other three died from heart attacks when they were drinking. Some alcoholics become mentally disordered and were sent to asylums. Prostitution became prosperous in Dongfeng Town long with the rubber boom in the last decade, resulting in spread of STDs (sexually transmitted diseases) in surrounding communities. According to an herbalist in Baka, more than 100 patients with STDs visited him for private treatment in recent years. None of these happened ten years ago. A few villagers from Baka or nearby Bohe died from AIDS and more are diagnosed HIV positive. AIDS would become an epidemic in Xishuangbanna in the near future if no effective measures are carried out soon.

5.5.6 Rubber plantation and belief system

Though animist beliefs of the Akha were suppressed and most sacred forests were destroyed during Mao-era, some sacred forests (e.g. cemetery) and sites remained as *yawkhawr* or taboo. However, most of these remained sacred forests (including cemetery hills) and sites were further replaced with rubber plantations in the last decade. The sacred (or *yawkhawr*) forests/sites were reserved under the name of *naevq* (spirits). Those who dare to challenge the animist belief are usually young generations whose ages are in their 30s and 40s. When I asked them why they dare to claim these sacred lands, they said that they did not believe that there were such things as *naevq* or spirits. They believe that money is omnipotent, like a popular Chinese saying "qian neng shi gui tui mo," literally meaning "money can make ghosts mill." So even if there were *naevq*, they have become to believe that power of money surpasses that of *naevq*. Accordingly, rubber trees are called money trees, and it is okay to replace these sacred forests with rubber trees, because it is the economic growth in terms of cash income that has been employed by the state as a primary, if not the sole, indicator of social progress and development of a people;the Akha need to help themselves to upgrade their social status through "processing culture" (you wenhua) and "improving quality" (tigao suzhi in Chinese) with means of materialism (Sturgeon, 2010).

Of course, there are people, especially elders, who still believe in the power of *naevq*. It happens that the wife of a man who cleared a sacred forest for rubber plantation got eye problems in Baka Village. People explain that she has got a punishment from *naevq* because her husband broke the Akha law. Despite of their disagreement on sacred forests vs. rubber plantations, rubber trees become the most favorite cash crop in Xishuangbanna, though they were disliked by the Akha people when they were first introduced in the state farms. The Akha (and other local people as well) disliked the smell of wasted rubber too. They used to hold their breath whenever they were passing a latex collection station where a strong smell of wasted rubber was emitted, but now, they have gotten used to it, as Baka villagers joke, "we can not sleep well without the smell now."

5.5.7 Rubber plantation, social status and cultural traditions

Increased cash income from rubber plantation has promoted social status, or "quality" (Sturgeon, 2010) and acceptance of the Akha people in Xishuangbanna, reflected in the increased ratio and pattern of inter-marriage between Akha and Han. Prior to the 1980s, there were five Akha women from Baka Village married out to Han men workers in the neighbor state farm, while no single Han married into Baka Village, because it was believed not only that one married up by marrying a Han Chinese, but also that a social status of a state farm worker was higher than a farmer. It was easier for an Akha woman (especially a beautiful one) to marry a single Han worker in the farm than other way around. However, there have been ten Han men and six Han women married into Baka Village since the 1980s especially late 1990s when Baka villagers started to tap their own private rubber trees. But no single Baka villager married out to the state farm workers during the same period of time, because villagers with private rubber plantations are now believed wealthier than the state farm workers now, which was also observed by other scholars (Sturgeon, 2010).

Increased cash income from rubber plantation has enabled Baka villagers (and many other villagers as well) to not only revitalize some of their traditional cultural festivals (Akha New Year Festival or *Kartanrpar*), but also celebrate them at larger scales. Improved living standards have also liberated Akha women from many heavy traditional duties such as fetching water and carrying firewood, which allows them to have more time to make traditional costumes for the festival celebrations. Hand-weaving traditional cotton cloth has even become a kind of competition among these Akha women. For instance, according to 2006 Baka household survey, there were 247 *yar* ❶ cotton cloth woven in the village in 2005. If this presents average amount of cloth woven in Baka each year, it could produce enough cloth to make costume for every villager in two years. Since this trend has continued for some years, there is actually a lot of excessive cotton cloth in Baka Village, though it is not evenly distributed among the households.

5.5.8 Rubber plantation and biological resources

Baka Village has preserved about 3,000 mu (equals to 200 ha) collective

---

❶ *yar* is a length unit of cloth in Akha. One *yar* of cloth could be made a set of Akha costume for an adult.

forests, adjacent to state forests on Bohe Mountain (see Figure 16). Although they were once cleared for rice cultivation in 1990 and 1991 in order to cover the food shortage in Baka, these collective forests have been regenerated well. Despite that the villagers constantly attempt to encroach into the state forests, no one ever tried to cut a single tree from the collective forests without permission from the village authority. The reason given by the villagers is that so called "state forests" had been local people's forests for many generations until the early 1980s when the state declared its ownership over them. Therefore, morally speaking, it is all right for the villagers to get back their ancestors' resources through encroachment. On the other hand, since the collective forests are under their control, the villagers could manage it well without being destroyed.

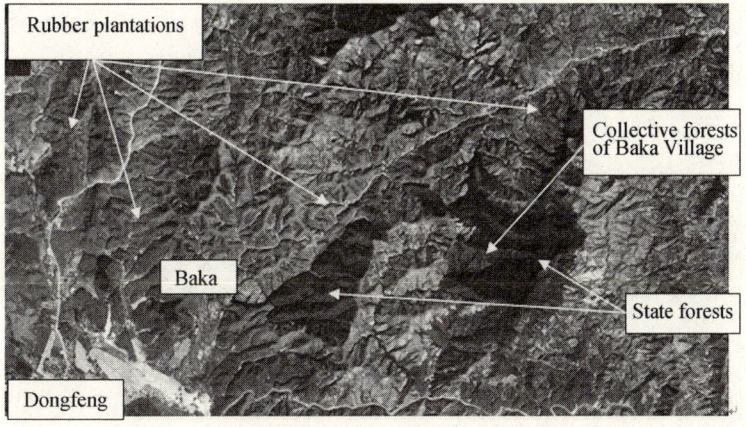

Figure 16　Map of Current Land Uses in Baka Village

According to the villagers, most local plant species are preserved in the forests. However, the forests are not only fragmented, like an island in a sea of rubber plantations, but also too small to accommodate any big animals for the long term. Therefore, as most forests surrounding Baka Village have been replaced with rubber plantations, almost all big animals and most birds have disappeared in this area. Application of chemical pesticide and herbicide in rubber plantations has also killed fish and crabs in the streams. Some of the local fish species such as *ngaqbawlaw* (in Akha) disappeared completely. Most important NTFTs (Non-Timber Forest Products) in traditional Akha economy such as bamboo shoots, bamboo worms, and mushrooms have been reduced dramatically along with expansion of rubber plantations.

The state farms had been disliked by the Akha people (and by the local people in general) since the 1960s because the former appropriated a lot of arable lands from the latter. As a form of revenge, local people often stole livestock (particularly chickens) and vegetables as well as rubber from the state farms, which resulted in social conflicts between local communities and the state farms. Once a while, the conflicts evolved into physical violence, which even caused death. The conflicts sharpened in the 1980s and 1990s when the villagers started to take "waste rubber" from the state farms after the farm workers collected rubber for the day. Rubber trees are usually tapped with a half circle cut of rubber bark every another day in Xishuangbanna. Latex usually flows out from each cut for a few hours and received with a bowl, but the latex is usually collected before it completely stops flowing for the purpose of processing before it is coagulated, in order to make a better quality rubber. The latex that flows out after the first collection continued to be received in the bowl, but will not be collected until right before the next cut, when it is coagulated. This kind of coagulated rubber is called "fei jiao", literally meaning "waste rubber". But it is not wasted; rather, it will be processed for market, though the quality is lower. The "waste rubber" is like a bonus to the state farm workers. However, local villagers went to collect the "waste rubber" without permission from the state farms in the 1980s and 1990s. Some people even stole normal rubber before it was collected.

This had been the cause of conflicts between the state farms and the local communities. Some local people got arrested and punished with serious fines or even jailed as they stole the rubber. When I asked Baka villagers why they did so, they answered that the state rubber trees were planted on the local people's forested lands, which used to provide them a lot of NTFPs, and they did not get benefits from the plantations. Now, they were very poor, they needed more and more money to pay for their children's education, medical care, and food from markets. Since their private rubber plantations did not produce rubber until the late 1990s, they had no other choices but to collect the "waste rubber" to meet their urgent need of cash. It seemed all right for them to collect some rubber from the state plantations, as they used to get NTFPs in the forests before. But from the state farms' point of view, local people's behavior was theft. Majority of local villagers stopped "collecting"/ "stealing" the "waste rubber" from the state farms when they started to tap their own rubber trees by the end of the 1990s. Only a few elders and some poor families continued to "collect" it as part of their livelihood. As long as they did not steal the "normal rubber," their collection was tolerated by the state farms. The tension between the state farms and the local communities has been lightened since then.

Disappearance of local forests has encouraged Baka villagers to preserve some important plants in their homegardens. There are 170 useful plant species found in their homegardens, 44.1% of which are introduced directly from local forests. Therefore, if managed correctly, homegardens could become an effective method of *ex situ* conservation of plants. However, the swidden crop bio-diversity has been lost along with rubber plantations in Baka.

5.6　Conclusion

Rubber plantation in Xishuangbanna was promoted by the state for the sake of national security and the defense industry. On the one hand, rubber was an urgently needed strategic material for defense industry of the newly established People's Republic of China. On the other hand, the state needed to control over local natural resources and people particularly ethnic minorities in Xishuangbanna, a newly integrated frontier. More specifically, rubber plantation—perceived as "modern" (productive in terms of taxability) and "legible" (controllable in terms of accountability)—was promoted to replace traditional swidden agriculture, which was regarded "primitive" (unproductive in terms of taxability) and "illegible" (uncontrollable in terms of accountability) by the state. Accordingly, the local ethnic minorities, particularly those highlanders like Akha who practiced swidden agriculture, were regarded "backward" and lack of "quality" to perform "advanced" work required by the state. In other words, from the state's point of view, local natural resources were "wasted" and local people (particularly ethnic minorities) were not "cultured", both which needed to be "utilized" and "mobilized" for the state building. For the state, the best way to solve these problems was to replace local swidden agriculture with rubber plantations and, in doing so, transform local ethnic minorities into rubber farmers. This would allow the state to kill two birds with one stone—to gain control over local resources and people, on the one hand, and on the other hand, to produce more rubber with little or no cost from the state.

Therefore, rubber plantations under various schemes—state farms, collective enterprise, joint-operation (between state farms and local communities), and private enterprise were developed. Development of these various types of rubber plantations was prioritized by the state, in the order listed above, for the purpose of control. The government planned to maintain a predominant role of the state farms in rubber production, supplemented by the collective and joint-operation plantations, while assigning these small holdings to the lowest priority and to a trivial position in rubber production. Notwithstanding the state's intention, however, the total area of min ying or people-run plantations — including collective, joint-operation and private — surpassed that of the state farms in Xishuangbanna by 2004. Moreover, almost all of the rubber plantations under the collective enterprise and joint-operation schemes have been privatized and distributed among the local households in Xishuangbanna by the 2000s. Furthermore, as the local people like Akha were forced to abandon traditional swidden agriculture gradually, those who live in lower slopes adopted rubber trees — a new crop that was intentionally employed by the state to control over local resources and people — and resisted the state's control by using the same crop. Like tea trees in Mengsong, rubber trees became weapons of the weak to encroach the "state forests". The villagers also always underreport their rubber plantations in order to avoid real or potential taxes on them, which is also a form of resistance (Scott, 1990).

Indeed, rubber trees have become the most favored cash crop for the local farmers in Xishuangbanna because rubber trees could not only generate unprecedented cash income to local farmers, but also provide other important resources for rural livelihood such as firewood (dead branches), timber and animal feed (rubber seeds). No other cash crops could compete with rubber trees for these versatile uses. These side-benefits have been an important reason for the recent expansion of private rubber plantations. However, replacement of local forests with rubber plantations in Baka area has reduced availability of NTFPs for collection, not to mention the disappearance of wild animals and loss of agricultural biodiversity. Drinking water has also been polluted by chemical pesticide and herbicide used in the rubber plantations in Baka Village.

As we observed in Baka, Xishuangbanna is experiencing fast economic growth mainly due to rubber plantations. Increased cash incomes has enabled Baka villagers to build better houses, get better health care and have greater mobility (with motorbikes and other vehicles), access to broader information and entertainment mainly through public media, revitalize some cultural traditions with new resources, and liberate local people, especially women, from heavy labor such as transporting agricultural products, animal fodder, and firewood that were carried on their backs and now are transported by tractors. Improved living standards with accumulated wealth from rubber have also helped to lift the social status of Akha people. This is indicated in significant increase in number of inter-marriages between Akha and more dominant Han and Dai ethnic members in the last decade. However, an economic boom based on rubber plantation is a double-edged sword, in both economic-social-cultural and ecological senses. Economically, households are more vulnerable as rubber farmers than as swidden farmers to unfavorable weather conditions, such as cold winters and storms, pests and diseases, and to fluctuations of international rubber price. This vulnerability is not a direct effect of rubber plantations *per se*, but rather from the homogeneity of landscapes — the simplification of livelihood created by monoculture of rubber trees. What is worse is that Baka villagers are so locked in rubber plantations that they do not know any other way out in case of a rubber crisis except going back to shifting cultivation by cutting rubber trees. High dependency of household and village economies on rubber has also been accompanied by social stratification and other social-cultural problems such as competitive consumption, gambling, alcoholism, and spread of STDs through prostitution.

Ecologically, expansion of rubber plantations combined with deforestation during the commune period had seriously destroyed natural habitats of various kinds of wildlife. As a result, big predators like tigers and leopards began coming to prey livestock in the villages at a very high frequency, or even attacking people more often in Xishuangbanna in the 1950s and 1960s. Baka village unprecedentedly caught eight tigers and leopards in their traps around the village during that period of time. According to the Akha informants I interviewed, most big wild animals such as tigers, leopards, bears, monkeys, deer (except muntjac), and antelopes had disappeared in most Xishuangbanna areas except in those natural reserves by the end of 1970s. They attribute this to two major reasons: on the one hand, a substantial numberof wild animals were killed by the workers of the state farms in their organized hunting;on the other hand, the remaining populations had fled to neighboring Burma and Laos as a result of loss of their habitats, destruction of their natural food chrains, and threats of human predators. The nature of the organized hunting is essentially different from those traditional ones conducted by the indigenous peoples like the Akha. First, the methods were different. The state farm workers were equipped with modern weapons (i. e. , semi-or fully automatic machine guns) and trained hunting dogs, making their hunting more active, effective, and destructive, compared with those traditional hunting methods. Second, the purposes were different. Being supplementary to their swidden agriculture, hunting and fishing had been part of Akha's traditional livelihood. However, though the workers of the state farms also consumed the meat of the killed, they had another mission in their organized hunting because many wild animals (such as tigers, leopards, bears, and boars) were labeled as "bandits" who came to steal people's properties such as livestock and crops, or even threaten people's lives and needed to be eradicated along with those human bandits (remained Nationalist troops) who were active along the border with Burma in the 1950s and 1960s (also see Sturgeon 2005). Many state farm officials were transferred army officials and many state farm workers were veterans who had multiple missions. Third, the extents of the killings were different. Having not been restricted from those hunting taboos and regulations as the Akha did, the state farm workers killed any animals and birds out of protection list without limitation of numbers in any seasons. Some of Akha's sacred animals such as pangolins were even their favorite games because they were believed to have high medical value in the Chinese medicine system. Similarly, more destructive fishing methods such as using chemical poisons as well as electric shocking machines were introduced by the state farm workers.

Disappearance of natural forests has also led to economic, social, and cultural consequences. Economically, availability of the NTFPs (Non-Timber Forest Products) to the Akha and other indigenous populations had dramatically decreased, which forced the Akha and local people to "steal" rubber from the state rubber farms and/or vegetables from the state farms, another form of resistance against the state, as the way they collected NTPs in the forests before. This had been a major source of social tension and conflicts between the indigenous populations particularly Akha and the state farms, which was not eased until by the end of twentieth century when the Akha and other local populations started to tap their private rubber trees in substantial numbers. Disappearance of natural forests and its concomitant depletion of NTFPs had also raised awareness and increased the practice of preserving botanical resources both in their collective forests and in their home gardens. Disappearance of natural forests also let some Akha, particularly young generations, to believe that the natural spirits are disappearing or their power is weakening. Instead, they need to deal with and please the newly emerged more powerful *naevq*, New China and the Han; therefore, it is possible to replace those traditional sacred sites reserved for natural spirits with rubber trees, a new crop and a new plant that was preferred by the new powerful *naevq*. Again, as in the case of Mengsong, replacement of natural forests with rubber plantation does not end the Akha belief in spirits or *naevq* ;instead, they coped with the transformations of the landscapes, both bio-physical and social-political, through granting new meanings to their existed concept *naevq*, an old tradition and cultural mechanism to adapt to changing environments.

Chapter 6

Conclusions

6.1 Revisiting Contested Landscapes in China

In conclusion, contrary to the common perception of shifting cultivators as deforesters, the Akha had sustainably managed their natural resources and played an undeniable role in conserving local biodiversity until the onset of China's modernization programs in the 1950s (Wang et al., 1999; Wang, 2001). Their success was achieved through effectively embedding their traditional ecological knowledge in their landscapes and religious representation of their management system.

The management of natural resources through religious representations was not only prevailing among traditional Akha society, but also widely practiced by the indigenous peoples such as Dai (Tai Lue), Bulang and Jinuo in Xishuangbanna (Gao, 1999; Pei, 1996). For instance, there were over 1,000 holy hills protected by the Dai (Tai Lue) people prior to 1958; these holy hills made up about 5% of the total lands of Xishuangbanna (Gao, 1999). It is evident that the indigenous people of Xishuangbanna had sustainably managed their natural resources and created/maintained very high level of biodiversity along with rich cultural diversity (Pei, 1996; Wang, 2001). However, their historical contributions to natural reserves and biodiversity conservation have been erased along with the replacement of their sacred landscapes by the state landscapes of productivity and control. This was achieved through a pair of contradictory state policies: environmental imperialism and scientific conservation, by the means of which the country takes control over the local resources and indigenous peoples.

6.1.1 Environmental Imperialism of Chinese states

The environmental imperialist tradition holds that humans are superior to, and hold dominion over nature (White, 1967: 1205). Expansion of Chinese (e.g., Han) agricultural civilization and political territory can be understood as a result of environmental as well as economic-political imperialism through domesticating and transforming of their environments, and "civilization" of the "barbarians" they encountered. Tremendous deforestation is evident in China's history (Tuan, 1969; Elvin, 1973, 2004; Anderson, 1988, 1996). Development of intensified agriculture to support its huge populations is the major reason for the deforestation; and both Yi-Fu Tuan (1969) and Mark Elvin (2004) demonstrated a positive correlation between expansion of the Chinese farm economy and deforestation. Besides cleared for farming, mountains and mountains were denuded of their trees one after another for providing (1) timbers to build splendid ancient Chinese emperors' palaces, and numerous growing cities and towns; (2) fuel for cooking and heating; (3) pulp mill materials for making paper used by huge bureaucracy; and (4) soot for the making of black ink. Edward. H. Schafer (1967) argued that the most civilized of all arts was responsible for the deforestation of much of North China. The art was the art of writing, which required soot for the making of black ink. The soot came from the burnt pine. "Even before T'ang times, the ancient pines of the mountains of Shantung bad been reduced to carbon, and now the busy brushes of the vast T'ang bureaucracy were rapidly bringing baldness to the T'a-hang Mountains between Shansi and Hopei" (299-300). Deforestation continued as the Chinese territory expanded, and as a result, though about half of the Chinese domain could have been forested at onetime, forests occupied only 8.5% of China in the early 1950s, two-thirds of them was in the northern Manchuria and much of remainder lied in mountains of the Southwest (Tuan, 1969: 31, 195). The reasons for this forest distribution pattern is that when the Manchu ruled China Northern Manchria was reserved for themselves and forbidden territory to Chinese, while not until 1420 did Yunnan and Guizhou (*Kuei-chou*) become Chinese provinces (Tuan, 1969: 32, 139). But only the lake basins of Yunnan (i.e., Kunming and Dali areas) were sinicized through the agricultural efforts of garrison troops and of civilians who had been forcibly sent there from the Yangtze delta, while much of the minority populations lived mountainous areas of Southwestern China, including northwest Guizhou (Yi), south and southwest Sichuan (Yi and Tibetan), north and northeast Yunnan (Yi), northwest Yunnan (Tibetan and Naxi), south Yunnan (Hani and Yi), southwest Yunnan (Dai), and were not ruled effectively by Chinese until the establishment of the People's Republic of China in 1949 (Harrell, 1995). It explains why the biggest tropical rainforests of China remained in Xishuangbanna, which became a small prefecture of Yunnan Province in 1950 (Hsieh, 1995), but not in the economically advanced tropical southeast and south coast of China (e.g., Fujian and Guangdong Provinces).

Chinese environmental imperialism was backed up by classical Chinese culture that valued culture over nature (Elvin, 1973, 2004). Agricultural fields and irrigation works were all valued as part of culture, while uncultivated lands and mountains were all called as "huang di" and "huang shan" meaning *wasted* lands or mountains. These wasted lands and mountains needed to be cultivated. Forests were useless rather than providing for timber, fuel, and other materials, and wild plants were useless and ugly if they could not provide these materials. Thus wild forests and plants needed to be replaced by the landscapes of production for the good of human beings. Although scientific tradition of forestry and conservation have old roots in China as well (which will be discussed in next section), environmental imperialism had been dominant in the history of China. As Tuan (1969) admits, Chinese forestry serviced to meet Chinese economic and aesthetic needs, not because of love of nature or ecological consideration.

"The best-known illustration of Chinese knowledge of forestry and of their desire for *aesthetics* and *products* is the tree grove in the temple compounds. Almost every large village has a temple with its well-managed cluster of trees, and in particular is this true of temples and monasteries located in the mountains. Certain trees appear to have special religious significance and receive special care as, for example, the maidenhair tree (*Ginkgo biloba*), the white-barked pine (*Pinus bungeana*), and the peacock pine (*Cryptomeria japonica*). These are rarely seen in the wild state. Other trees are the chestnut for the Taoists, and later the Buddhists, and the linden (*Tilia mandshurica*) for the Buddhists, to replace the tropical peepul tree (*Ficus religiosa*) of India" (ibid: 34-35).

Tuan concluded that vegetation regimes in most parts of China except for north Manchuria, Mountainous Southwest, and Hainan Island, had been transformed by human activities. Thus, logically, I was not surprised when Elvin (1973: xvii) concluded that "classical Chinese culture was as hostile to forests as it was fond of individual trees".

This tradition continued in People's Republic of China, in which trees were extensively planted in answer to dire economic need but also for aesthetic reasons (Tuan 1969), on the one hand; and on the other hand, more natural forests were destroyed, particularly during the Commune Period. The most salient example may be the great development of rubber tree plantations in Hainan Island, and south and southwest Yunnan (e. g. , Xishuangbanna and Hekou respectively) at the expenses of the last two tropical rainforests in this country since the 1950s. The newly born government of China needed to produce this strategic but unavailable industrial material rubber within its own territory for the sake of national security during the Cold War. From the state's point of view, Xishuangbanna tropical natural forests were wasteful that needed to be reclaimed and traditional swidden agriculture was unproductive that needed to be replaced, and both were uncontrollable (untaxable). Rubber plantations were justified by the belief of Chinese that the plantations were forests which would also provide environmental/ ecological services as those natural forests did. So it was just "forests for forests" and would kill two birds with one stone. Therefore, numerous state rubber plantation farms have been established in Xishuangbanna under the Reclaim Bureau of Yunnan Province since 1956, which were co-operated into ten county-level state farms by the early 1980s.

Since these tropical areas were home of numerous indigenous peoples, the state control over local resources was achieved along with control over local people through objectification and marginalization of them — by using an evolutionary theory of modes of production, adopted from the Soviet Union (Gladney, 1997: 72). The Akha (as a branch of the Hani Minority Nationality) along with their shifting cultivation, were rated as a primitive mode of production; they were seriously "behind" and backward in their social development. Therefore, "[t]he state project, dominated by Han, was then to "help" Akha farmers learn to be productive and advance into socialist modernity" (Sturgeon, 2005: 27 – 28). Such state classifications were a "technology of power" (Keyes, 1994) that enclosed peoples into a new nation in marginalized and disempowered positions. Since local indigenous people were viewed as backward and thus unqualified for this new job of modern productivity, the farm workers were recruited from Han populations in other parts of China, and indeed most of the first workers were retired veterans. Thus rubber plantations seemed to be a perfect new technology which would allow the state to exercise control over both local resources and indigenous people. In other words, the state started imposing its landscapes of productivity and rule (Neumann, 1998: 19) over the existed sacred landscapes of the Akha and the other indigenous peoples.

These contested landscapes, or "tensioned landscapes-in-movement" as Bender (2001) called them, are not only resulted from Chinese environment imperialism, but also resulted from the internal colonialism of the Chinese state in general, reflecting tensions and movements among different groups involved. It has been suggested that the process of colonization could be analyzed in terms of landscapes of power: the technology of control and the power of the colonizers to distance, objectify, attempt to control "the other" —whether people or land (Bender 2001). The process by which the Chinese state objectified and gained control over its subjects through creating 56 nationalities under the name of "civilization" is well elaborated by Dru C. Gladney (1991) and others (Harrell, 1995, 2001; Litzinger, 2000; Mueggler, 2001). Subjects the state tries to control are anything but passive. At the beginning, the Akha had a hostile, and even fearful, attitude toward rubber trees and rubber tree plantation because they represented the dominant power of the state and/or the Chinese Han (for the Akha, the two are often interchangeable), and thus of "Others", as of spirits. But such an attitude changed when the Akha started to grow rubber trees as their main cash crops in the early 1980s, in other words, the rubber trees have become "domesticated" and thus have become part of Akha's inside domain. The Chinese Government has tried to stop the local people from expanding their private rubber tree plantations since the 1990s as they have realized the negative environmental consequences of the plantations, but these efforts have not been successful because the rubber tree has become the favorite cash crop for the most local people including Akha. I interpret this as a form of resistance of the peasants, following James Scott (1985) in his *Weapons of the Weak*.

In conclusion, great expansion of rubber plantations, which had been achieved at the expense of rainforests as well as of forested lands used for shifting cultivations by local people, allowed Xishuangbanna to become the second national biggest base for rubber production but forced local people to farm less desirable lands, and indeed left less land — not enough for continuing traditional swidden agriculture in many Akha villages. The rural reform in the early 1980s, particularly the Household Contract Responsibility System, further limited swidden lands within demarcated areas, which forced many Akha communities like Baka with lower altitudes (lower than 1000 meters above sea level) to abandon swidden agriculture and adopt rubber plantations. Their culture and life styles have also become adaptive to rubber plantations. Since rubber plantations become unprofitable at higher altitudes, replacement of swidden agriculture in higher mountains of Xishuangbanna was achieved more forcefully through "stick and carrot" policies. On the one hand, the logging ban under the Natural Forest Protect Project in 1998 which forbade cutting any natural trees also meant to forbid shifting cultivation as it required cutting trees. On the other hand, the Land Conversion Project provided incentives for shifting cultivators to adopt monoculture plantations of cash crops particularly tea and Chinese fir or even rubber trees. However, since the project in particular and the government in general favored economic benefits over ecological ones, much natural forest had been replaced with monoculture plantations, which greatly jeopardized ecological goals of the project.

Despites criticism from both domestic sources and abroad, Chinese environmental imperialism will continue as long as the ideology is still taught in the Chinese national education system. Those who have experienced Chinese education from primary through graduate schools like me may forget most of the details taught in the schools such as formulas and literatures, but everybody would remember one thing that the purpose of science is to *renshi ziran, zhengfu ziran, gaizao ziran* ("认识自然,征服自然,改造自然"), literally meaning "KNOW nature, CONQUER nature, TRANSFORM nature", since we have been indoctrinated by this "philosophy" again and again in any classes of history, science, history of science, and the like.

6.1.2 Scientific Conservation Tradition

Scientific conservation tradition has old roots in China. In the *Chou Li* or *Rites of Chou* (3rd century BC), we find two classes of officials whose duties were concerned with conservation. One was the Shan-Yu, inspectorate of mountains, and the other the Lin-Heng, inspectorate of forests (Tuan, 1969: 34). Another ancient literary reference to conservation practice was in the *Mencius* (1979: 164-165). The sage advised King Huai of Liang that he would not lack for wood if he allowed the people to cut trees only at the proper time. Roadside planting is also an ancient practice in China and dates back to the Eastern Chou (722 BC – 222 BC) and Qin (Ch'in) (221 BC – 207 BC) periods. Common species traditionally used for roadsides include the poplar (*Populus simonii*), pines (especially Pinus tabulaeformis), willows (*Salix babylonica*, *S. matsudana*), chestnut (*Aesculus chinensis*), elm (*Ulmus parvifolia*), and the Chinese scholar tree (*Sophora japonica*) (Tuan, 1969:34). *Feng-Shui* is another classic example of the Chinese science of proper arrangement of elements in a landscape to ensure harmony (Anderson 1996). Chinese farmers have also developed one of the most intensified agricultures in the world, which successfully feeds one-fifth of the world's population on only seven percent of the world's arable land — and at the same time have developed a renowned cuisine (Anderson, 1988; Wen and Pimentel, 1986a, 1986b).

Scientific conservation tradition continued in the People's Republic of China, as demonstrated in establishment of natural reserves. There are 1799 natural reserves established by China's governments at various levels ranging from county, prefectural, provincial, and national; among which 187 are national natural reserves. Many natural reserves at various administrative levels have been also established in Xishuangbanna. First, the Xishuangbanna Natural Reserve is the third earliest established natural reserve in China; it was established in 1958 by Yunnan Provincial Government and was upgraded as a national natural reserve in 1986. Xishuangbanna Natural Reserve comprises seven separated areas with a total area of 242,510 hectares, making up 12.68% of Xishuangbanna territory. Please recall that a group of scientists was dispatched to investigate the feasibility of rubber plantation in Xishuangbanna in the early 1950s. Besides accomplishing their task by submitting a feasibility report of rubber plantation to the government, these scientists also submitted another proposal to Yunnan Provincial Government in 1958, suggesting establishing natural reserves in Xishuangbanna to protect the last pieces of tropical rain forests in the territories of China from rubber plantations and other human exploitation. The proposal was approved; and initially, four natural reserves❶ were established in Xishuangbanna in October 1958. However, one of them, Damenglong Natural Reserve was destroyed during the "Great Leap Forward" and the "Great Prdetarian Cultural Revolution" movements. Another two natural reserves❷ were added when the communes were dissolved in 1980. For the purpose of better administration, all these seven natural reserves were united under the umbrella name as Xishuangbanna Natural Reserve by Yunnan Provincial Government in 1981 and it was upgraded as a national natural reserve in 1986 (Forestry Bureau of Xishuangbanna Prefecture 1998; Bureau of Xishuangbanna National Natural Reserve 2010). Another natural reserve, Nanbanhe Natural Reserve, was established in Xishuangbanna as a provincial natural reserve in 1991, and was upgraded as a national natural reserve in 2000. With a total area of 26,600 hectares, Nanbahe Natural Reserve is the first national natural reserve that was established according to the watershed bio-sphere model, to conduct experiments on how the ethnic groups of Dai (Tai Lue), Hani (Akha), Bulang, Lahu, and Yi sustainably utilize the natural resources and live with their environments harmoniously. At the prefectural level, the Bulong Natural Reserve was established in 2009. It has an area of 35,485 hectares. At the county level, eight natural reserves with total area of 47,258 hectares and five natural reserves with total area of 49,600 hectares were established in

---

❶ These four natural reserves were Damenglong, Mengyang, Mengla, and Menglun respectively. The last one comprised three fragmented patches. Therefore, the total number of six areas was established in 1958.

❷ These two natural reserves were Shangyong and Mangao.

Jinghong Municipality and Menghai County respectively in the 2000s (Bureau of Xishuangbanna National Natural Reserve 2010). Therefore, by 2009, the total area of natural reserves in the Xishuangbanna reaches 401, 453 hectares, making up 21% of the prefectural territory. It means 8.31% of the national lands of Xishuangbanna have been assigned for natural reserves in the last two decades; most of these lands were covered by state forests including *Sanqpaqbarwar* (the Community Rattan Forest) and Watershed Protection Forest in Mengsong. Except the national natural reserves, all of these local natural reserves have to do with the Logging Ban enacted in 1998 and the following twin projects of the Natural Forest Protection and the Land Conversion in early 2000, which required the roles of the forestry bureau to switch from mainly logging to protecting forests (Zhao et al., 2001).

All these new developments show that the China's government now takes environmental issues seriously and take them into account in development plans. However, like rubber plantation at the beginning, many of these new natural reserves were established through expropriating forest lands from local populations. For instance, the community rattan forest *Sanqpaqbarwar* was expropriated as state forests in the early 1980s and then was declared as part of the Bulong Natural Reserve in 2009 by the prefectural government of Xishuangbanna. The *Sanqpaqbarwar* forest conditions have been degrading under the state control and management since the 1980s; because outsiders (mostly lowland Dai people) were allowed to log in the forest with permission from the Damenglong Forestry Station. A rattan weaving factory was established in Mengsong by Damenglong Township Government in 1986, which depleted the rattan resources dramatically. Without being able to protect and get benefits from their common resources protected by their ancestors for generations, Mengsong villagers also started encroaching the forest by clearing the understory and planting tea trees. Berkes (1999) hypothesizes that "a conservation ethic can develop if a resource is *important or limiting, predictable and depletable*, and if it is effectively under the control of the social group in question so that the group can reap the benefits of its conservation" (p95). In contrast, "tragedy of commons" happens under open-access conditions. Berkes' hypothesis is well supported by the case of *Sanqpaqbarwar*. In most of these natural reserves (except Nanbanhe) local people are not allowed to access and/or participate in management. As a result, incorporation of *Sanqpaqbarwar* into a state natural reserve may stop logging effectively, but it could not guarantee no encroachment from local people, either in the form of hunting, or of transforming it into tea agro-forest. Therefore, co-management and sustainable uses of the resources, such as what the Mengsong community had done in the case of *Sanqpaqbarwar* for generations, is probably the key to achieve bio-diversity conservation.

6.2 Cultural (Mal)adaptations to Frontiers by the Akha

Akha society has been evolving as its members adapt to two sets of environments: bio-physical (i.e. natural) and social-political. They have been building/maintaining two sets of boundaries in their interactions with these two sets of environments. The first set of boundaries is between Akha society (such as a village) and their bio-physical environment; I call it B-boundary[1]. A B-boundary divides the traditional territory of an Akha village (or chiefdom) into two domains: the humans (*tsawr*) and the spirits (*naevq*),

---

[1] It is an abbreviation of bio-physical boundary. I did not use the term "natural boundary" because this boundary is culturally constructed and/or perceived.

Sacred and Contested Landscapes

as demonstrated in Chapter 3. The second set of boundaries is between Akha society and their outside social-political environment; and I call it S-boundary. S-boundary has two levels: village and pan-ethnic. An S-boundary at the village level (I called Sv-boundary) is between a village and its outside environment; this boundary is usually perceived to mark a territory of a village. In other words, the Sv-boundary is the boundary among villages. An S-boundary at the pan-ethnic level (I call it Sp-boundary) is between the pan-Akha society and other people. In other words, the Sp-boundary is the boundary between the traditional Akha identity❶ and the others. A schematic map of Akha society is illustrated in Figure 17 below.

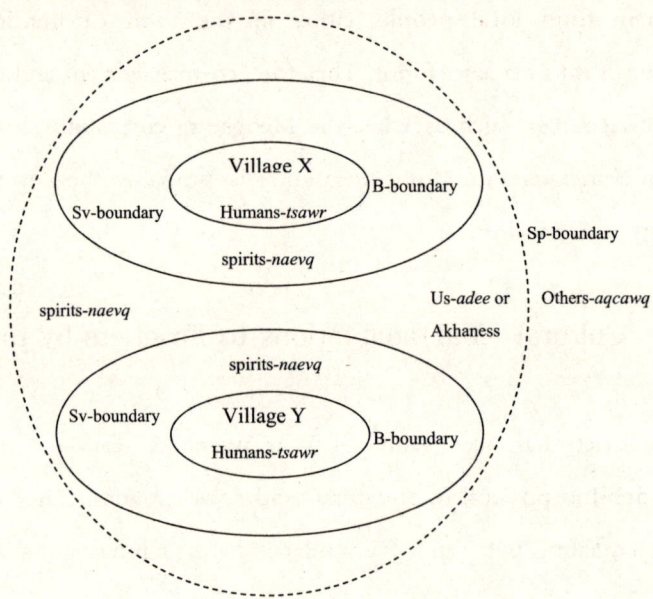

Figure 17   A Schematic Map of Akha Society

---

❶ Definition of Akha identity is subject to debate among scholars as well as among Akha people themselves, see Alting von Geusau (2000), Kammerer (1990), Tooker (2004), Toyota (2003), and Li Haiying (2012) for the detailed debate. I am using a more traditional way that the Akha identified themselves as a people who carried the ancestor's ways of life according to the *Ghanrsanrkhovq*.

I argue that Akha society has evolved as its members constantly construct and reconstruct these boundaries. These boundaries presented frontiers (following Tsing 2004) where Akha people come to contact and interact with two sets of environments. The concept *naevq* has two meanings in Akha culture: one is "spirits"; the other is "the others", particularly stronger people; both could be interpreted as "perceivable outside force beyond one's control". Therefore, I believe that the notion of spirits (both *naevq* and *sanr*) was adopted by the hunting-gathering forbearers of the Akha as they noticed that nature had its own force uncontrollable by humans at will. In other words, the natural forces (or natural laws as modern scientists might call them) were interpreted as forces managed by spirits, who along with humans were all governed by the supreme God or Creator. This could be the origin of animist belief and community-of-being worldview. Notions of us (*adee*) and the others (*aqcawq*) could also be developed as various foraging bands came into contact with each other; and the boundary among bands was the prototype of S-boundary. In the meanwhile, the notion of the inside and the outside of the band should be developed as well; and the boundary was more materialized and formalized as the Akha ancestors became agriculturalists and adopted more permanent residency (hamlets or villages). This "historical transition" was described by the Akha as their ancestors separated from *naevq*. In this process, the B-boundary along with a binary worldview was formed; and boundaries among villages became S-boundaries. As society of the Akha ancestors grew to enclose multiple villages, a prototype of Sp-boundary was constructed to distinguish between us and the others. Eventually, a strong Sp-boundary was constructed along with the formation of the Akha identity in the process of building and defending Jadae polity. The Sp-boundary was based on a territory and defended by the Jadae polity back then. Though Akha society involved in political fragmentation as they migrated into Zomia after fall of Jadae polity, the Sp-boundary was maintained through the "genealogical and alliance system" (Alting von Geusau, 2000).

During the Diasporic Period, most Akha populations lived in a small independent chiefdom called *pu* (or village) in Akha. A *pu* was led by a *dzoeqma* (chief) and governed by a Village Elder's Council (*pulanr tsawrmawq tsawrkhav*); and each village had a well defined B-boundary and Sv-boundary. However, when the Sv-boundaries among the Akha villages overlapped or merged, a supra-village political structure would be expected, such as in the case of Mengsong. As Mengsong community grew and split into several independent villages, the split villages did not move out of Mengsong, which resulted in overlapped Sv-boundaries, or the Sv-boundaries were not clear cut among villages. This situation required a supra-village figure to mediate among the *dzoeqma* of each village, in order to manage some important common resources such as rattan and irrigating water, as well as to maintain the complicated Sv-boundaries. As the Akha society integrated into the lowland Tai State of Sipsongpanna, a dual political system was formed, in which the *dzoeqma*- led Village Elder's Council continued to manage internal affairs through maintaining the B-boundary, while the *jawrbavr -naqngeq* system was created to deal external affairs such as collecting taxes for the lowland Tai lords in order to maintain the Sv-boundary with the Tai state. Sometimes the *dzoeqma* and the *jawrbavr* were the same person. In that case, he had a dual status and a dual duty; when he performed the *dzoeqma* duties, he was called *dzoeqma*; when he performed the *jawrbavr* duties, he was called *jawrbavr*. In places where the outside state power did not exist, there was no *jawrbavr-naqngeq* system.

As long as the Sv-boundary of a village was not contravened by outside force, a typical traditional Akha village with a well-functional *dzoeqma* - led Village Elder's Council could manage their natural resources through regulating various landscapes according to the ancestral customary law *Ghanrsanrkhovq* as described in Chapter 3. But if the Sv-boundary was broken or intruded upon, or if the *dzoeqma* -led Village Elder's Council did not function well, the Akha ecology of sacred landscapes would be disturbed or even broken down. For instance, during the commune period, the Sv-boundaries were seriously broken down as all the lands and crops (such as teas) were collectivized regardless the traditional Sv-boundaries; the B-boundaries were also broken down along with the dissolution of the *dzoeqma*-led Village Elder's Council and abandonment of the *Ghanrsanrkhovq* ; these had led to huge destruction of sacred landscapes of the Akha (and forests in general) in Xishuangbanna. As the boundaries were restored roughly in the 1980s, an improvement of forest management was observed in Mengsong. However, the traditional boundaries were still broken, for instance, the community rattan forest *Sanqpaqbarwar* was assigned as state forest, meaning the Sv-boundary was undermined. This change justified exploitation of the resources (rattan and timber) by the state. As a protective as well as resistant response, Mengsong Akha also started to collect rattan in the forest and grow tea trees under the forest. Another example is that the Logging Ban (and Shifting Cultivation Ban) in 1998 seized at least 3, 000 mu (200 hectares) of fallow lands with well regenerated forests in Mengsong. A rumor saying that these forested lands would be declared as state forests soon made a lot of Mengsong families nervous of losing their lands. According to the following twin projects, the Natural Forest Protection Project and the Land Conversion Project introduced in the early 2000s, these forested lands should be subsidized by the government. But the project agency refused to compensate for it, by reasoning that it could not be subsidized because the farmers did not put any labor in reforestation. Combination of fear of losing the lands and hope to gain the state subsidy had pushed the families to clear the forests[1] and planted tea trees according to the standardized technology without any natural covers because this was the only way get the state subsidy, not in the traditional way of agroforestry. Similarly, about 80% of swidden lands in Mengsong (about 18,000 *mu* or 1,200 *ha*) were converted into tea plantations in modern style (see Figure 11). Many Mengsong traditional agricultural lands (about 25,000 *mu* or 1,667 *ha*) were declared as the state wastelands in the early 1980s; Mengsong villagers also used this opening policy and converted almost all these lands into tea plantations. In the fear of losing their forests, many families also cleared parts or all of their freehold forests and planted tea trees. In other words, when the Sv-boundary was compromised, the Akha would extend the B-boundary to protect their interests. Though only 4,940 *mu* (329 *ha*) or roughly 10% of the tea plantations in Mengsong had been recognized and subsidized by the Land Conversion Project, the more importance was to reclaim their traditional lands back.

Recall the Akha traditionally managed their natural resources through making a balance between the Inside and the Outside domains. In case of swidden agriculture, they needed to "rent" the lands from the *naevq* (representative of nature or natural force) temporarily and transformed them into the Inside domain temporarily as they were cultivating the lands; then "returned" them back to the *naevq* when they were fallowed. Only the

---

[1] Cutting trees was allowed again with the introduction of the Land Conversion Project.

domesticated landscapes such as paddy fields and fenced gardens would become the Inside domain and the private property. Therefore, the Inside domain is correlated to the private ownership in Akha culture. Since the tea trees under the agro-forests were "domesticated" and became part of the Inside domain, and thus became private property;while the wild trees still belonged to the community. In the same logic and same way, Mengsong villagers reclaimed their ownership over the lost wastelands by "domesticating" them (i. e. planting tea trees). Mengsong villagers also solidified their private ownership over their swidden lands by converting them into tea plantations, that is, domesticating and transforming them into the Inside domain permanently. The same logic would explain their actions in converting their freehold forests. Swidden lands and freehold forests were granted land titles to the individual families; and yet, domestication (i. e. , the traditional way of claiming the private tenure) would provide the villagers more secured sense than the legal land title granted by the state. Similarly, in Baka Village, their traditional swidden lands at Badar were declared as the state wastelands in the early 1980s. A nearby Dai (Tai Lue) village submitted an application to the Forestry Bureau of Jinghong Municipality, asking permission to plant rubber trees in the early 2000s. Baka villagers immediately claimed that those lands were their traditional swidden lands and they should be granted permission to grow rubbers on the lands too. As the Dai village did not have much upland to grow rubber trees, the government granted half of the lands to each village in order to pacify both sides. So in this case, Baka villagers also successfully reclaimed their traditional lands through rubber plantations. Baka villagers were also constantly encroaching the nearby state forests by planting rubber trees, while they remain their collective forests untouched.

The Akha villagers from both Mengsong and Baka have been using cultural mechanisms to protect their interests when these came to contest with those of the state. The mechanism is to maintain a balance between the Inside and the Outside domains; when the Outside domain intrudes on the Inside domain, the Inside domain should also expand into the Outside domain in order to re-establish the balance. The Akha notion of the Inside (*lavqkhoer*) and the Outside (*lavqnyir*) is not absolute but, rather, relative. Even though outside the village gates is usually understood as the Outside while the inside as the Inside, this contrasting pair of spatial domains could, relatively, go beyond in both micro and macro scales. On the one hand, to the micro scale, inside the house is the Inside domain for a family while outside of it is the Outside domain; within the house, the women's part is the Inside domain while the men's part is the Outside domain (Tooker, 1988, 2012). On the other hand, to the macro scale, outside of a village's traditional territory is the Outside domain while the within of it is the Inside domain. In this latter sense, the owner of the Outside would also become *naevq*, who has power/force out of the Akha people/society's control. Therefore, we could conclude that

1) Akha societies have involved as they adapt to two sets of environments, biophysical and social-political;

2) Akha societies have managed their natural resources through a cultural mechanism to maintain a balance between the Inside and the Outside domains defined by the biophysical boundary and the social-political boundary (i. e. the territory boundary) respectively;

3) Akha societies are more likely to adopt a more sustainable natural resource management regime when their traditional territory (i. e. the Social-political boundary) is secured and thus the bio-physical environment is the

main external force with which they have to deal;

4) When social-political environment becomes the main force with which they have to deal and particularly when their traditional territory (i. e. the Socio-political boundary) is not secured or is intruded upon, Akha societies will adopt a natural resource management system that would protect their best interests, through expanding the Inside domain — which might have to be achieved at the expenses of natural environment and bio-diversity.

6.3 Discussions and Suggestions on Sustainable Development and Bio-diversity Conservation in Xishuangbanna and Beyond

As it was mentioned earlier, China's government started taking environmental issues seriously after the Yangtze River flooding in 1998. Xishuangbanna Prefectural Government also responded well to the central government's call to preserve natural forests and protect environment — through converting shifting cultivation to permanent economic and/or ecological forests, as demonstrated in their establishment of numerous natural reserves at various levels as well as in their efforts to eliminate shifting cultivations. But if our goal is sustainable development and biodiversity conservation in Xishuangbanna and beyond, some lessons could be learned from this study.

6.3.1 Management of natural reserves

The earlier established Xishuangbanna National Natural Reserves were seven pieces of fragmented forests. These newly established natural reserves in the last two decades are very important as they have provided bases for building corridors to connect those fragmented national reserves in the future.

Connections of these natural reserves through corridors are very important to restore the overall ecosystems of Xishuangbanna, and are particularly vital for long term survival of big wildlife such as elephants and tigers. However, these new natural reserves (and old ones as well) were established on the traditional territories of local indigenous populations, though they might had been expropriated as state forests in the early 1980s, such as the Community Rattan Forest *Sanqpaqbarwar* in Mengsong. In this case, participation of local communities in managing the natural reserves might be vital to achieve both sustainable development and biodiversity conservation. If local communities were excluded, they would become "thieves" or "encroachers", as happened in *Sanqpaqbarwar* since it was declared a state forest in the early 1980s. So, local communities should be invited to become co-managers and protectors. Successful Traditional models of management, such as that of *Sanqpaqbarwar*, could also be applied with adjustment into the new management system.

Co-management also means that the local communities are allowed to use certain resources in the natural reserves according to specified regulations. The dynamic view of ecosystem renewal should be observed in the management of certain natural reserves. It is evident that appropriate use of resource could maintain healthy and productive ecosystems. For example, the tropical forest ecosystem can absorb the perturbation of long-fallow shifting cultivation, and in fact flourishes with it. Thus, if the objective is to conserve tropical forests, a strategy of focusing on resilience, through knowledge of regeneration cycles and ecological processes, such as plant succession, may be the key to tropical forest sustainability (Lugo, 1995; Holling et al., 1995). Another example, the best population of a protected tree *xevxeer* (*Calophyllum polyanthum*) in China is preserved in *Sanqpaqbarwar* in Mengsong. The reason I was told by the villagers is that a mature *xevxeer* tree needs to be cut in order to allow more seedlings to grow; if the mature tree were not cut, all the seedlings would die out before they could grow big.

Similarly, the local governments could also invite local communities to co-manage those yet incorporated state forests and wastelands in order to prevent from being encroached. This could be arranged in many forms, such as community preservation forest, or revival of traditional sacred landscapes. For instance, the state forests at Bohe Mountain nearby the Baka Village have been encroached all the time, while the collective forests of the village are maintained untouched. If the governments allow the Baka and other communities to co-manage the state forests, I believe that they could be maintained better. There are actually some Akha cultural sacred sites in the state forests on Bohe Mountain. If the local governments assist local communities (not just Baka) to revitalize the Akha sacred landscapes on the Bohe Mountain, its state forests could be protected better by the local communities. Since these remaining state forests and collective forests are sources for building further corridors to connect those natural reserves, protecting and even recovering them are remained equally important.

6.3.2 Restoration of traditional sacred landscapes

Although many sacred forests and landscapes were destroyed during the Commune Period, a substantial numbers of them still remained, albeit in more fragmented forms. It is also evident that dry monsoon rainforests in Xishuangbanna only exist in the holy hills protected by the Dai people (Wang, 2001). However, many of these sacred forests and landscapes have become out of protection due to the dissolution of the traditional managing institutions. Therefore, it is urgent to restore these sacred forests along with revitalization of the traditional management system where it is possible before both knowledgeable persons and the forests themselves are gone. Restoration of the traditional sacred landscapes is significant for four reasons: first, it has cultural and ecological educational value; second, it could serve as a core area to establish a bigger natural reserve at the village level or above; third, it could serve as material basis for revitalizing and/or maintaining traditional ecological knowledge and its management institute. Since traditional ecological knowledge was embedded in the landscapes, if the landscapes were gone, the knowledge would also be prone to loss. Then last, but not least, the traditional sacred forests and landscapes could serve as an entry and/or anchor point for connecting to the global religious communities in conservation (Tucker, 2003; Tucker and Grim, 1994; Darlington, 2012) or spiritual ecology (Sponsel, 2012).

Since the first Earth Day on April 22, 1970, whole scientific and academic fields have developed with a focus on environmental questions, problems, and issues — such as environmental economics, environmental education, environmental ethics, environmental history, environmental law, environmental literature, environmental philosophy, and environmental studies (Collett and Karakashian, 1996). These and many other traditional human ecological approaches — such as cultural ecology, political ecology and historical ecology — are certainly necessary. Indeed, they are contributing significantly to reducing some environmental problems. Yet, the ecocrisis not only persists, but is becoming even worse. In a belief that secular approaches have proven insufficient to resolve the environmental crisis, a quite different approach to the ecocrisis, spiritual ecology, has grown rapidly since the 1990s and it has demonstrated positive effects already (Sponsel, 2012: ibid). Advocates of spiritual ecology consider the ecocrisis to result from human alienation from nature combined with the disenchantment, objectification, and commodification of nature, as Sponsel describes,

"Increasingly nature is considered as simply a warehouse of resources to be extracted in order to not only meet basic human needs, but also to try to satisfy the apparently unlimited greed for profit of rampant predatory capitalism coupled with the associated modern fixation of many people and societies on materialism and consumerism. Ultimately such rapacious selfishness is no less than ecocidal for the biosphere and accordingly also suicidal for the human species" (ibid: xvi).

Alternatively, "spiritual ecology is the recognition of the considerable relevance of religions and spiritualities in dealing constructively with the ecocrisis" (ibid: xvii).

Sponsel calls spiritual ecology as a revolution because its proponents view ecocrisis as far more than merely a social, economic, political, governmental, legal, scientific, and/or technological matter, but ultimately as a much deeper cultural, moral, ethical, and spiritual crisis as well (Tucher, 2003; Anderson, 1996). Therefore, to solve the crisis, or at least to substantially reduce it and the associated risks and dangers, our societies need to rethink about "spiritual and ecological questions such as: What is nature? What is human nature? What is the place of humans in nature? What should be the place of humans in nature?" (Sponsel, ibid: xvii). Sponsel does not give an explicit answer, but I believe the answer is that the revolution requires our societies to switch a view of nature from "commodity belonging to us" to "community to which we belong". As I have demonstrated in this study, a community-of-being worldview would allow our society to treat nature and non-human beings respectfully.

Dove et al. (2011) criticizes environmentalists interested in sacred forests for tending to ignore cultural ecological history. In Java and elsewhere in

Southeast Asia, the sacralization of fragments of forest often, and of individual trees almost always occurs as part of a wider process of deforestation and landscape transformation (Block, 1995; Dove, 2003). In other words, sacred trees and groves in and around villages actually symbolize the forest that the village ancestors cut down. Therefore, Dove et al. (2011) criticizes that characterizing "the partial end products of this historical process as evidence of spiritually driven conservation artificially abstracts what is happening on a small part of the landscape as a whole over a long period of time". While I agree with Dove et al that we need to understand the cultural ecological history, the formation of the sacred forests in Xishuangbanna is different from the process described by them. The sacred forests in Xishuagbanna were formed before they got fragmented. In other words, they were sacralized not because they were fragmented, but because they were culturally and ecologically important, and as thus, they were maintained while the others were cut down.

6.3.3 Biodiversity Conservation

As it was demonstrated in Chapter 3, swidden agriculture was characterized with very high level of biodiversity, at genetic level, species level, and ecosystem level. However, the Shifting Cultivation Ban in 1998 and the Land Conversion Project in the early 2000s have ended almost all shifting cultivation in Xishuangbanna. For instance, there are only a few families in Hongqi Village, and some families in Ake, Yakou and Lahu villages in Mengsong still practicing it, as they have little or no irrigated paddy fields to farm. It means that agro-biodiversity has dramatically decreased in the last decade. If swidden agriculture were totally stopped, all of this agro-biodiversity would be lost. During my fieldwork in 2008, those families who were still practicing swidden agriculture asked me to help them to get permission from the local governments to allow them to continue it. I approached to local authorities to propose that an experiment area needs to be set up for *in situ* preservation of agro-biodiversity of swidden agriculture and Aka and Yakou would be an ideal place to conduct such an experiment because they had lands and some families were willing to do it. But the local authorities did not approve our proposal. An alternative to *in situ* conservation is collecting seeds of the crops and saving them in seed bank.

Another location of high biodiversity is homegardens. In contrast to swidden agriculture, homegardens have been thriving both in Mengsong and Baka, more so in the former than the latter. Collecting wild plants and growing them in managed patches such as homegardens for food, medicinal and cultural purposes had a long history among indigenous peoples in Xishuangbanna and other tropical regions (Long, 1993; Wang et al., 1999; Long and Li, 2006; Fu et al., 2006). The local people have accumulated abundant knowledge about collection, utilization, and management of local plant resources. The diverse collection includes many vulnerable and endangered species and also endemic species. It is evident that homegardens are not only important to maintain local people's livelihood and culture, but also significant for *ex situ* biodiversity conservation in human-dominated areas (Gao et al., 2012). Since local indigenous people produce organic food such as vegetables in the homegardens, the local governments should protect the price of their products, so that they could compete with those produced in the industrialized and chemicalized fields.

6.3.4 Sustainable development

In conclusion, Akha societies and their natural resource management system have evolved as they have adapted to dynamic changes of two sets of forces. When natural forces are the major challenges, Akha natural resource management system tends to be more sustainable since ecological balance is not taken less as important than those of economic and cultural benefits; when social-political forces surpassed natural forces, Akha people tend to adopt a new strategy of natural resource management which would provide best protection for their lives, in doing so, negative ecological consequences may follow if the social-political forces (such as those of Chinese government policies) favor economic or political benefits over ecological ones. Thus, in order to achieve a sustainable resource management regime and a sustainable development, stakeholders, especially those with power and influence such as governments and international organizations/societies, should create favorable conditions that allow local communities to adopt ecologically friendly strategies. For instance, the Chinese government and the Natural Forest Protect Project should pay Mengsong communities for their contributions to forests conservation; instead of incentivizing them to replace natural forests (swidden lands in fallow) with tea plantations. Of course, the government also needs to consider the economic development of local communities. But, there exist other options for promoting economic development in Mengsong. For instance, protection of the market price of their organic tea from their traditional tea trees under natural forests is more helpful than blind expansion of tea plantations without any protection. If the government could stabilize and protect the market price of their organic tea, Mengsong actually would not need that much in the way of new tea plantations; as in Reed's (1997) demonstration that collecting yerba mate and rubber in forests by the Guaraní people in Paraguay is not only more profitable but also more sustainable than monoculture of cash crops and ranching. As contributers of one of the key water sources for lowland paddy fields in Damenglong Basin, Mengsong could be also compensated for their contributions to forests conservation by the lowlanders who benefit from it through government differentiated taxation and its redistribution system. The government should also discourage commercial mining and logging from outsiders in such ecologically important areas like Mengsong where local communities have received little economic benefit. These government-approved activities not only destroyed local forests and ecology, but also injured local people's hearts as their generations-long investment was easily reaped by unrelated others without any compensation. Local people were further cheated and harmed by the government in its dam construction in Mengsong. All of these problems arose from the lack of participation of local communities in decision-making. Equal and fair participation in decision-making is the key prerequisite for a sustainable development (WCED, 1987). China is yet far from establishing such a political system.

In order to achieve a sustainable development in indigenous people centered areas like Xishuangbanna, China should respect local people's culture and rights to their own resources; should return to them stewardship and ownership;should allow them to join the management of natural resources with their traditional ecological knowledge and wisdom; and should not allow this traditional ecological knowledgeand agro-biodiversity to disappear without any effective measurement to protect and conserve it.

Southeast Asian governments particularly those of Laos and Myanmar who are eagerly expanding rubber plantations under influence of China should take the lessons from Xishuangbanna. Local communities and governments might get economic benefits from rubber plantations, but a substantial proportion of forests need be preserved for animals as well as for local people's livelihood (e. g. collecting or even reasonable hunting). Economic activities need also to be diversified to reduce the high risk created by the monoculture of cash crops like rubber trees as they are entering global market economy. Reciprocal social and cultural services as well as relevant educational services need to be provided to local communities in order for them to prepare for exposure to modern societies.

REFERENCES

[1] Agrawal, Arun. State Formation in Community Spaces? Decentralization and Control over Forests in the Kumaon Himalaya, India[J]. *Journal of Asian Studies,* 2001, 60 (1): 9 – 40.

[2] Alting von Geusau, Leo G. M. 2000. Akha Internal History: Marginalization and the Ethnic Alliance System[M]//in Civility and Savagery: Social Identity in Tai States, edited by Andrew Turton. Richmond: Curzon Press, 2000: 122 – 158.

[3] Ecologies of the Heart[M]. New York and Oxford: Oxford University Press, 1996.

[4] Anderson, Eugene N. The Food of China[M]. New Haven: Yale University Press, 1998.

[5] Anderson, Eugene N. and Felix Medina Tzuc. Animals and the Maya in Southeast Mexico [M]. Tucson: University of Arizona Press.

[6] Backus, Charles. The Nan-chao Kingdom and T'ang China's South Western Frontier[M]// Cambridge Studies in Chinese History, Literature and Institutions. New York: Cambridge University Press, 1981.

[7] Examination of A Place Name "Guha" in Hani Oral History and Southward Migration of the Hani[J]. Yunnan Normal University Journal, 2013 (2): 138 – 149.

[8] Bai, Yongfang. Historical Memories in Traditional Hani Costumes: A Case Study of Wo-tuo-bu-ma, Luchun County, Yunnan Province[D]. Ph. D. dissertation. Central University for Nationality (of China) (Zhongyang Minzu Daxue), 2009.

[9] Bai, Zhonghe. A Supplementary Study of History of Yuan Jiang[EB/OL]. Yunan National Culture, 2008. [引用日期](发布日期). http://www. ynmw. org/news. asp? ProdId = 0000686.

[10] Baidu Baike. 2013a. Tianshan. Published at an online Baidu encyclopedia (in Chinese) at http://baike. baidu. com/view/20630. htm. Retrieved on May 9, 2013.

[11] Baidu Baike. 2013b. Aidinghu. Published at an online Baidu encyclopedia (in Chinese) at http://baike. baidu. com/view/67406. htm. Retrieved on May 9, 2013.

[12] Baidu Baike. 2013c. Huoyanshan. Published at an online Baidu encyclopedia (in Chinese) at http://baike. baidu. com/view/4573. htm. Retrieved on May 9, 2013.

[13] Baidu Baike. 2013d. Tianshan Tianchi. Published at an online Baidu encyclopedia (in Chinese) at http://baike. baidu. com/view/10092. htm. Retrieved on May 9, 2013.

[14] Baidu Baike. 2013e. Caiwobaohu. Published at an online Baidu encyclopedia (in Chinese) at http://baike. baidu. com/view/454149. htm. Retrieved on May 9, 2013.

[15] Baidu Baike. 2013f. Huyang. Published at an online Baidu encyclopedia (in Chinese) at http://baike. baidu. com/view/54006. htm. Retrieved on May 9, 2013.

[16] Baidu Baike. 2013g. Chuanguan (Boat-shaped coffin). Published at an online Baidu encyclopedia (in Chinese) http://baike. baidu. com/view/469370. htm. Retrieved on May 20, 2013.

[17] Ban, Gu (AD 32-92). *Han Shu* [*History of the Former Han*], reprinted by Zhonghua Shujuk, 1962.

[18] Basso, Keith H. Wisdom Sits in Places: Landscape and Language Among the Western Apache [M]. Albuquerque:University of New Mexico Press, 1996.

[19] Bender, Barbara. Introduction [M]//*Contested Landscapes: Movement, Exile, and Place*. Barbara Bender and Margot Winer. eds. Oxford: Berg,2001.

[20] Berkes, Fikret. Sacred Ecology: Traditional Ecological Knowledge and Resource Management [M]. Philadelphia, PA: Taylor & Francis,1999.

[21] Blackburn, Thomas C. and Kat Anderson, Before the Wilderness: Environmental Management by Native Californians[M]. Menlo Park, CA: Ballena Press, 1993.

[22] Blaikie, Piers, and Harold Riverfield. Defining and Debating the Problem [M]//Land Degradation and Society. Piers Blaikie and Harold Riverfield, eds. London: Methuen, 1987: 1 – 26.

[23] Blu, Karen. "Where Do You Stay At?": Home Place and Community Among the Lumbee [M]//Senses of Place. Steven Feld and Keith Basso. Santa Fe & New Mexico, School of American Research Press, 1996.

[24] Bradley, David. Proto-Loloish[M]. London and Malmo:Curzon Press, 1979.

[25] Bureau of Xishuangbanna National Natural Reserve. Chronicle of Natural Reserves in Xishuangbanna Dai Autonomous Prefecture[M]. Kunming: Yunnan Science and Technology Press, 2010.

[26] Callicott, J. Baird, and Michael P. Nelson. American Indian Environmental Ethics: An Ojibwa Case Study[M]. Upper Saddle River, NJ: Pearson Prentice Hall, 2004.

[27] Chang, Qu (AD 291 – 361). Huayang Guo Zhi (Chorography of Huayang Country)[M]. Reprinted by Qi Lu Shu She, 2010.

[28] Chen, Chuankang. On Question of Development and Natural Conservation in Xishuangbanna[M]//Proceedings of Symposium on Utilization of Tropical Resources. Ministry of Agricultural Reclamation & Association of Tropical Crops of China, 1979.

[29] Chen, Shanyang, Xu Jianchu, Pei Shengji. Rattan Resource Management and Extersion in Mengsong Hani Swidden Agroecosystem[M]//Collected Research Papers on Biodiversity in Swidden Agroecosystems in Xishuangbanna. Pei Shengji, Xu Jianchu, Chen Sanyang, Long Chun-lin, edited. Kunming: Yunnan Education Press, 1997.

[30] Cohen, Paul T. Resettlement, Opium, and Labour Dependence: Akha-Tai Relations in Northern Laos[J]. *Development and Change*, 2000, 31 (1): 179 – 201.

[31] Cohen, Paul T. and Chris Lyttleton. The Akha of Northwest Laos: Modernity and Social Suffering[M]// Challenging the Limits:Indigenous Peoples of the Mekong Region. Prasit Leepreecha, Don N. McCaskill, and Kwanchewan Buˉadæˉng. Chiang Mai: Mekong Press, 2008: 117 – 142.

[32] Cold Injury Investigation Office of Agricultural Reclamation Bureau of Yunan Province. Reports on Cold Injury on State Rubber Farms in Yunnan[M]//Selections of Paper on Development and Ecological Balance in Yunnan Tropicals. Republished in Theories and Practices of Rubber Plantations at Tropical North Edges and High Altitudes of Yunnan (paper collections), Yunnan Agricultural Reclamation Cooperation Ltd. and Yunnan Association of Tropical Crops, 2005: 112 – 190.

[33] Collett, Jonathan, and Stephen Karakasian. Greening the College Curriculum: A Guide to Environmental Teaching in the Liberal Arts[M]. Washington, D. C. : Island Press, 1996.

[34] Daly, Herman E. Steady-State Economics (2nd ed.) [M]. Washington, D. C.: Island Press, 1991.

[35] Darlington, Susan M. The Ordination of a Tree:The Thai Buddhist Environmental Movement [M]. Albany: State University of New York Press, 2012.

[36] Day, Kristen A. China's Environment and the Challenge of Sustainable Development[M]. Armonk, New York, London: M. E. Sharpe, 2005.

[37] Diamond, Jared, New Guineans and their natural world[M]//The Biophilia Hypothesis. S. R. Kellert and E. O. Wilson. Washington, D. C. : Island Press, 1993: 251 - 71.

[38] Dove, Michael R. The Banana Tree At The Gate[M]. New Haven & London: Yale University Press, 2011.

[39] Dove, Michael R. Comments on Peter Brosius's Analysis and Interventions, Anthropological Engagements with Environmentalism[M]. Current Anthropology, 1999 (40): 290 - 291.

[40] Dove, Michael R. , Percy E. Sajise, and Amity A. Doolittle. Beyond the Sacred Forest: Complicating Conservation in Southeast Asia[M]. Durham: Duke University Press, 2011.

[41] Douglas, Mary. Purity and Danger[M]. London:Routledge and Kegan Paul, 1966.

[42] Duan, Shuqiao. New Explanation of Yelang in Yelang Guo[EB/OL]. Published online by Southwest University for Nationalities at http://222. 210. 17. 136/mzwz/news/8/z_8_52425. html, on December 3, 2011.

[43] Economy, Elizabeth C. The River Runs Black: the Environmental Challenge to China's Future [M]. Ithaca&London: Cornell University Press, 2004.

[44] Elvin, Mark. The Retreat of the Elephants: An Environmental History of China[M]. New Haven: Yale University Press, 2004.

[45] Elvin, Mark. The Pattern of the Chinese Past[M]. Stanford: Stanford University Press, 1973.

[46] Fan, Chuo. AD 863. Manshu (The Book of the Southern Barbarians)[M]. Reprinted by Zhonghua Shuju, 1962.

[47] Fan, Ye (AD 398 - 445). Hou Han Shu (History of Later Han Dynasty). Reprinted by Zhonghua Shu Ju in 2009.

[48] Feld, Steven. Waterfalls of Song: An Acoustemology of Place Resounding in Bosavi, Papua New Guinea[M]//Senses of Place Steven Feld and Keith Basso, Santa Fe & New Mexico, School of American Research Press, 1996.

[49] Forde, C. Daryll. Habitat, Economy and Society: A Geographical introduction to Ethnology [M]. London: Methuen, 1934.

[50] Forestry Bureau of Xishuangbanna Prefecture[J]. Land Conversion Plan of Xishuangbanna Prefecture, 2000.

[51] Forestry Bureau of Xishuangbanna Prefecture. Forestry Chronicle of Xishuangbanna Prefecture [M]. Kunming: Yunnan Nationality Press, 1998.

[52] Fu, Yongneng, Guo Huijun, Chen Aiguo, and Cui Jingyun. Household Differentiation and

on-farm Conservation of Biodiversity by Indigenous Households in Xishuangbanna [J]. China Biodiversity Conservation, 2016 (15): 2687 − 2703.

[53] Gao, Jie, Tianhua He, Qiao-Ming Li. Traditional Home-garden Conserving Genetic Diversity: A Case Study of Acacia Pennata in Southwest China [J]. Conserv Genet 2012 (13): 891 − 898.

[54] Gao, Lishi. Studies of Dai Traditional Irrigation and Environmental Preservation in Xishuangbanna [M]. Kunming: Yunnan People's Press, 1999.

[55] Gladney, Dru. Muslim Chinese: Ethnic nationalism in the People's Republic [D]. Cambridge, MA: Council on East Asian Studies, Harvard University, 1991.

[56] Grossman, Lawrence S. The Political Ecology of Bananas: Contract Farming, Peasants, and Agrarian Change in the Eastern Caribbean [M]. Chapel Hill and London: The University of North Carolina Press, 1998.

[57] Gunderson, L. H., C. S. Holling, and S. S. Light. Barriers and Bridges to the Renewal of Ecosystems and Institutions [M]. New York: Columbia University Press, 1995.

[58] Hallowell, Irving. Ojibwa World View and Disease [M] //Man's Image in Medicine and Anthropology. Edited by Iago Galdston. New York: International Universities Press, 1963: 258-315.

[59] Hansson, Inga-Lill. A Phonological Comparison of Akha and Hani [J]. *Linquistics of the Tibeto-Burman Area*, 1982 (1): 63 − 115.

[60] Hansson, Inga-Lill. Death in an Akha Village [M] //*Highlanders of Thailand*. John McKinnon and Wanat Bhruksasri. Kuala Lumpur: Oxford University Press, 1983: 278 − 290.

[61] Harrell, Stevan. Ways of Being Ethnic in Southwest China [M]. Seattle and London: University of Washington Press.

[62] Hansson, Inga-Lill. Chinese Historical Microdemography [M]. Berkeley: University of California Press, 1995.

[63] Harvey, Graham. Animism: Respecting the Living World [M]. New York: Columbia University Press, 2006.

[64] Hawkes, Jon. The Fourth Pillar of Sustainability: Culture's Essential Role in Public Planning [M]. Melbourne: Common Ground P/L, 2001.

[65] Holling, Crawford. S. The resilience of terrestrial ecosystems: local surprise and global change [M] //Sustainable Development of the Biosphere. W. C. Clark and R. E. munn, eds. Cambridge: Cambridge University Press, 1986: 292 − 317.

[66] Hsieh, Shih-chung. On the Dynamics of Tai/Dai-Lue Ethnicity: An Ethnohistorical Analysis [M]//Cultural Encounters on China's Ethnic Frontiers, Stevan Harrel, ed., Seattle and London: University of Washington Press, 1995: 301 – 328.

[67] Huang, Shaowen. From Nuomaamei to Ailao Mountain: Hani Nationality Cultural Geographic Research[M]. Kunming:Yunnan Nationality Press, 2007.

[68] Huang, Xianfan. Nong Zhigao[M]. Nanning: Guangxi People's Press, 1983.

[69] Huang, Zerun, Gu Xijin, Li Yikun, and Wang Ke. Current Status and Suggestions on Future Development of Rubber Industry in Xishuangbanna [M]//Selections of Paper on Development and Ecological Balance in Yunnan Tropicals. Republished in Theories and Practices of Rubber Plantations at Tropical North Edges and High Altitudes of Yunnan (paper collections), Yunnan Agricultural Reclamation Cooperation Ltd. and Yunnan Association of Tropical Crops, 2005: 781 – 797.

[70] Hunn, Eugene. Nch'i-Wana, the Big River[M]. Seattle:University of Washington Press, 1990.

[71] Huntington, Ellsworth. Mainsprings of Civilization [M]. New York: John Wiley & Sons, 1945.

[72] Hansson, Inga-Lill. Civilization and Climate[M]. New Haven: Yale University Press, 1920.

[73] Jiang, Dingzhong. 哈尼族史志辑要(Hani Zu Shi Zhi Ji Yao, or A Summary of Historical Records on Hani Nationality)[M]. Kunming: Yunnan Nationality Press, 2007.

[74] Jin, Zheng, Liao Guoqiang, Jin Zhenggu, Lan Minghong, and Li Quanzhong. The Hani as Descendents of A Major Military Tribe of Dali Kingdom - A New Hypothesis on Origin and Migration of Hani Nationality In Collection Papers of the Fifth International Conference on Hani/Akha Culture [Mojiang, Yunnan, China, 8 – 12 April, 2005], eds., Liu Shuncai and Zhao Dewen, Yunnan Nationality Press, 2007.

[75] Shida and Ahai, eds. Migratory Epic of Yaniya (Ya Ni Ya Ga Zan Ga in Chinese)[M]. Kunming: Yunnan People's Press, 1992.

[76] Johnson, Leslie M. and Eugene S. Hunn (eds.). Landscape Ethnoecology[M]. New York & Oxford: Berghahn Books, 2010.

[77] Kahn, Miriam. Your Place and Mine: Sharing Emotional Landscapes in Wamira, Papua New Guinea[M]//Senses of Place, eds., Steven Feld and Keith Basso, Santa Fe & New Mexico, School of American Research Press, 1996.

[78] Kammerer, Cornelia A. Spirit Cults among Akha Highlanders of Northern Thailand[M]//

Founder's Cults in Southeast Asia: Ancestors, Fertility, and Polity, Cornelia A. Kammerer and Nicola Tannenbaum, eds. Monograph Series, 52. New Haven: Yale University Southeast Asia Studies, 2003.

[79] Kammerer, Cornelia A. Descent, Alliance, and Political Order Among Akha[J]. American Ethnologist, 1998, 25 (4): 659 – 674.

[80] Kammerer, Cornelia A. Begging for Blessing Among Akha Highlanders of Northern Thailand [M]//Merit and Blessing in Mainland Southeast Asia in Comparative Perspective, Cornelia A. Kammerer and Nicola Tannenbaum, eds. , 79 – 97. Monograph Series, 45. New Haven: Yale University Southeast Asia Studies, 1996a.

[81] Kammerer, Cornelia A. Discarding the Basket: The Reinterpretation of Tradition by Akha Christians of Northern Thailand[J]. Journal of Southeast Asian Studies, 1996B (27): 320 – 322.

[82] Kammerer, Cornelia A. Territorial Imperatives: Akha Ethnic Identity and Thailand's National Integration[M]//Hill Tribes Today: Problems in Change, eds. John McKinnon and Bernard Vienne. Bangkok: White Lotus-Orstorm, 1989: 259 – 301.

[83] Kammerer, Cornelia A. Gateway to the Akha World: Kinship, Ritual, and Community Among Highlanders of Thailand[D]. Ph. D. dissertation, University of Chicago, 1986.

[84] Keyes, Charles F. The Nation-State and the Politics of Indigenous Minorities: Reflections of Ethnic Insurgency in Burma[J]. Paper presented at Tribal Minorities and the State, organized by the Harry Guggenheim Foundation, Istanbul, 1994 (2): 21 – 25.

[85] Kormondy, Edward J. Concepts of Ecology[M]. 4th edition. Upper Saddle River, NJ: Prentice hall, 1996.

[86] Kukaewkasem, Yotsaphong. A Study of Linguistic Features in Akha Personal Names[J]. Paper Presented at the Sixth International Conference on Hani/Akha Culture, Luchun, Yunnan, China, 2008 (11).

[87] Kunstadter, Peter (ed.). Southeast Asia Tribes, Minorities, and Nations[M]. Princeton, New Jersey: Princeton University Press, 1967.

[88] Lando, Richard. The Gift of Land: Irrigation and Social Structure in a Toba Batak Vilage[D]. Ph. D. dissertation. Dept. of Anthropology, University of California, Riverside, 1979.

[89] Lansing, J. Stephen. Priests and Programmers: Technologies of Power in the Engineered Landscape of Bali[M]. Princeton, N. J.: Princeton University Press, 1991.

[90] Leach, Edmund Ronald. Political systems of highland Burma: A study of Kachin social

structure[D]. Cambridge: Harvard University Press, 1954.

[91] Lee, Kai N. Compass and Gyroscope: Integrating Science and Politics for the Environment [M]. Washington, D. C. : Island Press, 1993.

[92] Lewis, Paul. Akha Oral Literature[M]. Bangkok: White Lotus Press, 2002.

[93] Lewis, Paul. Basic Themes in Akha Culture[M]//. The Highland Heritage: Collected Essays on Upland Northern Thailand, edited by Anthony Walker. Singapore: Suvarnabhumi Books, 1992: 207-224.

[94] Lewis, Paul. Akha-English-Thai Dictionary[M]. Chiang Rai, Thailand: Development and Agricultural Project for Akha (DAPA), 1989.

[95] Lewis, Paul. Ethnographic Notes on the Akhas of Burma[M]. New Haven: Human Relations Area Files, 1969-1970.

[96] Lewis, Paul W. and Bai Bibo. Hani Cultural Themes[M]. Bangkok: White Lotus, 2002.

[97] Li, Haiying. Traditionalist Movements: A Case Study of A Multi-Religious Akha Community in Northern Thailand[D]. A paper presented at the 2nd International Conference on International Relations and Development, Chiang Mai, Thailand, 2012-07-26. Available at http://www.icird.org/2012/abstracts_authors.html.

[98] Li, Yikun and Wang Ke. People Run Rubber Plantation in Yunnan[J]. Rural Development Studies (in Chinese), 1989 (133).

[99] Liang, Zhaotao, Chen Qixin and YangHeshu (eds). Introduction to Chinese Ethnology[M]. Kunming: Yunnan People's Press, 1985.

[100] Litzinger, Ralph A. Other Chinas: the Yao the politics of national belonging[M]. Durham, NC: Duke University Press, 2000.

[101] Liu, Long, Hu Tongyuan, Yangshucai, Liu Wenwei, and Guo Ruixiang. A Report of National Land and Economic Investigationin Xishuangbanna [Xishuangbanna Guotu Jingji Kaocha Baogao][M]. Kunming: Yunnan People's Press, 1990.

[102] Long, Chun-lin. Collected Research Paper of Tropical Botany[D]. Kunming: Yunnan University Press, 1993(2): 66-67.

[103] Long, Chun-lin and Li ML. Status and Conservation Strategies of Community Plant Genetic Resources - A Case Study in Manlun, a Dai Village in Xishuangbanna[M]. Chinese Bulletin Botany, 2006(23): 177-185.

[104] Long, Chun-lin, Wang Jieru, Li Yanhui, and Pei Shengji. Traditional Tea-garden Ecosystems

of Xishuangbanna [M]//Collected Research Papers on Biodiversity in Swidden Agroecosystems in Xishuangbanna. Edited by Pei Shengji, Xu Jianchu, Chen Sanyang, and Long Chun-lin. Kunming: Yunnan Education Press, 1997.

[105] Ma, Lajia. Sichuan Yi Studies: Exploring Mysteries of Sanxingdui Cultural Relics [M]. Chengdu: Sichuan Nationality Press, 2002.

[106] Ma, Tingzhong, Jiang Dingzhong, Li Weiji, and Wang Ersong, edt. A Brief History of Hani Nationality (Hani Zu Jian Shi)[M]. Beijing: Nationality Press, 2008.

[107] Mao, Youquan. On Four Hypotheses of Hani Origins [J]//Si Xiang Zhan Xian (The Ideological Front, a Chinese Journal), 1992 (5).

[108] Mason, Otis. Technogeography, or the Relation of the Earth to the Industries of Mankind [J]. American Anthropologist. 1894 (2): 137 − 161.

[109] Meadows, D. H., D. L. Meadows, J. Randers, and W. W. Behrens III. The Limits to Growth [M]. New York: Universe Books, 1972.

[110] Mencius. Mencius [M]. D. Lau, trans. Harmondsworth, UK: Penguin, 1979.

[111] Michaud, Jean. Historical Dictionary of the Peoples of the Southeast Asian Massif [M]. Latham, Md., Scarecrow, 2006.

[112] Michaud, Jean. Turbulent Times and Enduring Peoples: Mountain Minorities in the Southeast Asian Massif [M]. Curzon, Richmond, England, 2000.

[113] Montesquieu, Charles Baron. The Spirit of the Laws [M]. New York: Hafner, 1949.

[114] Morton, Micah. Negotiating the Changing Zomia of Mainland Southeast Asia: A Preliminary Discussion of the Role of Language in Akha Identitarian Politics [J]//International Journal of Thai Studies, 2010.

[115] Mueggler, Erik. The Age of Wild Ghosts: Memory, Violent, and Place in Southwest China [M]. Berkeley: University of California Press, 2001.

[116] Munasinghe Institute for Sustainable Development, 2007. Sustainable Development Triangle [M]//Encyclopedia of Earth. Eds. Cutler J. Cleveland (Washington, D. C.: Environmental Information Coalition, National Council for Science and the Environment).[First published in the Encyclopedia of Earth January 29, 2007; Last revised Date March 21, 2013; Retrieved April 30, 2013 <http://www.eoearth.org/article/Sustainable_development_triangle>

[117] Murray, Frank. Potential Impacts of Climate Change and Regional Air Pollution on Biodiversity and Landscape Use. Biodiversity Conservation Corridors Initiative (BCI),

International Symposium, 2006 (4): 27 – 28, Bangkok, Thailand. Available at http://www. gms-eoc. org/CEP/Comp2/docs/Thailand/BCI_Frank_Murray. pdf.

[118] Myers, Fred R. Pintupi Country, Pintupi self: Sentiment, Place, and Politics among Western Desert Aborigines[M]. Berkeley, Los Angeles, and London: University of California Press, 1991.

[119] Nelson, Richard K. Make Prayers to the Raven: A Koyukon View of the Northern Forest [M]. Chicago: University of Chicago Press,1983.

[120] Neumann, Roderick P. Imposing wilderness: struggles over livelihood and nature preservation in Africa[M]. Berkeley: University of California Press,1998.

[121] Nightingale, Jean. Without A Gate[M]. Singapore: Overseas Missionary Fellowship,1990.

[122] Ostrom, Elinor. Governing the Commons: The Evolution of Institutions for Collective Action[M]. Cambridge: Cambridge University Press,1990.

[123] Padoch, Christine. Monitoring the Demise of Swidden in Southeast Asia: Local Realities and Regional Ambiguities [D]. A presentation paper at the Society of Ethnobiology 27th Annual Conference, UC Davis, 2004(3): 24 – 27.

[124] Panadda Boonyasaranai. Revival and Construction of Akha Ethnic Identity in Thailand and Neighboring Countries [M]//Identity Discourse. Bangkok: OS Printing House. (in Thai),2004.

[125] Panadda Boonyasaranai. Akha: Uncivilized and Poor but Attractive[M]//Identity, Ethnicity, and Marginality. ed. Pinkaew Luangaramsri. Bangkok: OS Printing House. (in Thai),2003.

[126] Paulson, Susan, Lisa L. Gezon, and Michael Watts. Locating the Political Ecology: An Introduction[J]. Human Organization,2003 (3): 205 – 217.

[127] Peet, Richard, and Michael Watts. Production: Development Theory and Environment in an Age of Market Triumphalism[J]. Economic Geography,1993(69): 227 – 253.

[128] Pei, Shengji. Indigenous Knowledge and Conservation of Biodiversity in the Mountain Ecosystems[M]//Environment and Biodiversity: In the Context of South Asia. Katmandu, Nepal: Ecological Society,1996: 51 – 58.

[129] Pu, Chongxiu. Origin of the Name "Yuan Jiang" [EB/OL]. Published online by Yunnan Nationality Culture, available at http://sinayn. com. cn/article/180/16637. Html. 2008.

[130] Qin, Yazhou. Ye-lang Guo: Unanswered Questions of Millennia Left by Sima Qian? (in Chinese)[EB/OL]. Published at Xinhuanet on May 24, 2005. Available online at http://

news. xinhuanet. com/focus/2005-05/24/content_2995445. htm. 2005.

[131] Rao, Raghavendra R. Traditional Knowledge and Sustainable Development: Key Role of Ethnobiologists[J]. *Ethnobotany*, 1996(8): 14 – 24.

[132] Reed, Richard K. Forest Dwellers, Forest Protectors: Indigenous Models for International Development[M]. Boston: Allyn and Bacon, 1997.

[133] Reid, Walter V., and K. R. Miller. Keeping Options Alive: the Scientific Basis for Conserving Biodiversity[M]. New York: World Resources Institute, 1989.

[134] Roux, Henri. The Akha and Phu Noi: Minorities of Laos in the 1920s [Originally published in 1924 as: Deux Tribus de la Région de Phongsaly (Laos septentrional), *Bulletin de l'Ecole Française d'Extrême Orient,* Vol. 24, No. 1, pp. 373 – 500, Plates IX - XVII]. Translated by Walter E. J. Tips, Bangkok: White Lotus, 2011.

[135] Roux, Henri and Tran-Van-Chu. Quenques minorities ethniques du Nord-Indochine, I. A-kha ou Kha-kô[J]. *France-Asie*, 1954 (92 – 93): 152 – 233.

[136] Sauer, Carl. The Morphology of Landscape[J]. University of California Publications in Geography. Berkeley: University of California Press, 1925(2): 19 – 54.

[137] Schafer, Edward H. Ancient China[M]. New York: Time-Life Booksd.

[138] Scott, James C. The Art of Not Being Governed: An Anarchist History of Upland Southeast Asia[M]. New haven & London, Yale University Press, 2009.

[139] Scott, James Domination and the Arts of Resistance: Hidden Transcripts[M]. New Haven and London: Yale University Press, 1990.

[140] Sheridan, Thomas E. Where the Dove Calls: The Political Ecology of a Peasant Corporate Community in Northwestern Mexico[M]. Tucson: The University of Arizona Press, 1998.

[141] Shi, Junchao. Descendents of Plateau and Coast Cultures - Examining Migratory Epics of Hani[M]//Collection of Hani Studies. Kunming: Yunnan University Press, 1991: 31 – 40.

[142] Shi, Weiyi. Rubber Boom in Luang Namtha: A Transnational Perspective. A report for GTZ RDMA (Rural Development in Mountainous Areas), Lao-German Development Cooperation, 2008.

[143] Sima, Qian. Shiji [*Records of the Grand Historian*], reprinted by Zhonghua Shuju in 1959.

[144] Song, Lian et al. (comp.) (AD 1310 – 1381). Yuan Shi [History of the Yuan], reprinted by Zhonghua Shuju in 1976.

[145] Sponsel, Leslie E. Spiritual Ecology: A Quiet Revolution[M]. Santa Barbara: Praeger, 2012.

[146] State Forestry Bureau of China. State Natural Forest Protection Project,1998.

[147] State Forestry Administration of P. R. China. Criteria of Identifying Ecological or Economic Forests in Land Conversion Project. Available at http://www. tghl. gov. cn/zcfg/zc_02_08. htm. 2001.

[148] State Forestry Administration of P. R. China. Ten Years of Xishuangbanna Natural Forest Protect Project, at http://www. forestry. gov. cn/distribution/2008/09/11/lyyw-2008-09-11-18606. html. 2008.

[149] State Office of Land Conversion Project. Compensation and Subsidy Policy for Land Conversion Project. Available at http://www. tghl. gov. cn. 2000.

[150] Statistic Bureau of Xishuangbanna Prefecture. Xishuangbanna Statistics Book 2004 [M]. Kunming: Yunnan News Press,2005.

[151] Strang, Veronica. Uncommon Ground: Cultural Landscapes and Environmental Values [M]. Oxford and New York: Berg,1997.

[152] Steinberg, David, ed. In Search of Southeast Asia: A Modern History [M]. Honolulu: University of Hawai'i Press,1987.

[153] Stivers, R. The Sustainable Society: Ethics and Economic Growth [M]. Philadelphia: Westminster Press,1976.

[154] Sturgeon, Janet C. Governing Minorities and Development in Xishuangbanna, China: Akha and Dai Rubber Farmers as Entrepreneurs [J]. *Geoforum*, 2010(41): 318 – 328.

[155] Stivers, Janet. Border Landscapes: The Politics of Akha Land Use in China and Thailand [M]. Seattle: University of Washington Press,2005.

[156] Stivers, Janet. Practices on the Periphery: Marginality, Border Powers, and Land Use in China and Thailand [D]. Ph. D. dissertation, Yale University,2000.

[157] Sun, Guansheng. Ancient, Mythical, Magnificent - Exploring Origins of Hani Culture [M]. Kunming: Yunnan People's Press,1991.

[158] Sun, Shimei and Chen Zhengbiao. Preliminary Exploration on Bronze Culture of Tanglang Mountain in Qiaojia [M]. Cross-Century Explorations in Yi Studies. Guizhou Provincial Association of Yi Studies, and Guizhou National Archaic Texts Sorting Office, edited. Guiyang: Guizhou Nationality Press,2009.

[159] Sutton, Mark Q. and Eugene N. Anderson. Introduction to Cultural Ecology [M]. 2nd edition. Plymouth, UK: AltaMira Press,2010.

[160] Swain, Margaret B. Native Place and Ethnic Relations in Lunan Yi Autonomous County, Yunnan[M]//Perspectives on the Yi of Southwest China, ed. , Stevan Harrell, Berkeley, Los Angeles, and London: University of California Press,2001.

[161] Tambiah, Stanley J. World Conqueror and World Renounce[M]. Cambridge: Cambridge University Press,1976.

[162] Tax, Sal. An Appraisal of Anthropology Today[M]. Chicago: University of Chicago Press, 1953.

[163] Tian, Xiaoxiu. Modular Modernity: Shifting Forms of Collective Identity Among the Akha of Northern Thailand[J]. *Anthropological Quarterly*, 2004 (2): 243 – 288.

[164] Tian, Xiaoxiu. History of Chinese National Development (Zhonghua Minzu Fazhan Shi *in Chinese*)[M]. Beijing: Huaxia Press, 2001.

[165] Tong, Enzheng. Ancient Ba Shu[M]. Chengdu: Sichuan People's Press, 1979.

[166] Tooker, Deborah Ellen. Space and the Production of Cultural Difference among the Akha Prior to Globalization: Channeling the Flow of Life [M]. Amsterdam: Amsterdam University Press, 2012.

[167] Tooker, Deborah Ellen. Modular Modernity: Shifting Forms of Collective Identity Among the Akha of Northern Thailand[J]. Anthropological Quarterly, 2004 (2): 243 – 288.

[168] Tooker, Deborah Ellen. 1996a. Irrigation Systems in the Ideology and Ritual Practices of Akha Shifting Agriculturalists, paper presented at the Second International Conference on Hani-Akha Culture, Chiang Mai and Chiang Rai, Thailand, 12 – 18 May.

[169] Tooker, Deborah Ellen. 1996b. No Longer the "Other". Hani-Akha Conference. IIAS Newsletter 9, Summer 1996. International Institute for Asian Studies, Leiden, The Netherlands. (http://www. iias. nl/iiasn/iiasn9/soueasia/akha. html)

[170] Tooker, Deborah Ellen. Putting the Mandala in its Place: A Practice-based Approach to the Spatialization of Power on the Southeast Asian "Periphery" - The Case of the Akha[J]. *The Journal of Asian Studies* : 1996, 55 (2): 323 – 358.

[171] Tooker, Deborah Ellen. Identity Systems of Highland Burma:'Belief', Akha-zang and a Critique of Interiorized Notions of Ethno-Religious Identity[J].*Man* , 1992, 27 (4): 799 – 819.

[172] Tooker, Deborah Ellen. 1988. Inside and Outside: Schematic Replication at the Levels of *Village, Household and Person among the Akha of Northern Thailand. Ph. D* dissertation, Harvard University.

[173] Toyota, Mika. Contested Chinese Identities Among Ethnic Minorities in the China, Burma and Thai borderlands[J]. Ethnic & Racial Studies, 2003 (2): 301 – 320.

[174] Toyota, Mika. Cross border mobility and social networks: Akha Caravan Traders[M]// Where China Meets Southeast Asia: Social and Cultural Change in the Border Regions, ed. Grant Evans et al. Singapore: ISEAS, 2000: 204 – 221.

[175] Toyota, Mika. Cross Border Mobility and Multiple Identity Choices: The Urban Akha in Chiang Mai, Thailand[D]. Unpublished Ph. D. thesis, University of Hull, 1999.

[176] Tsing, Anna L. Friction: An Ethnography of Global Connection[M]. Princeton, N. J. : Princeton University Press, 2004.

[177] Tuan, Yi-Fu. China[M]. Chicago: Aldine Publishing Company, 1969.

[178] Tucker, Mary Evelyn. Worldly Wonder: Religions Enter Their Ecological Phase[M]. Chicago: Open Court Publishing Company, 2003.

[179] Tylor, Edward. Primitive Culture, Researches into the Development of Mythology, Philosophy, Religion, Language, Art and Custom[M]. London: John Murray, 1871.

[180] UCLG (the United Cities and Local Governments). Culture and Sustainable Development: Examples of Institutional Innovation and Proposal of A New Cultural Policy Profile. Report 4 of the Agenda 21 for Culture. The report is available online at http://www.cities-localgovernments.org and http://www.agenda21culture.net. 2009.

[181] Van Driem, George. Neolithic Correlates of Ancient Tibeto-Burman Migrations[M]// Archaeology and Language II, Roger Blench and M. Spriggs. London: Routledge, 1999: 67 – 102.

[182] _____. Tibeto-Burman Phylogeny and Prehistory: Languages, Material Culture and Genes [M]//Examing the Farming/Language Dispersal Hypothesis. Peter Bellwood and Colin Renfrew. Cambridge: McDonald Institute for Archaeology. 2002: 233 – 249.

[183] Van Schendel, Willem. Geographies of Knowing, Geographies of Ignorance: Southeast Asia from the Fringes [R]. paper presented at the workshop Locating Southeast Asia: Genealogies, Concepts and Prospects, Amsterdam, 2001 (3): 29 – 31.

[184] Vayda, Andrew P., and Bradley B. Walters. Against Political Ecology[J]. Human Ecology, 1999 (1): 167 – 179.

[185] Wang, Hui. Buyi Culture Will Reveal Mystery of Ancient Yelang State. Published online by Hainan News at http://www.hinews.cn/news/system/2011/02/14/012004378.shtml,

2011-02-14.

[186] Wang, Jianhua. Applications of Indigenous Knowledge in Natural Forest Conservation in Xishuangbanna [M]//Research Reports on Natural Forest Conservation and Land Conversion Program in Yunnan Province of China. Zhao Juncheng, XuJianchu, and Qi Kang. Kunming: Yunnan Science and Technology Press, 2001: 494 − 502.

[187] Wang, Jianhua. Cultural Practices and Indigenous Knowledge of Swidden Cultivation in Mengsong Akha Communities, Xishuangbanna, South Yunnan, China[M]//Links between Cultures and Biodiversity: Proceedings of the Cultures and Biodiversity Congress 2000 Yunnan, P. R. China. Jianchu Xu (ed.), Kunming: Yunnan Science and Technology Press, 2000: 633 − 639.

[188] Wang, Jianhua. A Preliminary Study of Hani Agricultural Cultivation Culture in Xishuangbanna [M]//A Collection of Essays on Hani Culture, the Hani Research Committee of Yunnan Nationalities Association (ed.), Kunming: Yunnan Nationalities Press, 1999: 350 − 387.

[189] Wang, Jianhua. Traditional Cultural and Biodiversity Management of Mountain Ethnic Group in Xishuangbanna: A Case Study of Mengsong Hani Community [R]. master thesis, Kunming Institute of Botany, Chinese Academy of Sciences, 1998.

[190] Wang, Jianhua and Huang Rongsheng. Genealogies, Jadae Polity and Formation of Akha People[R]. paper presented at the sixth International Conference on Hani/Akha Culture, Luchun, Yunnan, China, 2008 (11): 1 − 6.

[191] Wang, Jianhua, Xu Jianchu, Pei Shengji. Study on Indigenous Knowledge System for Management of Ecosystem Diversity in Mengsong Hani Community, Xishuangbanna[J]. Chinese Journal of Ecology, 2000 (19): 36 − 41.

[192] Wang, Jichao. Historical Relationships of Yi Nationality and Yelang Ancient State. Published online by Southwest University for Nationalities at http://222. 210. 17. 136/mzwz/news/2/ z_2_22849. html, 2009-10-04.

[193] Wang, Zhijun. Inventory of Bird Diversity in Mengsong, Xishuangbanna[M]//Collected Research Papers on Biodiversity in Swidden Agroecosystems in Xishuangbanna. Pei Shengji, Xu Jianchu, Chen Sanyang, and Long Chun-lin. Kunming: Yunnan Education Press, 1997.

[194] WCED (World Commission on Environment and Development). Our Common Future [M]. Oxford: Oxford University Press, 1987.

[195] Wen, Duzhong and David Piementel. Seventeenth Century Organic Agriculture in China, Part I: Cropping Systems in jiaxing Region[M]. Human Ecology, 1986 (1): 1 – 14.

[196] Wen, Duzhong Seventeenth Century Organic Agriculture in China, Part II: Energy Flows Through an Agrosystem in Jiaxing Region[M]. Human Ecology, 1986 (1): 15 – 28.

[197] White, Lynn Jr. The Historical Roots of Our Ecologic Crisis[J]. Science, 1967 (155): 1203 – 1207.

[198] Wiens, Herold. Han Chinese Expansion in South China[M]. The Shoe String Press, Yale University, 1967.

[199] Wilkinson, Endymion (ed.). Chinese History: A Manual Revised and Enlarged[D]. the Harvard University Asia Center for the Harvard-Yenching Institute, 2000.

[200] Wolf, Eric. Europe and the People Without History[M]. Berkeley: University of California Press, 1982.

[201] Wu, Wenyi. Yelang Culture. Online publishing at Baibu Baike, available at http://baike.baidu.com/view/484490.htm. Retrieved on May 15, 2013.

[202] Xinhuanet Yunnan Channel. Understanding Mojiang, available at http://www.yn.xinhuanet.com/live/2007-04/26/content_9899151_1.htm. 2007.

[203] Xishuangbanna Bureau of Ethnic and Religious Affairs. Ethnic and Religeous Chronicles of Xishuangbanna. Kunming: Yunnan Nationality Press, 2006.

[204] Xishuangbanna Prefecture. Gateway to ASEAN: Xishuangbanna Jinghong Industrial Zone [M]. An Advertisement Book Distributed by Xishuangbanna Prefectural Government, 2008.

[205] Xu, Jianchu, 2006. The Political, Social, and Ecological Transformation of a Landcape: The Case of Rubber in Xishuangbanna, China[J]. Mountain Research and Development, 2006, 26 (3): 254 – 262.

[206] Xu, Jianchu, Chen Sangyang, Li Yanhui, and Pei Shengji. Crop and Variety Diversity in Mengsong Swidden Agroecosystems[M]//Collected Research Papers on Biodiversity in Swidden Agroecosystems in Xishuangbanna. Pei Shengji, Xu Jianchu, Chen Sanyang, and Long Chun-lin. Kunming: Yunnan Education Press, 1997.

[207] Xu, Zaifu. Fig Trees - the Key Plants in the Ecosystem of Tropical Rain Forest in South Yunnan[J]. Biodiversity, 1994 (1): 21 – 23.

[208] Yang, Liujin. Genealogies of Hani Nationality in Honghe (Honghe Hani Zu Pu Die *in*

Chinese)[M]. Beijing: Nationality Press, 2005.

[209] Yang, Wanzhi. A Study of Hani Hieroglyphic Symbols, Honghe Nationality Studies (in Chinese), 1991 (3): 43 – 49.

[210] Yang, Yuda. On Formation of Nanzhong Great Clans and Changes of Han Society during Han and Wei Dynasties[J], Nationality Research, 2003 (5).

[211] Yang, Zhongming. A Brief History of Hani Nationality in Xishuangbanna (Xishuangbanna Hani Zu Jian Shi *in Chinese*)[M]. Kunming: Yunnan Nationality Press, 2010.

[212] You, Zhong (ed.). Colloquium on National History of the Southwest (Xinan Minzu Shi Lun Ji *in Chinese*)[M]. Kunming: Yunnan Nationality Press, 1982.

[213] You, Zhong. National History of Southwestern China (Zhongguo Xinan Minzu Shi *in Chinese*)[M]. Kunming: Yunnan People's Press, 1985.

[214] You, Zhong. National History of Yunnan (Yunnan Minzu Shi *in Chinese*)[M]. Kunming: Yunnan University Press, 1994.

[215] Yunnan Agricultural Reclamation Cooperation Ltd. and Yunnan Association of Tropical Crops, 2005. Theories and Practices of Rubber Plantations at Tropical North Edges and High Altitudes of Yunnan (paper collections).

[216] Yunnan Provincial Editorial Committee on Local Chronicles (云南省地方志编纂委员会). Yunnan Provincial Chronicles: Ethnographies (云南省志·民族志)[M]. Kunming: Yunnan People's Press, 2002.

[217] Yunnan Provincial Government. Yunnan Sheng Xingzheng Quhua Jiance 2006 (A Brief Handbook of Administrative Division of Yunnan Province 2006)[M]. Kunming: Yunnan People's Press, 2006.

[218] Yunnan Provincial Office of Publication and Plan for Ethnic Minorities' Archaic Texts. Migrations of Hani Ancestors (Ha Ni A Pei Cong Po Po in Chinese), Kunming: Yunnan People's Press, 1986.

[219] Zhang, Xiaoming. Insights on the Origin, Migration, and Mixture of Hani Minority Nationality from Genetic Studies [R]. A presented paper at the Seventh International Conference on Hani/Akha Culture (ICHAC), Yuanjiang, Yunnan, China, 2012 (11): 24 – 28.

[220] Zhang, Xinshi. Towards Understanding of Biodiversity [M]. Advanced Researches on Biodiversity. Qian Yingqian et al eds. Beijing: China Science and Technology Publishing, 1995.

[221] Zhao, Juncheng, Xu Jianchu, Qi Kang, eds. Research Reports on Natural Forest Conservation and Land Conversion Program in Yunnan Province of China[M]. Kunming: Yunnan Science and Technology Press, 2001.

[222] Zhe, He. Textual Researches and Analyses on Hani (*Ha Ni Kao Bian* in Chinese)[M]. Kunming: Yunnan Nationality Press, 2010.

[223] Zheng, Shaoqian. Pu'er Fu Zhi [Gazetteer of Pu'er Prefecture], Daoguang of the Qing Dynasty, 1840.

[224] Zhou, Shengxian. Nation's forest out of the woods[N]s. *China Daily*, 2000-12-07.

Appendix I

Preferred Timber Trees in Mengsong

Akha Name	Scientific Name
Aqjiraqye pavqma	*Elaeocarpus austro-yunnanensis*
Aqjiraqye pavqzaq	*Elaeocarpus varunua*
Boeqsoev	*Eurya groffii*
Boercanq	*Phoebe sheareri*
Boercanq xeer	*Phoebe puwenensis*
Cirnawv	*Choerospondias axillaris*
Haqba	*Castanopsis calathiformis*
Khawrdmr sevnav	*Litsea chinpiengensis*
Lmrbor	*Nyssa javanica*
Panqlanr	*Paramichelia bailloni*
Pavqbuq ma	*Alseodaphne andersonii*
Pavqbuq zaq	*Litsea monopetala*
Siqbir	*Litsea cubeba*
Tseevqkav	*Castanopsis mekongensis*
Tseevqxaer	*Castanopsis hystrix*
Xevxeer	*Calophyllum polyanthum*
Xirsav ba	*Schima argeatea*
Xirsav neir	*Schima wallichiii*
Zeeq	*Toona ciliate*
Zivqkanq	*Styrax tonkinensis*

Appendix II

A List of Plants and Crops in Mengsong Swidden Fields
(156 species and varieties)

Akha Name	Scientific Name	Uses
Anrjirpavqdaw	Mentha haplocalyx	Vegetable
Aqcevq	Coix lachryma-jobivar. gigantea	Starchy food, medicine
Aqjuqnartor	Vitex quinata var. puberula	Shadowand support for rattan
Aqpaer-margawq	Prunus pashia	Fruit
Arbawr-manqcoer	Manihot esculenta	Starchy food, vegetable
Arbawr-marhecaer	Cyphomandra betacea	Vegetable
Ardu	Zea mays	Starchy food, fodder
Arganq	Thysanolaena maxima	Vegetable, making besom
Arhaq	Indosasa singulispicula	Vegetable
Arziv	Dioscorea cirrhosa	Starchy food
Baevkhawr	Psophocarpus tetragonolobus	Vegetable
Boeqtevq	Stachys sieboldii	Vegetable
Boerbav	Luffa cylindrica	Vegetable
Byaqxanq	Clerodendranthus spicatus	Medicine
Byaevyaq	Cucumis melo	Fruit
Bymq	Nephelium chryseum	Fruit
Bymqma	Colocasia esculenta	Vegetable, fodder
Caer	Oryza sativa var. spontanca	Staple food
Ciqcaq	Phyllanthus emblica	Fruit
Cirnawv	Choerospondias axillaris	Timber, fruit
Daeqxeer-jiyaw	Amorphophallus bannaensis	Vegetable
Darghmr	Calamus nambriensis var. alpinus	Making furniture, fruit, vegetable
Darghmr	C. nambariensis var. Damenglongensis	Making furniture, fruit, vegetable

Appendix II A List of Plants and Crops in Mengsong Swidden Fields

Continued

Akha Name	Scientific Name	Uses
Darghmr	C. nambariensis var. sishuangbannaensis	Making furniture, fruit, vegetable
Darghmr	C. obovoideus	Making furniture, fruit, vegetable
Dargmq	Centella asiatica	Vegetable
Darpirdarlanr	Croton hutchinsonianus	Hedge, medicine
	Croton crassifolius	Hedge, medicine
Durpyur	Bauhinia variegata	Vegetable
Eerpuq	Cucurbita pepo	Container, vegetable
Eerpuq	Lagenaria siceraria	Container, vegetable
Eerpuq	L. siceraria var. microcarpa	Adornment, religious use
Ghaeq	Prunus majestica	Fruit, hedge
Ghasawr	Coriandrum sativum	Spice
Ghawqbu	Raphanus sativus	Vegetable
Ghawqcaer	Fagopyrum tataricum	Vegetable
Ghawqcaer-saw	Fagopyrum esculentum	Vegetable
Ghawqhaq	Emilia prenanthoides	Vegetable
Ghawqloer	Solanum nigrum var. photeinocarpum	Vegetable
Ghawqpavq-haq	Brassica integrifolia	Vegetable
Ghawqpavq-pyur	Brassica chinensis	Vegetable
Ghawqpavq-pyurma	Brassica pekinensis	Vegetable
Ghawqpavq-siq	Brassica oleracea var. capitata	Vegetable
Ghawqyer neir	Amaranthus tricolor	Vegetable
Guqqir-guqdar	Allium hookeri	Spice
Haqbawr	Dendrocalamus sp.	Bamboo shoot, fencing
Haqciv	Plectrocomia himalayana	Making furniture, fruit, vegetable
Haqcoer	Dendrocalamus hamiltonii	Vegetable
Haqpaqoeqtsavq	Viola angustistipulata	Vegetable
Haqpaqoeqtsavq	Plantago erosa	Vegetable
Hawqnyawq	Oryza sativa var. glutinosa	Staple food
Jaqsawv	Erythrina lithosperma	Timber, hedge
Jaqsawv	Erythrina stricta	Timber, hedge
Jiroq or Jaroq	Mangifera indica	Fruit

Sacred and Contested Landscapes

Continued

Akha Name	Scientific Name	Uses
Jiyaw	Amorphophallus konjac	Medicine, food
Kataev	Ananas comosus	Fruit
Kawqlaeq	Melia toosenden	Timber, medicine
kmrtsov	Jatropha curcas	Oil
Laeqoq-nav	Morus alba	Fruit
Laevbawlaev	C. yunnanensisvar. intermedius	Making furniture, fruit, vegetable
Laevlaevnyoer	Calamus yunnanensis	Making furniture, fruit, vegetable
Laevlaevxeer	C. yunnanensisvar. densiflora	Making furniture, fruit, vegetable
Lanqloer	Setaria italica	Starchy food
Lanxar	Acorus calamus var. verus	Medicine
Laqbeeq-boeqtevq	Canna edulis	Starch
	Canna sp.	Starch
Laqbeeq-yarmovq	Crassocephalum crepidioides	Vegetable
Laqpir	Capsicum annuum	Spice, vegetable
Laqpir-xaer	Capsicum frutescens	Spice
Lawrba	Coix lachryma-jobi	Adornment
Lawrbawq	Camellia sinensis var. assamica	Beverage
Lawrdawq	Dendranthema indica	Aesthetics, medicine
Lawrdawq	Cosmos sulphureus	Aesthetics
Lawrtawq	Trema orientalis	Fibre
Lokalodu	Elscholtzia communis	Spice
Loq	Sterculia pexa	Fibre
Lupavq	Piper betle	Chewing stuff
Lupavq	Piper longum	Spice, chewing stuff
Maerpir	Alpinia galanga	Medicine
Maerxeer	Curcuma longa	Medicine, dyestuff
Manqcoer	Ipomoea batatas	Starchy food, fodder
Manqcoer-devga	Dioscorea alata	Starchy food
Manqcoer-ma	Dioscorea esculenta	Starchy food
Maqxir-neevma	Dolichos lablab	Vegetable
Mardae	Cucurbita maxima	Vegetable

Appendix II A List of Plants and Crops in Mengsong Swidden Fields

Continued

Akha Name	Scientific Name	Uses
Margawq	Purus spp.	Fruit
Marhe-caer	Lycopersicum esculentum var. cerasiforme	Vegetable
Marhe-joe	Solanum melongena var.	Vegetable
Marhe-miqxmr	Solanum melongena	Vegetable
Marhe-siqhaq	Solanum integrifolium	Vegetable
Marhe-tev	Solanum melongena var.	Vegetable
Marnaw	Sechium edule	Vegetable
Mawqsawr	Eryngium foetidum	Spice
Miqxuq	Pinus khasya var. lanbianensis	Timber
Narmanarpiawq	Helianthus annuus	Oil
Neevcoer	Vigna sesquipedalis	Vegetable
Neevde	Phaseolus vulgeris	Vegetable
Neevde mawyaevqu	Phaseolus sp.	Vegetable
Neevde yevqnav	Phaseolus coccineus	Vegetable
Neevganq	Vigna sinensis	Vegetable
Neevganq	Vigna radiata	Vegetable
Neevgaw	Vigna sinensis	Vegetable
Neevpanq	Arachis hypogaea	Oil
Neevpyav	Glycine max	Oil, spice, fodder
Ngabaev	Musa sapientum	Fruit, fodder, vegetable
Ngabaev-awv	Musa nana	Fruit
Nganeir	Musa acuminata	Fodder, vegetable
Ngapeer-siqtiv	Ensete glaucum	Fodder, adornment
Nmqsiq-mar	Perilla frutescens	Oil
Nmqsiq-xaer	Sesamum orientale	Oil
Oerpoe	Ficus hispida	Fodder
Parhaw	Houttuynia cordata	Vegetable
Pavliq	Castania mollissima	Dried fruit
Pawqcoer	Saccharum sinensis	Fruit
Pawqpir	Cymbopogon citratus	Spice
Pivrmavq	Ricinus communis	Oil

Sacred and Contested Landscapes

Continued

Akha Name	Scientific Name	Uses
Saerbawq	Allium fistulosum	Spice
Saerciv	Allium tuberosum	Vegetable
Saerguq	Allium bakeri	Vegetable
Saerpur	Allium sativum	Spice
Savlav	Dalbergia spp.	Timber, lacquer host
Savsm	Cunnighamia laceolata	Timber
Seeqliur	Punica granatum	Fruit
Sevzanr-ngabaev	Carica papaya	Fruit
Siqcaq	Purus salicina	Fruit
Siqhoq	Cucumis sativus var. xishuangbannaensis	Fruit
Siqhoq-haq	Momordica charantia	Vegetable
Siqhoq-tsawvq	Cucumis hystrix	Fruit
Siqloer-jur	Citrus reticulata	Fruit
Siqloer-puq	Citrus grandis	Fruit
Siqloer-saw	Citrus medica	Fruit
Siqloer-xayae	Citrus medica var. sarcodactylis	Fruit
Siqmanq	Canarium album	Vegetable, fruit
Siqmavq	Rhus chinensis	Spice, religious use
Siqpuv	Ficus racemosa	Vegetable, fruit
Siqpuv-lavqghawq	Ficus auriculata	Vegetable, fruit
Siqxor	Baccaurea ramiflora	Fruit
Siqymq	Prunus persica	Fruit
Taevma	Psidium guajava	Fruit
Tanqhoq	Benincasa cerifera	Vegetable
Tanrbuvq	Acacia pennata	Vegetable
Tsanqtseevq	Zingiber officinalis	Spice, vegetable, medicine
Tsaqder	Pisum sativum	Vegetable
Tsaqdur	Vicia faba	Vegetable
Tseevqcir	Polygonum hydropiper	Spice
Tseevqkav	Castanopsis mekongensis	Timber, acorn nut
Tseevqxaer	Castanopsis argyrophylla	Timber, acorn nut

Appendix II A List of Plants and Crops in Mengsong Swidden Fields

Continued

Akha Name	Scientific Name	Uses
Tseevqxaer	Castanopsis hystrix	Timber, acorn nut
Wosoer	Lactuca sativa	Vegetable
Wuvqdzan-pavqma	Artocarpus lacucha	Vegetable
Wuvqjil	Imperata cylindrica	House construction material
Xarlanq	Sorghum vulgare	Starchy food
Yaevma	Dilichandrone stipulata	Vegetable
Yaqyoir	Solanum tuberosum	Vegetable
Yavhawq	Nicotiana tabacum	Tobacco
Zivqbuvq	Toona sinensis	Vegetable

Appendix III

A List of Plants in Mengsong Homegarden
(227 species and varieties)

Akha Name	Scientific Name	Uses
Anrbiq	Buddleia candida	Hedge, honey resource, religious use
Anrjirpavqdaw	Mentha haplocalyx	Vegetable
Anrpaw	Buddleia officinalis	Edible dyestuff, honey resource
Arbawr-manqcoer	Manihot esculenta	Starchy food, vegetable
Arbawr-marhecaer	Cyphonamdra betacea	Vegetable
Ardu	Zea mays	Starchy food, fodder
Arjir-pawqcoer	Chasalia curviflora	Hedge
Arjir-dzanqlavq	Evodia austro-sinensis	Medicine
Armar	Phyllostachys mannii	Musical instrument, aesthetics, religious use
Arpavqnanq	Euphorbia pulcherrima	Aesthetics
Aqbeevr	Diospyros kaki var. sylvestris	Fruit, dyestuff, dope
Aqgan	Opuntia monacantha	Hedge, aesthetics, medicine
Aqgan-aryaev	Rosa chinensis	Aesthetics
Aqgan-ciryaev	Rosamultiflora	Aesthetics, hedge
Aqgher	Sapindus rarak	Hedge, scour
Aqmaeraqta	Juglans regia	Food
Aqpaer	Pyrus pashia	Fruit
Beqleq	Zingiber purpurea	Medicine
Boeqbaev	Melastoma polyanthum	Wild fruit, aesthetics
Boeqbaev-nican	Memorialis hirta	Medicine
Boeqsoev	Eurya groffii	Religious use
Boeqtevq	Stachys sieboldii	Vegetable
Boerbav	Luffa cylindrica	Vegetable

Appendix III A List of Plants in Mengsong Homegarden

Continued

Akha Name	Scientific Name	Uses
Bupavq-boeqtevq	Maranta arundinacea	Starchy food
Byaqxanqtiv	Artemisia argyii	Medicine
Byaqyaevlawrgar	Plumbago zeylanica	Medicine
Bymq	Nephelium chryseum	Fruit
Bymqma	Colocasia gigantea	Fodder, vegetable
Bymqma zaq	Colocasia esculenta	Vegetable, fodder
Caedzanrlaeqoq	Myrica esculenta	Fruit
Caevqpartsawq	Eupatorium coelesticum	Medicine
Canqpavq	Crinum asiaticum var. Sinicum	Aesthetics
Cirhaq-neevpyav	Cajanus cajan	Vegetable, beverage
Cirnawv	Choerospondias axillaris	Timber, fruit
Daema-kmrtsov	Vernicia montane	Hedge, oil
Darghmr	Calamus nambariensis	Making furniture, fruit, vegetable
Darghmr	Calamus nambriensis var. alpinus	Making furniture, fruit, vegetable
Darghmr	C. nambariensis var. Damenglongensis	Making furniture, fruit, vegetable
Darghmr	C. nambariensis var. sishuangbannaensis	Making furniture, fruit, vegetable
Darghmr	Calamus obovoideus	Making furniture, fruit, vegetable
Dargmq	Centella asiatica	Vegetable
Darpirdarlanr	Croton crassifolius	Medicine
Darpyavdarmuv	Asparagus filicinus	Medicine
Dovqyawr	Lobelia clavata	Medicine
Durpyur	Bauhinia variegata var. candida	Vegetable, hedge
Dziq	Cannabis sativa	Fibre
Dziqmyanq	Laggera pterodonta	Medicine
Eerpuq daw	Lagenaria siceraria	Container, vegetable
Eerpuq joe	Lagenaria sicerariavar. hispida	Container, vegetable
Eerpuq zaq	L. siceraria var. microcarpa	Container, adornment, religious use
Ghaceiqmiqxaer	Piper polysyphorum	Medicine
Ghaeq	Prunus majestica	Hedge, aesthetics
Ghasaeq	Macropanax undulatum var. simplex	Vegetable
Ghasawr	Coriandrum sativum	Spice

Continued

Akha Name	Scientific Name	Uses
Ghawq	Caryota ochlandra	Starchy food, aesthetics
Ghawqbu	Raphanus sativus	Vegetable
Ghawqcaer	Fagopyrum dibotrys	Vegetable
Ghawqkanr	Trachycarpus fortunai	Fibre
Ghawqloer	Solanum nigrum var. photeinocarpum	Vegetable
Ghawqloer-zoq	Solanum spirale	Vegetable
Ghawqmyavq	Crataeva uniloculeris	Vegetable
Ghawqpavq-haq	Brassica integrifolia	Vegetable
Ghawqpavq-pyur	Brassica chinensis	Vegetable
Ghawqpavq-siq	B. oleracea var. capitata	Vegetable
Ghawqyer	Amaranthus hypochondriacus	Vegetable
Ghawqyer aqgan	Amaranthus spinosus	Vegetable
Ghawqyer neir	Amaranthus tricolor	Vegetable
Ghaxaerbuqhaq	Adhatoda vasica	Vegetable
Guqcir	Allium hookeri	Spice
Hawqtanqtaerlaev	Elaeagnus conferta var. Menghaiensis	Fruit
Haqboer-aryaev	Tithonia diversifolia	Hedge, aesthetics
Haqghmr-daeqciq	Clerodendron japonicum	Medicine, aesthetics
Haqciv	Plectrocomia himalayana	Making furniture, fruit, vegetable
Haqcoer	Dendrocalamus hamiltonii	Bamboo shoot
Haqnaq	Chenopodium bryoniaefolium	Vegetable
Haqyanr	Alocasia macrorrhiza	Medicine, aesthetics
Jaqbuqluyaev	Celosia argentea var. cristata	Aesthetics
Jaqgulumyanq	Ocimum basilicum	Spice
Jaqsawv	Erythrina lithosperma	Timber
Jaqsawv ba	Erythrina stricta	Timber
Jeiqcml	Measa montana	Medicine
Jeiqnav	Indosasa sp.	Fencing, bamboo shoot
Jiroq	Mangifera sylvatica	Fruit
Jiyao	Amorphophallus konjac	Medicine, food
Jiyao ma	Amorphophalluskerrii	Food, medicine

Appendix III A List of Plants in Mengsong Homegarden

Continued

Akha Name	Scientific Name	Uses
Jurdovq	Acanthopanax trifoliatus	Vegetable
Kanqbor	Iresine herbstii	Medicine
Kawqlaeq	Melia toosenden	Hedge, timber, medicine
Keeqcaqngacaer	Tetrastigma planicaulum	Fruit, vegetable
Keeqseq	Polygala arillata	Medicine
Laeqoq	Rubus ellipticus var. obcordatus	Fruit
Laeqoq-gannav	Rubus foliosus	Medicine
Laeqoq-nav	Rubus alceaefolius	Fruit
Laeqoq-bawrnav	Morus alba	Hedge, fruit
Laeqpirsav	Cinnamomum glanduliferum	Spice, timber
Laev laevnyoer	Calamus yunnanensis	Making furniture, fruit, vegetable
Laev laevxeer	C. yunnanensis var. densiflora	Making furniture, fruit, vegetable
Laev bawlaev	C. yunnanensis var. intermedius	Making furniture, fruit, vegetable
Lanhaqlanma	Phlogacanthus curviflorus	Medicine, aesthetics
Laqbeeq-aryaev	Hibiscus mutabilis	Aesthetics
Laqbeeq-aryaev	H. mutabilis f. Plenus	Aesthetics
Laqbeeq-aryaev	H. rosa-sinensis	Aesthetics
Laqbeeq-aryaev	H. rosa-sinensis var. rubro-plenus	Aesthetics
Laqbeeq-aryaev	H. schizopetalus	Aesthetics
Laqbeeq-aryaev	H. syriacus	Aesthetics
Laqbeeq-boeqtevq	Canna edulis	Starchy food
Laqbeeq-ghasawr	Foeniculum vulgare	Vegetable
Laqbeeq-yarmovq	Crassocephalum crepidioides	Vegetable
Laqpir	C. frutescens	Spice
Laqpir nyoer	Capsicum annuum	
Laqpir daw	Capsicum annuum var. cerasiforme	Spice
Laqpir ja	C. annuum var. longum	Vegetable, Spice
Laqpir ma	C. annuum var. grosum	Vegetable
Laqpir tivr	Capsicum annuum var. conoides	Spice, vegetable
Lawrbawq	Camellia sinensis var. assamica	Beverage

Continued

Akha Name	Scientific Name	Uses
Lawrcawr	Elscholtzia kachinensis	Vegetable
Lawrdawq	Tagetes erecta	Aesthetics
Lawrdawq neir	Cosmos sulphureus	Aesthetics
Liya	Clerodendron serratum	Medicine
Lmrbor	Nyssa javanica	Timber, fruit
Loqhaeq	Boehmeria nivea	Fibre, fodder
Luma	Althaea rosea	Aesthetics, medicine
Lupavq	Piper betle	Chewing stuff
Maercoev	Alpinia kastumadai	Vegetable
Maerganq	Costus specious	Medicine
Maerlawv	Amomum maximum	Fruit
Maernyoer	Curcuma aromatica	Medicine
Maerpir	Alpinia galanga	Medicine
Maerxeer	Curcuma longa	Dyestuff
Maeryaev	Hedychium coronarium	Aesthetics
Maeryaev-xeer	Hedychium chrysoleucum	Aesthetics
Manqcoer	Ipomoea batatas	Starchy food, fodder
Manqcoer-devga	Dioscorea alata	Starchy food
Manqsawr	Eryngium foetidum	Spice
Manqsiqhaq	Solanum torvum	Vegetable
Mardae	Cucurbita maxima	Vegetable
Mardawq	Canna indica	Aesthetics
Margawq	Pyrus pyrifolia	Fruit
Marhe	Solanum melongana	Vegetable
Marhecaer	Lycopersicum esculentum	Vegetable
Marhecaer zaq	L. esculentum var. carasiforme	Vegetable
Marhesiqhaq	Solanum integrifolium	Vegetable
Marmiq	Artocarpus heterophylla	Fruit
Marnaw	Sechium edule	Vegetable, fodder
Marsav	Broussonetia papyrifera	Fodder, hedge, vegetable
Maqxirneevma	Dolichos lablab	Vegetable

Appendix III A List of Plants in Mengsong Homegarden

Continued

Akha Name	Scientific Name	Uses
Miqcaelae	Debergeasia orientalis	Fodder, fibre
Miqlaeju	Oreocnide frutescens subsp. orientalis	Fodder, fibre
Miqxuq	Pinus khasya var. Lanbianensis	Timber, lighting
Miqyaer-pavqtsaev	Passiflora wisonii	Medicine
Mqcivxawq	Mirabilis jalapa	Aesthetics
Myanq	Baphicacanthus cusia	Dyestuff
Naevqdzawvq	Zanthoxylum armatum	Medicine
Narma-narpyawq	Helianthus annuus	Oil
Ngabaev	Musa sapientum	Fruit, fodder, vegetable
Ngabaevawv	Musa nana	Fruit
Nganeir	Musa acuminata	Fodder, vegetable
Ngapeer-seqtiv	Ensete glaucum	Fodder, adornment
Nibuvq	Erythropalum scandens	Vegetable
Nmqsiq-mar	Perilla frutescens	Oil
Nmqsiq-xaer	Sesamum orientalis	Oil
Paerlov	Spondias purpurea	Spice
Parhaw	Houttuynia cordata	Vegetable
Pavliq	Castanea mollissima	Food
Pavqbyavq	Anoectochilus roxburghii	Medicine
Pavqcae	Agave sisalana	Aesthetics
Pavqgevq	Sansevieria trifaciata	Aesthetics
Pavqtaev	Pandanus furcatus	Fibre for weaving
Pavqtaev zaq	Pandanus tectorius	Fibre for weaving
Pavqtevq	Bryophyllum pinnatum	Medicine
Pawqcoer	Saccharum sinensis	Fruit
Pawqpir	Cymbopogon citratus	Spice
Pirlaq	Brassica caulorapa	Vegetable
Pivrmavq	Rucinus communis	Oil
Puqtaw	Vitis vinifera	Fruit
Saerbawq	Allium fistulosum	Spice
Saerbyaevr	Polygonum barbatum	Vegetable

Continued

Akha Name	Scientific Name	Uses
Saerciv	Allium tuberosum	Vegetable
Saerguq	Allium bakeri	Spice, vegetable
Saerpur	Allium sativum	Spice
Saerpurneir	Eleutherrine plicata	Edible dyestuff
Sanqgar	Blumea balsamifera	Medicine
Savciq	Anredera cordifolia	Medicine
Savsm	Cunnighamia laceolata	Timber
Sawq	Morus macroura	Timber, fruit
Seeqliur	Punica granatum	Fruit
Seqgawr	Brugmansia arborea	Hedge, aesthetics
Seqgawr zaq	Datura stramonium	Medicine
Sevxanxeer	Dendrobium sp.	Aesthetics, medicine
Siqbir	Litsea cubeba	Medicine, spice
Siqcaq-haq	Prunus salicina	Fruit
Siqguq	Ficus sp.	Chewing stuff
Siqhaqtsuv	Solanum indicum	Vegetable
Siqhaqtsuv	S. indicum var. recurvatum	Vegetable
Siqhoqhaq	Momordica charantia	Vegetable
Siqloer-jur	Citrus reticulata	Fruit
Siqloer-puq	Citrus grandis	Fruit
Siqloer-xayae	Citrus medica	Fruit
Siqmavq	Rhus chinensis	Spice, religious use
Siqpuv-lavqghawq	Ficus auriculata	Vegetable, fruit
Siqpuv-tev	Ficus oligodon	Vegetable, fruit
Siqymq	Prunus persica	Fruit
Taevma	Psidium guajava	Fruit, medicine
Tanrbuvq	Acacia pennata	Vegetable
Tsanqtseevq	Zingiber officinalis	Spice, vegetable, medicine
Tsaqder	Pisum sativum	Vegetable
Tsaqdur	Vicia faba	Vegetable
Tsawrghaqtsawrpir	Cinnamomum tamala	Spice, medicine

Appendix III A List of Plants in Mengsong Homegarden

Continued

Akha Name	Scientific Name	Uses
Tseevqcir	Polygonum hydropiper	Spice
Tseevqkav	Castanopsis mekongensis	Timber, dried fruit
Tseevqmyaevq-dzardovq	Evodia lepta	Vegetable, medicine
Wosoer	Lactuca sativa	Vegetable
Wuvqjir	Imperata cylindrica	House construction material
Xaevqni	Melodinus sp.	Medicine
Xipalaeq	Passiflora edulis	Fruit
Xivqpavqdunyov	Paris polyphylla var. yunnanensis	Medicine
Xmlciq	Pogostemon glabra	Medicine
Xmlxivr	Stereospermum colais	Timber
Xuqlir	Grevillea robusta	Hedge, aesthetics
Yaerlaq	Ligustrum lucidum	Aesthetics, hedge
Yaerlaqxav	Cestrum nocturnum	Hedge, aesthetics
Yaevbyavq	Belamcanda chinensis	Medicine
Yarkajeiqdawvq	Artemisia austro-yunnanensis	Medicine
Yavhawq	Nicotiana tabacum	Tobacco
Xawqlawrzaq	Homalomena occulta	Medicine
Zeeq	Toona ciliata	Timber
Ziqbuvq	Toona sinensis	Vegetable

Appendix IV

The Twelve Annual Ancestor Offerings of the Akha

1) *Khmqxeevq Aqpoeq Dzaqbae*, performed on the last day of the third lunar month *Boeqzoq*, is the celebration of the end of Leisure (or off-farming) season, *Jawrla yamq*, and approaching a new spring. *Khmq* means spring while *xeevq* means new. Sticky rice cake (*hawqtanq*), rice liquor (*jirbaq jirsiq*), and tea (*lawrbawq*) are offered to ancestors.

2) *Khmqxeevq Aqpoeq Lawrdav*, performed on the first day of the fourth lunar month *Khmqxeevq*, is the celebration of starting a new spring. All Akha priests (*Boermawq*), shamans (*Nyirpaq*), and blacksmiths (*Bajiq*) perform renewal/restoration ceremonies for their paraphernalia and tools. It is also the day when masters of political, religious, and technician personnel officially take new apprentices. Sticky rice cake (*hawqtanq*), glutinous dumplings (*jalae*), chicken, rice liquor, and tea are offered to ancestors. Each family also needs to boil reddish dyed eggs and give them to own children as well as any children who visit their family. Similar to the Easter. All Akha people take a day off work next day, called *Khmqxeevq Khmqjeiq Lan-e*, meaning "New Spring Thunder God Day", asking for spring rain. A collective hunting is usually organized on that day.

3) *Khmqmir Aqpoeq*, performed on the day after the New Spring Thunder God Day, is the celebration of arrival of the new spring. Next day, the greater village chief (*Dzoeqma*) will kill a pig and hold a feast to all

villagers (usually only elders and VIPs attend though). This festival is called *Dzoeqyan Lawr-e* in Akha, meaning village chief's feast. This is a form of redistribution of the chief's wealth that has been accumulated throughout the year when he receives tributes from the villagers (recall the front legs of game were given to him). All villagers celebrate the festival by performing a bamboo dance from one family to another starting from the village chief's house.

4) *Caerka Aqpoeq*, is performed on the first buffalo day of the fifth lunar calendar *Tsaqngawq*, before the Rice Sowing Initiate Ceremony (*caer kadawvq-e*) is conducted by the village chief. This ceremony is a marker of beginning a new farming season (or raining season), *Yaerghanr yamq*. Any wedding ceremonies are usually not allowed after the Rice Sowing Initiate Ceremony, because Akha people believe that it is other beings (*aqcawq zaq-e*, including spirits, animals, and birds) breeding season. After *Khmqxeevq Aqpoeq* and before *Caerka Aqpoeq* is a transit period between the Leisure (off-farm) season and the Raining season.

5) *Yaerkuq Aqpoeq Dzaqbae*, performed on the ninth buffalo day after the Rice Sowing Initiate Ceremony, is to cherish memory of and offer an honor to an Akha hero *Yaerkuq*, son of the Supreme God *Aqpoeq Miqyaer*. *Yaerkuq* is believed to sacrifice his life for the Akha people in a fight against a severe pest in ancient times. The next day, a huge swing, called *Lavqceq*, will be lifted to celebrate the victory of Akha people over the pest. So it is also called Swing Festival. This festival is celebrated after the second round of weeding is completed in the agricultural fields.

6) *Yaerkuq Aqpoeq Lawrdav* is the second ancestor offering performed on the day after the swing is lifted during the Swing Festival.

7) *Ghola (Zola) Aqpoeq*, is performed on next buffalo day after the

Swing Festival. The next day, all *Dzoeqzaq* (lesser village chiefs) will kill pigs and hold feast for all villagers, called *Dzoeqzaq Yanlawr-e* in Akha, meaning lesser village chiefs feast. In the past, a water buffalo needed to be sacrificed at the Holy Buffalo Sacrificing Post (*nyoqsaevq aqgher bawrdaw*), for ancestors in this festival.

8) *Ghaciv (Zaciv) Aqpoeq* , performed on the first sheep day after the *Ghola Aqpoeq* , is an offering to seven generations of one's ancestors.

9) *Karyaev Aqpoeq* , literally meaning " Rice Flowering Festival ", is performed on the next buffalo day after *Ghaciv Aqpoeq* . Second day, all village children are painted colorfully and chase evil spirits from house to house, starting with the greater village chief's house, out of the houses and village. On their chasing parade, they make a lot noise by beating house walls and fences with painted wooden machetes and weapons. When the children march reaches a house, the house owners will set off firework and fire their guns toward the sky if they have guns. The house owner also scatters candies for kids picking up freely. All these make this festival a lot of fun to children. In the meanwhile, adult male villagers gather at the house of the greater village chief and make a master huge wooden machete of 2 – 3 meters length, called *Tawvma* . After children have finished chasing all the houses, their wooden machetes and weapons will be gathered at the house of greater village chief, and then will be shown off outside the village lower gate, *dzanrdanq lanrkanw* . The *Tawvma* is also put over on two posts lifted outside of the same village gate. So, this gate is also called *Tawvma Lanrkanq* , meaning " Master Machete Gate ". This festival is also called Akha Minor New Year, or *Khovqzaq Par-e* in Akha, after which wedding ceremonies can be performed again.

10) *Hawqxeevq Aqpoeq* , meaning New Rice Festival, is performed to

offer the first rice and first fruits to ancestors, expressing their sincere thanks to their ancestors who have looked after their crops (rice) well. It is performed when the rice is ready for harvest.

11) *Kartanr Aqpoeq Dzaqbae*, usually performed on the last buffalo day of the year, is to celebrate the harvest and mark the end of a farming season. All the financial affairs need to be cleared and particularly all the old debts in the past year need to be paid off, on the next day. In Akha, this is called *Jeiqpav karkhawq mr-e*.

12) *Kartanr Aqpoeq Lawrdav*, performed the day after *Jeiqpav Karkhawq Mr-e*, is a celebration of beginning of a new year.

Appendix V

Akha Lunar Calendar
(khovqtovq latovq)

Akha societies have their own lunar calendars (*khovqtovq latovq*, literally meaning "tracing years and months"). The lunar calendars vary slights in terms of names of the lunar months and/or order of some months among various subgroups or even between different villages within the same subgroups. It is believed that Akha ancestors used the same calendar and the same set of *ghanrsanrkhovq* (belief system and practices, way of life, and customary law) back in the Jadae polity, and that the variations of the *ghanrsanrkhovq* (including calendar) are occurred in the process of oral transmission and practices by various subgroups in centuries-long migrations and settlements in different locations. Therefore, representatives of Akha cultural specialists, scholars, and leaders standardized the Akha calendar based on a version passed down through the ruling lineage of the Jadae polity, at an ad hoc workshop, held in Jinghong, Yunnan, China, from December 30, 2008 to January 2, 2009. The description of the Akha lunar calendar here is the standardized version from the workshop.

The Akha uses the number 12 as a unit to count time, called *yei*. Therefore, an Akha week comprises 12 days, called *nan-yei* (*nan* means "day"). Similarly, a 12-year cycle is called *khovq-yei* (*khovq* means "year" here). Twelve animals are employed to name each year and each day of the circle. Six of these animals are domestic including horse, sheep, rooster, dog, pig and buffalo, and another six are wild or mysterious including dragon, termite, monkey, rat, tiger, and rabbit. Since Akha people believe that the sky was created on the day of dragon (*Lanq* in Akha) before anything else, so the day of dragon is the first day of the 12-day week/cycle. The order of the twelve animals in Akha is *Lanq* (dragon), *Xaer* (termite), *Manq* (horse), *Yawr* (sheep), *Myovq* (monkey), *Ha/Gha/Za* (rooster), *Keeq* (dog), *Ghavq/zavq* (pig), *Ho* (rat), *Nyoq* (buffalo), *Khaqlaq* (tiger), and *Tanqlav* (rabbit). Traditionally Akha people do not work in agricultural fields on the days of sheep and tiger, similar to the concept of weekends in the western calendar.

There are usually twelve lunar months in a year. The name of the twelve lunar months in Akha in order are 1) *Ghaeqla* (*Khovqxeevq*), 2) *Oerla* , 3) *Boeqzoq/Boeqyuvq* , 4) *Khmqxeevq* , 5) *Tsaqngawq* , 6) *Ghanrla*, 7) *Tseirla* , 8) *Cawqla* , 9) *Zola/Ghola* , 10) *Siqyaev/Siqyei* , 11) *Nanqyaev/Nanqyei* , and 12) *Tanrla* . There are six greater lunar months containing 30 days and six lesser lunar months containing 29 days. An extra lunar month called *Ghorla* is added after *Tanrla* roughly every three years. More precisely, there are 7 *Ghorla* lunar months in every 19 years.

An Akha year is divided into three seasons *Jawrla Yamq* (leisure or off-farming season), *Yaerghanr Yamq* (raining season), and *Tsanqgav Yamq* (cool season). *Jawrla Yamq* is composed of the four months of *Ghaeqla, Oerla* , *Boeqzoq* , and *Khmqxeevq* . *Yaerghanr Yamq* is composed of *Tsaqngawq* , *Ghanrla* , *Tseirla* , and *Cawqla* . *Tsanqgav Yamq* is composed of *Zola* , *Siqyaev* , *Nanqyaev* , *Tanrla* , and *Ghorla* . Below is a brief description of the thirteen months with major cultural-social and agricultural activities identified.

No.	Akha Name of the Lunar Month	Selected Characterizations of the Month	Cultural-social and Agricultural Activities
1	Ghaeqla (Khovqxeevq) (between late Dec. -early Feb. ;mostly in January)	Ghaeq mavq yaev-e tiq la (month of cherry blossom) Xmrtaev bala (month of making iron tools) Khovqxeevq yarxar bala (month of land selection)	Making iron tools Selecting a land plot Youths traveling to look for lovers Building new houses
2	Oerla (mostly in February)	Oermr bala (month of wedding ceremony)	It is the best time to hold wedding ceremonies in a year.
3	Boeqzoq (mostly in March)	Boeqzoq sanqxir bala (month of fallen leaves)	Cutting trees for swidden fields
4	Khmqxeevq (mostly in April)	Japyur teir-e bala (month of making rice dumplings)	Akha Spring Festival Paraphernalia renewal Village gates renewal
5	Tsaqngawq (mostly in May)	Circa bala (month of sprouting)	The Rice Sowing initiating ceremony Rice planting
6	Ghanrla (mostly in June)	Aqiq arho ghanrlar-e bala (month of ants and termites getting mature)	The first round weeding Offering to deities of the sky, earth, and water❶
7	Tseirla (mostly in July)	Boeqbaev yaevbyar mr (month of Melastoma blossom) Nyoqpeer naqkhanq deiq (too much rain makes water buffalo hang their ears down)	Offering to swidden fields'spiritual lord and Rice Goddess The second round of weeding
8	Cawqla (mostly in August)	Cawqo bymq-e tiq la (month of rice pregnancy) Daqyuq daevq-e tiq la (month of daqyuq cicada singing) Haqbyeivq purdzmr xaer (month of new bamboo shoots sprouting)	The second round weeding (cont.) The Swing Festival
9	Ghola (Zola) (mostly in September)	Nyoqpeer tsov-e tiq la (month of sacrificing water buffalo for ancestors) Ganma daevq-e tiq la (month of ganma cicada singing) Byeivq jaq xawq-e tiq la (month of bamboo shoots growing into young bamboo)	The Water Buffalo Sacrificing Festival The Chicken Sacrificing Festival The third round of weeding The Rice Flowering Festival (Akha minor new year)

❶ In Thailand and some parts of Myanmar, the offering to the Sky God, the Earth Goddess, and Water God is performed before the Rice Sowing Initiate Ceremony in the fourth lunar month *Khmqxeevq*.

Appendix V Akha Lunar Calendar

continued

No.	Akha Name of the Lunar Month	Selected Characterizations of the Month	Cultural-social and Agricultural Activities
10	Siqyaev (Siqyei) (mostly in October)	Caergeeq tevq-e tiq la (month of the first rice festival)	The First Rice Festival Starting rice harvest
11	Nanqyaev (Nanqyei) (mostly in November)	Jirdzm dav-e tiq la (month of harvest)	Threshing rice Storing dried rice in a new barn
12	Tanrla (Khovqoer) (mostly in December)	Khovqoer jirghov piq-e tiq la (month of ending the farming season)	Akha New Year Festival
*	Ghorla (mid December–early January)	Haqniq tiq ghor sar-e bala (month of health)	Seven extra lunar months Ghorla (meaning " month of the health ") are added every 19 years

Appendix VI

Dynamics of Mengsong Land Uses

1. Dynamics of zone I —*pu* (villages) and zone II —*putsanq* (village fence forests)

Traditional Land Use Zones	I. *Pu* (villages)		II. *Putsang* (village fence forests)
Types of Landscapes	Residency	Home gardens	Village protection forests
Period I (1950 – 1977)	Growing	Fluctuating	Destroyed
Period II (1978 – 1998)	Growing	Growing	Partially recovered and became scenic forests (Feng jing lin)
Period III (1998 – up to date)	Growing	Shrinking	Some remained as scenic forests; Partially became tea agroforests.

2. Dynamics of zone III —*ghaqtsanq* (protected forests)

Traditional Land Use Zones	III. *Ghaqtsanq* (protected forests)				
Types of Landscapes	Watershed forests	*Sanqpaq-barwar*	Cemetery groves	Earth Lord groves	Holy Water site
Period I (1950 – 1977)	Protected	Protected	Partially destroyed	Destroyed, partially became fruit orchards	Destroyed
Period II (1978 – 1998)	Became state forests	Became state forests	Partially recovered	Became part of collective or household forests	Not restored
Period III (1998 – up to date)	Becoming tea agroforests	Becoming tea agroforests	Remained	Became tea agroforests	Not restored

Appendix VI Dynamics of Mengsong Land Uses

3. Dynamics of zone IV—*miqkhaevlavqghaw aqganq* (firewood forests)

Traditional Land Use Zones	IV. *Miqkhaevlavqghaw Aqganq*- firewood Forests	
Types of Landscapes	Timber, firewood forests	Tea agroforests
Period I (1950 – 1977)	Maintained	Developing
Period II (1978 – 1998)	Became collective and household forests	Developing
Period III (1998 – up to date)	Most of them became tea agroforests	Expanding

4. Dynamics of zone V — *nyoqjawrkmrteev Aqganq* (fenced buffalo forests)

Traditional Land Use Zones	V. *Nyoqjawrkmrteev Aqganq* (fenced buffalo forests)	
Types of Landscapes	Pasture Lands	
Period I (1950 – 1977)	Partially maintained	Partially became fruit orchards
Period II (1978 – 1998)	Partially remained; Partially became "Lun xie di"	Maintained
Period III (1998 – up to date)	Most became tea plantations	Some remained as fruit orchards; Most became tea plantations

5. Dynamics of zone VI—*yarmrjawqxmq aqdae* (agricultural lands)

Traditional Land Use Zones	VI. *Yarmrjawqxmq Aqdae* (agricultural lands)		
Types of Landscapes	Irrigated Paddy Fields	Swidden Fields	Sacred Sites
Period I (1950 – 1977)	Developing	Expanding	Mostly destroyed, became farming lands
Period II (1978 – 1998)	Developing	Partially became "Lun xie di" The rest declared as state wastelands (25, 000 mu = 1, 666. 7ha)	Some remained as farming land; some were abandoned
Period III (1998 – up to date)	Mostly remained; Some destroyed by mining; Some submerged under the new Mengsong reservoir.	Most became tea plantations; Some became rubber plantations; Some became irrigated paddy fields; A small proportion remained as swidden fields.	Became rubber or tea plantations; The rest remained abandoned

Acknowledgement

This book is based my Ph. D dissertation, which was accomplished in August 2013. Above all, I would like to thank World Heritage Administration Bureau of Honghe Hani and Yi Autonomous Prefecture (WHAB-HHYAP), Yunnan Province, who has funded the publication of this book; and Prof. Zhang Hongzhen, ex-official head of WHAB-HHYAP and director of Research Center for Honghe Hani Terrace Conservation and Development, Honghe University, without whose encouragement, I could not turn my Ph.D. dissertation into this book. For accomplishment of Ph.D. dissertation, I would like to give my heartfelt gratitude to the institutes and persons mentioned below.

First of all, I would like to thank the Department of Anthropology, University of California at Riverside (UCR) for accepting me as a Ph.D. student, and the Graduate Division of UCR for granting me the Dean's Fellowship Award (2002 – 2006), without which I could not have started this study at the first place. My preliminary fieldwork was funded by the Humanities Graduate Student Research Grant, UCR (2004), and my main one-year fieldwork was funded by the Pacific Rim Research Grant, University of California (2005 – 2006). My supplementary fieldwork was supported by various grants including the Subaltern - Popular Dissertation Research Award, University of California at Santa Barbara (2006 – 2007), the Graduate Dean's Dissertation Research Grant of UCR (2007 – 2008), and the Sustainable Mekong Research Network (Sumernet) Fellowship, the Stockholm Environment Institute (SEI) - Asia (2008 - 2009). Dissertation writing was supported by both the Sumernet Fellowship and the Visiting Scholar Fellowship at the Regional Center for Social Sciences and Sustainable Development (RCSD), Faculty of Social Sciences, Chiang Mai University (CMU) (2009 – 2010). I also benefited greatly as a manager of the project on "Documentation of Akha Cultural Traditions" funded by the U. S. Ambassadors Fund for Cultural Preservation (AFCP), the U. S. Department of State (2010 – 2012). My sponsors in China were Dr. Yang Yongping, then deputy director of Kunming Institute of Botany (KIB) and Dr. Chen Jin, director of Xishuangbanna Tropical Botanical Garden (XTBG), Chinese Academy of Sciences (CAS). My studies, dissertation research and writing were not possible without all of this institutional and financial support.

 Second, I would like to give my wholehearted thanks to my advisor Dr. Eugene N. Anderson, a great mentor and the most knowledgeable person I have ever happened to know in my life. His great mentorship with unbelievable knowledge about almost everything has guided me to sail without becoming lost in the academic ocean in general and anthropological sea in particular. His constant support, encouragement, and endless patience to me, a slower learning student, have helped me to survive in the unusually long journey of my PhD study. My sincere thanks also go the other members of my dissertation committee, Dr. David B. Kronenfeld and Dr. David A. Biggs, without whose generous supports and guidance, I could not accomplish my studies. My thanks also go to Dr. Sally Ness, an ex-member of my dissertation committee but who could not serve on it at the end because of her sabbatical leave out of the country. I benefited much from her seminar on Anthropology of Landscape. Other mentors who have guided me to grow in academic world include, but are not limited to, Prof. Pei Shengji and Dr. Xu Jianchu (both were advisors of Master studies in Botany at KIB-CAS who led me to enter the field of ethnobotany, which paved a path for me to enter into anthropology eventually), Prof. Li Yanhui (who taught me botanic taxonomy), Dr. Leo Alting von Geusau (the founder and ex-director of the Southeast Asian Mountain Peoples' Culture, Development and Education Foundation, from which the Inter Mountain Peoples Education and Culture in Thailand Association and the Association for Akha Education and Culture in Thailand developed later, who introduced me to the broad network of Akha people particularly knowledgeable elders in Mengkong River region), Dr. Louis Lebel (then director of the Unit for Social and Environmental Research (USER), CMU, who mentored me when I was the Sumernet fellow), Dr. Chayan Vaddhanaphuti and Dr. Yos Santasombat (the former is director of RCSD and the latter is professor of anthropology at CMU, both were mentors of me when I was a visiting scholar at RCSD, CMU), Dr. Timmi and Dr. Maruja Salas Tillmann (an anthropologist couple who shared much their wide anthropological knowledge from other parts of the world and supported me as good colleagues and close friends since 1996), Dr. David Feingold and Dr. Heather Peters (another anthropological couple who have been supportive in various ways). I would like to give my cordial thanks to all these persons, without whose endless support, sharing, guidance, and encouragement, I could not complete my Ph.D. studies and become a successful anthropologist.

The next group to whom I would like to give my devotional respects and cordial thanks are my Akha cultural teachers including, but are not limited to, *Aqbawr Kandzer Ghoeqlanqguq*, *Aqbawr Jargaw Ghoeqlanqguq*, *Ardov*

Arhae Ghoeqlanqguq, *Aqpiq Xaevdeer Ghoeqlanqma*, *Aqbawr Liqcaq Jeirbeeqguq*, *Aqpiq Parpaq Ghoeqlanqma*, *Aqbawr Tutsaq Pyawqsaerguq*, *Aqbawr Heeqpyawq Aqghawr (Jawrban) guq*, *Aqghawr Panrlov Nyawrbyeivqguq*, *Aqcan Lawqpir Pyawqsearguq*, *Aqbawr Govlawq Meeqbanguq*, *Aqbawr Jarghuq Byanlaeqguq*, *Ardov Aqzir Jeirbeeqguq* (from China); *Aqbawrhaq Saeduqguq*, *Aqbawrbaeq Saeduqguq*, *Pirma Arkev Ceimeeqguq*, *Ardov Kawqtsaq Lartavguq*, *Ardov Lawqgaw Manqpovguq* (from Thailand); *Ardov Jaqtee Ceimeeqguq* (from Myanmar); *Boermawq Lansar Danyirguq*, *Boermawq Beeqganr Lawqyanqguq* (from Laos). Most historical, cultural, and ecological knowledge documented here were taught by these great teachers, whose mentorship has guided me to become an Akha student in the fullsense.

I also would like to thank my colleagues and friends who have helped in various ways. Though I cannot list all of their names, I still would like to mention Dr. Prasert Trankansuphakon (director of the Indigenous Knowledge and People, Chiang Mai, Thailand), Mr. Sakda Saemi (director of the Inter Mountain Peoples Education and Culture in Thailand Association), and Mr. Aju Jupoh (ex - director of the Association for Akha Education and Culture in Thailand) who had provided me with much collaboration and convenience when I was working and living in Chiang Mai, Thailand in the past six years. My sincere thanks also go to my Hani − Akha colleagues and friends, such as Mr. Huang Rongsheng who companioned me to do my fieldwork in Laos and Myanmar; Mr. Li Er who provided me some convenient transportations at the beginning of my fieldwork in China; Dr. Bai Yongfang and Mr. Pu Yaqiang who have provided me with much second hand data on the Hani - Akha history and culture; Mr. *Maerlanq Ghoeqlanqguq* who has studied Akha culture and traditional knowledge together with me since 1997; Mr. Zhang Xiaoming who helped me make all the maps used in the dissertation;

Mr. Li Jie who provided me information on the natural reserves in Xishuangbanna; Mr. *Cirtuq Byevtseirguq*, Mr. *Cirjoe Byevtseirguq*, and Mr. *Zalanq Mazevguq* who arranged my fieldtrip to Akha communities in Eastern Shan State of Myanmar safe and convenient. Special thanks go to a special colleague and friend Mr. Micah Morton who has been very supportive by providing references I need. Mr. Tao Guoda and Mr. Wang Hong helped me to identify all the plants. I am also thankful to all of my colleagues and friends not listed here due to space limits, but always in my heart and I remember your support and encouragement all the way coming along. Without generous help from these colleagues and friends, I could not complete my dissertation.

I also own huge debts to the leaders and all villagers of my two major research sites in China, Mengsong and Baka, as well as my extended research site in Thailand, Doi Chang. I would like particularly thank Mr. *Nyirer Pyawqsaerguq* (the head of Baka village), Mr. *Dzerguq Ghoeqlanqguq* (the head of Hongqi village), Mr. *Ketuq Ghoeqlanqguq* (the head of Hongxing village), Mr. *Xovsav Jeirbeeqguq* (the accountant officer of Mengsong Administrative Village—MAV), Mr. Li Chengdong (then the official head of MAV), Mr. Laoer *Dancanguq* (the official head of MAV after Mr. Li), and Mr. He Yongneng (the official head of MAV after Mr. Laoer), Mr. Somsak Phisailert (the official head of Doi Chang village); all of them facilitated the smooth process of my fieldwork.

Then last, but not least, I own my heartfelt thanks to my wife Miju, son Eugene, daughter Mulan, parents and extended families both in China and Thailand, without whose love, understanding, support, patience, and encouragement, I could not endure all the challenges and overcome all the difficulties in the long journey of accomplishing my studies and dissertation.